Global Trade and the Transformation of Consumer Cultures

The oceanic explorations of the 1490s led to countless material innovations worldwide and caused profound ruptures. Beverly Lemire explores the rise of key commodities across the globe and charts how cosmopolitan consumption emerged as the most distinctive feature of material life after 1500 as people and things became ever more entangled. She shows how wider populations gained access to more new goods than ever before and, through industrious labour and smuggling, acquired goods that heightened comfort, redefined leisure and widened access to fashion. Consumption systems shaped by race and occupation also emerged. Lemire reveals how material cosmopolitanism flourished not simply in great port cities like Lima, Istanbul or Canton, but increasingly in rural settlements and coastal enclaves. The book uncovers the social, economic and cultural forces shaping consumer behaviour, as well as the ways in which consumer goods shaped and defined empires and communities.

BEVERLY LEMIRE is Professor and Henry Marshall Tory Chair at the University of Alberta, Canada. She publishes widely in textile history, gender and economic development, and material history and was founding Director of the University of Alberta's Material Culture Institute. She was elected a Fellow of the Royal Society of Canada in 2003.

New Approaches to Economic and Social History

Series Editors

Marguerite Dupree (University of Glasgow)

Debin Ma (London School of Economics and Political Science)

Larry Neal (University of Illinois, Urbana-Champaign)

New Approaches to Economic and Social History is an important new textbook series published in association with the Economic History Society. It provides concise but authoritative surveys of major themes and issues in world economic and social history from the post-Roman recovery to the present day. Books in the series are by recognized authorities operating at the cutting edge of their field with an ability to write clearly and succinctly. The series consists principally of single-author works – academically rigorous and groundbreaking – which offer comprehensive, analytical guides at a length and level accessible to advanced school students and undergraduate historians and economists.

Global Trade and the Transformation of Consumer Cultures

The Material World Remade, *c*.1500–1820

BEVERLY LEMIRE
University of Alberta

CAMBRIDGE
UNIVERSITY PRESS

CAMBRIDGE
UNIVERSITY PRESS

University Printing House, Cambridge CB2 8BS, United Kingdom

One Liberty Plaza, 20th Floor, New York, NY 10006, USA

477 Williamstown Road, Port Melbourne, VIC 3207, Australia

314–321, 3rd Floor, Plot 3, Splendor Forum, Jasola District Centre, New Delhi – 110025, India

79 Anson Road, #06–04/06, Singapore 079906

Cambridge University Press is part of the University of Cambridge.

It furthers the University's mission by disseminating knowledge in the pursuit of education, learning, and research at the highest international levels of excellence.

www.cambridge.org
Information on this title: www.cambridge.org/9780521192569
DOI: 10.1017/9780511978814

First published 2018

Printed in the United Kingdom by TJ International Ltd. Padstow, Cornwall.

A catalogue record for this publication is available from the British Library.

Library of Congress Cataloging-in-Publication Data
Names: Lemire, Beverly, 1950– author.
Title: Global trade and the transformation of consumer cultures, 1500–1820 : the material world remade / Beverly Lemire, University of Alberta.
Description: Cambridge, United Kingdom ; New York, NY : Cambridge University Press, 2018. | Series: New approaches to economic and social history | Includes bibliographical references and index.
Identifiers: LCCN 2017053763| ISBN 9780521192569 (hardback : alk. paper) | ISBN 9780521141055 (paperback : alk. paper)
Subjects: LCSH: Consumption (Economics) – History. | Commerce – History. | International trade – History.
Classification: LCC HC79.C6 L46 2018 | DDC 306.309/03–dc23
LC record available at https://lccn.loc.gov/2017053763

ISBN 978-0-521-19256-9 Hardback
ISBN 978-0-521-14105-5 Paperback

For Morris, for everything

Contents

Colour plates are to be found between pp. 174 and 175

Figures

Maps

Plates

Acknowledgements

The research and writing of this book took years, and I incurred countless debts in the process. My formal involvement with global history began with the conferences and events organized by the Global Economic History Network (2003–2007), in particular the global cotton project based at the London School of Economics. This enterprise was headed by Patrick O'Brien, Centennial Professor of Global History at the LSE, and funded by the Leverhulme Trust. The presentations and discussions that arose during the conferences and symposia helped me rethink the material transformations that arose after 1500 and enriched my understanding of historical change regionally and globally. At the same time, my role in the International Economic History Association (2006–2012) allowed many conversations with colleagues whose broad perspectives on historical processes were important. My visits to the University of Warwick's Global History and Culture Centre added further to my understanding of global history. These opportunities provided an enviable tutorial, as did my visits to other institutions around the world. I thank all those who shared their thoughts and ideas and in particular Maxine Berg, Bruno Blondé, Huw Bowen, Robert DuPlessis, Margot Finn, Price Fishback, Pat Hudson, Colleen Kriger, Bronwyn Labrum, Bozhong Li, Anne McCants, Conal McCarthy, Philippe Minard, Patrick O'Brien, Giorgio Riello, Prasannan Parthasarathi, Om Prakash, Olivier Raveux, Tirthankar Roy, George Bryan Souza, Kaoru Sugihara, Masayuki Tanimoto, Ilja Van Damme, Jan Van Luiten and Grietjie Verhoef. As well, I thank Janet Hunter and Penelope Francks for involving me in their mission to publish the first history of Japanese consumerism. It was a privilege to work with them and the other contributors.

Over the years, I benefitted from the talent and energy of research assistants including Caroline Lieffers, Kristine Kowalchuk, Katie Pollock, Yuxian Song and Anran Tu who made critical contributions.

My doctoral students Meaghan Walker, Kristina Molin Cherneski and Ashley Sims also earn thanks for the support they provided at key moments. My students were a vital part of this broad project: discussing concepts with them was rewarding. I also passed hours with friends and colleagues trying to work through ideas, often while assessing objects in museum collections. I profited from these occasions and thank those I met in various parts of the world like Phillip Buckner, Anne De Stecher, Sara Fee, Janice Helland, Adrienne Hood, Dana Leibsohn, Peter McNeil, Lynne Milgram, Lesley Miller, Rosemary Ommer, Ann Smart Martin, Renate Piper, Vivienne Richmond, Miki Sugiura, Karen Tranberg Hansen and Sophie White. Maxine Berg, Prasannan Parthasarathi and Giorgio Riello also fit in this special category of thanks. Indeed, it may seem like I spent years in conversation, rather than quickly writing this book. That is pretty much true and the benefits were mine. A friendly sounding board is of inestimable value when working through historical questions. In recent years the team of the Object Lives research project further enriched my professional life: www.objectlives.com. Our collaborative interdisciplinary team is advancing the methodology of historical object study, as well as adding critical analysis of the colonizing and decolonizing processes as expressed in objects that circled the globe, emerging and returning to northern North America. I am indebted to this team for their investment in this venture, which in turn influenced many parts of this book: Laura Peers, Anne Whitelaw, Sarah Carter, Susan Berry, Judy Half, Sara Komarnisky, Jonathan Lainey, Cynthia Cooper, Laurie Bertram, Sarah Nesbitt, Katie Pollock and Julie-Ann Mercer. Our work is reshaping understanding of historical change and object agency in this region and time period.

Special thanks are due to Michael Watson, Executive Publisher, History and Area Studies, Cambridge University Press. His patience and counsel were invaluable and the anonymous reader's comments on manuscript drafts made this a stronger book.

The University of Alberta provided critical support including from the Office of the Provost, the Department of History and Classics and the Faculty of Arts. I am grateful for this unflagging commitment. I thank the Social Sciences and Humanities Research Council of Canada for funding that allowed me to pursue my questions at overseas archives, libraries, museums and conferences. In addition, All Souls College, University of Oxford, provided a visiting fellowship at a crucial time in the gestation of this volume, as did the Research Department, Victoria and Albert Museum, London. Versions of Chapter 6 were presented as a keynote address at the Canadian Women Artists History Initiative conference, 2015 and at the Seventh Annual Burge Lecture at the University of British Columbia, 2017. Elements from Chapter 6 were also published in the *Encyclopedia of Asian Design*, vol. 4 (2017).

Local colleagues and friends inspired me on many occasions, and I am indebted to them too. Melanie Marvin facilitated many of my related projects over these years with a professional élan that made these activities more rewarding. Many instructive conversations took place with Ehud Ben Zvi, Sarah Carter, Heather Coleman, Lesley Cormack, Andrew Gow, Jaymie Heilman, John-Paul Himka, Ann McDougall, Lianne McTavish, Ken Mouré, Arlene Oak, Michael Polushin, Julie Rak, Jane Samson and Susan Smith among others, plus with my former colleague Aloka Parasher-Sen. I count the time considering historical conundrums as time well spent. The power of history is apparent everywhere, including in Canada, as we grapple with the consequences of colonialism and its long-run toxic legacy. The Report of the Truth and Reconciliation Commission of Canada points to the importance of inclusive histories and critical analyses in our shared pasts. Their calls to action point the way forward, a weighty matter for historians of this generation and beyond.

Morris Lemire was my constant companion in this long endeavour: reader, advisor, travel buddy. My debts are too large for simple thanks. But I offer my thanks wholeheartedly.

1 | Early Globalization, Rising Cosmopolitanism and a New World of Goods

In the autumn of 2011, newspapers in Western Canada announced that a seventeenth-century Chinese coin had been unearthed 250 kilometres northwest of Whitehorse, Yukon, on the site of a planned gold mine. Its location traces a line deep inland from the arc of the Gulf of Alaska. Exposed with the first turn of the archaeologist's shovel, the physical features of the coin revealed its formal history: it had been minted in Qing China's northeast province of Zhili between 1667 and 1671.[1] This is one of three Chinese coins, dating from the 1400s to the 1600s, discovered in this region in recent years. The paths they followed to northwest North America speak to networks linking China's powerful market to northern peoples instrumental in the North Pacific fur trade, echoing long-run exchanges between Chinese, Siberian and North Pacific societies. Archaeological evidence demonstrates the scope and variety of trade routes criss-crossing the globe, webs that thickened and diversified from the 1500s onwards, linking disparate peoples through the goods they bought, sold and desired. Such coins served many purposes aside from currency and were sometimes used as adornments and charms, offering functional and symbolic protection. An example of eighteenth-century Tlingit armour, Figure 1.1, made in a northwest Pacific Coast society, was sewn with deep horizontal lines of Qing-minted coins from the reigns of four emperors.[2] This object memorializes the sustained networks along the North Pacific littoral and its hinterlands, ties that were transformed as the centurieis proceeded.

---

[1] The defeat of the Han-based Ming regime by Manchurian warriors heralded the beginning of the Qing era (1644–1912). www.cbc.ca/news/canada/north/17th-century-chinese-coin-found-in-yukon-1.1072367

[2] Diana D. Loren, *Archaeology of Clothing and Bodily Adornment in Colonial America* (Gainesville: University of Florida Press, 2010), pp. 69–70.

Figure 1.1 Tlingit hide armour (walrus skin or moose) with Qing Dynasty coins from four consecutive emperors.
© President and Fellows of Harvard College, Peabody Museum of Archaeology and Ethnology, PM# 69–30-10/2065.

The Chinese market was a massive vortex drawing in goods from afar[3] – indeed, access to this market and its commodities inspired the landmark voyages of both Christopher Columbus and Vasco da Gama in the 1490s as both strived to reach this apogee of enterprise. The size and capaciousness of Chinese demand powered connections of many sorts, pulling seafarers to these ports and merchants to their cities from across continents and oceans, stimulating linkages very distant from their borders.[4] The context of these exchanges altered dramatically

[3] Jonathan Schlesinger explores this phenomenon for the Qing era, noting the coining of new words for the many new products that appeared: 'the lexicon of earlier times simply could not account for the bounty.' *A World Trimmed with Fur: Wild Things, Pristine Places, and the Natural Fringes of Qing Rule* (Stanford: Stanford University Press, 2017), p. 11.

[4] For the expansion of Chinese merchants and peoples through Southeast Asia, see Ng Chin-keong, *Trade and Society, the Amoy Network on the China Coast, 1683–1735* (Singapore: Singapore University Press, 1983); Leonard Blussé, 'Chinese Century. The Eighteenth Century in the China Sea Region' *Archipel 58*

over the 1500s once routine global oceanic ties were in place. The Tlingit armour and the flow of Chinese coins that defined this artefact signal the commercial systems that became more expansive in scale and more relentless in tempo as, generation-by-generation, goods and people were drawn more closely together into ever denser circuits of exchange. This early modern globalism elicited and shaped new consumer practices in diverse world regions, with new material meanings advancing stedaily. The result was a cosmopolitan material culture unlike any previous era that redefined material life, social practice and commercial enterprise.

An array of actors fashioned this new world of goods as the flow and range of objects multiplied and commercial routes expanded. As direct and indirect relations evolved, the history that followed included a growing shared knowledge of other polities. Equally, governments and their subjects encountered commodities that sparked new administrative and collective agendas as they reacted to the potential of new trade, the reality (or threat) of new plebeian fashions and the insurgent material preferences of citizenry. Imperial histories traditionally traced the political edifices that grew over this period, including European, Ottoman, Safavid, Mughal and Qing 'gunpowder' empires, as they affected proximate regions and the later nation states. More recently, attention was directed to gender, racial and subaltern forces shaping empires, as well as the complexities affecting those living within imperial settings.[5] Global history has attracted growing interest, including among imperial historians, who address the interactions between empires and wider world

(1999): 107–129; Anthony Reid, 'An "Age of Commerce" in Southeast Asian History' *Modern Asian Studies* 24:1 (1990): 1–30; Craig Lockard, '"The Sea Common to All": Maritime Frontiers, Port Cities, and Chinese Traders in the Southeast Asian Age of Commerce, c. 1400–1750' *Journal of World History* 21:2 (2010): 219–247.

[5] The literature on this subject is vast. For early modern empires, see Sanjay Subrahmanyam, 'Holding the World in Balance: The Connected Histories of the Iberian Overseas Empires, 1500–1640' *American Historical Review* 112:5 (2007): 1359–1385; for the new 'imperial turn', see Durba Ghosh, 'Another Set of Imperial Turns?' *American Historical Review* 117:3 (2012): 772–793; for new perspectives on the British Empire, see Tony Ballantyne, 'The Changing Shape of the Modern British Empire and its Historiography' *The Historical Journal* 53:2 (2010): 429–452; Catherine Hall and Sonya O. Rose, eds., *At Home with the Empire: Metropolitan Culture and the Imperial World* (Cambridge: Cambridge University Press, 2006). And for an example of the new archaeological treatment of colonialism, see Tim Murray, *The Archaeology of Contact in Settler Societies* (Cambridge: Cambridge University Press, 2004).

movements, including the dramatic impact of European colonialism.[6] Global processes shaping material life are the focus of this study, which takes account of imperial administrative and commercial apparatus as these shaped, or attempted to shape, the material options and priorities of discrete world peoples.

Global history is currently a subject of passionate interest, perhaps the result of our obsession with present-day global affairs.[7] The noted specialist of world history, William McNeill, observes that 'Historians approach their subject from the moving platform of their own times, with the result that the past changes shape continually.'[8] Historians are more attentive to the global past than in previous generations, even as they debate fundamental issues. They recognize that the global links that entwine us in the present day cannot be unwound, though some would have it so. What can be offered is clearer attention to the innumerable shared material experiences as the early modern global era advanced, with equal attention paid to specific practices and consequences as a result of these newly forged ties. Major shifts in material culture and consumer practice attended each step in the early modern globalizing course.

[6] For example: A. J. R. Russell-Wood, *The Portuguese Empire: A World on the Move, 1415–1808* (Baltimore: Johns Hopkins University Press, 1998); D. Fairchild Ruggles, ed., *Women, Patronage and self-Representation in Islamic Societies* (Albany, NY: SUNY Press, 2000); Tony Ballantyne and Antoinette Burton, eds., *Bodies in Contact: Rethinking Colonial Encounters in World History* (Durham, NC: Duke University Press, 2005); Linda Colley, *The Ordeal of Elizabeth Marsh: A Woman in World History* (New York: Pantheon Books, 2007); Emma Rothschild, *The Inner Life of Empire: An Eighteenth-Century History* (Princeton: Princeton University Press, 2011); Tony Ballantyne, *Webs of Empire: Locating New Zealand's Colonial Past* (Vancouver: University of British Columbia Press, 2012).

[7] For examples of interest in major museums with these issues note the major exhibition at the Metropolitan Museum of Art 'Interwoven Globe'. See also, Amelia Peck, ed., *Interwoven Globe: The Worldwide Textile Trade, 1500–1800* (New York: Metropolitan Museum of Art, 2013); Donna Pierce and Ronald Otsuka, eds., *At the Crossroads: The Arts of Spanish America and Early Global Trade, 1492–1850* (Denver: Denver Art Museum, 2010); Isabel Mendonça, ed., *As Artes Decorativas e a Expansão Portuguesa: Imaginário e Viagem, Actas do II Colóquio de Artes Decorativas*, (Lisbon: FRESS/CCCM,i.p., 2010). See also, Arturo Giraldez, *The Age of Trade: The Manila Galleons and the Dawn of the Global Economy* (Lanham, MD: Rowman and Littlefield, 2015).

[8] William H. McNeill, 'The Rise of the West after Twenty-five Years', preface, *The Rise of the West: A History of the Human Community* (Chicago: University of Chicago Press, 1991), p. xv.

Kenneth Pomeranz assessed the commonalities shared by parts of northwest Europe and southeast China over much of this period, naming the nineteenth century as the time of 'the Great Divergence': a sequence of political, economic and technological events after 1820 when British industrialization recast economic aptitudes. Then and only then, he insists, did advanced segments of the world diverge economically.[9] The Pomeranz hypothesis revised several debates on the nature of global development and continues to be assessed and reassessed, including in these chapters.[10] However, there is little dispute that the industrial revolution that began in Britain and concurrent Western imperial projects led generations of Western scholars to view the preceding centuries through a distorted lens. The West's temporal (and temporary) pre-eminence was considered by them to have been a permanent state of affairs. The power of this teleological perspective was enormous and long running. The singularity of nineteenth-century industrial events, and the concurrent racial hierarchies and racialized colonial policies set in place, warped perceptions of earlier centuries and non-Western societies. From this proceeded the widely held belief in the inevitability of Western supremacy in all aspects of industry and commerce, science and technology, past and present, a view that dominated academic disciplines until recently and still remains a powerful trope in some circles.[11] A Eurocentric perspective distorts the histories of past centuries and the complexities of global events. This volume continues the revision of these powerful essentialist views.

For some decades, historical analyses of consumerism and changing material patterns of life were dominated by a focus on Western societies and economies. This perspective was subject to trenchant criticisms with significant interventions by scholars exploring diverse world regions and multi-focal forces of change.[12] Fashion, consumerism and evolving

---

[9] Kenneth Pomeranz, *The Great Divergence: China, Europe, and the Making of the Modern World Economy* (Princeton: Princeton University Press, 2000).

[10] See, for example, the special issue of *Economic History Review* 'Asia in the Great Divergence' 64:S1 (2011).

[11] Naill Ferguson, *Empire: The Rise and Demise of the British World Order and the Lessons for Global Power* (London, 2002) and *Civilization: The West and the Rest* (New York, 2012); Gregory Clark, *A Farewell to Alms: A Brief Economic History of the World* (Princeton: Princeton University Press, 2007).

[12] For example,Peter Burke, 'Res et verba: Conspicuous Consumption in the Early Modern World' in John Brewer and Roy Porter, eds., *Consumption and the World of Goods* (London: Routledge, 1993), pp. 148–161; Craig Clunas,

material politics are now understood to be diagnostic phenomena of economic development, discernable in a number of locales; they are important indicators of material, cultural and economic changes.[13] I demonstrate the swelling scale of commercial enterprise over these centuries and the new cosmopolitan material cultures that emerged, which were tied to the proliferation of new global consumables that were adopted and adapted at every compass point. The accelerating pace of material change was not limited to one world precinct; indeed, research points to shared commonalities in this process with China, among many other regions, a full participant.[14] I focus on changing consumer culture

'Modernity Global and Local: Consumption and the Rise of the West', *American Historical Review* 104:5 (1999): 1497–1511; Jack Goody, *The Theft of History* (Cambridge: Cambridge University Press, 2006). For examples of scholarship see note below.

[13] R. Bin Wong, *China Transformed: Historical Change and the Limits of European Experience* (Ithica, NY: Cornell University Press, 1997); Pomeranz, *Great Divergence*, pp. 114–165; Craig Clunas, *Superfluous Things: Material Culture and Social Status in Early Modern China* (Cambridge: Polity Press, 1991); S. A. M. Adshead, *Material Culture in Europe and China, 1400–1800* (New York: St Martin's Press, 1997); Donald Quataert, ed., *Consumption Studies and the History of the Ottoman Empire, 1550–1922* (Albany, NY: SUNY Press, 2000); Antonia Finnane, 'Chinese Domestic Interior and "Consumer Constraint" in Qing China: Evidence from Yangzhou' *Journal of the Economic and Social History of the Orient* 57 (2014): 112–144. Recent Chinese-language works include: Wu Jen-shu, *Pinwei shehua: wanming de xiaofei shehui yu shi dafu* (*Taste and Extravagance: Late Ming Consumer Society and the Gentry*), (Beijing: Zhonghua Book Company, 2008); Li-yueh Lin, 'Costumes and Customs: The Vogue and Opinion on Luxury Clothes of Ordinary People in Late Ming China' (*'Yishang yu fengjiao: wan Ming de fushi fengshang yu fu-yao yilun'*), *New Historical Studies* (*Xin shixue*), vol.10, No.3 (1999): 111–157; His-yuan Chen, 'Sleepless in China: Carnivalesque Celebration of the Lantern Festival and Official Regulation of Everyday Life during the Ming-Qing Period, ' ('Zhongguo ye wei mian: Ming Qing shiqi de yuanxiao, yejin yu kuanghuan'), *Bulletin of Central Sinica History and Language Division* (*Zhongyang yanjiu yuan lishi yuyan suo jikan*), 75.2(2004): 283–329; Hui-min Lai, 'The Kyakhta Trade in Russian Textiles in the Nineteenth Century' ('Shijiu shiji qiaketu maoyi de e'luosi fangzhi pin'), *Bulletin of Modern History Institute at Academia Sinica*, Vol.79 (2013): 1–46; Jin-min Fan, 'Suzhou with Its Style and Mode as a Fashion Leader in the Ming and Qing Dynasties' ('"Suyang", "Suyi": Ming Qing Suzhou ling chaoliu') *Journal of Nanjing University (Philosophy, Humanities and Social Sciences)* No. 4 (2013): 123–141. Also, Dorothy Ko, 'Skill as Luxury in Early Modern Global China', unpublished paper presented at the conference 'Luxury East and West: Geographies of Luxury', University of Warwick, May 2014; Schlesinger, *World Trimmed with Fur*.

[14] Clunas, 'Things in Between'.

globally, demonstrated by new types of consumables, new rituals of life and the material cosmopolitanism that redefined this period. These alterations are demonstrable, even as many suffered extraordinary pains in the provision of these commodities.

The Agency of Things and Cosmopolitan Consumption

A new material cosmopolitanism emerged from the new channels of trade set in place as, generation after generation, material life altered across the ecumene. I define the cosmopolitanism of this early global era as a wider habitual involvement in diverse material media resulting from global commerce, including commodities like tobacco, plus the new situational activities arising from global trade. These traits were not the purview of metropolitan elites but became widely diffused over time, an occurrence demonstrable in the mink robe of an unknown Qing man (Plates 3.2 A and B), the work of a West African ivory carver (Plate 5.1), or the needlework of (Huron) Wendat embroiderers (Plates 6.6 and 6.7). Attention to the flow of goods and the meanings assigned these wares are critical to this story. Thus, I include archaeological and material evidence in my analysis. Object study is invaluable in parsing the intent, meaning and impact of goods; it is also invaluable in tracking the spread and reception of commodities and assessing the shifting context of makers and users across cultures. This interdisciplinary methodology is now more widely employed by historians.[15] Likewise, the agency of things

---

[15]   For example, Edward S. Cooke, *Making Furniture in Preindustrial America: The Social Economy of Newtown and Woodbury, Connecticut* (Baltimore: Johns Hopkins University Press, 1996); Helen Clifford, 'A Commerce with Things: The Value of Precious Metalwork in Early Modern England' in Maxine Berg and Helen Clifford, eds., *Consumers and Luxury: Consumer Culture in Europe 1650–1850* (Manchester: Manchester University Press, 1999), pp. 147–169; Laurel Thatcher Ulrich, *The Age of Homespun: Objects and Stories in the Creation of an American Myth* (New York: Knopf, 2001); Adrienne D. Hood, *The Weaver's Craft: Cloth, Commerce and Industry in Early Pennsylvania* (Philadelphia: University of Pennsylvania Press, 2003); Ann Smart Martin, *Buying into the World of Goods: Early Consumers in Backcountry Virginia* (Baltimore: Johns Hopkins University Press, 2008); Karen Harvey, ed., *History and Material Culture: A Student's Guide to Approaching Alternative Sources* (London: Routledge, 2009); Janice Helland, Beverly Lemire and Alena Buis, eds., *Craft, Community and the Material Culture of Place and Politics, 19th–20th Century* (Aldershot, UK: Ashgate, 2014); Anne Gerritsen and Giorgio Riello, eds., *Writing Material Culture History* (London: Bloomsbury, 2015); and for a collaborative interdisciplinary object study, see www.objectlives.com

is an accepted paradigm advanced by scholars such as Alfred Gell, and is, in Chris Gosden's words, 'part of an emerging attempt to take the material world seriously in terms of how it affects human relations'. This includes the 'effects that things have on people'.[16]

The 'agency of things' is a concept employed within and outside of the academy. A business group recently adopted this designation, aiming to help 'consumer brands embrace the Internet of Things (IoT)'.[17] Currently, many scholars explore the social relationships of 'things' in societies – individuals and the objects that animate their lives. Things might offer spiritual protection, define status or challenge hierarchy, as with the Tlingit armour referenced above. Objects are recognized for their capacities to affect events, rather than being inanimate dust-collectors – the impact of Asian floriated commodities on worldwide consumers and embroiderers (addressed below) is a case in point. 'As knots of socially sanctioned knowledge, things shape the temporal structures, allowing for social order to be stabilized and reproduced.'[18] Things could also be disruptive. Goods of various sorts featured in spiritual, social, cultural and economic practices in ways not easily parsed one from the other. Ceremonies of life employed objects with tangible power – objects from the natural world or human made. Rituals from gift giving to the redressing of slaves demonstrated the capacity of objects to touch with incontrovertible force.[19] The dynamism of this period altered contexts of

---

[16] Chris Gosden, 'What Do Objects Want?' *Journal of Archaeological Method and Theory* 12:3 (2005), pp. 193, 196. Alfred Gell, *Art and Agency: An Anthropological Theory* (Oxford: Clarendon Press, 1998).

[17] http://sharpendagency.com/ accessed 15 September 2016.

[18] Alex Preda, 'The Turn to Things: Arguments for a Sociological Theory of Things' *Sociological Quarterly* 40:2 (1999), p. 347.

[19] Loren, *Archaeology of Clothing and Bodily Adornment*; Susan E. Whyman, 'Sir Ralph Verney: Networks of a Country Gentleman – The Gifts of Venison' in *Sociability and Power in Late-Stuart England: The Cultural Worlds of the Verneys 1660–1720* (Oxford: Oxford University Press, 1999), pp. 14–37; Ann Rosalind Jones and Peter Stallybrass, 'Introduction: Fashion, Fetishism and Memory in Early Modern England and Europe' in *Renaissance Clothing and the Materials of Memory* (Cambridge: Cambridge University Press, 2000), pp. 1–14; Michelle Maskiell and Adrienne Mayor, 'Killer Khilats, Part 1: Legends of Poisoned "Robes of Honour" in India' *Folklore* 112 (2001): 23–45; Kathleen DuVal, '"A Good Relationship and Commerce": The Native Political Economy of the Arkansas River Valley' *Early American Studies* 1:1 (2003): 61–89. For 'redressing' and its practice see Robert DuPlessis, *The Material Atlantic: Clothing, Commerce, and Colonization in the Atlantic World, 1650–1800* (Cambridge: Cambridge University Press, 2016).

object use, transforming the kinds of goods on hand and the volume of things circulating along sea lanes and cross roads. The objects I assess in this study enrich archival findings and illuminate historiographic trends, bringing time, place and materiality more vividly to life.

Some scholars suggest objects wielded a 'secondary agency' distinct from that of individuals or social groups, though nonetheless powerful enough to induce emotions and instigate actions. This interpretation works 'to bridge the Cartesian divide between people as active subjects and inert passive objects, to better reflect how things provoke and resist human actions through their "secondary agency."'[20] Thus, the value of things cannot be enumerated simply through account ledgers – though these, too, have a major analytical role. We must be attuned to the qualities deemed desirable or powerful in various objects, in different cultures, at different times. That issue was enormously consequential in early contacts between Europeans and Native American peoples, for example, when Native American spiritual valuation of colour and reflective substances underpinned their exchange priorities with newcomers.[21]

The period I explore in this volume was distinguished by intensified, routinized and systematic contact and connections between communities of people formerly linked by intermediaries, if linked at all. Notably, the Americas and their peoples were abruptly and insistently absorbed into new, sustained geopolitical systems as European colonization was gradually enforced. Colonization was a long-run process and was not wholly complete by the end of the period covered by this volume. As these connections were extended and colonial systems set in place, the world's indigenes and colonizers were enmeshed in new geopolitical structures embedded in global networks. As well, for the first time, the influence of the Americas extended systematically into the wider world, which is evident in the impact of Indigenous travellers or

[20] Bill Sillar, 'The Social Agency of Things? Animism and Materiality in the Andes' *Cambridge Archaeological Journal* 19:3 (2009), pp. 369–370.

[21] The term 'contact zone' was coined by Mary Louise Pratt, who defines it as 'social spaces where cultures meet, clash, and grapple with each other, often in the context of asymmetrical relations of power, such as colonialism, slavery, or their aftermaths.' Pratt writes of the nineteenth century, but her concept is valuable for earlier eras as well. *See Imperial Eyes: Travel Writing and Transculturation* (London: Routledge, 1992), p. 4. For discussion of the Native American aesthetics in the early colonial period as revealed in bead preferences, see Loren, *Archaeology of Clothing and Bodily Adornment*, 56–62.

the circulation of American tobacco and chocolate cultures.[22] The influence of Native American technologies and material systems permeated world communities in unprecedented ways. Over time, this global paradigm knitted together *all* inhabited continents, generating an inexorable confluence of people and products, and causing a material *métissage* of unparalleled scope. This was more than simple 'mixing', as it created myriad new systems founded on multi-ethnic exchange. This history is differentiated from all previous eras.

Network building took place in alliance with other structural developments: growing imperial administrations and 'the rise of large "gunpowder" empires' quickened, funded by the profits of heightened long-distance trade. Systematic contact and connection produced increasingly powerful mercantile institutions in various world regions, including Europe, that were allied to expansive colonial endeavours which moved people as well as goods through voluntary and involuntary migration. Capitalism expanded relentlessly over this era as the potential for commodity profit was realized. In fact, one of the signature traits of the early global era was the rising power of commercial capitalism and the spread of capitalist markets, with growing populations entangled in this system as consumers, whether accessing goods through formal or informal circuits, and whether paying with currency or in kind. This era saw more people in contact with more things (and more different things) than ever before, with objects that enticed, confused, upset and enriched new populations. Others were enslaved and dispossessed in the making and transmission of these things. Yet, even enslaved and colonized populations touched, used and acquired goods of various sorts and shaped their meanings. The agency of subject peoples is a recurring theme in this volume, people active in the creation of new cultural forms. With each generation, more were affected by the confluence of things. Material life altered in response. Cosmopolitan consumption

---

[22] Ross W. Jamieson, 'The Essence of Commodification: Caffeine Dependencies in the Early Modern World' *Journal of Social History* 35:2 (2001): 269–294; Marcy Norton, 'Tasting Empire: Chocolate and the European Internalization of Mesoamerican Aesthetics' *American Historical Review* 111:3 (2006): 660–691 and *Sacred Gifts, Profane Pleasures: A History of Tobacco and Chocolate in the Atlantic World* (Ithaca: Cornell University Press, 2008); Jace Weaver, 'The Red Atlantic: Transoceanic Cultural Exchanges' *American Indian Quarterly* 35:3 (2011): 418–463; Coll Thrush, *Indigenous London: Native Travelers at the Heart of Empire* (New Haven: Yale University Press, 2017).

emerged as the most distinctive feature of material life in the centuries after *c.* 1500, a phenomenon shared in all world regions.[23]

Cosmopolitanism is a trait usually assigned to social elites, diplomats and merchants, denoting a distinctive worldliness.[24] Familiarity with the foreign is a major aspect of this attribute, acquired by living in a multi-ethnic society, travelling widely or enhanced connections with people, goods and ideas diffused from alien parts.[25] Jonathan Schlesinger observes that, by the eighteenth-century Qing era, 'Even for those who never traveled, a world of goods was at hand: Scholars studied them in guides, gazetteers, *material medica*, and personal accounts; ordinary consumers inspected them in the marketplace.'[26] Cosmopolitanism took many material forms. More robust commercial capitalism encouraged new sensibilities and priorities – whether small farmers took up tobacco growing for the market in Japan or Africa, or European women took up new employment to secure the modest luxuries they desired, like Indian chintz. I show how a wider range of plebeian men and women acquired cosmopolitan sensibilities through knowledge of global commodities, adoption and adaptation of foreign goods, and creative amendments to their material lives. New expressive material patterns are apparent across rank and ethnicity, across latitudes and cultures. I recently explored the ways deep-sea, long-distance European sailors enacted the cosmopolitan

---

[23] Dana Leibsohn, 'Colonial / Cosmopolitan: Dressing Up in Spanish America' Plenary Address presented at the conference Dressing Global Bodies, University of Alberta, July 2016; Julia Binter, 'African Cosmopolitanism: Trade, Transculturation and Imperial Encounters in the Nineteenth-Century Niger Delta', presented at the Colonial Objects and Social Identities conference, National Museum, Copenhagen, September 2016.

[24] Margaret C. Jacob, *Strangers Nowhere in the World: The Rise of Cosmopolitanism in Early Modern Europe* (Philadelphia: University of Pennsylvania Press, 2006); Alison Games, *The Web of Empire: English Cosmopolitanism in an Age of Expansion, 1560–1660* (Oxford: Oxford University Press, 2008); Jennifer Mori, *The Culture of Diplomacy: Britain in Europe, 1750–1830* (Manchester: Manchester University Press, 2011); Fernando Rosa Ribeiro, *The Portuguese in the Creole Indian Ocean: Essays in Historical Cosmopolitanism* (Basingstoke, UK: Palgrave Macmillan, 2015); Minghi Hu, ed., *Cosmopolitanism in China, 1600–1950* (Amherst, NY: Cambria Press, 2016).

[25] 'cosmopolitan, adj. and n.',. OED Online, Oxford University Press. www.oed .com.login.ezproxy.library.ualberta.ca/view/Entry/42259?redirectedFrom=cos mopolitan (accessed 14 October, 2016).

[26] Schlesinger, *World Trimmed with Fur*, p. 10.

spirit of the age through their access to and use of foreign wares. Similar claims could be made for other communities, as more geographic links were forged and societal connections broadened. Cosmopolitan knowledge can be found among Native American consumers, African slaves in the Americas and multi-ethnic families within the Indian Ocean world.[27] The material lives they devised epitomized the spirit of this early global age.

Material cosmopolitanism flourished not simply in great port cities like Lima, Batavia or Istanbul, but increasingly in rural towns and coastal enclaves served by networks of pedlars or coastal vessels; folk remote from capital cities also became enamoured of novelties, new luxuries or goods soon conceived as necessities. Thus, tobacco appeared in the inland Chinese province of Yunnan by about 1600, and the shards from Chinese ceramics can be dated in New Mexico from about the same date.[28] Cosmopolitan consumption epitomized this period, previously identified in histories of individual commodities: the spread of caffeinated drinks into Ottoman and European regions with accompanying ceramic accoutrements; tobacco's course through Africa and Eurasia; and the new webs of textile exchange that brought a heightened complexity to world markets.

Cosmopolitanism became a shared trait among global communities, though regional rituals of consumption prevailed. This phenomenon is exemplified in Chinese soldiers' rapid embrace of the tobacco pipe, elite

---

[27] Arthur J. Ray, 'Indians as Consumers' in Carol M. Judd and Arthur J. Ray, eds., *Old Trails and New Directions: Papers of the Third North American Fur Trade Conference* (Toronto: University of Toronto Press, 1980), pp. 255–271; Jean Gelman Taylor, 'Meditations on a Portrait from Seventeenth-Century Batavia' *Journal of Southeast Asian Studies* 37:1 (2006): 23–41; Lockard, '"The Sea Common to All"'; Sophie White, '"Wearing Three or Four Handkerchiefs around His Collar, and Elsewhere about Him": Constructions of Masculinity and Ethnicity in French Colonial New Orleans' *Gender and History* 15:3 (2003): 528–549 and 'Geographies of Slave Consumption' *Winterthur Portfolio* 45:2/3 (2011):229–248; Karol K. Weaver, 'Fashioning Freedom: Slave Seamstresses in the Atlantic World' *Journal of Women's History* 24:1 (2012): 44–59; Beverly Lemire, '"Men of the World": British Mariners, Consumer Practice, and Material Culture in an Era of Global Trade, c. 1660–1800' *Journal of British Studies* 54:2 (2015): 288–319.

[28] Carol Benedict, *Golden Silk Smoke: A History of Tobacco in China, 1550–2010* (Berkeley: University of California Press, 2011), pp. 27–29. George Kuwayama, *Chinese Ceramic in Colonial Mexico* (Los Angeles: Los Angeles County Museum of Art and University of Hawaii Press, 1997), p. 22; Linda R. Shulsky, 'Chinese Porcelain in Old Mobile' *Historical Archaeology* 36:1 (2002): 97–104.

Native Americans' integration of tea in their social rituals or the many routes taken by Indian printed handkerchiefs, which became staples through Africa, colonial America and Europe in different stylistic vintages.[29] The visual culture of design was also transformed.

Imperial political structures of East and West form the contextual backdrop of this volume; but formal politics spend more time in the wings than on centre stage. Imperial networks are foregrounded with particular attention to the informal and illegal exchange that shadowed collective formal enterprises, noting the contingent ways in which goods were circulated or acquired. Additionally, more time is spent with a cast of plebeian players – slave and free, women and men – whose lives intersected with the burgeoning global era of things. Historians now take wider social, ethnic and geographic foci in studying consumer trajectories, a radical alteration since the first iterations of this topic. In the section that follows, I assess how the historiography of consumer practice evolved.

Historical Perspectives: Setting the Framework

Why did the study of consumerism become a major enterprise over the past generation? What are the roots of this project and its trajectory? The study of consumer behaviour is not just a contemporary concern nor is it just the focus of market researchers, consumer associations and business faculties. In recent decades historians joined anthropologists, art historians and other scholars in the study of material life as a way to uncover the characteristics of past societies that touched women and men before and during industrial modernity.[30] In postwar Europe, Fernand Braudel emerged as a luminary in the Western academy with

---

[29] Addressed in Chapters 2, 4 and 5 of this volume.

[30] Influential anthropological works include Marcel Mauss, *The Gift: Forms and Functions of Exchange in Archaic Societies*, translated by Ian Cunnison, (London: Cohen and West Ltd., 1954) original French edition 1925; Mary Douglas and Baron Isherwood, *The World of Goods: Towards an Anthropology of Consumption* (New York: Basic Books, 1979); Mary Douglas, *Thought Styles: Critical Essays on Good Taste* (London: Sage Publications, 1996); Grant McCracken, *Culture and Consumption: New Approaches to the Symbolic Character of Consumer Goods and Activities* (Bloomington, IN: Indiana University Press, 1987); Daniel Miller, *Material Culture and Mass Consumption* (Oxford: Blackwell, 1987); Pierre Bourdieu, *Distinction: A Social Critique of the Judgment of Taste*, translated by Richard Nice (French edition 1979, Cambridge MA: Harvard University Press, 1987); Arjun Appadurai, ed.,

a legacy that resounds to this day. One of his largest projects, *Civilization and Capitalism, 15th–18th Century*, assessed the economic history of pre-industrial Europe in a multi-volume publication that extended its gaze across the globe. Volume 1 in his series, *The Structures of Everyday Life*, set the template for study of material life for generations to come, not least through his identification of singular societal formations as large-scale commercial capitalism advanced.

Braudel acknowledged that, 'the more research I did, the more disconcerted I became ... because ... [the economic realities] did not seem to fit, or even flatly contradicted the classical and traditional theories of what was supposed to have happened.' He noted how 'complicated' he found early modern economic activity, an observation worthy of serious reflection, for

there were not one but several economies. The one most frequently written about is the so-called market economy, in other words the mechanisms of production and exchange linked to rural activities, to small shops and workshops, to banks, exchanges, fairs and (of course) markets. It was on these 'transparent' visible realities ... that the language of economic science was originally founded ... But there is another shadowy zone, often hard to see for lack of adequate historical documents, lying underneath the market economy: this is that elementary basic activity which went on everywhere and the volume of which is truly fantastic. This rich zone, like a layer covering the earth, I have called for want of a better expression *material life* or *material civilization*.

At a further 'exalted level', above the market economy, Braudel outlined the world of large-scale international trade, the most 'favoured domain of capitalism'.[31] Braudel's identification of this tripartite structure did not overturn all previous economic theories: not at all. But, it did offer what few had acknowledged – the existence of systems, including *material life*, founded upon disparate cultural and social experiences, systems which were entangled with the other two 'visible' levels of the economy.

   The Social Life of Things: Commodities in Cultural Perspective (Cambridge: Cambridge University Press, 1986).

31 Fernand Braudel, *Civilization and Capitalism, 15th–18th Century, The Structures of Everyday Life*, vol. 1 translated by Siân Reynolds (New York: Harper & Row, 1985), pp. 23–24. French edition *Les structures de quotidian: le possible et l'impossible*, 1979. Laurence Fontaine further advances analysis of the early modern European economy and the functioning of markets and credit, domestic and commercial life. *The Moral Economy: Poverty, Credit and Trust in Early Modern Europe* (Cambridge: Cambridge University Press, 2014).

Braudel encouraged a rethinking of standard categories, stepping away from the heated debates founded on long-standing political divisions 'which the explosive word *capitalism* always arouses'.[32]

Braudel's best-selling three-volume work incorporated extensive data on Eurasian trade, recognizing the obvious impact of Asian products and markets on European growth. However, the entire work proceeded from a profoundly Eurocentric perspective. Eurocentrism was the intellectual offspring of European imperialism – belief in the permanent unequalled might of Europe in the world – views that permeated Western society and the academy in that period. Most notably, he claimed that the material world 'stood still' outside the small constituency of European elites who were able to enjoy material improvements. In his view, stasis was the norm for all others, especially non-Western peoples. He emphatically denied the existence of fashion or material change among the great urbanized commercial centres of Eurasia – China, Japan, India, Persia and Turkey – and refuted any suggestion that there was an interest in material change except 'as a result of political upheavals'.[33] Braudel also denied any substantive material innovation among Europe's peasantry and working classes. His views were buttressed by his reputational weight and his statements on this question were echoed for generations, even as discursive battles ensued.

Civilization and Capitalism, a mammoth flawed project, was as important for its strengths as its weaknesses. Braudel gave credence to thematic topics long denied space in academic precincts. He gave serious attention to housing, food, clothing and fashion, subjects seldom addressed by prominent historians at this time. In fact, he challenged his colleagues to think differently about these issues. In time, a growing number of historians addressed these neglected subjects and more attention was given to questions of demand. But the Braudelian worldview remained stubbornly persistent. Disruptions occurred gradually over time.

Joan Thirsk exemplifies the disruptive, innovative thinking that increased from the 1970s onwards, unearthing key features of material life among the common people of Europe and colonial America.[34] Thirsk noted the acceleration of small trades in rural and urban

---

[32] Braudel, *Structures,* p. 25. I address this theme more fully in Chapter 4.
[33] Braudel, *Structures,* pp. 312–314.
[34] For example, Lois Green Carr and Lorena S. Walsh, 'Inventories and the Analysis of Wealth and Consumption Patterns in St. Mary's County, Maryland,

English settings, often wholly new sectors offering waged employment to women and children, bringing more money into families. Thirsk demonstrated the power of fashion, a contagion that burned through English communities in the late 1500s and 1600s, sparking regional manufacturing in items like hosiery where none previously existed.[35] Thirsk's findings challenged existing interpretations of life among the working poor; far from being in material inertia, the early modern period witnessed exceptional vitality entirely at odds with Braudel's claims. Yet, as the leader of the *Annales* and celebrated for his many achievements, Braudel's conclusions were only slowly revised among the generality of scholars.

Thirsk began by challenging her male compatriots in economic history. In her 1975 Ford Lectures, at Oxford University, Thirsk proposed 'the development of a consumer society in early modern England', a groundbreaking claim. She urged her listeners and (later) readers to think again about the

criteria by which some [issues] have been judged more important and others less [that] have been laid down by our menfolk. Starch, needles, pins, cooking pots, kettles, frying pans, lace, soap, vinegar, stockings do not appear on their shopping lists, but they regularly appear on mine. They may ignore them, but could they and their families manage without them?[36]

1658–1777' *Historical Methods* 13 (1980): 81–104; Carole Shammas, 'Consumer Behavior in Colonial America' *Social Science History* 6 (1982): 67–86 and *The Pre-Industrial Consumer in England and America* (New York: Oxford University Press, 1990); Lorna Weatherill, *Consumer Behaviour and Material Culture in Britain 1660–1760* (London: Routledge, 1988); Micheline Bauland, Anton J. Schuurman and Paul Servais, eds., *Inventaires Après-Decès et Ventes de Meubles: Apports à une histoire de la vie économique et quotidienne (XIVe–XIXe siècle)* (Louvain-la Veuve: Académia, 1988); Beverly Lemire, 'The Theft of Clothes and Popular Consumerism in Eighteenth-Century England' *Journal of Social History* 24:2 (1990): 255–276; Cary Carson, Ronald Hoffman and Peter J. Albert, eds., *Of Consuming Interests: The style of Life in the Eighteenth Century* (Charlottesville: University Press of Virginia, 1994); Stana Nenadic, 'Middle-Rank Consumers and Domestic Culture in Edinburgh and Glasgow, 1720–1840' *Past and Present* 145 (1994): 122–156.

35 Joan Thirsk, *Economic Policy and Projects: The Development of a Consumer Society in Early Modern England* (Oxford: Clarendon Press, 1978) and 'The Fantastical Folly of Fashion: the English Stocking Knitting Industry, 1500–1700' in N. B. Harte and K. G. Ponting, eds., *Textile History and Economic History: Essays in Honour of Miss Julia de Lacy Mann* (Manchester: Manchester University Press, 1973), pp. 50–73.

36 Thirsk, *Economic Policy and Projects,* pp. 22–23.

In measured and pointed prose, Thirsk upended historical 'certainties', offering a wealth of evidence to bolster her claims. She discovered rising household demand for items from pins to combs, ribbons to starch, linked to the upsurge in new small-scale industries with products aimed at common folk. She concluded that while 'it has become convention to treat the mass market for consumer goods as a product of the Industrial Revolution, insignificant before the later eighteenth century ... Reality was more complex.'[37] Her observations were radical and they were not universally applauded. In fact, she encountered difficulty in securing publication of her Ford lectures, though publication from these events was routine. Editors at Oxford University Press doubted if readers would be interested in the little things that employed the poor, stocked pedlars' packs and embellished humble homes and people.

Thirsk's concept of consumerism – fomented among the working poor and lower middle classes – introduced a new historical model, challenging long-held assumptions of static traditional societies before industrialization. Multilingual, with experience in many European cultures, Thirsk was deeply attuned to the importance of trade and cross-cultural influences that shaped the appearance of new commodities in northwest Europe. Indeed, she suggested research agendas requiring more careful perusal of pan-European and extra-European forces. More historians of Europe began looking outward for transformative influences. By 2000, it was widely accepted that material changes in Europe occurred over a long timeframe, well before steam-powered mills and factories dotted the landscape, change powered by consumer demand among wage-earning women and children.[38] It was also clear that other dynamic regions provided critical stimuli to this western region of Eurasia.[39] More scholars concurred that great

---

[37] Thirsk, *Economic Policy and Projects*, p. 125.

[38] A viewpoint extrapolated by Jan de Vries, *The Industrious Revolution: Consumer Behavior and the Household Economy 1650 to the Present* (Cambridge: Cambridge University Press, 2008), p. 7.

[39] Quataert, *Consumption Studies*; Richard Goldthwaite, *The Building of Renaissance Florence: An Economic and Social History* (Baltimore: Johns Hopkins University Press, 1980), p. 44; 'The Empire of Things: Consumer Demand in Renaissance Italy' in F. W. Kent, Patricia Simons and J. D. Eade, eds., *Patronage, Art and Society in Renaissance Italy* (Oxford: Clarendon Press, 1987) and *Wealth and the Demand for Art in Italy, 1300–1600* (Baltimore: Johns Hopkins University Press, 1993); Evelyn Welch, *Shopping in the Renaissance: Consumer Culture in Italy, 1400–1600* (New Haven: Yale University Press, 2005).

historical processes were best understood by adjusting the analytical lens to its widest setting.

However, the sustained critiques that began with Thirsk and others in her generation took time to become mainstream. A hefty volume, *Consumption and the World of Goods* (1993), reflected another effort to understand material change. Yet, the editors devoted virtually the whole volume to Western topics, with a few notable exceptions. One reviewer observed that 'the contrast between the constantly repeated global metaphor of a "world" of goods and the rigorously localized context in which the discussion takes place [offers] . . . at best a British Empire, of goods.'[40] *Consumerism in World History,* a volume published in 2001, offered another Braudelian tale, unchanged through its two editions.[41] Peter Stearns concludes that only late eighteenth-century England reflected the *true* traits of consumerism, as industrialization took hold. He dismisses the possibility of fashion-based, economically significant consumer demand before full-fledged industrialization in the 1800s. For Stearns, too, the material world 'stood still' outside the West before the modern age. Most astonishing of all was his misrepresentation of long-distance trade (1500–1800) as simply 'consumer products for the upper classes'.[42] He wholly discounts early modern plebeian demand, in or out of Europe; misses the significance of the new materials circling the globe; and overlooks the spread of fashions outside court circles before 1800. In sum, he does not assess the period between 1500 and 1800 on its own terms, judging it instead against later industrial levels of production and the 'full-blown' consumerism of the industrial age. He essentially repurposes the Braudelian worldview.[43] Stearns acknowledges that 'there were vital signs of consumerism in Asia and Africa, before the Western form emerged.' But he insists that 'What is sometimes called "Westernization" involves the spread of consumer behaviors.'[44] He does not address histories of the non-Western world.[45] Rather, he defines 'consumerism' in such a manner that only

---

[40] Craig Clunas, 'Modernity Global and Local', p. 1503.
[41] Peter N. Stearns, *Consumerism in World History: The Global Transformation of Desire* (New York: Routledge, 2001 and 2006).
[42] Stearns, *Consumerism in World History,* p. 3.
[43] Stearns, *Consumerism in World History,* p. 1.
[44] Stearns, *Consumerism in World History,* p. ix.
[45] Historians such as Donald Quataert, 'Clothing Laws, State and Society in the Ottoman Empire, 1720–1829' *International Journal of Middle East Studies*

a nineteenth-century Western industrial iteration can be authentic. This judgement cannot stand.[46]

Recent generations of scholars continue to struggle against the tenacious Braudelian worldview of plebeian Europeans and other world peoples.[47] Among the various distorted claims proposed by Fernand Braudel was the telling assertion that 'to be ignorant of fashion was the lot of the poor the world over.'[48] Daniel Roche likewise sees the sartorial world of *ancien régime* France as distinguished in part by 'inertia and immobility, especially among the lower classes and in the countryside'.[49] These hypotheses might seem feasible to some for some regions; however, interpretive realignments are well advanced. Culturally significant embellishments were made with little cost, with the adaptation of modest fittings like ribbons or new low-cost textiles.[50] Further, Ulinka Rublack argues against Daniel Roche's view that drab clothes were the lot of early modern plebeian populations, dismissing the idea that they languished in a colour-starved state until

29:3 (1997): 403–425 and *Consumption Studies*; Suraiya Faroqhi, *Subjects of the Sultan: Culture and Daily Life in the Ottoman Empire* (New York: I.B. Tauris & Co, 2000 and 2005); Craig Clunas, 'Books and Things: Ming Literary Culture and Material Culture' in Frances Wood ed., *Chinese Studies, British Library Occasional Papers* 10 (London, 1988), pp. 136–143, *Superfluous Things*, and 'The Art of Social Climbing in the Ming Dynasty' V&A/Arts Club Lecture, *The Burlington Magazine,* 133, no 1059 (1991): 368–377; Adshead, *Material Culture in Europe and China.*

46 Antonia Finnane provides an astute critique of recent scholars who refuse to acknowledge 'fashion' outside the West and, more particularly, in China. Finnane observes of one scholar that 'when fashion is defined very narrowly on the basis of particular empirical detail about a "particular sort of society," the possibility of any other clothing culture being described as "fashion" is by definition excluded.' *Changing Clothes in China: Fashion, History, Nation* (New York: Columbia University Press, 2008), p. 9.

47 There is an extensive historiography on this subject, including most recently: DuPlessis, *Material Atlantic*; Peck, *Interwoven Globe*; Giorgio Riello and Prasannan Parthasarathi, eds., *The Spinning World: A Global History of Cotton Textiles* (Oxford: Oxford University Press, 2009).

48 Braudel, *Civilization and Capitalism*, vol. 1, p. 313.

49 Daniel Roche, *The Culture of Clothing: Dress and Fashion in the Ancien Regime*, translated by Jean Birrell (Cambridge: Cambridge University Press, 1994), p. 56.

50 Olivier Raveux, 'Fashion and Consumption of Painted and Printed Calicoes in the Mediterranean during the Later Seventeenth Century: The Case of Chintz Quilts and Banyans in Marseilles', *Textile History*, 45:1 (2014): 49–67 and 'La difusió de les indianes a l'Europa mediterrània a la segona meitat del segle XVII', *barcelona quaderns d'història*, 17 (2012): 31–50.

the unleashing of industrial production.[51] Colour options were numerous and treasured from Europe to Japan and beyond, and were available through the use of rich local dye stuffs, in addition to the enormous visual variety attainable in patterned stripes, checks and tie-dyeing.[52] Assumptions concerning a grey, monochrome pre-industrial citizenry do not survive close scrutiny. Dynamic retailing was also crucial in these undertakings.[53] The force of fashion touched many lives outside courts and elite circles. Daniel Miller observes that 'however oppressed and apparently culturally impoverished, most people nevertheless access the creative potential of the unpromising material goods about them.'[54] In the era of advancing global contacts and intensified commerce, even those lumped into the vast heterogeneous category of 'the poor' enjoyed the possibility of fashion or material amelioration. Larger and larger populations experienced changes in their material lives. Braudel was inattentive to cloth, ribbons and pins and changing everyday habits, as were many of his academic heirs. His theory of material stasis is now wholly overturned.[55]

Cross-cultural exchange was unleashed in distinctive ways: as merchants met and mingled, mariners rolled in and out of ports, Indigenous Americans negotiated with sojourners and settlers, and enslaved Africans marked their new environments through their creative interventions as millions were carried to new lands.[56] Material borrowing,

---

[51] Ulinka Rublack, *Dressing Up: Cultural Identity in Renaissance Europe* (Oxford: Oxford University Press, 2010), pp. 261–265.

[52] For the use of red-heeled footwear in Copenhagen see Signe Groot Terkelsen and Vivi Lena Andersen, 'Red Heels. The Symbol of a Power Shift in 17th-Century Copenhagen' *Archaeological Textiles Review* 58 (2016); Karen Diadick Cassleman, *Lichen Dyes: The New Source Book*, 2nd ed. (Mineola, NY: Dover Publications, 2001). The variety of indigo patterning is demonstrable in the traditional pattern books of master dyers and weavers in Kyoto. Personal observation. See, for example, www.aizenkobo.jp/

[53] Laurence Fontaine, *History of Pedlars in Europe*, translated by Vicki Whittaker (Cambridge: Polity Press, 1996).

[54] Daniel Miller, 'Appropriating the State on the Council Estate', quoted in Sophie White, 'Geographies of Slave Consumption' *Winterthur Portfolio* 45:2/3 (2011), p. 236.

[55] The critique of Braudel on this subject is addressed more fully in this chapter.

[56] For example, Meagan Vaughan, *Creating the Creole Island: Slavery in Eighteenth-Century Mauritius* (Durham, NC: Duke University Press, 2005); Judith A. Carney and Richard Nicholas Rosomoff, *In the Shadow of Slavery: Africa's Botanical Legacy in the Atlantic World* (Berkeley: University of California Press, 2009); Sophie White, *Wild Frenchmen and Frenchified*

adjusting and translating shaped the influx of goods in world centres. Historians of China, such as Kenneth Pomeranz, claim an important comparable (and even precursive) prosperity in the highly developed parts of East Asia, on par with or superseding that of the developed parts of early modern Europe. His important perspective challenges claimed European advantages before the Great Divergence of Asia and Europe that came with nineteenth-century industrialization.[57] I address this and other critical historical paradigms, while exploring the materials of trade.

World histories are being reassessed in light of a heightened interest in the material past. Of course, this subject does not receive equivalent attention in all national and regional historiographies. Historians of the Indian subcontinent, for example, determined this a less interesting subject than others, a viewpoint only beginning to change. Likewise, the history of consumerism in Japan attracted sustained attention relatively recently.[58] Interest in this issue varies, challenging easy transnational comparisons. Moreover, it is clear that intellectual concepts carry within them inherent assumptions and presuppositions. The 'rise of consumerism' (pre-1800s) cannot be transposed holus-bolus to all geographic and chronological settings without caveats and cautions. Equally, the use of chronological terms steeped in assumptions of linear progress – early modern and modern – have been critiqued. However, some historians of the non-Western world see advantage in assessing 'early modern' traits.[59]

Indians: Material Culture and Race in Colonial Louisiana (Philadelphia: University of Pennsylvania Press, 2013).

[57] Pomeranz, *Great Divergence.*

[58] For a later period see Douglas E. Haynes, Abigail McGowan and Tirthankar Roy, eds., *Towards a History of Consumption in South Asia* (Oxford: Oxford University Press, 2010). The first volume on consumerism in Japan was published in 2012, with a Japanese language edition in 2016. See Janet Hunter and Penelope Francks, eds., *The Historical Consumer: Consumption and Everyday Life in Japan, 1850–2000* (Basingstoke, UK: Palgrave Macmillan, 2012); Andrew Gordon, *Fabricating Consumers: The Sewing Machine in Modern Japan* (Berkeley: University of California Press, 2012). And for a scholarly initiative addressing the consumption of cloth and clothing, see www.lccg.tokyo/events/ (accessed 12 June 2016).

[59] The terminology 'early modern' is addressed in a cogent fashion for the seventeenth- and eighteenth-century Ottoman Empire in James Grehan, 'Smoking and "Early Modern" Sociability: The Great Tobacco Debate in the Ottoman Middle East (Seventeenth to Eighteenth Centuries)' *American Historical Review* 111:5 (2006): 1352–1377. For a critique of the use of the term 'early modern' see Jack A. Goldstone, 'The Problem of the "Early Modern"

James Grehan is one of a number of scholars of non-Western regions to see the wider circulation of new things as a defining feature of this time period. He asks, 'Were there any overarching cultural movements, beyond those specific to Western Europe ... that might have produced common "early modern" responses?' His conclusion is noteworthy.

One likely catalyst was the worldwide diffusion of new commodities that, winning almost instant favour, would later be integral to the creation of a modern consumer culture. This history of early modern consumption is still being reconstructed, and outside northwestern Europe and colonial North America, it remains particularly obscure. What seems certain, however, is that throughout much of Eurasia, growing numbers of consumers were indulging a taste for entirely new luxuries.[60]

Western perspectives powerfully shaped the academic agenda of the history of consumerisms, fashion and material practice. I work to correct long-standing Eurocentric and *presentist* perspectives offered by Braudel and his acolytes. I work to give voice to a wide variety of peoples pursuing their interests. Thus, the following chapters do not trace the conspicuous consumption of the leisured elites, although they figure occasionally. I devote the most space to the material lives of middle-ranked and common peoples of many ethnicities and circumstances. Separated by distance and culture, they shared more material experiences over time: a puff, a knotted cloth or stitched symbol that might bridge cultural distance among communities, or enable communication where none previously existed, augmenting cosmopolitan knowledge. The goods touched by these women and men became defined and redefined by local cultures, becoming part of their cultural landscape whatever the origins of these things.[61]

Historians like Thirsk, who appeared early in this field, left powerful legacies emphasizing the significance of ostensibly modest changes in 'scattered and undistinguished communities', and the tremendous cumulative importance of cheap fripperies and small inessentials that added pleasures to life and enhanced opportunities for survival.[62] Early

World' *Journal of the Economic and Social History of the Orient* 41:3 (1998): 249–284.

[60] Grehan, 'Smoking and "Early Modern" Sociability', pp. 1353–1354.

[61] Nicholas Thomas, *Entangled Objects: Exchange, Material Culture, and Colonialism in the Pacific* (Cambridge, MA: Harvard University Press, 1991), p. 7.

[62] Thirsk, *Economic Policy and Projects*, pp. 7–22.

on, Joan Thirsk defined the significance of 'the development of consumer society' with attention to the mundane, the local and the seemingly insignificant, set amidst powerful political agendas. The focus of her research was England; the model she devised illuminates world locales. I rely on this historiographic quilt with old and new parts; the chapters that follow balance the meanings and changing significance of goods, amidst rising commodity flows after 1500.

Book Chapters

Common themes are woven throughout this volume, most particularly the effect of new global connections on the genesis of a more cosmopolitan material culture, a shared phenomenon. New commodities and new habits, as well as heightened conduits of exchange, created a new expressive consumerism reflected in materials of life, more intensively realized in vibrant economic centres from Japan and southeast China to the urban districts of Turkey and northwest Europe. I trace 'industrious' practices across a similarly wide terrain. Industriousness was identified by Jan de Vries as a key ingredient in European economic development in the early modern period. De Vries points to the greater number of women and children who worked for wages in order to acquire new consumables and augment family comforts.[63] Industriousness of an equally generative kind involved ever-wider populations (including women of all kinds) as agents in small and medium scale commercial enterprises linked to the market. Thus, industriousness was manifest not only in waged work but also in the intensified entrepreneurial involvement of women and men across a wide social level: selling, trading and bartering in increased numbers with heightened capacity, manipulating things to best effect. More intensive, sustained commerce opened possibilities for small and mid-range endeavours, for remaking and recycling – income-generating actions that powered markets and economies. These activities augmented the capacity for the material improvement of life, whether by a slave in Jamaica selling goods at a Sunday market or the expanded retailing of cheap fur garments in an Istanbul bazaar or the sale of broken peppercorns swept from a ship's hold. Over these centuries, industriousness took more dynamic forms, handling more diverse resources.

[63] De Vries, *Industrious Revolution*.

Material priorities shifted as a consequence, including among the fur trading populations of North America. Compensations provided to these and other heterogeneous people aligned them more closely to a globalized commercial system while transforming their material options in profound ways. Chronologies of empire often shaped the outcome in these events. The impacts of empires and colonies figure prominently throughout this volume as facets of this emerging global system, revealed through apparatus of power shaping (or attempting to shape) habits of consumption and hierarchies of material life.

Chapter 2 explores the 'cloth era', a foundational commerce.[64] This period is defined by the striking worldwide integration of textile trades, augmenting commerce and consumption. I emphasize the architecture of legal traffic in this chapter, laying out the new junctures that arose. Heightened connections saw the exchange of American silver for Chinese silks and North American pelts bartered for wool and cotton cloth from both Europe and Asia. Trade networks were redrawn through the integration of the Americas in this world system that encompassed the extraordinary dimensions of the fur trade and the growth of the adjunct cloth trade. The links between furs and fabrics and their dynamic intersection across continents are a major focus in this chapter. In this way, I problematize categories of 'old' and 'new' luxury, as furs became a widespread consumer commodity, even as the old-style customary uses of peltry remained. Tensions between local and foreign fabrics were another hallmark of the age, fomenting disputes of many sorts. Yet, despite protectionist interventions by various governments, they could not halt the rise of cosmopolitan consumer knowledge or the demand for new goods that ensued.

Bodily embellishment is a cornerstone of societal practice, the focus of wide-ranging investment among all social classes, eliciting edicts from rulers of all descriptions. Chapter 3 considers clothing, perhaps the most hotly debated and widely legislated consumer product. Members of early modern world communities saw the advance of fashion as threat or opportunity, an issue of heightened importance as materials flowed. Regulations multiplied as officials attempted to control the sometimes-anarchic material

---

[64] For a discussion of the importance of cloth and clothing, see DuPlessis, *The Material Atlantic*, pp. 3–5; Hood, *Weaver's Craft: Cloth*, pp. 1–7; Colleen E. Kriger, *Cloth in West African History* (Latham, MD: AltaMira Press, 2006), pp. 1–7.

order.[65] I explore the sumptuary politics and practice of clothing and the creative insurgency of populations from Tokugawa Japan to colonial America. Cosmopolitanism was nowhere more contentious than in the self-selected dress of subaltern groups. The secondhand trade was a vital feature of these clothing ecosystems, enabling wider consumer access as well as broader industrious potential for entrepreneurial women and men. Finally, the mass production of readymade goods marked the new capacity of imperial and corporate livery systems. Sailors, soldiers and slaves caught up in Western imperial institutions represented a growing mass of 'involuntary consumers', whose apparel augured a new regulated status.[66] Consumer choice was constrained in this context, a paradoxical outcome amidst enhanced technologies of production and trade.

The consumer circuits I describe intertwined illegal with licit practices, for consumerism was typically reliant on multiple modes of exchange. Chapter 4 addresses the 'extralegality' of material life, as groups and individuals contested with authorities for access to commodities.[67] Informal *commerçant* clung limpet-like to formal commercial infrastructure. And, just as seagoing vessels were scraped of barnacles after months at sea, so regulatory agents laboured to dislodge illicit actors rooted in their networks, with limited success. The extralegal strategies so widely deployed set important parameters for the 'new world of goods'. Shells, pepper and wool cloth are my case studies. The *raison d'etre* of officialdom was to keep commerce in

---

[65] For example, Madeline C. Zilfi, 'Whose Laws? Gendering the Ottoman Sumptuary Regime' in Suraiya Faroqhi and Christoph K. Neumann, eds., *Ottoman Costumes: From Textile to Identity* (Istanbul: EREN, 2004), pp. 125–141; Colleen E. Kriger, 'Silk and Sartorial Politics in the Sokoto Caliphate (Nigeria)' in Beverly Lemire, ed., *The Force of Fashion in Politics and Society: Global Perspectives from Early Modern to Contemporary Times* (Aldershot, UK: Ashgate, 2010), pp. 143–166; Rublack, *Dressing Up*, pp. 265–270; Beverly Lemire, 'Fashion Politics and Practice: Indian Cottons and Consumer Innovation in Tokugawa Japan and Early Modern England' in Shoshana-Rose Marzel and Guy D. Stiebel, eds., *Dress and Ideology: Fashioning Identity from Antiquity to the Present*, (London: Bloomsbury Academic, 2014), pp. 189–210.

[66] John Styles, *The Dress of the People: Everyday Fashion in Eighteenth-Century England* (New Haven: Yale University Press, 2007), pp. 247–320.

[67] A concept discussed at length in Chapter 4. Alan Smart and Filippo M. Zerilli, 'Extralegality' in Donald M. Nonini, ed., *A Companion to Urban Anthropology* (John Wiley & Sons, 2014), p. 222. I thank Dr Lynne B. Milgram for generously bringing this work to my attention.

defined channels, controlling the handling, taxing and use of these wares. Consumers and their suppliers refused these directives. Fashions and new tastes were facilitated as a result of porous borders and unworkable regulations, as legal and 'extralegal' activities entwined to the benefit of buyers from all ranks.[68] Tradition figures as well in this scenario. Customary attitudes towards shipwreck, scavenging and the extraction of waste from maritime commerce brought larger flows of commodities into the hands of common people worldwide. Consumerism was augmented through myriad inventive strategies.

Tobacco – Native Americans' bequest to world cultures – is featured in Chapter 5. Europeans initially stumbled across this plant on their arrival in the Americas, a substance integral to the spiritual, diplomatic and social practice of America's first peoples. Thereafter merchants, mariners and missionaries conveyed this leaf to the world, moving it around the globe by 1600. I trace processes of transmission and adoption that occurred in Africa and Asia, as expressed in a variety of cultural forms, redefining sociability and communities of interest. Different configurations of tobacco consumption emerged in Western institutions, delimiting status, occupation and ethnicity. Two categories of labourers experienced distinctive consumer dynamics: plantation slaves and male workforces (mariners and voyageurs) moving long-distance, waterborne cargoes. Slave traders and plantocrats, sea captains and large-scale merchant enterprises enacted systems of coercive consumption to discipline communities critical to the functioning

---

[68] Smart and Zerilli, 'Extralegality'. For smuggling, see Anthony Disney, 'Smugglers and Smuggling in the Western Half of the *Estado Da India* in the Late Sixteenth and Early Seventeenth Centuries' *Indica* 26:1 & 2 (1989): 57–75; Nuala Zahedieh, 'The Merchants of Port Royal Jamaica and the Spanish Contraband Trade, 1655–1692' *William and Mary Quarterly* 43 (1986): 570–593 and 'Trade, Plunder and Economic Development in Early English Jamaica, 1655–1689' *Economic History Review* 39:2 (1986): 205–222; Robert J. Antony, ed., *Elusive Pirates, Pervasive Smugglers: Violence and Clandestine Trade in the Greater China Seas* (Hong Kong: Hong Kong University Press, 2010); Alan L. Karras, *Smuggling: Contraband and Corruption in World History* (Lanham, MD: Rowman & Littlefield, 2010); Paul A. Van Dyke, ed., *Americans and Macao: Trade, Smuggling and Diplomacy on the South China Coast* (Hong Kong: Hong Kong University Press, 2012); Peter Andreas, *Smuggler Nation: How Illicit Trade Made America* (Oxford: Oxford University Press, 2013); Michael Kwass, *Contraband: Louis Mandrin and the Making of a Global Underground* (Cambridge, MA: Harvard University Press, 2014); Felicia Gottmann, *Global Trade, Smuggling, and the Making of Economic Liberalism* (Basingstoke, UK: Palgrave, 2016).

of this global system. I reveal the dimensions of these disciplinary regimes. Racialized consumption was another element to emerge in European precincts, as citizens learned their roles in the new colonial system via representations and interactions with tobacco.[69] Tobacco advertising and material culture tutored metropolitan and Euro-American colonists in the racial politics of consumption and the re-ordering this entailed, as new racial hierarchies were set in place.

Chapter 6 focuses on the needle arts, one of the most plastic discursive forms that is able to measure the impact of commodities in a different register. A new visual vocabulary emerged as a response to contact, connection and exchange, with Asian floriated ceramics and textiles as catalyst goods. The movement of cargoes was augmented by the passage of people – Asian needleworkers, servants and slaves – who reinforced new styles and tastes in Europe and the colonial Americas. New styles of needlework ensued in both localities, giving voice to usually voiceless populations who reinterpreted existing botanic cultures in new ways. Object study is central to this analysis, focused on products that owed nothing to mechanization, but everything to the needle skills learned and revised in worldwide locales. This chapter offers a new perspective on the early globalizing process. Asian floral patterns were among the most powerful emblems of this era, readily translated, encouraging a new-style material discourse. In this widening marketplace, colonized Indigenous Americans negotiated their place through the embroidery of flowered souvenirs, housewares and fashions, as they too responded to globalized material culture. I digress outside the formal timeframe of this book to explore the exceptional creative responses of Native American needleworkers through the mid-nineteenth century. Globalized floral media had entered their communities and sparked new interpretive responses. Despite increased colonial constraints, Native American embroidery contributed to the fully cosmopolitan market that emerged from early globalization. Floral design and floral culture was translated and repurposed, a new visual *lingua franca* that claimed artistic space in a new world of exchange.

This history of consumerism is not a triumphalist saga leading to the apex of modern human development: the shopping mall. Rather I address pressing issues of historical change tied to the advent of new

[69] Thrush, *Indigenous London*, p. 36.

economic, social and cultural practices. The environmental impact of many aspects of this story can be inferred and is occasionally addressed; but that is not the focus of this study. Power was enacted across wider landscapes and new inequities thrived, evident in material practice. Nonetheless, agency is apparent amongst a wide range of historical actors whether tobacco smokers in Sierra Leone, voyageurs on North America's Great Lakes, or fashion-conscious townswomen in Edo, Japan.[70] Likewise, the needleworkers of Asia, Europe and the Americas offer a reassessment of the processes of early modern global communication. These and a host of middling and labouring peoples, through the Americas, Africa and Eurasia experienced the pains and potential of enhanced global commerce and consumption.[71]

Jan De Vries poses the question 'Have there been turning points or points of divergence in the evolution of consumption and consumer society?'[72] The answer is clearly 'yes'. The connections established

[70] Emİnegul Karababa and Gulİz Ger, 'Early Modern Ottoman Coffeehouse Culture and the Formation of the Consumer Subject'*Journal of Consumer Research* 37:5 (February 2011): 737–760; Grehan, 'Smoking and "Early Modern" Sociability'; Danielle van den Heuvel, 'The Multiple Identities of Early Modern Dutch Fishwives' *Signs: Journal of Women in Culture and Society*, 37:3 (2012): 587–594; Jamieson, 'The Essence of Commodification'; Smart Martin, *Buying into the World of Goods.*

[71] Literature addressing these themes includes Shammas, *Pre-Industrial*; Ruth Phillips, *Trading Identities: The Souvenir in Native North American Art from the Northeast, 1700–1900* (Seattle: University of Washington Press, 1998); Susan B. Hanley, *Everyday Things in Premodern Japan: The Hidden Legacy of Material Culture* (Berkley: University of California Press, 1997); Daniel Roche, *A History of Everyday Things: The Birth of Consumption in France, 1600–1800,* translated by Brian Pearce (Cambridge: Cambridge University Press, 2000); John E. Crowley, *The Invention of Comfort: Sensibilities and Design in Early Modern Britain and Early America* (Baltimore: Johns Hopkins University Press, 2001); Maxine Berg, *Luxury and Pleasure in Eighteenth-Century Britain* (Oxford: Oxford University Press, 2005); Marta V. Vicente, *Clothing the Spanish Empire: Families and the Calico Trade in the Early Modern Atlantic World* (New York: Palgrave Macmillan, 2006); Eiko Ikegami, *Bonds of Civility: Aesthetic Networks and the Political Origins of Japanese Culture* (Cambridge: Cambridge University Press, 2005); Riello and Parthasarathi, *The Spinning World*; Haynes, McGowan, Roy and Yanagisawa, *Consumption in South Asia*; Dana Leibsohn, 'Made in China, Made in Mexico' in Donna Pierce and Ronald Otsuka, eds., *At the Crossroads: The Arts of Spanish America and Early Global Trade, 1492–1850* (Denver: Denver Art Museum, 2012); Richard Ate, ed., *Behind Closed Doors: Art in the Spanish American Home* (New York: The Monacelli Press for the Brooklyn Museum, 2013).

[72] De Vries, *Industrious Revolution*, p. 4.

after 1500 pulled world communities closer together in new ways; and for the first time the Americas were drawn into direct and continuing contact with Asia, Africa and Europe, with influences rippling in flows and counterflows.[73] Connections forged new personal and commercial possibilities; and communication through new habits and material culture became more the norm, however unequal. I offer new interpretive paradigms to explain these processes. These diverse and capacious narratives integrate local and comparative perspectives from which a clearer history emerges of the material transformations we shared.

---

[73] The use of the term 'counterflows' is based on the work of Michael H. Fisher, *Counterflows to Colonialism: Indian Travellers and Settlers in Britain 1600–1857* (Delhi: Permanent Black, 2004).

2 | Fabric and Furs
A New Framework of Global Consumption

With Your Majesty's leave I will tell you what I feel about this Chinese trade which in my opinion is prejudicial and should be prevented because of the big profits they get from these [Philippine] Islands for a foreign kingdom. Most of what they [the Chinese merchants] bring is cotton cloth getting first the cotton from here and bringing it back woven when the natives can weave them here with their own cotton if they want to because they make them and even better than those coming from China. They can load them for Mexico. They can load up to four hundred thousand pesos worth. This way they would take care to cultivate and profit from the cotton without the Sangleys [Chinese] as middleman. The Sangleys also bring silk faulty and of poor quality except that which they bring raw and twisted which I am afraid if sent to the Kingdoms of Spain in big quantities will destroy the royal revenues of His Majesty on the silk of Granada, Murcia and Valencia which will not fail to be inconvenient.

'Letter of the Governor of Filipinas, Gómez Pérez Dasmariñas, ... to His Majesty, Philip II, 20 June 1592'[1]

[The Seneca] say that, a year or two ago, they requested, that they should receive a blanket and a piece of cloth for one beaver, to which they got no answer, than that we would tell them, when the ships came ... The Dutch cannot consent to what the brothers request, that we should give so much cloth ... for one beaver, as it has to come a great distance over the sea.

'The Director General to the Seneca ... Fort Orange (Albany) ... 25 July 1660'[2]

Textile usage defined comfort, social status and ethnic identity. Transformations in consumption marked historical eras. Textile

---

[1] 'Letter of the Governor of Filipinas Gómez Pérez Dasmariñas to His Majesty, Philip II, 20 June 1592, Manila' in Virginia Benitez Licuanan and José Llavador Mira, eds., *The Philippines under Spain: Reproduction of the Original Spanish Documents with English Translation*, vol. 5 (1590–1593) (Manila: National Trust for Historical and Cultural Preservation of the Philippines, 1994), pp. 390, 392.

[2] John Roymeyn Bordhead et al., eds., *Documents Relative to the Colonial History of the State of New York, vol. 13 (Albany, NY: Weed, Parsons and Co., 1881)*, pp. 184, 186. Please note: the original text has been faithfully reproduced here as in other quotations, including the inconsistencies of spelling.

production is one of the most significant achievements of industrial technology, while the trade in textiles was among the most important commercial sectors. Foreigners assessed other societies by the quality of their fabrics, the manner of their use and the size of trade in these goods. The new commercial networks forged after 1500 provided conduits for an enhanced circulation of textiles, including new consumer patterns within the Americas and between the Americas and other continents. The impact of expanding markets, with more involved in the making and trading of wares, transformed the material landscape in ways described as a consumer revolution. This terminology is much debated. In the centuries under review, new media were diffused, new commercial connections were enacted and material regimes were revised. New-style cosmopolitanism resulted.

The Spanish governor in Manila, whose letter is excerpted above, reflects an equivocal response to this early globalizing process. He begrudged the Chinese their roles as manufacturers of Philippine raw cotton and dreaded the fallout should Chinese silks appear in Spain. Imperial authorities jealously guarded their advantage. Authorities in Europe, the Middle East, China, Japan and Africa celebrated local industries and often feared competitors. Authorities also feared unfettered consumption across social ranks, legislating material order through sumptuary laws assigning specific material grades to designated groups. They made and remade regulations as commercial forces undercut their edicts. The dynamics of clothing consumption will be addressed in Chapter 3. In this chapter, I explore the meaning of the 'consumer revolution' as textile regimes advanced, attending to different world regions and the significance of the goods traded and consumed. These new patterns of textile exchange were instrumental in the more cosmopolitan material culture, which was the defining paradigm of this age.

Textiles provided a foundational traffic, constituting among the largest cargoes and most important commodities. Robert DuPlessis argues for the centrality of this commerce in the early modern Atlantic World, proving his claims with detailed assessments of the continents and peoples touched by these trades and defined by new habits of consumption.[3] The importance of this heterogeneous trade

---

[3] Robert S. DuPlessis, *The Material Atlantic: Clothing, Commerce, and Colonization in the Atlantic World, 1650–1800* (Cambridge: Cambridge University Press, 2016).

can be tracked further still, to other world reaches where Western European merchants played minor roles. I address the legal commerce in these goods and the new circuits set in place to which the informal and illegal accreted; extralegality and informal markets are subjects of a later chapter.[4] Dynamic demand and inventive consumer conduct characterized this era, an interpretation broadly accepted as historians parse different regions. Yet, this claim of material dynamism was once wholly denied.

Furs and fabrics are the focus of this chapter. I assess these commodities in the context of major interpretive theories, such as the 'industrious revolution', 'old luxury' and 'new', and the great divergence. The early global era forged new and tighter links, directing enhanced commodity flows. Societies with varying agendas shaped these processes, while, at the same time, greater material cosmopolitanism flourished among diverse peoples. Overall, popular tastes evolved as commerce quickened.

Foundational Eurasian/African Networks

This was the cloth age. Textile manufacturing employed vast populations in skilled and semi-skilled tasks, from raising silk worms to reeling threads from silk cocoons, from shearing sheep to spinning thread. Weaving, bleaching, dyeing and pressing were some of the many productive processes that preceded the sale of cloth, before it entered circuits of sale, use and reuse. In every quarter of the world, fibres of all kinds were manipulated into media suitable for garments, embellishments and furnishings, processes that varied from culture to culture, place to place. The business of these commodities was an economic barometer and a marker of regional capacity. Whether as gift or cargo, for open markets or specific castes, textiles evoked their origins and encouraged multiple meanings through their use, while augmenting rivers of commerce.[5]

---

[4] Alan Smart and Filippo M. Zerilli, 'Extralegality' in Donald M. Nonini, ed., *A Companion to Urban Anthropology* (John Wiley and Sons, 2014), pp. 222–238. I thank Dr. Lynne B. Milgram for this reference.

[5] For textiles as gift and for regional sale, see Colleen E. Kriger, *Cloth in West African History* (Oxford: AltaMira Press, 2006); and for silk as market commodity, see Shelagh Vainker, *Chinese Silk: A Cultural History* (Rutgers: Rutgers University Press, 2004).

Importantly, textiles served multiple roles not only as a commodity for sale and use, but also as an alternate currency at a time when the availability of specie was unreliable.[6] Monetization was only sporadically in place, and alternative currencies were essential to mediate exchange. Cloth acted as currency at several levels, including among large merchants over long-distances, enabling regions to interact through elaborate exchange systems. As well, at a second stage, goods were channelled into secondhand networks following initial purchase and use. Both practices contributed vital buoyancy to markets; but it is the former I emphasize here. In fifteenth- and sixteenth-century Korea, cotton cloth served as an official currency, facilitating market activity.[7] The relative functionality of cloth (for use or barter) was gauged within discrete trading zones, sometimes spanning vast spaces, where well-known stuff underwent sophisticated analysis for value and quality. It is essential to note the compound features embedded in these fabrics, as cloth *enabled* trade even as it draped or decorated end users and their abodes. The Indian Ocean and its adjacent territories were one such zone where, as Pedro Machado explains,

Gujarati textiles [from northwest India] had a critical function in African material exchange . . . as primary measure of value for which ivory, slaves and other commodities were exchanged across the Indian Ocean in areas that effectively constituted cloth currency zones of contact . . . These textiles served a critical and wide-spread function as currency in a largely non-monetized world.[8]

---

[6] Cotton cloth was used extensively as a currency in Korea from the fifteenth century, regionally, as well as in international trade and prior to the rise of cotton manufacturing hemp cloth served that role. S. M. Hong-Schunka, 'Exchange of Commodities between Korea and Ryūkū' in Angela Schottenhammer, ed., *Trade and Transfer Across the East Asian 'Mediterranean'* (Wiesbaden: Otto Harrassowitz KG, 2005), pp. 137–138. Indian cotton also figured as a major alternate currency in parts of Africa and Southeast Asia. Giorgio Riello and Tirthankar Roy, 'Introduction' in Giorgio Riello and Tirthankar Roy, eds., *How India Clothed the World: The World of South Asian Textiles, 1500–1850* (Leiden: Brill, 2009), p. 10. For East Africa see Pedro Machado, 'Cloths of a New Fashion: Indian Ocean Networks of Exchange and Cloth Zones of Contact in Africa and India in the Eighteenth and Nineteenth Centuries' in Riello and Roy, *How India Clothed the World*; for the Baltic, Scandinavia and Iceland, see Larry Allen, *The Encyclopedia of Money*, 2nd ed. (Santa Barbara, CA: ABC-CLIO, 2009), pp. 72–73.

[7] T'ae-jin Yi, *The Dynamics of Confucianism and Modernization in Korean History* (Ithaca: Cornell University Press, 2007), pp. 103–104.

[8] Machado, 'Cloths of a New Fashion', pp. 57, 59.

Thus, the persistence and expansion of textile traffic pulled together disparate peoples and satisfied diverse needs.

The Silk Road was another storied network, its labyrinth of tracks linking khanates and kingdoms across the expanse of Central Asia, touching the Caspian and Black Seas, its caravans animating cities like Isfahan, Baghdad, Damascus and Istanbul (Map 2.1). Importantly, these routes remained active even as other commercial systems were ignited, allied to long-established oceanic pathways that served large swaths of Eurasia and Africa.[9]

People, technologies and ideas, as well as richly varied cargoes, flowed through these intricate channels, a system that 'linked all regions of the Afro-Eurasian landmass'.[10] Immense quantities of silk passed along its tracks, along with cargoes of cotton, as Chinese, Indian and other merchants speculated on cloth requirements in regional and distant markets.[11] This web reached its apogee in the fourteenth century, before the traumas wrought by the Black Death buffeted civilizational exchange. During its heyday, silks moved widely, spawning imitations. Once extracted from the control of Chinese producers, silk production took hold in likely habitats along the many branches of the Silk Road, becoming one of the 'trans-civilizational exchanges'.[12] Thereafter, textiles of various sorts flowed east as well as west, north and south, with Persian, Indian and Byzantine silks becoming profitable commodities for Chinese merchants. One result was that foreign substitutes allowed wealthy Chinese merchants to evade sumptuary laws, lining their robes with purple satins from afar. At the western end of the Silk Road, Byzantine silks in royal purple draped Christian effigies of Jesus and the Virgin Mary. These connections would last for centuries, sparking further diffusions of Asian textile culture across the Mediterranean.[13] Land-based

[9]   For example, Stephen Frederic Dale, *Indian Merchants and Eurasian Trade,*
      1600–1750 (Cambridge: Cambridge University Press, 1994); Jagjeet Lally,
      'Rethinking the Geography of Global Economic History: Northwest Indian
      Cotton Cloth and Caravan Trade, c.1600–1900', unpublished paper presented
      at the Economic and Social History of the Premodern World, seminar, Institute
      of Historical Research, 30 May 2014.
[10] David Christian, 'Silk Roads or Steppe Roads? The Silk Road in World History'
      Journal of World History 11:1 (2000), p. 1.
[11] Stephen F. Dale, 'Silk Road, Cotton Road or ... Indo-Chinese Trade in Pre-
      European Times' *Modern Asian Studies* 43:1 (2009): 79–88.
[12] Christian, 'Silk Roads or Steppe Roads?', p. 5.
[13] Xinru Liu, *The Silk Road in World History* (Oxford: Oxford University Press,
      2010), pp. 89–92.

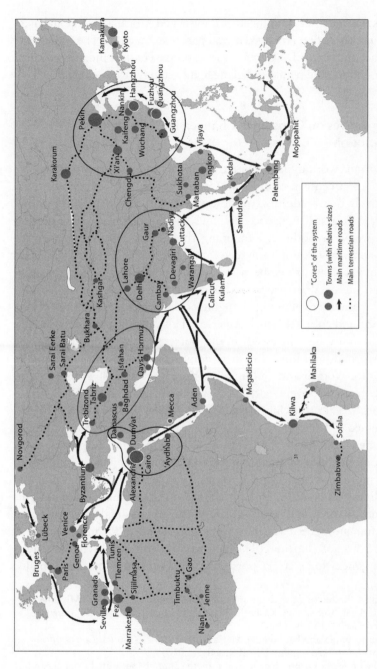

Map 2.1 *The Eurasian and African World-System in the Thirteenth and Fourteenth Centuries.* Philippe Beaujard, 'The Indian Ocean in Eurasian and African World-Systems before the Sixteenth Century' *Journal of World History*, 16:4 (2005), p. 428.

and seaborne routes knit together Eurasia and Africa, with regional overland networks that remained a vital part of exchange.[14] The Columbian
contact and Vasco Da Gama's arrival on the coast of India represented
profound turning points, changing textile cultures irrevocably.

Perspectives on Consumer Change: The Industrious Revolution

Historians work intensively to explain the unique elements of change
in the three centuries following 1500. The focus on consumerism is a
relatively recent addition to these efforts; consumerism in the global
context is a still more recent focus.[15] One of the most important
interpretive hypotheses explaining the rise of consumerism or the
'consumer revolution' emerged from one world region in the first
instance and has since been reassessed for its applicability in other
zones. Jan de Vries proposed the concept of an 'industrious revolution', a theory explaining changing consumer practices in northwest
Europe and colonial North America. This model carries such weight
that it must be addressed at the outset. De Vries argues for the
transformational impact of new employment patterns – principally
those for women and children – options that flourished most intensively from the seventeenth century onwards, well before industrialization.[16] This thinking owes a debt to the work of Joan Thirsk,
discussed in Chapter 1, who argued for the importance of innumerable new enterprises that employed the rural poor. Improved work
options encouraged greater plebeian consumerism, allowing them to
buy more and move further along the continuum from want and
neediness to comfort and pleasure. I must emphasize that in this
period, scarcity and want – brought on by seasonal cycles, natural
and human-made disasters – were still the norm for most people at
least some of the time. The opportunity for more reliable waged
employment for a larger portion of the population marked a major

---

[14] Lally, 'Rethinking the Geography of Global Economic History'; Michelle
Maskiell, 'Consuming Kashmir: Shawls and Empire, 1500–2000' *Journal of
World History* 13:1 (2002): 27–65.

[15] For example, Ina Baghdiantz-McCabe, *A History of Global Consumption:
1500–1800* (Abingdon, UK: Routledge, 2015).

[16] The timing of European economic growth cannot be separated from expanding
trade.

development, made more precious by the new material goods coming to hand. De Vries makes peace between formerly conflicting schools of thought: one emphasized stagnant or falling male wages, suggesting lower standards of living before industrialization; while the other documented rising ownership of new goods, even among labouring and lower middle-ranked families. De Vries argues that the reallocation of female and child labour into waged work enabled the increased purchase of more goods, which were often the products of new industries – goods soon deemed essential. The allocation of work hours was decided collectively as well as individually, depending on opportunities for single women and families. The heightened interest in consumer wares was a shared fascination that drove the desire for waged work among the largest sector of the population.

De Vries, Joan Thirsk and others emphasize the new industrial sectors that arose in this period, many of which were in the textile and clothing industries.[17] Choosing labour over leisure, women and children used their wages to acquire more and different things: captivating items, including ribbons, light wools and mixed-fibre cloth, hosiery, buttons and gloves. As De Vries observes, 'The industrious revolution had as its social pendant female earning power'.[18] This analysis moves the discussion of consumption away from a narrow focus on elites and their acolytes; it addressed the stimulus of growing cities and commercial connections, as well as enhanced

[17] Joan Thirsk, *Economic Policy and Projects: The Development of a Consumer Society in Early Modern England* (Oxford: Clarendon Press, 1978); Margaret Spufford, *The Great Reclothing of Rural England: Petty Chapmen and their Wares in the Seventeenth Century* (London: Hambledon Press, 1984); Pamela Sharpe, 'Literally Spinsters: A New Interpretation of Local Economy and Demography in Colyton in the Seventeenth and Eighteenth Centuries' *Economic History Review* 44:1 (1991): 46–65; Elizabeth C. Sanderson, *Women and Work in Eighteenth-Century Edinburgh* (Basingstoke, UK: 1996); Hester Dibbits, 'Between Society and Family Values. The Linen Cupboard in Early Modern Households' in Anton Schuurman and Pieter Spierenburg, eds., *Private Domain, Public Inquiry. Families and Life Styles in the Netherlands and Europe, 1550 to the Present* (Liversum: Verloren, 1996), pp. 125–145; Beverly Lemire, *Fashion's Favourite: The Cotton Trade and the Consumer in Britain, 1660–1800* (Oxford: Oxford University Press, 1991) and *Dress, Culture and Commerce: The English Clothing Trade Before the Factory* (Basingstoke, UK: Macmillan, 1997).

[18] Jan de Vries, *The Industrious Revolution: Consumer Behavior and the Household Economy, 1650 to the Present* (Cambridge: Cambridge University Press, 2008), p. 179.

rural employment. The case for this new pattern of labour and consumption is compelling and supported by deep research on changing individual and household practice, including the measurable transformation of material life.[19]

Historians of China, among others, were similarly engaged in explaining transformations in social and economic practice, including an enhanced ownership of goods. There was, for a time, a palpable tension as historians of these regions struggled to claim their place in discussions of consumption, when major works on comparative consumer history largely ignored discoveries outside the West.[20] From at least the 1990s, Craig Clunas, then curator at the Victoria and Albert Museum, London, noted the multiplication of delectable things in late

---

[19] Jan de Vries, 'The Industrial Revolution and the Industrious Revolution' *Journal of Economic History* 54 (1994): 249–270 and *The Industrious Revolution*. See also: Neil McKendrick, John Brewer and J. H. Plumb, *The Birth of a Consumer Society: The Commercialization of Eighteenth-Century England* (London: Hutchinson, 1983); Lorena S. Walsh, 'Urban Amenities and Rural Sufficiency: Living Standards and Consumer Behavior in the Colonial Chesapeake, 1643–1777' *Journal of Economic History* 43:1 (1983): 109–117; T. H. Breen, '"Baubles of Britain": The American and Consumer Revolutions of the Eighteenth Century' *Past & Present* 119 (1988): 73–104 and *The Marketplace of Revolution: How Consumer Politics Shaped American Independence* (New York: Oxford University Press, 2004); M. Baulant, A.J. Schuurman and P. Servais, eds., *Inventaires après-deces et ventes de meubles: Apport s á une histoire de la vie économique et quotidienne XIVe – XIX siècle* (Louvain-la Neuve: Academia, 1988); Daniel Roche, *La Culture des apparences* (Paris: Librairie Arthème Fayard, 1989); Carole Shammas, *The Pre-Industrial Consumer in England and America* (Oxford: Clarendon Press, 1990); Cary Carson, Ronald Hoffman and Peter J. Albert, eds., *Of Consuming Interest* (Charlottesville: University Press of Virginia, 1994); Maxine Berg, *Age of Manufactures 1700–1820: Industry, Innovation and Work in Britain*, 2nd ed. (London: Routledge, 1994), especially Chapter 7; Lorna Weatherill, *Consumer Behaviour and Material Culture in Britain, 1660–1760* (London: Routledge, 1996); Bruno Blondé, 'Tableware and Changing Consumer Patterns. Dynamics of Material Culture in Antwerp, 17th–18th Centuries' in Johan Veeckman, ed., *Majolica and Glass from Italy to Antwerp and Beyond. The Transfer of Technology in the 16th–Early 17th Century* (Antwerp: Stadt Antwerpen, 2002), pp. 295–311; Mark Overton, Jane Whittle, Darron Dean and Andrew Hann, *Production and Consumption in English Households, 1600–1750* (London: Routledge, 2004).

[20] See, for example, Craig Clunas, 'Modernity Global and Local: Consumption and the Rise of the West' *American Historical Review* 104:2 (1999): 1497–1511; Donald Quataert, 'Clothing Laws, State and Society in the Ottoman Empire, 1720–1829' *International Journal of Middle Eastern Studies* 29 (1997): 403–425.

Ming China (late sixteenth and early seventeenth centuries). The "superfluous things" he identified carried immense social weight.[21] His close study of Ming objects inspired new questions and new hypotheses. Clunas observed shared anxieties among Chinese and European authorities as their intractable citizens indulged in new commodities at odds with extant sumptuary legislation. New silks appeared during the late Ming era, for example, goods absent from older sumptuary codes and now favoured by stylish 'servant girls'. Clunas called for a reinterpretation of Chinese history, challenging the widespread assumption among historians of Europe that innovation in material culture and consumption was only to be found in Western climes – a holdover from the Braudelian view. Clunas noted that in the 1990s, 'social historians [of China] simply have not provided those of us who work with objects with a detailed enough picture to enable us to insert in their proper contexts the pieces which we have in our charge'.[22] Clunas produced his own explanations, attentive to urban dynamism, material richness and the complaints of moralistic Ming commentators scandalized by rising consumption. One pointed to the disruptive effects of 'the wealth of [the cities of] Suzhou and Hangzhou ... [and] the lavishness of life there, with jobs being created for all sorts of "boatmen, sedan chair carriers, singsong boys and dancing girls"'. It was these selfsame girls who were said to 'look down on brocaded silks and embroidered gowns'.[23] Hyperbole aside, Clunas saw vibrant patterns of consumer practice in China, equivalent to those described for early modern Europe.

Kenneth Pomeranz positions China within a paradigm that emphasized consumer practice. He addresses Qing China and assesses whether the concept of the industrious revolution fit this vast and complex polity. The absence of equivalent documents to those found in Europe precluded any easy quantitative comparison. Building on the findings of Clunas and others, Pomeranz concurs that 'De Vries' picture of Western Europe describes advanced areas of China as well'.[24] Pomeranz observes the increased importance of new consumables in these flourishing urban

---

[21] See, for example,Craig Clunas, *Superfluous Things: Material Culture and Social Status in Early Modern China* (Honolulu: University of Hawai'i Press, 1991) and 'The Art of Social Climbing in Sixteenth-Century China' *Burlington Magazine* 133:1059 (June 1991): 368–375.

[22] Clunas, 'Art of Social Climbing', p. 369.

[23] Clunas, *Superfluous Things*, p. 146, 154.

[24] Pomeranz, *Great Divergence*, p. 94.

regions of China, including new furnishings and bodily embellishments produced by textile industries. He necessarily couches his comparison with caveats, while drawing attention to women's earnings in the cotton sector and the popularity of newly fashionable commodities of various kinds. Links to commercialized, capitalized markets affected opportunities to consume, as well as opportunities to work in consumer industries. Importantly, the commoditization of popular fashion goods was well advanced in China, particularly among the eastern cities like Suzhou. And, as in Europe, expanded opportunities arose for female paid employment including in the flourishing embroidery trades that were a hallmark of this area. An estimated 100,000 female embroiderers congregated in the countryside outside Suzhou in the mid-Qing era, supplying an endless array of embroidered confections to urban retailers, who in turn served an urbane set of customers.[25] The sophisticated, urbanized sectors of Chinese society supported new facets of consumer practice, in ways still being assessed.[26]

The concept of an industrious revolution offers a valuable comparative template, one employed as well in the Ottoman context. Here, too, the 'democratization of consumption' among low-status citizens was a notable feature of early modern Ottoman society. Eminegül Karababa traces the cyclical appearance of new light fashionable textiles in probate records of elite and non-elite people in sixteenth- and seventeenth-century urban Anatolia. Here, too, textile choices increased, the result of expanding labour opportunities, commercial dynamism and networks of exchange.[27] In sum, the paradigm of the industrious revolution fits a range of sophisticated, commercialized, urbanized regions where new waged employment generated new choices, where consumer desires pushed against official restraints. These phenomena shaped gender options and family priorities in a number of world areas, exemplified in the rising tides of new cheap linens, light silks or pretty cottons. Some moralists decried these changes, seeing this as perverse luxury. The notion of 'luxury' is another salient point in this period,

---

[25] Rachel Silberstein, 'Eight Scenes of Suzhou: Landscape Embroidery, Urban Courtesans, and Nineteenth-Century Chinese Women's Fashions' *Late Imperial China* 36:1 (2015), p. 23.

[26] Pomeranz, *Great Divergence*, Chapters 2 and 3.

[27] Eminegül Karababa, 'Investigating Early Modern Ottoman Consumer Culture in the Light of Probate Inventories' *Economic History Review* 65:1 (2012): 194–219.

and my next focus is the question of luxuries old and new as I move into the study of a major sector of the material market: the fur trade.

The Fur Trade, 'Old Luxury' and 'New'

The appetite for furs burgeoned in many world communities, all of which displayed a seemingly inexhaustible desire for peltry. Of course, the demand for certain furs was customary among the elites, what Jan de Vries terms an 'old luxury'. These commodities were imbued with cultural meanings that aligned rare and sumptuous pelts with majesty and authority. Coronation and court robes in many kingdoms, for example, were embellished with ermine or sable, the most exceptional of furs for those of exalted inherited status. Kings and princes might joust for the best of these luxuries to demonstrate their magnificence; these narrow contests preoccupied very few and were approved by moralists as appropriate material manners. Such indulgences were approved as confirmation of social stasis. Tensions arose, however, when new luxury of a different sort emerged well beyond the court and courtiers' realm. As de Vries observes,

Rather than being defined by royal courts, the New Luxury was generated by urban society. Rather than presenting a coherent style and hegemonic cultural message, it consisted of heterogeneous elements. ... New Luxury, striving more for comfort and pleasure, lent itself to multiplication and diffusion ... [serving] more to communicate cultural meaning ... among participants in consumption'.[28]

There is great utility in this theoretical concept, categorizing consumer goods and the varied practices of consumption according to the social models they sustained. Indeed, the medieval Russian fur trade fed a predominantly old style of luxury, the skins carried from the far north along tracks to the Black Sea, thereafter dispersed east, west and south. In the fourteenth century, Ibn Battuta confirmed that 'ermine is of the best of the varieties of furs. One mantel of this fur is valued in the land of India at a thousand dinars'.[29] This noted Islamic scholar and pilgrim ultimately received a luxurious sable robe of his own, a gift from the Khan of the Chagatai Mongol khanate, marking the esteem in which

---

[28] De Vries, *Industrious Revolution*, pp. 44–45.
[29] Janet Martin, *Treasures of the Land of Darkness: The Fur Trade and Its Significance for Medieval Russia* (Cambridge: Cambridge University Press, 1986), p. 31.

Battuta was held and the eminence of the Khan.[30] Crowns and coronation and ceremonial robes disporting rare and costly furs made visible
the exalted status of the wearer. These patterns of use and gift exchange
exemplify the traditional roles of fur as a materialization of power and
patronage, the epitome of old luxury.[31]

However, the cultural politics of fur evolved, even as some of the old
practices remained. The new patterns of fur consumption, arising after the
1500s, do not fit neatly in the 'old luxury' category and particularly not
during the worldwide expansion of the fur trade, a time defined by rising
consumption of cloth, clothing and accessories. Fur certainly remained a
marker of status, with legislated standards of wear across Eurasian societies (whether or not these could be enforced). In France, for example,
magistrates were permitted to wear scarlet robes lined with ermine, a
mark of their august appointed rank.[32] But a passion for fur did not burn
only in patrician breasts, and the widening appetite for furs spurred the
sourcing, making and use of this medium. The 'new luxury' dimensions of
this fur trade included the newly wealthy, who played with the theatrics of
peltry, as well as the more humble middling and even labouring folk who
aspired to furs of other sorts for their looks and utility. Members of
wealthy commercial, professional and trading families hungered for fur,
men like Hans Fugger (1531–1598). A scion of the powerful Fugger
merchant family, based in Augsburg and Swabia, the middle-aged merchant took immense care to hunt down the necessary number and quality
of lynx pelts to make a coat in a particular Hungarian style. Winter was
approaching, and he set his heart on this garment, writing to correspon-
dents across Europe for the requisite skins.[33] The 1557 portrait of a
married woman from the Slosgin family of Cologne (Plate 2.1) exemplifies the rhetorical value of furs, her wide ermine sleeves contrasting
dramatically with the deep red velvet undersleeves of her ensemble. The
white ermine added a richly tactile element to her self-fashioning.

---

[30] Ibn Battuta, *The Travels of Ibn Battuta, A.D. 1325–1354* (Cambridge:
      Cambridge University Press, The Hakluyt Society, 1971), p. 560.
[31] For Russian and Tartar merchants in Bengal, in the 1500s, see Ralph Fitch, 'The
      Relations of Master Ralph Fitch' in E. Denison Ross and Eileen Power, eds., *The
      Broadway Travellers: The First Englishmen in India* (London: George
      Routledge and Sons, 1930), p. 59.
[32] Roche, *The Culture of Clothing*, p. 40.
[33] Ulinka Rublack, *Dressing Up: Cultural Identity in Renaissance Europe*
      (Oxford: Oxford University Press, 2010), pp. 52–53.

Was there a tacit challenge in the use of this storied fur by a woman of bourgeois rank? Ermine had long been associated with royal and noble equipage in Europe, in coronation robes, crowns and peer's robes.[34] Yet this woman was not reticent in her desires. The ermine she wanted was readily available to one of the prominent merchant families in the free imperial city of Cologne, a centre of vibrant commerce.[35] The choice of this peltry tested traditional uses and traditional hierarchies of consumption.[36]

Elite consumers continued with their customary usage of furs, marking dynastic or diplomatic events, while at the same time less august buyers stretched the boundaries of fur consumption, creating wider categories of use and enjoyment with different meanings assigned.[37] Humble and modest men and women pushed for their mite of fur, buying hats, collars, gloves and muffs with fur incorporated in myriad ways. More people draped shoulders and beds as they could with squirrel and rabbit, driving demand for greater quantities and qualities of fur from different beasts, stimulating fashion innovation. Aside from the look, fur possessed important functional qualities, offering

[34] Francis Sandford, *The History of the Coronation of James II, ... King of England, Scotland ...* (London: Thomas Newcomb, 1687), pp. 21–22, 33, 44; Robert Huish, *An Authentic History of the Coronation of His Majesty, King George the Fourth* (London: J. Robins and Co. Albion Press, 1821), pp. 15, 68–70; S. A. M. Adshead, *Material Culture in Europe and China, 1400–1800: The Rise of Consumerism* (Basingstoke, UK: Macmillan, 1997), pp. 90–91.

[35] Johannes Vermeer's portrait *Woman with a Lute* (1662–1663) likewise portrays a young bourgeois woman whose use of ermine is more restrained, a narrow trim at the neck and sleeves of her gown: www.metmuseum.org/collection/the-collection-online/search/437880?rpp=30&pg=1&ft=ermine&when=A.D.+1600–1800&pos=1, accessed 22 November 2015.

[36] This fashion was replicated in a later portrait of an affluent colonial woman, Mrs John Dart of Charleston, South Carolina (1772–1774): www.metmuseum.org/collection/the-collection-online/search/12794?rpp=30&pg=1&ft=ermine&when=A.D.+1600–1800&pos=5, accessed 22 November 2015. Mrs Dart did not own an ermine-trimmed robe; but with the compliance of the painter her garments were adapted to include an item that held singular cachet.

[37] Jean Baptiste DuHade describes a room in which the Chinese emperor stored 'many habits lined with various furs of foxes, ermine, or zibeline, which the emperor sometimes bestows on his servants'. DuHade, *The Chinese Traveller: Containing a Geographical, Commercial and Political History of China ...*, vol. 1, 3rd ed. (London: E. and C. Dilly, 1741), p. 120. See also, Jonathan Schlesinger, *A World Trimmed with Fur: Wild Things, Pristine Places, and the Natural Fringes of Qing Rule* (Stanford: Stanford University Press, 2017), Chapter 1.

essential warmth in cold climates, and was treasured for practicality as well as aesthetics. Peltry was invaluable in the winter months, and those who could afford the cost used fur throws and mantles as well as snug fur garments. In fact, the warmth of a rabbit-skin robe was vastly superior to its woven alternatives and, as a result, was widely used in many cultures.[38] The pelts of lynx and rabbit, squirrel and martin, otter and fox, sable and beaver, wolf, cat and dog offered variations in look, length, feel, weight and cost whether full pelts or off-cuts from feet and bellies. Moreover, there was not a simple hierarchy in furs and fur consumptions, as a king might also use rabbit fur to warm his winter nightwear.[39]

Country folk throughout Europe mastered skills as trappers and traded rabbit skins, squirrel and polecat pelts with pedlars. Some peripatetic dealers, like those based in Trondheim, Norway, amassed substantial quantities of skins as a matter of routine on their circuits through northern lands.[40] Trapping was widespread in many parts, where small prey could be snared and the skins harvested. Smallholders also raised rabbits for this purpose. A Scottish writer reiterated the value of such husbandry in 1777: 'if the rabbit is of the best sort, [its fur] is of such value as always to be sure of coming to a ready market'.[41] Raised or trapped, rabbit skins traded internationally, with Ireland exporting rabbit skins to Amsterdam, for example.[42] These instances sketch some of the myriad participants invested in this sector.[43]

---

[38]   David Yoder, Jon Blood and Reid Mason, 'How Warm Were They? Thermal Properties of Rabbit Skin Robes and Blankets' *Journal of California and Great Basin Anthropology* 25:1 (2005): 55–68.

[39]   Joan Thirsk, *Alternative Agriculture. A History from the Black Death to the Present Day* (Oxford: Oxford University Press, 1997), p. 269.

[40]   Camila Luise Dahl and Piia Lempiäinen, 'The World of Foreign Goods and Imported Luxuries: Merchant and Shop Inventories in Late 17th-century Denmark-Norway' in Tov Engelhardt Mathiassen, Marie-Louise Nosch, Maj Ringgaard, Kirsten Toftegaard and Mikkel Venborg Pedersen, eds., *Fashionable Encounters: Perspectives and Trends in Textile and Dress in the Early Modern Nordic World* (Oxford and Philadelphia: Oxbow Books, 2014), pp. 4–5.

[41]   James Anderson, *Essays Relating to Agriculture and Rural Affairs*, 2nd ed., vol. 2, (Edinburgh, 1777), p. 306.

[42]   George Macartney, *An Account of Ireland in 1773. By a Late Chief Secretary of the Kingdom.* (London, 1773), p. 119; *An Account of the Quantities and Species of Goods Imported into Ireland from Foreign Parts, for Seven Years, Ended the 25th of March 1783*, (Dublin, 1783), p. 5;

[43]   Spufford, *The Great Reclothing of Rural England*, pp. 51, 185; Laurence Fontaine, *History of Pedlars in Europe*, translated by Vicki Whittaker

Northern territories in Eurasia provided the best furs with the densest coats on that continent. The fur trade was a mainstay of these lands, the goods operating as a type of currency and with local hunting communities supplying pelts for trade goods. The northern and arctic regions received sustained attention from Europeans, not least in the hunt for the Northeast Passage between Europe and China after 1500.[44] The English Muscovy Company joined the ranks of Scottish and Dutch adventurers in the 1550s who were sailing north seeking a route to China, but settled instead for trade with Russia and the furs to be had for markets in Western Europe.[45] Russian influence reached ever deeper into Central Asia and Siberia, challenging the existing khanates. From the sixteenth through the eighteenth centuries, the Russian government supported the establishment of trading posts followed by settlements and towns, all in the service of this lucrative enterprise, another facet of the global linkages that characterized this era. Russians and their Indigenous allies ultimately crossed the Bering Strait to the northwest coast of America in pursuit of furs.[46] Russian political power and business acumen are exemplified in a late 1600s portrait of Prince Andrey Priklonskiy, who was sent as ambassador to Shah Suleiman of Persia in 1673 (Plate 2.2). Russia's iconic furs are evident in Priklonskiy's cape and hat, the cloth in his silk and velvet robes perhaps the manufacture of Persia.[47] It is not clear whether he is garbed in fur-lined garments or not; fur was certainly part of his political mandate in discussions with Persia. The silk trade

(Cambridge: Polity Press, 1996), pp. 8–34. For rabbit skins owned by a London furriers and dealers, see *Old Bailey Proceedings Online* (www.old baileyonline.org, version 7.0, accessed 9 July 2014), May 1790, trial of ELIZABETH FARROW (t17900526-48); *Old Bailey Proceedings Online*, January 1791, trial of MARY INGLES (t17910112-8); Dahl and Lempiäinen, 'The World of Foreign Goods', p. 5.

[44] Peter C. Mancall, 'The Raw and the Cold: Five English Sailors in Sixteenth-Century Nunavut' *William and Mary Quarterly* 70:1 (2013): 3–40.

[45] The wealth secured by Dutch merchants in the Russia trade helped fund the launch of Dutch ventures in the East Indies. Paul Bushkovitch, *A Concise History of Russia* (Cambridge: Cambridge University Press, 2012), p. 42.

[46] Janet Martin, 'The Land of Darkness and the Golden Horde: The Fur Trade Under the Mongols 13th–14th Centuries' *Cahiers du Monde russe et soviétique* 19:4 (1978): 401–421; Raymond Henry Fisher, *The Russian Fur Trade, 1550–1700* (Berkeley: University of California Press, 1943), pp. 8–23.

[47] Marika Sardar, 'Silk Along the Seas: Ottoman Turkey and Safavid Iran in the Global Textile Trade' in Amelia Peck, ed., *Interwoven Globe: The Worldwide Textile Trade, 1500–1800* (New York: Metropolitan Museum of Art, 2013), pp. 75, 77–79.

between Persia and Russia was growing in that era, involving the exchange of silks for rich peltry.[48]

The fur trade was a global system of environmental, commercial and cultural interaction, feeding diverse markets across Eurasia. Jewish dealers sold cheap furs in eighteenth-century flea markets in Istanbul. Though termed 'fake' by Muslim and Greek competitors, these tawdry goods nevertheless found willing buyers despite (or because of) their low quality and price.[49] Customers were happy with these wider options. One of the signature features of consumer markets in these centuries was the proliferation of midrange and inexpensive goods – new luxuries – offering a wider set of options for buyers, who interpreted these goods and their uses within their own calculus of value. The dynamism of the early modern global fur trade produced a widening breadth of commodities. Damascus marketplaces were stocked with a variety of fur goods of different qualities: rabbit, squirrel or cat sufficed for poorer shoppers, helping them to keep out the winter cold. Furs were valued in a multitude of dynamic commercial societies, holding richly varied significance.[50]

In China, the Manchu revived fur's fashionable status when they established the Qing dynasty (1644–1912). The northern Manchurian people held a particular love of furs from their ancestral lands, esteeming lustrous coats in particular (mink, fox, otter, sable), a taste adopted by their Chinese servants, administrators and military even before the formal conquest in 1644. Thereafter, these fashions flourished as nobles and courtiers adopted this mode. A prince of the first rank was assigned sable for court wear, with a fourth-rank prince allotted snow leopard and a first-rank bureaucrat approved to wear wolf.[51] Fur's success was likely encouraged by the effects of the little ice age in China, as well as elsewhere in the Northern Hemisphere, which were heightened by volcanic eruptions in Peru in the early 1600s. Further volcanic events recurred in the 1640s, bringing a period of cooler temperatures doubtless favourable to the use of peltry wherever

---

[48] Dale, *Indian Merchants and Eurasian Trade*, pp. 88–89.

[49] Suraiya Faroqhi, 'Introduction, or Why and How One Might Want to Study Ottoman Clothes' in Suraiya Faroqhi and Christoph K. Neumann, eds., *Ottoman Costumes: From Textile to Identity* (Istanbul: EREN, 2004), p. 35.

[50] James Grehan, *Everyday Life and Consumer Culture in 18th-Century Damascus* (Seattle: University of Washington Press, 2007), pp. 215–216.

[51] Schlesinger, *A World Trimmed with Fur*, p. 37.

possible.[52] In Qing China, the finest pelts were assigned to imperial and noble families as tribute, and sable was particularly esteemed, forming the basis of its early dynastic tribute system. As the natural stock of sable declined in some regions under heavy pressure, its rhetorical value to the Qing simply increased.[53]

The vast administration of the imperial household had a vested interest in these goods, as the profits from this virtual monopoly trade in quality furs were a major source of imperial revenue. Tribute in the form of sable, fox, ermine, mink and wolf pelts, as well as levies of designated furs, were funnelled into the imperial household from Mongolia and Manchuria. Thereafter, officials graded the pelts, assigning the best to their masters. Second-grade stuff was given as gifts by the emperor, and the lowest-grade furs were dispersed to provincial officials for sale.[54] Here, too, passions for furs ran high. Lower-ranked people enjoyed goods of lesser quality, a synonym of their status; still, these pelts allowed them to be warmed against wind and weather while making a statement. Plate 2.3 depicts a Manchu commoner about 1800, dressed for the cold in a full-length fur coat, one of several portrayals of Chinese fur-clad men produced by British artist William Alexander. Alexander crafted his portraits during Lord Macartney's embassy to Beijing in 1793. This depiction of perhaps a wealthy peasant sporting a rather shaggy fur garment may not be apocryphal, as squirrel, wolf and dog pelts were thought suitable for men of this rank. This image portrays the less august tastes a long way from the imperial court. This is in no way equivalent to the sumptuousness of the sable-lined robes beloved of the imperial family and was not intended as such; this image suggests how unassuming folk equipped themselves for the climate, perhaps their reward for industrious labours and a demonstration of material priorities. The enthusiasm for furs in Qing China ran deep, a material idiom of the dynasty. The politics of consumption and Qing sumptuary rules

---

[52] Adshead, *Material Culture in Europe and China*, pp. 90–91; Arturo Giraldez, *The Age of Trade: The Manila Galleons and the Dawn of the Global Economy* (Lanham, MD: Rowman and Littlefield, 2015), p. 89. The 'little ice age' is typically dated from *c.* 1350–1870 and, while cooler generally, included periods of intense cold weather.

[53] David A. Bello, *Across Forest, Steppe, and Mountain: Environment, Identity, and Empire in Qing China's Borderlands* (New York: Cambridge University Press, 2015), pp. 78–81, 87.

[54] Chang Te Ch'ang, 'The Economic Role of the Imperial Household in the Ch'ing Dynasty' *Journal of Asian Studies* 31:2 (1972), pp. 244, 251–261.

are addressed in Chapter 3, including the broad unquenchable appetite for peltry. The key point at this juncture is to note the capaciousness of this commerce, the networks serving this phenomenon and the new-style consumer tastes enabled by these ventures.

Russians were delighted to supply China with furs, as they received specie in exchange. Since the 1560s, silver from Americas flowed into Chinese coffers via the trans-Pacific Manila Galleon route, giving China handsome reserves of precious metals. As we saw in the opening extract, Chinese mercantile interests were closely focused on Manila, among other locales. Russia gradually developed formal relations with China, which began after the first diplomatic mission from Moscow to Beijing in 1654, with a treaty formalized in 1689.[55] China's demand for furs encouraged trapping and trading across Siberia and beyond, an enterprise managed by Russians and their intermediaries. Furs were a staple in the Russian state caravan trade to China, with the 1706 caravan earning a bumper profit of 270,000 roubles. Private merchants from Russia risked the ire of the tsar attempting to profit from this traffic, ultimately flooding Chinese markets with furs and driving down prices. Eventually, the free traders won out, and the state-sponsored caravans stopped in 1769.[56] The composition of these exchanges is suggested in the 1727 sale comprised of nearly 52,000 sable pelts and over 66,000 silver, red and cross fox skins valued at nearly 150,000 roubles.[57] This was one of several channels feeding Chinese demand. As fur-bearing animals were gradually depleted in easily accessible territories and demand continued undiminished, traders pushed further north, east and west, forging links with new communities of hunters and trappers. The city of Kyakhta, on the Mongolian-Russian border, grew by serving this traffic, first dealing with furs from more proximate forests and tundra and, next, the cargoes funnelled from the North Pacific, carried by river to this entrepôt. The environmental impact of this hunt yielded myriad consequences, effects evident on both sides of the Bering Strait, as well as throughout North America and farther

[55] Martha Avery, *The Tea Road: China and Russia Meet Across the Steppe* (Beijing: China Intercontinental Press, 2003), pp. 7, 9; R. E. F. Smith and David Christian, *Bread and Salt: A Social and Economic History of Food and Drink in Russia* (Cambridge: Cambridge University Press, 1984), pp. 228–229.

[56] Avery, *Tea Road*, pp. 90–91.

[57] Lai, 'Exotic Commodities'; Mikhail Iosifovich Sladoviskii, *History of Economic Relations between Russia and China*, translated from Russian (Jerusalem: Israel Program for Scientific Translation, 1966), pp. 30–32.

afield. Ultimately, in the 1780s, captains from many nations plumbed the broad South Pacific in the hunt for fur seals off Tasmania, New Zealand and Antarctic islands.[58] Chinese demand mirrored that in other parts of Eurasia, a driving force that pulled disparate lands, peoples and environments in contact with global markets. North America was another continent touched by this power.

Native North Americans' fur garments enthralled the Europeans who first arrived on their shores in the 1500s. In the early years, during repeated contacts along coastline and riverbanks, Europeans sometimes stripping Indigenous men of their fur robes, replacing these with whatever apparel was to hand.[59] Indigenous peoples found this behaviour puzzling. But these exchanges gradually formed the platform on which diplomacy and trade developed, particularly in the northern regions of the continent, where richly furred animals were plentiful and their pelts top quality. Europeans' commercial ardour shaped relations in contact zones along the littoral and across vast tracts fed by inland waterways.[60] The reasons for this passion is clear: the profits to be won from the growing markets for furs from the 1500s, including the making and wearing of felted fur hats, which were the epitome of style among early modern Europeans. The vogue for felted hats represented a new and growing sector, a major addition to those buying and using peltry, a new luxury that was open to 'multiplication and diffusion ... [serving] more to communicate cultural meaning ... among participants in consumption'.[61]

By the later 1500s, felting beaver hair into hat material was a flourishing enterprise, producing the best-quality felt hats available. Just as fur in pelt form was increasingly required, so too were goods manufactured from the undercoat of furred animals. Glossy, smooth, lightweight, resilient in fog, rain or sleet, the felted beaver hat was the best of its kind and the most

---

[58] Adshead, *Material Culture in Europe and China*, pp. 91–92.

[59] Johnson, 'Material Translation', Chapter 2, for the routine request to exchange clothing; Sherry Farrell Racette, 'Sewing Ourselves Together: Clothing, Decorative Arts and the Expression of Metis and Half Breed Identity', unpublished PhD, 2004, University of Manitoba, pp. 63–64; E.E. Rich, ed., *Hudson's Bay Copy Booke of Letters ...*, *1688–1696* (London: Hudson's Bay Record Society, 1957), p. 61.

[60] George R. Hamell, 'Strawberries, Floating Islands, and Rabbit Captains: Mythical Realities and European Contact in the Northwest During the Sixteenth and Seventeenth Centuries' *Journal of Canadian Studies / Revue d'études canadiennes* 21:4 (1987), pp. 81–84. For the premise of 'contact zones' see Pratt, *Imperial Eyes*, p. 4.

[61] De Vries, *Industrious Revolution*, pp. 44–45.

Figure 2.1 *Woman with High Crowned Hat c.* 1640s. Wenceslaus Hollar (1607–1677). Artwork from University of Toronto Wenceslaus Hollar Digital Collection, scanned by University of Toronto.

desirable European male fitment. Genteel and respectable European women also wore felted hats in the seventeenth and eighteenth centuries, a visual punctuation asserting their status and prestige. This portrait of a seventeenth-century English gentlewoman by Prague-born artist Wenceslaus Hollar exemplifies this essential headwear, a sign of this woman's cosmopolitan tastes and another product of global systems of supply and consumption (Figure 2.1). Various centres served the European market for felted hats, with London being one. Its workshops supplied Europeans, as well as colonists in the Americas and the Caribbean, reaching peak exports of over 700,000 hats annually in 1736, of which 83 per cent were beaver. Men and women of lower status relied on hats made from a combination of fibres like sheep, goat or rabbit, with perhaps a little beaver hair adding a modicum of quality. More of the cheaper sort of hats was exported to the colonies.[62] Head

---

[62] David Corner, 'The Tyranny of Fashion: The Case of the Felt-Hatting Trade in the Late Seventeenth and Eighteenth Centuries' *Textile History* 22:2 (1991), pp. 155–156.

coverings were vital accessories for all ranks of men and women, being crucial mediators of gender norms including male expressions of hat honour.[63] The routine uncovering of the head by men, a stylized expression of their obeisance, involved a set of choreographed gestures, whether participants were genteel or plebeian, military or secular. The hat was the centrepiece of this polite semaphore, as suggested in this German instructional guide below (Figure 2.2). This pantomime was so ubiquitous that it became the target of radical seventeenth-century Protestants, like the English Quakers, who denounced hat deference to any but God, decrying the 'artificial, feigned, and strained art of Complement, consisting ... of fopperies ... crouchings and cringings ... [and] uncovering their heads'.[64] This critique reveals the centrality of headwear in European social practice. The proliferation of hats was another aspect of the new luxury sweeping numerous world communities. Securing raw materials for this accessory was of great moment, promising great profits.

Russians first mastered the manipulation of beaver undercoat or 'wool', a secret they struggled to keep. They learned how to comb out the thick pelt for later processing, the hairs making a densely cohesive fabric of the best kind.[65] As beaver populations plunged in Europe, the hunt moved further into northern Eurasia and across the Atlantic to the Americas, driving colonial priorities in northern reaches.

The St Laurence River, long frequented by Basque, French, Portuguese and English fishers and whalers, became a major gateway to fur trading

---

[63] Lai, Hui-min, 'Japanese Products and Everyday Life in Suzhou, 1736–1795', ('Suzhou de dongyang huo yu shimin shenghuo, 1736–1795') *Papers Collection of Modern History Institute of Academic Sinica (Zhongyang yanjiu yuan jindai shi yanjiu suo jikan)*, 63(2009)1–48; Huimin Lai, 'The Exotic Commodities and Banner People's Daily Life in Beijing during Qianlong and Jiaqing Reign 1735–1820' ('Qian Jia shidai Beijing de yanghuo yu qiren richang shenghuo') in Wu Jen-shu, Paul Katz, and Lin May-li, eds., *The City and Chinese Modernity, (Cong chengshi kan zhongguo de xiandai xing).* (Taipei: Institute of Modern History, Academia Sinica, 2010), p. 17; Veronika Hyden-Hanscho, 'Beaver Hats, Drugs and Sugar Consumption in Vienna around 1700: France as an Intermediary for Atlantic Products' in Veronika Hyden-Hanscho, Renate Piper and Werner Stadgl, eds., *Cultural Exchange and Consumption Patterns in the Age of Enlightenment: Europe and the Atlantic World* (Bochum: Verlag Dr. Dieter Winkler, 2013), pp. 153–168.

[64] Benjamin Furly, *The Worlds Honour Detected, and, for the Unprofitableness Thereof Rejected ...* (London: Robert Wilson, 1663), p. 7.

[65] E. E. Rich, 'Russia and the Colonial Fur Trade' *The Economic History Review* 7:3 (1955): 307–328.

Habillemens Berlinois

1. *Gala* 2. *Cavalier* 3. & 4. *Négligé*

Figure 2.2 Illustration for 'Coiffures and Fashion' (*Koptputz und Kleidungen*), *c.* 1779. Daniel Nikolaus Chodowiecki (1726–1801). Danzig, Germany. 55.102.410. Los Angeles County Museum of Art. https://collections.lacma.or g/node/232004

country for the best quality pelts. Fishing led to trading. An estimated 350 to 380 European ships frequented the Gulf of St Laurence and St Laurence River in 1578, according to one English seaman of the day. Laurier Turgeon, using French notarial records, thinks this contemporary estimate understates the size of multi-national fleets. Fishers soon became fur traders, dealing with Indigenous peoples as a matter of course. All sojourners in northeast American coastal waters gave greater attention to the fur trade after 1550, with the Basques persisting in this commerce despite French claims of territorial sovereignty over this part of North America. Basque skills at bartering were noted by a French royal cosmographer, who wrote of the 'fine and beautiful pelts' the Basque acquired.[66] The lure of this business was as strong as the lure of riches in more southerly latitudes and the wide St Laurence River was a major route to this wealth. Turgeon notes that at the turn of the 1600s, 'far from being a fringe area worked by only a few fishermen, the northern part of the Americas was one of the great seafaring routes and one of the most profitable European business destinations in the New World'.[67] Map 2.2 reflects the formalized knowledge acquired by European cartographers in their representation of North America. This 1650 map was prepared by Nicolas Sanson d'Abbeville, geographer to the French king Louis XIV. It demonstrates the imperial ambitions of European competitors and their territorial claims, while at the same time noting the placement of Indigenous American allies and enemies: Haudenosaunee (Iroquois), Anishinaabeg (Odawa and Ojibwe) and Wendat (Huron), along with the Mi'kmaq (Souricois) resident on northeast interior and coastal lands. These mappings denote the immense attention given this region and the potential it represented to European powers and their citizens.

Fur enticed the Dutch to the Hudson River Valley in 1611, with four Dutch trading companies jostling for priority by 1614.[68] The Dutch

---

[66] Laurier Turgeon, 'French Fishers, Fur Traders and Amerindians during the Sixteenth Century: History and Archaeology' *William and Mary Quarterly* 55:4 (1998), p. 598.

[67] Turgeon, 'French Fishers, Fur Traders and Amerindians', p. 593.

[68] Mark Meuwese, 'The Dutch Connection: New Netherlands, the Pequots, and the Puritans in Southern New England' *Early American Studies* 9:2 (2011): 295–323; Jacobs Jaap, *New Netherland: A Dutch Colony in Seventeenth-Century America* (Leyden: Brill, 2005); Janssonius Jansz and Johannes Jan, *Belgii Novi, Angliae Novae et Partis Virginiae* (New Netherland, New England and parts of Virginia) 1650.

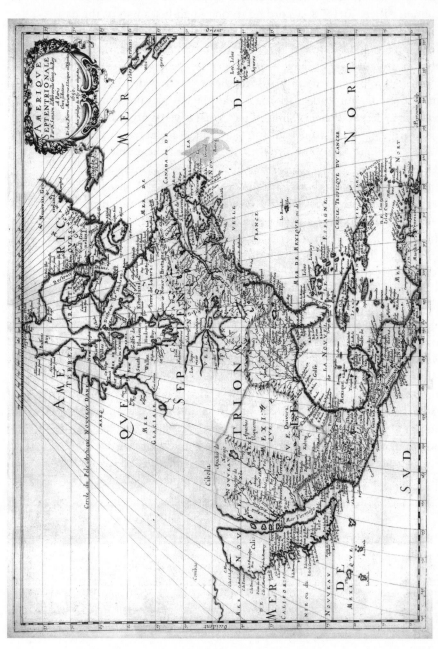

Map 2.2 *Amerique Septentrionale.* Nicolas Sanson (1600–1667). Historic Map Works LLC and Osher Map Library, Getty Images.

Figure 2.3 Iroquois engaging in trade with Europeans, 1722. Claude-Charles Bacqueville de la Potherie (1663–1736). Printed in *Histoire de l'Amérique septentrionale* (Paris: Jean-Luc Nion and François Didot, 1722), p. 22.

merchants of New Netherlands are recorded in the 1650 map. Meanwhile, the English consolidated their claims in New England; Swedes fixed New Sweden on the shores of the Delaware River; and the French claimed coastal Acadia, the St Laurence River basin and its hinterland. Figure 2.3 presents an early eighteenth-century French perspective of the Haudenosaunee reaction to fur-trade goods, showing Native American men modelling linen shirts and testing the drape of wool cloth, with one assessing his appearance in a mirror. Absent from this image, but haunting its frame, was European avidity for furs driving imperial ambitions. This, too, drove consumerism in the early global era.

Diplomatic alliances among Europeans and regional Indigenous peoples ordered the commerce in these lands. Alliances insured the relative safety of European merchants and settlers and afforded in-comers more profitable relations. Native American allies, in turn, received the trade goods they desired through what has been termed 'material diplomacy'.[69] The result of these engagements was massed cargoes of furs shipped across the Atlantic Ocean.[70] Beaver rapidly became a 'staple fur', with routine massive harvests of 300,000 pelts arriving annually at French ports in the 1700s from New France. Slightly further south, the colony of New York persisted in its fur trading, even as they extended colonial agricultural settlements, sending '364 bundles, 77 cases, 10 tierces and 26 hogsheads' of furs back to England in 1698.[71] Collectively, these resources supplied the major hatting industries of France, Russia, the Netherlands and Britain, which in turn sustained innumerable markets. The beaver hat was emblematic of new-luxury commodities in the Atlantic World, a token of colonial interactions on a global stage. More practically, beaver hats held their value, and well-worn examples were used as barter for slaves on the coast of West Africa, a commercial stratagem of Spanish and Portuguese slavers.[72]

Ultimately, fur trade networks encompassed much of the globe.[73] With extensive interests in Siberia and Alaska by the 1700s, Russia remained a redoubtable force in this sector, serving European and Asian markets with the aid of Indigenous allies and labourers.[74] Until the late 1700s, Western Europeans focused predominantly on the fur trading zones opening on to the Atlantic Ocean and Hudson's Bay. Here, too, it was critical to provide trade goods acceptable to Indigenous partners. In the first generations of contact, Native Americans wanted goods that were 'predominantly ceremonial and ideological', incorporating these

---

[69] Christian Ayne Crouch, *Nobility Lost: French and Canadian Material Cultures, Indians, and the End of New France* (Ithaca: Cornell University Press, 2014), p. 2.

[70] Jaap, *New Netherland*, pp. 20–25.

[71] Rich, 'Russia and the Colonial Fur Trade', p. 309.

[72] Susan Sleeper-Smith, 'Cultures of Exchange in a North Atlantic World' in Susan Sleeper-Smith, ed., *Rethinking the Fur Trade Cultures of Exchange in an Atlantic World* (Lincoln: University of Nebraska Press, 2009), p. xvii

[73] South American nutria skins were used as substitutes for beaver or adulterants in the fur industry in the 1700s, along with muskrat and rabbit. The fur trade from the coast of California to China offered another region of robust profits for Americans and Russians in the early 1800s.

[74] Kent G. Lightfoot, 'Russian Colonization: The Implications of Mercantile Colonial Practices in the North Pacific' *Historical Archaeology* 37:4 (2003): 14–28; John Bockstoce, *Furs and Frontiers in the Far North* (New Haven: Yale University Press, 2009).

into extant systems of meaning. Lustre and colour held profound importance for northeast Native American communities, reflected in their taste for red, blue and black, 'aesthetic attributes that qualified them for a significant place in the Indian metaphysical world'.[75] For Europeans, it was a bargain worth making, for they were utterly dependent on Indigenous men and women as military allies, hunters and skin processers.

Thereafter, in many parts of the continent the 'made beaver' became the commercial currency, the pelt cleaned, treated and ready for trade. In the 1630s, in northeast North America, the Oneidas, part of the Haudenosaunee confederacy, negotiated for advantage with the Dutch, stating that if assured of 'four hands of long cloth for each large beaver' (plus other goods), they would return to the Dutch outpost in the spring, rather than treat with the French.[76] Commerce was cast within shifting cultural patterns that evolved over generations, set within globalized networks.[77] Gift exchange long figured in ceremonies among Indigenous groups as adjuncts to renewed alliances.[78] Treaties between Europeans and Indigenous allies were also formalized through gifts, the majority of which were textiles by the later 1600s. Gifting was essential, especially during extended periods of war over the eighteenth century, as the British and French jockeyed for advantage in an imperial gavotte played out over the North American continent.[79] Commercial scenarios in the fur trade differed over time and location, with the spread of western settlement and

---

[75] Christopher L. Miller and George R. Hamell, 'A New Perspective on Indian-White Contact: Cultural Symbols and Colonial Trade' *Journal of American History* 73:2 (1986), pp. 325–327. See also, Hamell, 'Strawberries, Floating Islands'. For further discussion of the roles of beads in colonial America, see Diana D. Loren, *Archaeology of Clothing and Bodily Adornment in Colonial America* (Gainesville: University Press of Florida, 2010), Chapter 4.

[76] Daniel K. Ritcher, *The Ordeal of the Longhouse: The Peoples of the Iroquois League in the Era of European Colonization* (Chapel Hill, NC: University of North Carolina Press, 1992), p. 92.

[77] For a seminal study of indigenous women's roles in 'fur trade society', see Sylvia Van Kirk, *Many Tender Ties: Women in Fur-Trade Society, 1670–1870* (Norman: University of Oklahoma Press, 1980). Also, Elizabeth Mancke, *A Company of Businessmen: the Hudson's Bay Company and Long-Distance Trade, 1670–1730* (Winnipeg: Rupert's Land Research Centre, 1988).

[78] Bruce Trigger, *Natives and Newcomers: Canada's 'Heroic Age' Reconsidered* (Montreal and Kingston: McGill-Queen's University Press, 1985), pp. 186–188.

[79] Timothy J. Shannon, 'Dressing for Success on the Mohawk Frontier: Hendrick, William Johnson, and the Indian Fashion' *William and Mary Quarterly* 53:1 (1996): 13–42.

missionary interventions. These factors determined the opportunities and constraints faced by America's Indigenous peoples. However, some elements remained consistent: the pre-eminent barter of fur for cloth and the values assigned these goods. In this way, as Susan Sleeper-Smith explains,

Furs from North America's interior landscape became enmeshed in a spider web of seventeenth- and eighteenth-century exchange processes. Indians continued to control the landscape where the richest peltry was harvested, and their demand for specific goods determined what Europe produced for North American exchange. For two centuries ... indigenous demand for specific types of finished goods, especially cloth, influenced the goods ... produced for shipment to North America.[80]

Heavy woollen blanket cloth called stroud was one of the most important fabrics manufactured in Britain (and elsewhere in Europe), aiming to meet the criteria set by Indigenous North Americans. Over these centuries, their preferences decided the weight, colours and decorative touches incorporated into these goods with utilitarian and symbolic properties that became their preferred garments. Wool industries in Britain and other locales thrived provisioning these fabrics for this defined consumer market.[81] And where Indigenous men adopted shirts, they did so on their own aesthetic terms – over leggings, hanging loose, as exemplified in Figure 2.3.

The fur trade in the Hudson's Bay region forged another link in the global chain, connecting with communities deep in the interior and routinizing the flow of globally sourced commodities through vast inland territories whose rivers emptied into Hudson's Bay. The English crown granted commercial trading rights to the Hudson's Bay Company (HBC) in 1670, claiming the territory of Rupert's Land, as they called it, for their own. French and then American fur traders persistently disputed these imperial claims, as did resident Indigenous populations – no treaties were initiated with local First Nations in accord with these claims, not for two centuries. Map 2.3 denotes the vast tract claimed by the HBC. York Factory (est. 1684) was among the early trading posts fixed to the coast of Hudson's Bay; inland-trading forts took generations to be approved. From the outset, the HBC dispatched cargoes of the world's useful and attractive goods

[80] Sleeper-Smith, 'Cultures of Exchange in a North Atlantic World', pp. xvii–xviii. See also, DuPlessis, *Material Atlantic*.
[81] Cory Willmott, 'From Stroud to Strouds: The Hidden History of a British Fur Trade Textile' *Textile History* 36:2 (2005): 196–234.

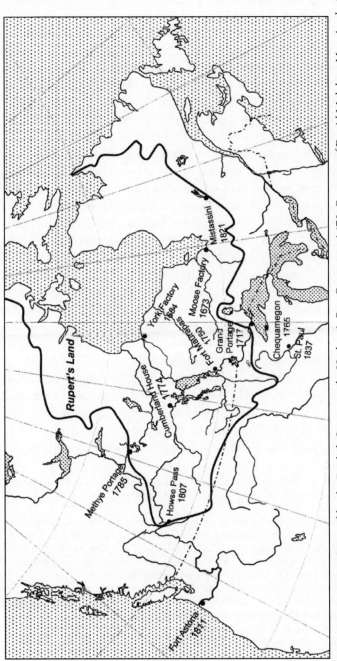

Map 2.3 *Territory Granted by the English Crown to the Hudson's Bay Company, 1670.* Courtesy of David Malaher, *Map Analysis Handbook for the Historian* (Centre for Rupert's Land Studies, University of Winnipeg, 2016), p. 6.

to entice Indigenous hunters to their door. The York Factory account book itemizes the goods mediated by European merchants. In 1689–1690 these included wares from the Indian subcontinent: for example, 'Romall handkerchiefs', 'white calico Shirts', 'Painted calico shirts', silk and herba longee sashes, and printed chintz and herba longee in the piece.[82] However, wool fabrics of various kinds, ribbed and plain weave, red, blue, grey and black, were the most critical to this reciprocal commerce and the most desirable to Native American consumers.

Arthur Ray first proposed the concept of 'Indians as consumers' in 1980, understanding this diverse population not as passive dependents within a European colonial scenario, but as active and demanding actors shaping fur trade society over generations. Ray's focus was the HBC territory of Rupert's Land, the Great Northern Plains and subarctic, sites of often intense competition among English, French and American traders for the loyalty of Indigenous hunters and trappers. Ray's analysis 'reveals the Indians as shrewd consumers who knew how to take full advantage of the economic opportunities offered to them'.[83] Enticements were offered by competing merchant groups, at posts scattered along inland rivers and lakes, as well as on the margins of the Hudson's Bay. All sought to attract the best hunters with the best pelts. Bargaining was routine, and these middlemen struggled to provide the quality and quantity of goods demanded by Indigenous partners.

Merchants, factors and *coureurs des bois*[84] scrambled to align their trade. Little business could be done if wool cloth or blankets were thin, short, poorly dyed, or missing essential decorative selvage stripes. The hue, weight and design of cloth determined the outcome of seasonal negotiations. In the mid-1700s, inferior Montpellier wool fabric was

---

[82] Hudson's Bay Company Archives (HBCA), B239/d/2 fo.1, fo. 2. I consider this subject more fully in Chapter 6, as globalized Asian designs affected Indigenous needlework.

[83] Arthur Ray, 'Indians as Consumers in the Eighteenth Century' in Carol M. Judd and Arthur J. Ray, *Old Trails and New Directions' Papers of the Third North American Fur Trade Conference* (Toronto: University of Toronto Press, 1980), p. 267. Ray offers an explicit attack on the Eurocentric Braudelian view of unchanging material culture outside European elites in this period.

[84] *Coureur de bois* ('runner in the woods') were French male settlers men who learned the techniques of woodland and water travel from First Nations peoples and headed inland in search of fur trade wealth, from the later 1600s. They ventured in defiance of French colonial laws, within a fiercely competitive environment; these adventurers and entrepreneurs depended on alliances with Indigenous communities.

substituted for the better English strouds, a ploy immediately noted and denounced by the Native Americans at the fort. These men would not accept lesser quality cloth.[85] Strouds were now a vital commodity, appreciated as well by Indigenous women for whom this marked an important addition to their material resources.[86] These women, skilled in fibre arts, also used wool cloth in its parts as, when worn, the thread added to traditional basketry and weavings.[87] Cloth was a sign of prosperity and an object of display, valued not least for its symbolic meanings in a system of values 'serially and systematically reinterpreted, restructured, or even replaced [to] ... better fit the present reality'.[88]

To maximize trade, company factors appointed 'captains', the most able and charismatic Indigenous men who organized their community to hunt and trade with the HBC or other commercial bodies. Captains enjoyed a formal status cemented with the gift of a well-trimmed wool captain's jacket of suitable colour, a notable object that reinforced their status. *The Red Lake Chief* is an early nineteenth-century depiction of a formal meeting at the inland Red River trading fort in what is now Manitoba, Canada (Plate 2.4). Peter Rindisbacher aimed to capture the material lives of his subjects and produced this representation in the ethnographic style. For our purposes, his sharp eye for detail is invaluable, situating these people within a global matrix of material culture and politics.[89] The most prominent Indigenous men are notable by their appearance: a captain's coat of European-made wool and enhancements, though often amended by Indigenous artisans; distinctive (beaver?) hats worn by a number of this company; and a fine compass-rose blanket sported by the most prominent Indigenous leader, with some of his followers draped in the best wool cloth. This image, with its formal elements of greeting and bodily embellishment, recapitulates the many other meetings in fur trade culture for political and commercial purposes. Indigenous leaders proved their merit by bringing others to trade with quality furs and bargained for the best outcome for their labours, employing

---

[85] Willmott, 'From Stroud to Strouds'; Smith, 'Something More Than Mere Ornament', pp. 15–17.

[86] Van Kirk, *Many Tender Ties*, p. 6.

[87] Laurel Thatcher Ulrich, *The Age of Homespun: Objects and Stories in the Creation of An American Myth* (New York: 2001), pp. 42–57.

[88] Hamell, 'Strawberries, Floating Islands', p. 80.

[89] Laura Peers, '"Almost True": Peter Rindisbacher's Early Images of Rupert's Land', 1821–26' *Art History* 32:3 (2009): 516–544.

their well-honed discursive skills to wring concessions from the trad-ing companies and their employees.[90] In 1772, a Cree chief, Wapinesew, famously demanded that the Fort York factor 'give us good measure of cloth; let us see the old measure; do you mind me? The young men loves you, by coming so far to see you; ... give them good goods; they like to dress and be fine'.[91]

Ann Carlos and Frank Lewis addressed the commercial patterns at HBC posts over the 1700s, pushing further the analysis of 'Indians as consumers'. They assessed the uptake of several categories of goods over time, including what they term 'other luxuries'.[92] Their characterization of 'luxury' is different from that of De Vries' division of old and new luxuries; rather, they describe the sorts of new luxuries that many other world communities enjoyed in whole or in part – non-essentials which enriched material lives and for which men, women and children laboured. Carlos' and Lewis' luxury grouping included cloth and items like pistols, buttons, beads, handkerchiefs, hats, lace, rings and combs – quintessential new luxuries as defined by de Vries – though the meanings assigned these goods, by these people, would be framed differently than by other consuming polities.[93] Pistols were not a prominent choice at that time and place; in 1740 at York Factory, for example, 26 pistols were bought compared to 189 blankets. But other categories of these wares exhibited a remarkable increase between 1716 and 1766, rising from 15 to 30 per cent of trade goods acquired at Fort York. Indigenous con-sumers were selective, rejecting items deemed shoddy or unappealing. James Isham, chief factor at York Factory and later governor of the post in the 1730s, amassed a detailed catalogue of the likes and dislikes of his commercial partners, urging London administrators to address these concerns. Isham also included samples of those things 'which is pleasing

---

[90] Toby Morantz, 'Economic and Social Accommodation of the James Bay Inlanders to the Fur Trade' in Shepard Krech, ed., *The Subarctic Fur Trade: Native Social and Economic Adaptations* (Vancouver: University of British Columbia Press, 1984), pp. 64–66.

[91] Edward Umfreville, *The Present State of Hudson's Bay: Containing a Full Description of that Settlement* ... (London: Charles Stalker, 1790), pp. 63–64.

[92] The use of the term 'luxury' is somewhat problematic, as scholars note the spiritual and social meanings assigned and the normative sharing of goods.

[93] This category excluded tobacco and alcohol. Ann Carlos and Frank D. Lewis, *Commerce by a Frozen Sea: Native Americans and the European Fur Trade* (Philadelphia: University of Pennsylvania Press, 2010), pp. 94–95. Alcohol was not accounted a major trade item, with sales in 1740 at Fort York less than half that of cloth.

to Indians'.[94] The HBC learned through experience, working assiduously with Yorkshire cloth manufacturers, for instance, who began including 'patterns' in their exchange of letters to ensure that goods fit the bill.[95] Wool fabrics and blankets, cotton and linen shirts, patterned calico, rolls of braid and ribbon transformed the textile consuming options of Native North Americans over generations, reshaping the material culture within the long trading and colonial periods, even as their hierarchy of values persisted and evolved over time.[96] In this respect, new luxuries and industriousness are manifest in fur trade societies in new ways.

The 'industriousness' of Native Americans – hunters, trappers and fur-processing women – was critical to the fur trade and is set within a different paradigm in the Americas. Though no wages traded hands, the 'made beaver' functioned as a common currency and encouraged new patterns of commercial hunting, commercial exchange, plus collective and community-directed consumerism. These represent an important new capacity, tied into global networks. At the same time, the colonial context carried a weight far beyond simple commercial relations, as it bore down on Native American populations. Yet, industriousness was manifest in profound ways by Indigenous Americans, to facilitate material exchange though in a different cultural guise.

Fur trading companies (French, British and American) pushed across the continent over generations, competing fiercely with each other for furs and the loyalty of Indigenous peoples that ensured their profits. They were the advance guard of later colonial settlement and imperial administrations. Native Americans attempted to secure strategic advantage, allying with one company, searching for best possibilities. From the late 1700s, large numbers of Haudenosaunee (Iroquois) ranged across the continent from their home territory in the eastern

---

94 Carlos and Lewis, *Commerce by a Frozen Sea*, pp. 99–100.
95 Willmott, 'Stroud to Strouds', pp. 210–211.
96 Additional histories of material transformation can be found in: Richard White, *The Middle Ground: Indians, Empire and the Republics in the Great Lakes Regions, 1650–1815*, 20th anniversary edition (Cambridge: Cambridge University Press, 2011), pp. 94–141; Shannon, 'Dressing for Success on the Mohawk Frontier'; Sophie White, *Wild Frenchmen and Frenchified Indians: Material Culture and Race in Colonial Louisiana* (Philadelphia: University of Pennsylvania Press, 2013); Sherry Farrell Racette, 'My Grandmothers Loved to Trade: The Indigenization of European Trade Goods in Historic and Contemporary Canada' *Journal of Museum Ethnography* 20:20–21 (2008): 69–81.

Great Lakes and St Lawrence River, some ultimately settling in the Columbia River territory. A number of these adventurers acted as 'free trappers' on the lookout for lucrative deals, to the discomfort of company agents. Alexander Ross described the Haudenosaunee trappers in the Columbia district as a 'discordant headstrong, ill-designed set of rascals', disliking their intractable independence.[97] Their stance was the outcome of rising pressures on Native Americans through colonial land seizures and the equivocal nature of the fur trade as fur-bearing animals declined in many regions. In the more southerly climes of the Mississippi Territory, Choctaw and Creek moved further west across the Mississippi River by 1800, pushed by encroaching settlers. They strived to maintain their seasonal hunting and trading tradition enacted over generations, bringing furs and skins to trading posts into the early 1800s. But these men and women also took up seasonal work on new cotton plantations that channelled mountains of raw cotton to newly industrialized mills in Britain and New England.[98] They were paid for their labour in customary 'blankets, stroud, handkerchiefs and worsted binding of various colours'.[99] Time-honoured material exchanges persisted in many regions, though tempered by powerful new political and economic forces.

Adaptive Systems of Trade and Consumption

Fur trade history traces the emergent patterns of this new global era, focusing on northern latitudes and their ties to wider world markets. This traffic demonstrates the new material ambiguities that appeared, challenging formerly settled categories of consumption. Old luxury was superseded in size by new, more democratic luxury, apparent in the incorporation of furs in clothing and furnishings, as the tempo of

---

[97] Jan Grabowski and Nicole St-Onge, 'Montreal Iroquois *Engagés* in the Western Fur Trade' in Theodore Binnema, Gerhard Ens and R. C. MacLeod, eds., *From Rupert's Land to Canada* (Edmonton: University of Alberta Press, 2001), p. 42.

[98] The industrialization of cotton production in Britain, the United States and Europe is the subject of extensive literature. It, too, is the culmination of the early global system that first enhanced trade between Europe and Asia, as I will show below. Europeans then sought to copy Asian textiles and compete in their production, resulting in expanded colonial plantation systems and industrialized manufacturing.

[99] Daniel H. Usner, Jr., *American Indians in the Lower Mississippi Valley: Social and Economic Histories* (Lincoln: University of Nebraska Press, 1998), p. 80.

consumption accelerated and numbers of participants soared. New material culture overwhelmed the old through the massive harvest of natural resources, the growing scale of this commerce, the distinctiveness of the new commodities and the capacity of new consumer wares to serve diverse markets and enact a plethora of meanings. This sector also demonstrates in real terms the 'industriousness' of those handling furs in world regions, increasingly linked to markets locally and internationally. The industriousness I describe for Native Americans is not fully aligned with that emphasized by Jan de Vries, who pointed to wage labour as a key stimulus of popular consumption. Rather, I emphasize that industriousness, involving men and women rooted in community-directed trapping and trade, was now entwined with globalized commercial networks. The labours of these peoples facilitated wholly new material habits. Moreover, the fur trade could not be detached from the trade in wool cloth and other textiles; these interdependent sectors transformed global habits of consumption in fundamental ways. These processes represented a convergence of sorts, according to some world historians, marking off this period from its predecessors.[100]

In the section that follows I address the further developments of this textile system, premised on new commercial links and heightened commodity access. There is now a vast interdisciplinary scholarship exploring the trade and consumption of cloth, considered from regional, comparative and global perspectives.[101] Features of early globalization are still

---

[100] There is debate about the timing of world convergences. Convergence is undoubtedly valuable concept with respect to periodization, however. David Northrup, 'Globalization and the Great Convergence: Rethinking World History in the Long Term' *Journal of World History* 16:3 (2005): 249–267.

[101] Some of the many sources on this subject include: Lillian M. Li, *China's Silk Trade: Traditional Industry in the Modern World, 1842–1937* (Cambridge, MA: Harvard University Press, 1981); James C. Y. Watt, *When Silk Was Gold: Central Asian and Chinese Textiles* (New York: Metropolitan Museum of Art, 1997); Vainker, *Chinese Silk, A Cultural History*; Liu, *Silk Road in World History*; Luca Mola, *The Silk Industry of Renaissance Venice* (Baltimore: Johns Hopkins University Press, 2000); A. P. Wadsworth and Julia de Lacy Mann, *The Cotton Trade and Industrial Lancashire 1600–1760* (Manchester: Manchester University Press, 1931); Serge Chassange, *Le coton et ses patrons en France, 1760–1840* (Paris: Editions de l'Ecole des hautes etudes en sciences sociales, 1991); Deepika Shah, *Masters of the Cloth: Indian Textiles Trades to Distant Shores* (New Delhi: Garden Silk Mills, 2005); Olivier Raveux, 'Space and Technologies in the Cotton Industry in the Seventeenth and Eighteenth Centuries: The Example of Printed Calicoes in Marseilles' *Textile History* 36:2

being assessed, though the significance of this phenomenon is indisputable. The history of cotton textiles is a case in point, a long-established staple of Indian Ocean and Eurasian trade.[102] These expressive fabrics ignited broader market activity as they moved into Western Europe and its colonies. The Portuguese first intruded into the sophisticated commercial system centred on the Indian Ocean and China Seas, and they rapidly realized the centrality of Indian cottons as currency in the spice trade. Without this cloth it was impossible to acquire spice from merchants in the Indonesian archipelago. Access to Chinese silks was likewise enticing for the Portuguese, a commodity better known to them than was cotton. As familiarity with cottons increased, the Portuguese realized their many uses in the Indian Ocean world and beyond. Quantities of fabric were shipped back to Lisbon via the *Carreira da índia* (India Run), initially as the stuff of private trade directed by enterprising captains and

(2005): 131–145; Marta V. Vicente, *Clothing the Spanish Empire* (Basingstoke: Palgrave Macmillan, 2006); Giorgio Riello and Prasannan Parthasarathi, eds., *The Spinning World: A Global History of Cotton Textiles, 1200–1850* (Oxford: Oxford University Press, 2009); Beverly Lemire, *Cotton* (Oxford: Bloomsbury, 2011); Giorgio Riello, *Cotton. The Fabric that Made the Modern World* (Cambridge: Cambridge University Press, 2013); Sven Beckert, *The Empire of Cotton: A Global History* (New York: Alfred A. Knopf, 2014); John Picton and John Mack, *African Textiles* (London: British Museum Press, 1979); Kriger, *Cloth in West African History* ;Pat Hudson, *The Genesis of Industrial Capital. A Study of the West Riding Wool Textile Industry, c. 1750–1850* (Cambridge: Cambridge University Press, 1986); Carla Rahn Phillips and William D. Phillips, *Spain's Golden Fleece: Wool Production and the Wool Trade from the Middle Ages to the Nineteenth Century* (Baltimore: Johns Hopkins University Press, 1997); G. L. Fontana and G. Gayot, eds., *Wool: Products and markets 13th–20th centuries* (Padova: Cleup, 2005); Brenda Collins and Philip Ollerenshaw, eds., *The European Linen Industry in Historical Perspective* (Oxford: Oxford University Press, 2003); Adrienne Hood, *The Weaver's Craft: Cloth, Commerce, and Industry in Early Pennsylvania* (Philadelphia: University of Pennsylvania Press, 2003); Jane Gray, *Spinning the Threads of Uneven Development: Gender and Industrialization in Ireland During the Long Eighteenth Century* (Oxford: Lexington Books, 2005); Willmott, 'From Stroud to Strouds'; Robert S. DuPlessis, 'Cloth and the Emergence of the Atlantic Economy' in Peter A. Cocolanis, ed., *The Atlantic Economy during the Seventeenth and Eighteenth Centuries: Organization, Operation, Practice, and Personnel* (Columbia, SC: University of South Carolina Press, 2005); Manuel Llorca-Jaña, *The British Textile Trade in South America in the Nineteenth Century* (Cambridge: Cambridge University Press, 2012); Carlos and Lewis, *Commerce by a Frozen Sea*; Peck, *Interwoven Globe*; and most recently, DuPlessis, *Material Atlantic*.
[102] Ruth Barnes, *Indian Block-Printed Textiles in Egypt: The Newberry Collection in the Ashmolean Museum, Oxford* (Oxford: Clarendon Press, 1997), 2 vols.

ships' officers. As the sale of these goods advanced, the carriage of silks and cottons became the prime focus of the *Carreira da índia*. The look, feel, colour and designs of these goods were a revelation to Portuguese sojourners and those they supplied. For, as well as fine and elegant wares, Indian cottons were made in a wide variety of qualities suited to almost every potential customer and her needs – the quintessential new luxury. Plain, fine, coarse, printed, painted and embroidered cottons arrived in remarkably greater quantities over the 1500s, filtering from Lisbon through the courts and ports of Europe. As James Boyajian observes, 'the carreira, much more so than Levantive trade, exposed Europeans to the extraordinary richness of Asian societies'.[103] This 'richness' included fabrics at every price point.

Specialist shops selling Indian wares sprang up in Lisbon and other Portuguese towns, while at the same time Portuguese pedlars moved Indian calicoes up through the Iberian Peninsula and beyond.[104] Clerics in Lisbon added patterned Indian fabrics to their vestments as early as 1508, perhaps as a result of personal or fraternal enterprise during missions in Asia.[105] Clerics showed acute commercial instincts in these and other markets, moving their own stocks through private circuits. This textile incursion was the beginning of a disruptive, creative period as Europeans and colonial populations reacted to these malleable, useful and often beautiful fabrics. Further, the costs of these goods made them accessible to humble shoppers. These new luxury fabrics opened a new world of material opportunity to many, an unsettling textile without equal in Europe. Linen producers in the Basque country were the first to protest the arrival of printed Indian cottons in their neighbourhoods; there, in the 1550s, public meetings were held by officials to consider the impact of the 'Portuguese men ... selling some clothes they called calicús'.[106] Cotton represented opportunity and threat. Its wide appeal seemed to endanger existing

---

[103] James C. Boyajian, *Portuguese Trade in Asia Under the Hapsburgs, 1580–1640* (Baltimore: Johns Hopkins University Press, 1993), p. 51.

[104] Lemire, *Cotton*, pp. 23–24.

[105] John Guy, *Woven Cargoes: Indian Textiles in the East* (London: Thames and Hudson, 1998), p. 9; Boyajian, *Portuguese Trade in Asia*, pp. 29–30; Barbara Karl, '"Marvellous Things Are Made with Needles": Bengal *Colchas* in European Inventories, c. 1580–1630' *Journal of the History of Collections* 23:2 (2011): 301–313.

[106] Lemire, *Cotton*, p. 24.

European goods. Cotton's success also encouraged ever-increasing importation from India to Europe, a focus of Portuguese enterprise.

By the 1550s, Portugal had a foothold on the eastern coast of the Indian subcontinent and the western coastal state of Goa, claiming as well the island of Ceylon. These sites, among others, gave the Portuguese ready access to key textile districts on the Indian subcontinent, plus major trading ports. They established a determined commercial and territorial presence in both the Indian Ocean and China Seas, intent on profiting from the textiles in that region, which were among the most diverse mass-made manufactured goods of that era. The Portuguese next carved a niche for themselves as intermediaries, carrying goods to China (in the mid-1500s) and Japan (after 1543), bringing items including Indian cottons to the designated ports of Macao off the coast of Canton and Nagasaki on the southwest island of Kyushu, Japan. They profited mightily. Indeed, the Portuguese maintained a major presence in Nagasaki from the 1570s as buyers and suppliers of consumer wares until expelled from Japan in 1639, by which time other European competitors vied with them for commercial prominence in Asia.[107]

In the early 1600s armed Dutch and English merchantmen challenged the Portuguese dominance of oceanic Asian sea routes, with trade in textiles a point of contention. The Portuguese traffic in this commodity was a major source of wealth, standing at between 60 and 70 per cent of the registered value of the *carreira* trade between Asia and Europe.[108] The Dutch East India Company (*Vereenigde Oostindische Compagnie*) or VOC quickly took up the task of carrying Indian cottons and other wares to Nagasaki, a role for which they received a monopoly from Tokugawa authorities in 1641. This privilege generated exceptional profits and a coterie of rivals. I noted previously that Spain, Portugal's long-time Iberian competitor, seized the Philippine port of Manila in the 1560s – Spain would not be cut out of the rich Asian traffic. Manila thereafter was the Spanish hub on the trans-Pacific Acapulco-Manila route, opening the massive movement of Spanish American silver to Asia in return for Asian wares.[109] The passion for Asian-made textiles was unquenchable in Europe and

---

[107] Boyajian, *Portuguese Trade in Asia*, p. 139.
[108] Boyajian, *Portuguese Trade in Asia*, p. 139.
[109] And, as I showed, above, the Chinese fur trade was powered by American silver.

Spanish America, funded by American silver, with huge rewards for those directing this exchange.[110]

In 1585, an enthusiastic Spanish treasury official in Manila assured his counterpart in Spain that: 'There is greater profit investing in Chinese goods than in gold'.[111] Throughout the 1600s, in excess of fifty tons of silver arrived in Manila annually from Acapulco, bargained for Chinese silks of all kinds, plus Indian cottons and other useful and luxurious goods that were then shuttled across the Pacific into the hands of an insatiable colonial clientele.[112] The scale of this worldwide trade is arresting. Hundreds of kinds of regionally made Asian fabrics, ribbons, handkerchiefs, coverlets and cushions were dispersed along ocean routes under the aegis of the Portuguese and then Spanish, Dutch, English, Danish, French, Austrian and Swedish merchants, sometimes competing, sometimes collaborating. Competition was frequently fierce, according to English reporting from Edo in 1615: '[the] Dutch [are] enabled to sell both raw and wrought silk cheap, being in the habit of plundering the China Junks; A Force to be employed by the Spaniards at Manilla against the Dutch in the Molluccas'.[113] Merchants from Surat to Canton, Macao to Manila, educated Europeans in the practice and potential of commerce in their regions and in the qualities of their merchandise, with cycles of cooperative commerce and fierce hostilities as each strived for advantage.[114] Asian

---

[110] Dennis O. Flynn and Arturo Giráldez, 'Born with a "Silver Spoon": The Origins of World Trade in 1571' *Journal of World History* 6:2 (1995): 201–221; Boyajian, *Portuguese Trade in Asia*, pp. 64–65. Between 1580 and 1640, the Portuguese and Spanish crowns were united and official peace reigned between the two powers.

[111] Virginia Benitez Licuanan and José Llavador Mira, eds., *The Philippines under Spain: A Compilation and Translation of Original Documents*, vol. 4 (Manila: National Trust for Historical and Cultural Preservation of the Philippines, 1993), p. 249.

[112] Dennis O. Flynn and Arturo Giráldez, 'Cycles of Silver: Global Economic Unity through the Mid-Eighteenth Century' *Journal of World History* 13:2 (2002), p. 398. Smuggling significantly increased the outflow of silver on many occasions.

[113] India Office Records, G/12/15, 23 October 1615. British Library.

[114] Wang Gungwu, 'Merchants without Empire: The Hokkien Sojourning Communities' in James D. Tracy, *The Rise of Merchant Empires: Long Distance Trade in the Early Modern World* (Cambridge: Cambridge University Press, 1990), pp. 400–422; K. S. Mathew, 'Indian Merchants and the Portuguese Trade on the Malabar Coast during the Sixteenth Century' in Teotonio R. De Souza, ed., *Indo-Portuguese History: Old Issues, New Questions* (New Delhi: Xavier Centre of Historical Research, 1984), pp. 1–12.

Figure 2.4 *Port of Acapulco*, 1685–1714. Thomas Doesburgh. Printed in *Orbis habitabilis oppida et vestitus. Des waerelds inhabited towns and Dragten* (Amsterdam, Carel Allard, *c.* 1685). RP-P-1889-A-15210. Rijksmuseum, Amsterdam.

merchants, in situ, also worked to profit from this generative commercial environment.

The Spanish devised a distinctive geography of trade, using Manila as the pivot point, whereby Pacific traffic to the Americas generated unique profits. The 1685 rendering of the Mexican port of Acapulco, by a Dutch artist, signals the prominence of this Pacific harbour in the Spanish Empire, a port that was important, too, in the new global commercial networks (Figure 2.4). The Dutch craved nautical knowledge in these years, codified in atlases and graphic collections by artists and cartographers who fed this obsession with representations of this globalizing world. In this depiction, ships approach on the horizon, and local traders and slaves (at the bottom left) carry cargo down to the quay in the foreground. A fortification overlooks the anchorage, acknowledging the value of this enclave at a time when colonial commerce was contested by force of arms. This is one of several Dutch illustrations of Manila and Acapulco created for a society steeped in international trade. The importance of these Pacific ports was immense.[115] The resulting trans-Pacific traffic inaugurated new manifestations of cosmopolitanism in the material culture of Spanish America, furnishing colonial communities in more complex ways, with world markets bound more closely together in the process.

The influx of fabric disconcerted mercantile regimes and debates mounted in many regions about whether to accept or ban this traffic – the sentiments expressed in the opening quotation typify these concerns. Merchants of New Spain who were affiliated with Spanish suppliers despaired at the quantity and diversity of imported Chinese goods flooding colonial markets. They insisted Asian textiles were 'very worthless, [but] since they are cheap, the people buy them and the prices of the silk that comes from Spain are affected. … [and] if this were to continue, it would no longer be necessary to send silk from Spain [to her colonies]'.[116] The cheapness, variety and quality of Asian goods were a perpetual conundrum to Western authorities with each decade that passed. But, as Robert DuPlessis demonstrates, the residents of Spanish American colonies maintained a passion for silks that persisted through the centuries and shaped their material habits. Settlers were distinguished by this silken allegiance, a visual contrast to Indigenous and enslaved populations among whom they lived.[117]

The Manila–Acapulco connection produced a distinctive material ecosystem in the Americas, with New Spain and the Viceroyalty of Peru exceptionally supplied, and the influence of Asian materials apparent across social and racial hierarchies. Manila galleons, filled and overfilled with cargo, channelled goods into legal and extralegal networks that spread across the Spanish colonies. Indeed, the (illegal) off-loading of these overburdened vessels began even before ships reached the coast. Official distribution took a more structured turn. Once at anchor, the ships were unladen, bales and barrels unpacked and stalls stocked for the Acapulco fair. Merchants flocked there to buy the newest stock, thereafter carrying merchandise from Acapulco to Mexico City, along the dusty 286-mile *Camino de China* or China Road. Once in the capital, transactions took place at seasonal fairs and everyday markets and

---

[115] Flynn and Giráldez, 'Born with a "Silver Spoon"'.
[116] Licuanan and Llavador, *Philippines under Spain*, vol. 4, p. 370.
[117] DuPlessis, *Material Atlantic*, p. 205.

shops, the influx of newly arrived stock enlivening shopkeepers and buyers alike.[118] The Plaza Mayor in Mexico City was the focal point of commercial life in New Spain, notable for its plethora of stalls; a new retail complex was built in 1703 and named the Parián, the term given the Chinese mercantile quarter in Manila.[119] Rich and poor, indigenous and newcomer frequented these outlets, sometime served by transplanted Chinese or Filipino artisans.[120] Similar fairs took place in Panama and Veracruz. Something new emerged: a distinctive cloth environment founded on transnational links, interpreted in heterogeneous colonial households.

Cotton was part of this equation. Cotton fabrics of different kinds had long been made in homes and workshops in the Aztec Empire, comprising part of the tribute system. Cloth making continued to take place for the household and the market, embedded in Indigenous gift culture, as well as being made for trade.[121] Asian wares intersected with complex Indigenous and European textile systems, with a vibrant mingling of influences. A distinctive material mélange defined Spanish colonial regions, the scale of trade through the Manila route being vast and sustained. This complicated provisioning served the equally complicated consumption process, whereby the Native American, African, Creole or newcomer selected the fabrics suited to their taste and their circumstance, as utility and expressive priorities were served. Scholars now explore the shared materiality of Chinese/Spanish shawls and the concurrent development of their different geographies of fashion and embodied patterns of wear.[122] These textiles exemplify the ways in

[118]   William J. McCarthy, 'Between Policy and Prerogative: Malfeasance in the Inspection of the Manila Galleons at Acapulco, 1637' *Colonial Latin American Historical Review* 2/2 (1993): 163–183; Shirley Fish, *The Manila-Acapulco Galleons: The Treasure Ships of the Pacific* (Central Milton Keynes: AuthorHouse, 2011), pp. 263–268, 434–435.

[119]   Dana Leibsohn, 'Made in China, Made in Mexico' in Donna Pierce and Ronald Otsuka, eds., *At the Crossroads: The Arts of Spanish America and Early Global Trade, 1492–1850* (Denver: Denver Museum of Art, 2012), pp. 16–18.

[120]   Louise Schell Hoberman, *Mexico's Merchant Elite, 1590–1660: Silver, State, and Society* (Raleigh: Duke University Press, 1991), pp. 26–32, 127–129; Walton Look Lai and Chee Beng Tan, eds., *The Chinese in Latin America and the Caribbean* (Leiden: Brill, 2010), pp. 13–14.

[121]   Frances F. Berdan, *Aztec Archaeology and Ethnohistory* (Cambridge: Cambridge University Press, 2014), pp. 98–107.

[122]   Sarah Cheang, 'Wearing the Chinese/Spanish Shawl: Fashion, Geography and Embodiment' and Amalia Ramirez Garayzar, 'Rebozos, Pañones and Perrajes: Women's Clothing in Colonial Latin America and the Manila Galleon',

which meanings and patterns of use emerged as cargoes were absorbed into diverse settings over generations. Local selection of new luxuries was shaped by spiritual and cultural aesthetics as well as by political and gendered ideals, actively creating the hierarchical creolized societies in the Americas expressed in cloth as culture.[123]

Colchas, embroidered coverlets or hangings, became one of the most celebrated Hispanic American crafts, praised not only for their beauty but also for their storied colonial heritage. They symbolize early modern globalism, with a lineage originating in the Indian subcontinent. It took a while for Europeans to discover all the textile treasures of Asia. Over time, quilts of great beauty were carried back to Europe in greater numbers, perhaps first used to charm kings and courtiers. By the late 1500s, Indian embroidered quilts (cotton and silk) poured into European ports by the hundreds and then by the thousands, their popularity growing throughout the seventeenth century.[124] Royal and aristocratic buyers, who admired the dextrous embroidery, were the initial collectors of these coverlets. Indian embroiderers modified designs for European buyers, though usually blending customary design idioms in their work (Plate 2.5), including the inclusion of coats of arms. Agents on site in India, working for European trading companies, struggled to find adequate supplies of quilts to meet demand. By the 1600s, the frenzy for these goods had spread among merchants and wealthy metropolitans who sought to bedeck their homes with reminders of Asian trade and its wonders. Auctions of East Indian wares, such as those in London, were sometime raucous affairs as bidders competed for embroidered cotton quilts, even those that were 'somewhat defective and stayned', so keen

---

unpublished papers presented at the conference 'Dressing, Global Bodies', July 2016, Edmonton, Canada.

[123] The term creole and creolization refer to the process of cultural creation in the New World, premised on several elements. First, the proximity of Europeans (termed 'Creoles') to Indigenous cultures and the potential changes these might effect. Then, the mixing of Indigenous, Africa (slave or free) and European cultures, creating new cultural forms and identities through a process called creolization. Charles Stewart, 'Creolization: History, Ethnography, Theory' in Charles Stewart, ed., *Creolization: History, Ethnography, Theory* (Walnut Creek, CA: Left Coast Books, 2007), pp. 1–24. For an example of the complexities of cloth and culture, see Sophie White, 'Geographies of Slave Consumption' *Winterthur Portfolio* 45:2 (2011): 229–248.

[124] Maria Jose de Mendonça 'Some Kinds of Indo-Portuguese Quilts in the Collection of the Museu de arte Antiga' in *Embroidered Quilts From the Museu Nacional de Arte Antiga, Lisboa* (London: Kensington Palace, 1978).

were buyers on new Asian furnishings.[125] These coverlets appeared at a time of rising interest in domestic comforts and new-style domestic spaces. Middle ranked and elite families in Western Europe were building houses with more bedrooms; beds and bedrooms assumed growing importance, as did soft furnishings, an interest shared in Europe and colonial settings. A search for comfort ensued, a goal that predominated among different confessional groups, well beyond the Anglosphere where this phenomenon was first identified.[126]

Colonists in Latin America found Indian embroidered quilts both useful and inviting and their access to these visual delights equalled that of Europe. 'By the 1580s no wealthy household of the Iberian overseas colonies would be without the finest cloths for furnishings – colchas (Indian bedspreads) and suitable wall hangings of various colours embroidered with silk'.[127] These goods were landed during illicit stops in Rio de Janeiro by Portuguese captains, as well as through the sanctioned trans-Pacific route.[128] In Spanish America, including at colonial outposts in New Mexico, creole women adapted the model of the fashionable Asian quilt, producing their own variants. Sheep, brought with missionaries and settlers as part of the colonization project, provided the fibre for production, adding to the textile rota already in place. Creole women of various ethnicities used local white wool cloth for the ground (rather than linen, cotton or silk) and employed brightly dyed wool, cotton or silk thread to embroider hybridized designs. These were likely collaborative projects, employing the skills and energies of the household mistress, her daughters and servants, women of varied ancestry. The results were quilts noted for 'marrying practical and aesthetic concerns'.[129] Plate 2.6 is a *colcha* from late eighteenth-century colonial Mexico, now in the collection of

---

[125] Lemire, *Cotton*, Chapter 5; John Irwin and Margaret Hall, *Indian Embroideries* vol. *II*, (Ahmedabad: Calico Museum of Textiles, 1973), p. 2.

[126] John Crowley first addressed the quest for comfort in Britain and their colonies. John Crowley, 'The Sensibility of Comfort' *American Historical Review* 104:3 (1999): 749–782; and for the breadth of this trend in Europe and its colonies see Lemire, *Cotton*, Chapter 5.

[127] Boyajian, *Portuguese Trade under the Hapsburgs,* pp. 141–142.

[128] Boyajian, *Portuguese Trade under the Hapsburgs,* p. 131; DuPlessis, *Material Atlantic,* pp. 78, 205.

[129] Kirstin C. Erickson, 'Las Colcheras: Spanish Colonial Embroidery and the Inscription of Heritage in Contemporary Northern New Mexico' *Journal of Folklore Research* 52:1 (2015), p. 2.

the Denver Art Museum. The ground is made of a distinctive fine, plain wool local cloth of that region called *sabinilla*. Cotton thread was used instead of local wool to make the design, a reflection of the more expansive cotton production by this date. The densely executed patterns nod to the original coverlets from India that were reinterpreted over generations.[130]

Wealthy settlers in Spanish America had many textile options for their homes and bodies. Europe remained a perennial source of supply for many of the fabrics valued by this community of consumers, like fine wool cloth for suiting, drapery that was especially esteemed.[131] In the pearl fishery island of Cubagua (now part of Venezuela), affluent buyers revelled in the luxury fabrics they acquired for their homes, 'second in importance, after jewels and precious objects in gold and silver, in early colonial households'.[132] They intended to establish a new aristocratic order and deployed luxury textiles to this end. But, at the lower end of the market, innumerable options were available to less august shoppers. New wares from Asia added additional components to the richly varied material culture arising from Indigenous American societies. There was a blending of aesthetic elements in textiles and embroideries produced by Native American peoples, a fact evident throughout the Americas.[133] This 'cultural mixing' was a potent, ever-present part of early colonial life.[134] The admixture of

---

[130] For more on the colonial heritage of *colcha*, see Suzanne P. MacAulay, *Stitching Rites: Colcha Embroidery Along the Northern Rio Grande* (Tucson: University of Arizona Press, 2000).

[131] DuPlessis, *Material Atlantic*.

[132] Jorge F. Rivas Pérez, 'Domestic Display in the Spanish Overseas Territories' in Richard Aste, ed., *Behind Closed Doors: Art in the Spanish American Home, 1492–1898* (New York: Brooklyn Museum and The Momacelli Press, 2013), pp. 55–56.

[133] Ray, 'Indians as Consumers'; Erica Smith, 'Something More than Mere Ornament: Cloth and Indian-European Relationships in the Eighteenth Century', unpublished MA, 1991, University of Manitoba; Ulrich, *Age of Homespun*, especially Chapter 1, 'An Indian Basket', pp. 41–74; DuPlessis, 'Cloth and the Emergence of the Atlantic Economy'; Willmott, 'From Stroud to Strouds'; Laura E. Johnson, 'Material Translations: Cloth in Early American Encounters, 1520–1750', unpublished PhD dissertation, 2010, University of Delaware and "Goods to Clothe Themselves': Native Consumers and Native Images on the Pennsylvania Trade Frontier, 1712–1760' *Winterthur Portfolio* 40:4 (2005): 47–76;White, *Wild Frenchmen and Frenchified Indians*; Pérez, 'Domestic Display in the Spanish Overseas Territories', pp. 56–57.

[134] Carolyn Dean and Dana Leibsohn, 'Hybridity and Its Discontents: Considering Visual Culture in Colonial Spanish America' *Colonial Latin American Review*

Chinese silks and Indian cottons, European linens and woollens, along with locally made cotton, wool and mixed-fibre cloth created distinct creolized[135] textile environments in Spanish, Portuguese and other Euro-American colonies that were revised and recreated over centuries.[136]

Map 2.4 mirrors knowledge acquired from many points of origin, accrued through generations of travel and exchange. This was synthesized in Europe in a visual medium that encapsulated the hard-won learning of those traversing many parts of these networks. However imperfect this mapping of maritime and land-based spaces, it nonetheless signifies the intensive interest in the world connections being forged and nowhere more so than in Europe. As cargoes arrived in European ports via the Cape of Good Hope, bales and bundles of European fabrics were being readied for shipment for Atlantic markets in Africa and the Americas. As Kathleen Brown observes, 'By the late seventeenth century, cloth had become the material lingua franca of Atlantic commerce'.[137] Supplying colonies – whether for the fur trade, settlers or expanding slave plantations – exerted a powerful economic stimulus in Europe, discernable in the growing scale of ports, warehouses, shipyards, retail and wholesale capacity, especially in western and northwestern Europe.[138] Textile production advanced in most European locales from the sixteenth through the eighteenth centuries with prominent silk making sectors in Italy, Spain, France, England and ultimately Sweden. Linen making flourished in Italy, the Germanic terri-tories, Spain, northern France, the Low Countries, Ireland, Britain, Russia and the Baltic regions, employing vast contingents. Wool and worsted fabrics were made in Spain, France, Britain and the Low Countries, and ultimately in Russia as well. And a hybrid cotton/linen manufacturing spread from northern Italian cities to the Rhineland, northern France,

12:1 (2003): 5–35; Rebecca Earle, '"Two Pairs of Pink Satin Shoes!!": Race, Clothing and Identity in the Americas (17th–19th Centuries)' *History Workshop Journal* 52 (2001): 175–195; White, 'Geographies of Slave Consumption'.

135   Stewart, 'Creolization', pp. 1–24.

136   Juan Carlos Sola- Corbacho, 'Urban Economies in the Spanish World: The Cases of Madrid and Mexico City at the End of the Eighteenth Century' *Journal of Urban History* 27:5 (2001), pp. 616–617.

137   Kathleen M. Brown, *Foul Bodies: Cleanliness in Early America* (New Haven: Yale University Press, 2014), p. 99.

138   For example, Nuala Zahedieh, *The Capital and the Colonies: London and the Atlantic Economy, 1660–1700* (Cambridge: Cambridge University Press, 2010); DuPlessis, *Material Atlantic*.

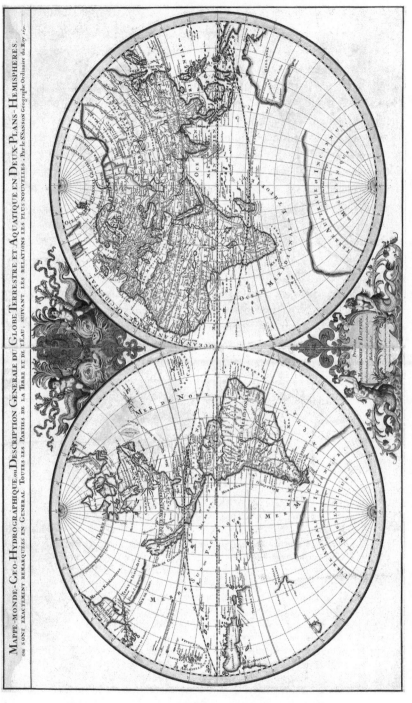

Map 2.4 *Mappe-monde Geo-Hydrographique ou Description Generale du Globe Terrestre et Aquatique en Deux-Plans-Hemipsheres ou son Exactement Remarquees en General Toutes les Parties de la Terre et de L'Eau, suivant les Relations les plus Nouvelles, par le S. Sanson Geographe Ordinaire du Roy.* H. Jaillot, Atlas Nouveau (Paris, 1691).

the Low Countries and Britain to add an important new ingredient to the options of working and middle-ranked consumers.[139] The growing employment available in these sectors, for children, women and men, marked what Jan de Vries defines as the 'industrious revolution'. As these industries grew they opened opportunities for common folk to earn income with which to add to their material comforts, to augment their stock of clothing and even indulge in occasional semi-luxury spending. The cumulative impact of this occasional spending was enormous. The results of enhanced production were evident in prosperous cities and industrious rural districts. Growing employment allied with urbanization and expanded retailing to support a rising population, with the spread of urban facilities through rural areas, structural changes associated with dynamic regions like the Netherlands and parts of Britain.[140]

Jan De Vries' concept of the industrious revolution was founded on European and colonial evidence, the augmented employment of women and children being a catalyst driving consumer industries, and plebeian consumerism.[141] Ribbons were among the inessentials whose production soared in the centuries after 1500. These may seem inconsequential notions; yet it was precisely these inexpensive and occasional pleasures that multiplied over time, with signal consequences. The prevalence of ribbons was so culturally significant they became the stuff of European poetry and plays, a pleasure recognizable to public audiences.[142] Ribbons,

---

[139] Maureen Mazzaoui, *The Italian Cotton Trade in the Later Middle Ages* (Cambridge: Cambridge University Press, 1981); Herbert Kisch, *From Domestic Manufacture to Industrial Revolution: The Case of the Rhineland Textile Districts* (Oxford: Oxford University Press, 1989); see also note 101 above on cotton.

[140] Jan de Vries and Ad van der Woude, *The First Modern Economy: Success, Failure, and Perseverance of the Dutch 1500–1815* (Cambridge: Cambridge University Press, 1997), Chapter 11.

[141] Jan de Vries, 'The Industrial Revolution and the Industrious Revolution' *Journal of Economic History* 54 (1994): 249–270; *The Industrious Revolution*; Craig Muldrew, *Food, Energy and the Industrious Revolution: Work and Material Culture in Agrarian England, 1550–1780* (Cambridge: Cambridge University Press, 2011) and ' "Th'ancient Distaff" and "Whirling Spindle": Measuring the Contribution of Spinning to Household Earnings and the National Economy in England, 1550–1770' *Economic History Review*, 65 (2012): 498–526. As noted earlier, claims for active consumerism based on dynamic urban markets are made for other developing world regions as well. Pomeranz, *The Great Divergence*.

[142] William Shakespeare, *The Winter's Tale* (1623). Catherine Richardson, *Shakespeare and Material Culture* (Oxford: Oxford University Press, 2011).

tape and braid could be sold relatively cheaply and were easily applied to apparel and furnishings of all sorts, affecting fashion. Haberdashers, mercers, shopkeepers and pedlars dispensed these accessories as a matter of course, items that would be more easily and repeatedly acquired by humble shoppers than large quantities of fabric. This seventeenth-century German trade card commemorates the enterprise of ribbon vendor, Mattheis Nair (Figure 2.5). The carefully crafted depiction of his clothing demonstrates the adornment potential of ribbons, from the bows on his shoes and breeches to the garnishes at his waist. Nair's left hand is filled with trimmings of different sorts and the coins in his right hand suggest their value. These embellishments enabled the 'fast fashion' of this age, giving voice to cultural aspirations. The Dutch ribbon loom (*lintmolen*), introduced in the early 1600s, allowed weavers throughout the Low Countries to make twelve to twenty-four ribbons simultaneously, expanding production enormously. This technology was carried to other regions across Europe, despite objections in some quarters.[143] Ribbon-making centres fed this seemingly inexhaustible demand, dispensing their products through Europe and its colonies. The ribbon trade, along with button-making, glove-making, hosiery-knitting and pin-making, offered the sorts of useful and decorative trifles first noted by Joan Thirsk and emphasized by Jan de Vries, goods essential to this consumerist change providing new sorts of employment and new systems of delight.

No sector was more vital to this interlinking dyad of work and consumption than cloth and clothing: the spinning, weaving, finishing, making, selling, repairing, remaking and reselling discussed in this chapter and the next. Spinning thread, in particular, brought critical additions to family incomes, especially as the use of spinning wheels spread across Europe. Spinning allowed women options, including a relatively independent life where cloth trades thrived or a critical addition to family incomes.[144] This iconic occupation employed young and old females alike, with women wielding drop-spindles or wheels. The spinning wheel augmented output and was one of the many steps towards greater mechanized production, as well as greater wage employment. Female spinning sustained the linen and wool trades of Europe, staples that served regional and global markets. These

---

[143] Wadsworth and Mann, *Cotton Trade and Industrial Lancashire*, pp. 98–102.
[144] Muldrew, '"Th'ancient Distaff" and "Whirling Spindle"'; Sharpe, 'Literally Spinsters'. See also the research project on spinning headed by John Styles, spinning-wheel.org/, accessed 12 June 2016.

Figure 2.5 Unknown, possible advertisement of Mattheis Nair, Ribbon Seller, 1600–1650 {nd}. Waddesdon (National Trust) Bequest of James de Rothschild, 1957; acc. No. 3686.4.41.70. Photo: University of Central England Digital Services © National Trust, Waddesdon Manor.

expanding sectors supported many European regions and represented greater possibilities of comparative plenty and comfort throughout the eighteenth century. Indeed, the textile trades were disproportionately powered by female industry; likewise, their consumerist impulses were directed to these new luxury wares. Enhanced waged work for women and children buoyed growing demand and also expand imperial commerce. The cargo just arrived from London, advertised in *The South-Carolina Gazette* in 1754, illustrates these dynamics, the goods including 'a large assortment of ribbons, ribbon laces, ferrits, none so pretties . . .'[145]

Fashion shaped the success of textile sectors globally, and such was the case in Europe. Old-fashioned heavy woollen cloth suffered, as the 'new draperies' lured away shoppers from the 1600s with lighter, cheaper, more varied fabrics in look, feel and texture. Linens also appeared in ever-greater varieties, with an expansion of utilitarian and finer goods, elegant patterning and subtle detail, serving dress and décor in new ways.[146] Silk, long transplanted from Asia, became the protected star of European textile technology – and an exceptional source of employment and revenue in Italy and Spain. The highest officials plotted for its advantage.[147] At the opening of this chapter, the Spanish Governor of the Philippines expressed the sorts of anxieties wracking European authorities when competitors threatened their silk industries. Jean Baptiste Colbert served as Louis XIV's finance minister from 1665 to 1683 and declared the dominance of French silks to be the aim of state policy; he promoted the recruitment of foreign workers while setting in place a legislative tariff wall to protect this sector.[148] His intent was clear. Protectionist policies abounded in Europe during this mercantilist era, aimed at monopolizing artisans and their skills, while the risks and

---

[145] *The South-Carolina Gazette*, 22 August 1754. Ferrit, or ferret, is a type of strongly made tape, often in cotton though also in silk.

[146] N. B. Harte, ed., *The New Draperies in the Low Countries and England* (Oxford: Oxford University Press, 1997); Collins and Ollerenshaw, *The European Linen*; Wadsworth and Mann, *Cotton Trade and Industrial Lancashire*.

[147] Mola, *The Silk Industry of Renaissance Venice*; Salvatore Ciriacono, 'Silk Manufacturing in France and Italy in the XVIIth Century: Two Models Compared', *Journal of European Economic History* 10:1 (1981): 167–172.

[148] Ina Baghdiantz McCabe, *Orientalism in Early Modern France: Eurasian Trade, Exoticism and the Ancien Regime* (Oxford: Berg Publishers, 2008), pp. 5–6, 101–102; Adam Geczy, *Fashion and Orientalism: Dress, Textiles and Culture from the 17th to the 21st Century* (London: Bloomsbury, 2013), pp. 37.

rewards of foreign trade were negotiated with other states.[149] Achieving the right balance of imports and exports preoccupied theorists and governments. The stakes were high. Success was not assured.

Among the great challenges facing European governments in the late 1600s were the commercial consequences of the globalism they themselves forged. Trade winds now carried ships from Asia to great ports along Europe's seaboard. The response of shoppers to these imports was instructive. First, they learned the qualities and characteristics of these textiles, a process begun in the 1500s and advanced over the next centuries. As they learned, they embraced these fabrics with growing enthusiasm for the choices and comforts they offered. Domestic interiors were the first areas fitted with new furnishings, as I noted with colonial *colchas*. Households were gradually equipped with a new genre of niceties: cotton coverlets, patterned silk cushions and washable white, printed, checked and striped cotton cloth used in curtains and napery.[150] In the 1600s, no European nation possessed the textile techniques equal to those of Asia, and it took centuries to command Asia's silk-making skills at the prices offered for sale. Limited indirect competition with Asia via overland trade could be borne.[151] Direct competition by sea presented pressing provocations. For, as these imported goods circulated, they revised Europeans' expectations about their needs and the quality and variety of Asian goods that fulfilled their needs. This sensory education changed the material environment and raised the bar for local European manufacturers, setting standards they could not yet meet. Local goods were at a disadvantage; local manufacturers and workers denounced the interloping goods, the traitorous merchants who brought them to their

---

[149]   For commerce between the German territories and Britain, see Margrit Schulte Beerbühl, *The Forgotten Majority: German Merchants in London, Naturalization, and Global Trade, 1660–1815*, translated by Cynthia Klohr. (London: Berghahn Books, 2007).

[150]   Beverly Lemire, 'An Education in Comfort: Indian Textiles and the Remaking of English Homes Over the Long Eighteenth Century' in Bruno Blondé and Jon Stobart, eds., *Selling Textiles in the Long Eighteenth Century: Comparative Perspectives from Western Europe* (Basingstoke: Palgrave Macmillan, 2014), pp. 13–29; *Cotton*, pp. 26–32.

[151]   For the European technological apprenticeship in printed cotton production, see Riello, *Cotton*, Chapter 5; Raveux, 'Space and Technologies in the Cotton Industry'; Maxine Berg, *Luxury and Pleasure in Eighteenth-Century Britain* (Oxford: Oxford University Press, 2005) and 'From Imitation to Invention: Creating Commodities in Eighteenth-Century Britain' *Economic History Review* 55:1 (2002): 1–30.

shores and the corrupt female consumers whose tastes unsettled the status quo. Indian cottons and Asian silks were immediate targets.

Tensions surged and complaints soared as industrialists protested the loss of their markets. The Sieur Chauvel, from the linen-making province of Normandy, complained bitterly to the French finance minister in the 1680s that the Indian cotton imports brought in by the French East India Company 'entirely ruined our manufactures of silk, of wool, and of linen'.[152] One government after another banned these goods. In 1686, France banned 'Cotton Linnen-Cloth, Printed in East-India, or Painted in the Kingdom; and other China and India Silks, Stuffs and Flower'd with Gold and Silver'.[153] This decree was translated and circulated widely in Europe, encouraging protests in other jurisdictions. Wool, linen and prestigious silk textiles remained cornerstones of Europe's manufacturing sector. Producers demanded shelter from the tide of competitive Asian manufactures pouring across their lands.

France inaugurated the first of many bans, decrees and enactments, to be followed by England, Spain, Prussia and many more, as officials attempted to shape their markets to suit their philosophy and protect local industry.[154] Spain's Philip V banned calicoes and other Asian fabrics from all his territories in 1718, desperate to protect Spanish dependents.[155] Prohibitions were instituted in most parts of Europe, excepting the Netherlands, which then flourished as a major entrepôt for textile smuggling. Riots broke out for extended periods in Britain and periodically in the Austrian Netherlands. Women in particular were targeted by mobs as corrupt acolytes of Indian imports: hundreds were beaten for their crimes, a subject discussed more thoroughly in

---

[152] Quoted in Michael Kwass, *Contraband: Louis Mandrin and the Making of a Global Underground* (Cambridge, MA: Harvard University Press, 2014), p. 54.

[153] 'A Decree of the Kings Counsel of State, concerning Cotton Linnen-Cloth ...' in Beverly Lemire, ed., *The British Cotton Trade* vol. 1 (London: Pickering and Chatto, 2010), p. 345.

[154] France 1686, with many subsequent decrees and enactments, England 1701 and 1721, Spain 1713, and Prussia 1713. These bans were consistent with other protectionist policies enacted to protect local textile industries, as with the burgeoning English linen trade. N. B. Harte, 'The Rise of Protection and the English Linen Industry, 1690–1790' in N. B. Harte and K.G. Ponting, eds., *Textile History and Economic History: Essays in Honour of Miss Julia de Lacy Mann* (Manchester: Manchester University Press, 1973), pp. 74–112.

[155] Vicente, *Clothing the Spanish Empire*, p. 11.

Chapter 3. Faced with bans, most consumers did not change their tastes. Local manufacturers struggled to supply the goods demanded at the quality required. And, during this transition period, a broad swath of consumers bought prohibited textiles as and when they could, turning to extralegal suppliers.[156] France was awash with smuggled Indian calico, as was Britain, Sweden and other localities.[157] Newspapers announced only occasional seizures of contraband.[158] Coastlines were imperfectly policed and retailers offered what would sell. Illicit trade advanced consumerism in this era, a point I address more fully in Chapter 4. The torrent of Asian wares might be redirected, but its effects could not be stopped.

The European textiles that succeeded in this period, and there were many, were adaptable to different circumstances and opportunities.[159] Wool strouds were a staple in the American fur trade, for example, a foundational ingredient in this commercial equation. European linen manufacturing flourished as well providing the various kinds of cloth now deemed essential by more social classes. In many instances, linens imitated Indian wares, adding to the diversity of material options. Cheap goods made for plebeian markets in Europe were successfully transplanted to the Americas, including as slave-wear in colonial plantations. European merchants also added these goods to their cargoes for the African slave trade, putting European-made linen/cottons in competition with Indian cottons in West African markets with initially only mixed success.[160] Textiles were culturally malleable commodities, as were all successful materials in this early global age. Fabrics such as these assumed different meanings as the societal context altered. Successful material (including furs) possessed qualities that

---

[156] The centrality of smuggling in this era of heightened consumerism is discussed in Chapter 4 of this volume.

[157] Kwass, *Contraband*, pp. 64–65; Riello, *Cotton*, pp. 121–123; H. S. K. Kent, *War and Trade in Northern Seas: Anglo-Scandinavian Economic Relations in the Mid-Eighteenth Century* (Cambridge: Cambridge University Press, 2008), pp. 103–109, 112–129. For more on the ubiquity of smuggling, see Chapter 4.

[158] Examples of newspaper entries of this sort are found in Beverly Lemire, ed., *The British Cotton Trade, 1660–1815*, vol. 3 (London: Pickering and Chatto, 2009), pp. 15–17.

[159] Belén Moreno Claverias, 'Luxury, Fashion and Peasantry: The Introduction of New Commodities in Rural Catalan, 1670–1790' in Beverly Lemire, ed., *The Force of Fashion in Politics and Society* (Aldershot, UK: Ashgate, 2010), pp. 67–93.

[160] Kriger, *Cloth in West African History*, pp. 35–39.

could be interpreted and revised across a range of cultures, feeding expressed needs, the essence of 'new luxury' commodities. Textiles were translated endlessly. Europe's challenge in the 1700s was to effectively imitate the most profitable of the Asian textiles, like Indian cottons, and bring it fully within their commercial repertoire, not simply as a trade commodity, but as a product of their industry.

Only after extensive trials, failures and experimentation did European manufacturers resolve production problems, opening a wholly new industrial era that served consumers at a different scale. In the interim, European nations competed directly with Indian cottons in colonial American and African markets, regions of growing importance to European industries in the 1700s.[161] The qualities established by Indian textiles remained the benchmark against which world consumers judged competing fabrics. The cosmopolitan knowledge they wielded shaped diverse consumer markets. The networks of global trade now woven could not easily be unwound.

Conclusion: Global Communities of Taste

Furs, silks, cottons, wools and linens – as well as ribbons and ties of all sorts – exemplify the dynamism of the early global age. These materials were fundamental in enhanced cosmopolitan consumer knowledge and sustained consumer change. My analysis supports and extends Kenneth Pomeranz's 'Great Divergence' paradigm, noting the nodes of shared economic activity in many world regions, activities aligned to growing consumer change. A greater density of regional and global networks sustained these nodes, creating a new system of connection and exchange. At the same time, 'industriousness' of various kinds was also realized on a wider global stage as people in many societies became more invested in commercial activities of many kinds, directed towards the acquisition of cloth and fittings, though material priorities varied.

The early global era relied on newly forged and improved linkages, with new geo-political ramifications and a cumulative impact across the globe. Over generations, material horizons expanded for more of the world's peoples than ever before. Social systems were tested with the flow of furs and fabrics, embraced in a host of circumstances and

[161] Riello, *Cotton*, pp. 151–159.

enabling new economic pursuits. The heightened attention to 'new luxuries' was reflected in the widespread procurement of furs and innovative adoption of peltry, as well as the multiplication and diffusion of fabrics of all sorts. The proliferation of wool blanketing in new locales; the passage of silks and cottons beyond their Eurasian homes; and the embellishment of garments and furnishings with ribbons and furbelows all fostered new fashions and norms. Material change was widespread: geographically and socially. It was an adjunct of dynamic urbanism, an extensive commerce stimulated by foreign novelties and contact with foreign peoples – plus the availability of new forms of waged work and commercial endeavours, combined with the willingness of women, children and men to labour for their pleasures.

One of the distinctive features of this age was the spread of adaptable textiles that gave voice to different cultural priorities among heterogeneous interests, a subject that will be explored in more depth in the chapters ahead. Goods that were easily implanted in new lands could be culturally translated with surprising facility. Indeed, new global links enabled the wider sharing of material culture, among divergent communities of taste, though often at odds with existing hierarchies of consumption. Many shades of material cosmopolitanism emerged in the process through fashions that were contested and embraced, a subject covered in the next chapter.

3 | Dressing World Peoples
Regulation and Cosmopolitan Desire

Ancient simplicity is gone. With the growth of pretence the people today are satisfied with nothing but finery, with nothing but what is beyond their station or purse. You have only to look at the way our citizens' wives and daughters dress. They can hardly go further. To forget one's proper place is to invite the wrath of heaven. ... But, of recent years, even since some ingenious Kyoto creatures started the fashion, every variety of splendid material has been used for men's and women's clothes, and the drapers' sample-books have blossomed in a riot of colour. ... One step further and we might have been wearing imported Chinese silks as working clothes.

Ihara Saikaku, *The Japanese Family*
Storehouse ... (1688)[1]

The most common of the two kinds of [ladies'] dress worn when they go aboard [in Lima], is the veil and long petticoat; the other is a round petticoat and mantelet. The former for church, the latter for taking the air, and diversions; but both in the prevailing taste for expence, being richly embroidered with silver or gold. The long petticoat is particularly worn on holy Thursday; as on that day they visit the churches, attended by two or three female Negro or Mulatto slaves, dressed in an uniform like pages.

Antonia de Ulloa, *A Voyage to*
South-America ... (1765)[2]

This afternoon we have a fair kept on the quarter-deck, of caps, neckcloths, waistcoats, drawers, shirts, stockings, shoes, etc. Most of the wares are

---

[1] Ihara Saikaku, *The Japanese Family Storehouse. Or the Millionaires' Gospel Modernized*, trans. G. W. Sargeant (Cambridge: Cambridge University Press, 1959), pp. 26–27, in Constantine Nomikos Vaporis, ed., *Voices of Early Modern Japan: Contemporary Accounts of Daily Life during the Age of the Shoguns* (Santa Barbara, CA: Greenwood, 2012), pp. 28–29.

[2] Antonia de Ulloa, *A Voyage to South-America: Describing at Large the Spanish Cities, Towns, Provinces etc* ... (Dublin: Alexander Ewing, 1765), vol. 2, p. 54.

sold, but not one penny paid: you could but ask for what you wanted and 'twas put into your hands – but mark the end on't.

The Diary of Henry Teonge, Chaplain on Board
H.M.'s Ships ... 1675–1679.[3]

Few media were as charged with meaning as clothing, and few elements of common use were as emblematic of evolving economic, social and political systems. Clothing and bodily adornment are termed the 'social skin', transmitting signs of status, age, ethnicity, gender and aspiration. As Terence Turner observes, 'the adornment and public presentation of the body, however inconsequential or even frivolous a business it may appear to individuals, is for cultures a serious matter: *de la vie sérieuse.*'[4] Developing societies approved material differentiation to express order and spiritual schema. With sustained transcultural contact, trade and economic progress came opportunities for more intensive fashioning of material culture, with cyclical amendments of hair, apparel or cosmetics, complicating social gradations. Hierarchy and its preservation were officially espoused in most developing regions of the world: thus, accelerated consumption opened a political process that challenged or mediated social orders. Religious injunctions, laws and edicts directed citizens and congregants to contain experimentation, adding moral weight to secular decrees.[5] Sumptuary rules worked to bolster or define existing hierarchies so that visual signs matched the rank of the wearer. Other statutes incorporated aspects of sumptuary control, as in the regulation of dress for African slaves or free people of colour in European colonies. Arjun Appadurai observes that 'sumptuary laws constitute an intermediate consumption-regulation device,

---

[3] G. E. Manwaring, ed., *The Diary of Henry Teonge, Chaplain on Board H.M.'s Ships Assistance, Bristol and Royal Oak 1675–1679* (London: Routledge, 1927), p. 210.

[4] Terence S. Turner, 'The Social Skin', reprinted in *HAU: Journal of Ethnographic Theory* 2:2 (2012), p. 486.

[5] For example, St Bernardino of Siena (1380–1444) became renowned for his public preaching against vanity and the bonfires of the vanities that ensued. Protestant and Catholic disputes in the sixteenth and seventeenth centuries were represented through highly charged print depictions of appropriate or immoral dress. Ulinka Rublack, *Dressing Up: Cultural Identity in Renaissance Europe* (Oxford: Oxford University Press, 2010), Chapter 3. Ottoman regulations likewise intended a clear visual hierarchy and differentiation among religious groups and among social ranks, with particular attention paid to women. Donald Quataert, ed., *Consumption Studies and the History of the Ottoman Empire, 1550–1922* (Albany, NY: SUNY Press, 2000).

suited to societies devoted to stable status displays in exploding commodity contexts, such as India, China, and Europe in the pre-modern
period.'[6] These laws were promulgated at a time when evolving material life unsettled existing order as global connections tightened, as new
luxuries multiplied and influences flowed. Fashion flourished in these
contexts and fashion actors routinely contested sumptuary regimes.
That is one focus of this chapter. Their apparel expressed the growing
cosmopolitan ethos of the age, interpreted by women and men living
with opportunity and constraint. Styles varied, but a spirit of material
innovation infused diverse populations.

Fashion relied on the energies of industry, the stimulus of disparate
populations and the vitality of commercial networks. It privileged
change over stasis and accepted innovations devised by non-elites.
Cities were a crucial setting for fashion practice, though commercial
meeting places also served this purpose in less populated areas.[7]
Friction was commonplace in populous centres. As Fernand Braudel
observed, early modern European cities served to 'increase tension,
accelerate the rhythm of exchange and ceaselessly stir up lives'.[8] His
claim applies as well to other centres, where global exchange tested the
limits of codified material culture. Tokugawa Japan included many
urban settings where 'drapers' sample-books ... blossomed in a riot
of colours', provisioning shoppers of many ranks. Ihara Saikaku
(1644–1693), the author of the opening extract, was an astute cultural
analyst. The son of a wealthy Osaka merchant, his popular poetry and
fiction focused on the fancies and fads of a sophisticated cohort.[9] He is
one of many to confirm the material disruptions underway, a phenomenon powered by early modern global trade and its consequences. I
focus on the disruptions of fashion and its effects on material change.

[6] Arjun Appadurai, 'Introduction: Commodities and the Politics of Value' in Arjun
Appadurai, ed., *The Social Life of Things: Commodities in Cultural Perspective*
(Cambridge: Cambridge University Press, 1986), p. 25.

[7] Cory Willmott argues for the role of trading posts as 'urban equivalents' in the
exchange of material goods, in the transfer of cultural knowledge and as
gestation sites of new styles and material uses. In regions of relatively low
population, such as the Great Plains of North America in this era, these sites are
arguably of immense cultural significance. Personal communication.

[8] Quoted in Catherine Richardson, 'Introduction' in Catherine Richardson, ed.,
Clothing Culture, 1350–1650 (Aldershot, UK: Ashgate, 2004), p. 19.

[9] Haruo Shirane, ed., *Early Modern Japanese Literature: An Anthology, 1600-
1900* (New York: Columbia University Press, 1893, reprinted 2008), pp. 21–23.

Clothing was profoundly influenced by globalizing forces, forces expressed in creative revisions of dress and the creolization of appearance.[10] Effects flowed from distant harbours through colonies to metropoles and back, in cycles of transculturation and evolution of style within shifting power dynamics.[11] Colonial, enslaved and Indigenous communities negotiated their apparel as men and women met, traded, fought and married – settler and traders, slave and free, missionary and acolyte. Coercion and conversion figured in these encounters, including direct attempts to undermine extant systems of dress and deportment among Native Americans, Africans and others.[12]

In this chapter I explore the politics of fashion within regimes of sumptuary law in Asian, European and colonial case studies. Plebeian people are centre stage, as they comprised the majority of the world's population and their aspiration for material change marked this era. Heightened industriousness and more waged labour for women and children affected consumption in many regions, as discussed in Chapter 2. The secondhand trade provided another critical means through which poor and middle-ranked people negotiated their resources to meet needs and desires, another focus of this chapter. Female industriousness was heightened through this trade in important ways, and consumer options widened. The readymade clothing trade is the final innovation I address. This sector, which was dependent on capitalist production and massed female labour, initially aimed to clothe sailors and soldiers and flourished as part of imperial policy. It inaugurated a high-water mark of production before the dawn of the factory.

---

[10] Charles Stewart, 'Creolization: History, Ethnography, Theory' in Charles Stewart, ed., *Creolization: History, Ethnography, Theory* (Walnut Creek, CA: Left Coast Books, 2007), pp. 1–24.

[11] Transculturation has been defined as a process producing 'cultural hybrids – the fusing of cultural forms' that 'never develop from "pure" cultural forms in the first place'. Quoting J.Lull in R. A. Roger, 'From Cultural Exchange to Transculturation: A Review and Reconceptualization of Cultural Appropriation' *Communication Theory* 16 (2006). p. 491.

[12] Bartolomé Yun-Casalilla, 'The History of Consumption of Early Modern Europe in a Trans-Atlantic Perspective: Some New Challenges in European Social History' in Veronika Hyden-Hanscho, Renate Pieper and Werner Stangl, eds., *Cultural Exchange and Consumption Patterns in the Age of Enlightenment: Europe and the Atlantic World* (Bochum: Verlag Dr. Dieter Winkler, 2013), p. 36; Robert DuPlessis, *The Material Atlantic: Clothing, Commerce, and Colonization in the Atlantic World, 1650–1800* (Cambridge: Cambridge University Press, 2016).

At the same time, uniform-style clothing defined the rising scale of 'involuntary consumers' and the new sorts of 'licensed' clothing they were assigned.[13] It heralded a disciplined, constrained choice enforced on sailors, soldiers and slaves, populations vitally important to imperial agendas. This disciplined dressing contrasts dramatically to the widening consumer options enjoyed by those untrammelled by these disciplinary apparatus. In all, new patterns of clothing consumption emerged even as regulators strained to keep buyers in approved avenues of material culture. These are the subjects I explore.

Regulation, Sumptuary Systems and Cosmopolitan Desires

The word 'fashion' is aligned with making and revising, beautifying and embellishing; it is also an aspirational force expressed in ways that shaped collective and individual material priorities. Its societal presence indicates a generative economy, though fashion might disrupt and disturb. Fashion is integrally connected to consumption, as style was materialized through textiles, ribbons, braid, lace, fur, feathers, embroidery, buttons and cosmetics. As bodily presentation was modified, priorities were revealed. Fashion inspired material change in large ways and small, despite secular and religious injunctions aimed at fixed temporal deportment. Arjun Appadurai contrasts the 'fashion system' with the 'license system'. The former is defined as an *'ever-changing universe of commodities'*, while the 'license system' required permission for the use of certain goods that were available only by agreement.[14] License and fashion collided repeatedly over these centuries, in many regions. Most governments strived to keep the upper hand in these contests, though total control was rarely achieved. These contests were a defining feature of early global fashion systems.

---

[13] John Styles importantly observed the numbers of poor consumers in eighteenth-century England whose clothing choices were few. Termed 'involuntary consumers' by Styles, they habitually received clothing as part of poor relief, charity or as part of their wages. This did not leave poor consumers powerless to shape their attire, but it did require a variety of strategies to affect preference. John Styles, *The Dress of the People: Everyday Fashion in Eighteenth-Century England* (New Haven: Yale University Press, 2007), pp. 247–320. The concept of 'involuntary consumer' is very useful when considering other populations supplied with basic apparel.

[14] Appadurai, 'Introduction: Commodities and the Politics of Value', p. 25 (emphasis in original).

In the license system, emblems defined rank. These recognizable symbols included all elements of attire – from rings to headwear, coloured coats to the choice of fur. Visual signals reinforced the status quo and were expressed through ceremonies and displays that incorporated these signs. The lord and his entourage, the judge in his court: each demonstrated status through garb and gesture. In this context, the wearing of clothing held deep meaning, for the donning of particular garments in defined rituals was held to transform the essence of that person. Enrobing imbued officeholders with authentic status and moral advantage: 'it was investiture, the putting on of clothes, that quite literally constituted a person as a monarch or a freeman of a guild or a household servant.'[15] Ceremonies of investiture celebrated these transformations with symbolic amendments of dress. The rank badge of an imperial civil servant or military officer was intended to signal standing in China, with birds for civilian and animals for military incumbents, the creatures tiered in meritorious order. The portrait of a mandarin in Plate 3.1 commemorates the material accoutrements of imperial service with the unnamed official garbed in a deep blue robe (the colour being representative of the Qing dynasty), with a rank badge specifying his place. Every facet of this attire bespeaks his service to the court, his field of responsibility and his authority, with the peacock feather attached to the finial of his hat serving as another confirmation of his standing. Officials of the fifth rank and higher wore peacock feathers confirming imperial approbation of their service, another sign linking the wearer to dynastic hierarchies.[16] Emblems of various sorts infused organizations, kingdoms and empires, both religious and secular.

Yet, divorced from their social context, in museum collections, for example, we cannot take these emblems at face value. There is recurring evidence of misrepresentation in the late Ming period, with those of lower rank claiming rank badges of a superior status, with at least one family commemorating this impertinence in a family portrait.[17] The intent behind

---

[15]   Ann Rosalind Jones and Peter Stallybrass, *Renaissance Clothes and the Materials of Memory* (Cambridge, 2000), p. 2.

[16]   Valery Garrett, *Chinese Dress from the Qing Dynasty to the Present* (Tokyo, Rutland, VT and Singapore: Tuttle Publishing, 2007), p. 73.

[17]   Sarah Dauncey, 'Illusions of Grandeur: Perceptions of Status and Wealth in Late-Ming Female Clothing and Ornamentation' *East Asian History* 25/26 (2003), pp. 49–50; Jonathan Schlesinger, *A World Trimmed with Fur: Wild Things, Pristine Places, and the Natural Fringes of Qing Rule* (Stanford: Stanford University Press, 2017), pp. 28–45.

Figure 3.1 *A Lady Going to Visit*, 1817. London. © Victoria and Albert Museum, London.

the official creation of these signs was clear. But, subtle defiance and overt self-assertion undermined the intent of this system within a context of heightened materiality and surging commoditization. Nonetheless, Qing court robes or the livery that enrobed a European or colonial servant carried his master's or mistress's authority in its colours, cloth or insignia – a tradition of dress that persisted through the eighteenth century and beyond, wholly removed from the fashion system. Wealthy European colonists routinely indulged in livery for servants or slaves as a sign of pre-eminence, as with a lady's attendants in Lima: 'three female Negro or Mulatto slaves, dressed in an uniform like pages.'[18] The small troop of African servants in Figure 3.1 were garbed in what was, by 1817, a set of antiquated costumes: the breeches and hose, plus heavily braided uniforms, signalled their servile status to onlookers, though a position in a wealthy household might have its benefits. Livery was a distinctive category of dress, often costly and archaic in form, demonstrating the power of tradition in every fold, while denoting the dependent affiliation of the wearer. Those inhabiting these servile roles were garbed by rule or custom, their personhood defined by this licensed apparel. Sumptuary

---

[18] Antonio de Ulloa, *A Voyage to South-America*, p. 54.

laws attempted to rein in the visual chaos represented by choice. And choice presaged an increased material anarchy over time. Ideally, the sight of a person passing through the city streets declared their status unambiguously, whether man or woman. But certainty eroded as the tempo of trade increased and the fashion ethos took hold.

Sumptuary laws increased within European precincts from the fourteenth century onwards, directed at the unregulated use of globalized commodities such as silk cloth and pearl jewellery among the ranks deemed unworthy of such luxuries. New laws were enacted as new products appeared, with legislators playing an endless game of catch-up. Daniel Roche sees sumptuary codes as one of the pillars of the French sartorial *ancien régime*, even as resistance to these edicts bubbled beneath the surface.[19] The growth of trade over these centuries elicited ever-longer lists of regulations in many quarters, with explicit, gendered laws to constrain men and women of different status.[20] Ottoman commentators in the sixteenth and seventeenth century decried the sight of commoners wearing clothing or accessories intended for elites. Their denunciations persisted even as local silk production increased, with goods taken up by local townspeople. Authorities were dismayed at the multiplication of commodities, with the appearance of new fabrics and the disappearance of old.[21] The efficacy of their rules varied. Clothing regulation in the Ottoman Empire addressed only the behaviour of subjects in public spaces: 'there were virtually no attempts to legislate what clothes or jewels people might put on in the privacy of their own homes.'[22] Importantly, new fashions made from new materials could be

[19] Daniel Roche, *The Culture of Clothing: Dress and Fashion in the 'Ancien Régime'*, translated by Jean Birrell (Cambridge: Cambridge University Press, 1994), pp. 23–43.
[20] Martha Howell, *Commerce Before Capitalism in Europe, 1300–1600* (Cambridge: Cambridge University Press, 2010), pp. 208–260.
[21] Eminegül Karababa, 'Investigating Early Modern Ottoman Consumer Culture in the Light of Bursa Probate Inventories' *Economic History Review* 65:1 (2012), pp. 199–200. Further studies of the politics of Ottoman dress include Donald Quataert, 'Clothing Law, State, and Society in the Ottoman Empire, 1720–1829' *International Journal of Middle East Studies* 29:4 (1997): 403–425; Suraiya Faroqhi and Christoph K. Neumann, eds., *Ottoman Costumes: From Textile to Identity* (Istanbul: EREN, 2004); James Grehan, *Everyday Life and Consumer Culture in Eighteenth-Century Damascus* (Seattle: University of Washington Press, 2007), Chapter 6, 'Fashion and Deportment'.
[22] Suraiya Faroqhi, 'Introduction' in Faroqhi and Neumann, eds., *Ottoman Costumes*, p. 23.

rehearsed in private, without fear of transgressing regulations. The details of sumptuary legislation differed from region to region, from regime to regime. Ulinka Rublack notes the complex laws in Central European cities where magistrates in sixteenth-century Nuremburg, for example, 'took mild views on sumptuary legislation.' In Leipzig, officials despaired at enforcing even modest restraints on burghers, as 'what people wear changes almost every year among the German Nation and from one to the other.'[23] Clothing was contentious as sumptuary regimes sought to order the flow of goods.[24] The 'fashion system' and the 'license system' collided repeatedly in these centuries, with many commoners determined to extend their clothing options despite the laws. Faced with a rising tide of goods, how was clothing culture shaped in world communities?

Tokugawa Regulation and Material Change

The Tokugawa (1603–1868) was a determined regime, mandating priorities across many sectors. One objective was to limit external influences and constrain Western trade, with Westerners confined to the port of Nagasaki. External influences circulated nonetheless, seeping through commercial labyrinths and incorporated into a lively material mix. A phenomenon termed 'indigenization' was a notable feature of this era, as in Japan and in other locales 'imported cultural elements ... [took] on local features as the cultural hybrids develop.'[25] In this period, the 'indigenization' or domestication of foreign goods flourished to an exceptional degree, helping to redefine Tokugawa material culture.

---

[23] Rublack, *Dressing Up*, p. 266.

[24] Alan Hunt, *Governance of Consuming Passions: A History of Sumptuary Law* (Basingstoke: Macmillan, 1996); Roche, *Culture of Clothing*; Beverly Lemire, *Dress, Culture and Commerce: The English Clothing Trade Before the Factory* (Basingstoke, UK: Macmillan, 1997); Antonia Finnane, *Changing Clothes in China: Fashion, History, Nation* (New York: Columbia University Press, 2008), Chapters 1 and 2; Wu Jen-shu, *Pinwei shehua: wanming de xiaofei shehui yu shi dafu (Taste and Extravagance: Late Ming Consumer Society and the Gentry)*, (Beijing: Zhonghua Book Company, 2008).

[25] James Lull, *Media, Communication, Culture: A Global Approach*, 2nd ed. (New York: Columbia University Press, 2000), p. 242, quoted in R. A. Rogers 'From Cultural Exchange to Transculturation: A Review and Reconceptualization of Cultural Appropriation', *Communication Theory* 16 (2006), p. 491. See Chapter 5 in this volume for examples of the impact of tobacco in Japan.

Emperor and nobles, a powerful shogun and samurai military, con-stituted the pre-eminent social architecture of Japan. Merchants and townsmen counted for little in this system, having scant prestige, while peasants were approved for their tireless labour. Despite the legislated barriers to material exchange, Edo Japan was infused with catalyst commodities from across the world. I use the term 'catalyst commod-ities' to denote commodities of exceptional cultural and economic vital-ity, things that sparked inventive uses as well as imitations. Catalyst commodities were widely embraced in Tokugawa Japan, including new elements of dress. This nation's dynamism came from its cities and its agricultural wealth, with commerce and industry also animating the economy.[26] Regions and cities were closely linked, as provincial lords or *daimyo* reported to the court at Edo in annual cycles, an alternative attendance that moved *daimyos* and their great entourages in distinctive ways.[27] Great and small cities thrived by providing staples, luxuries and entertainment to locals and travellers alike. The fast-growing capital of Edo reached over a million residents by 1720. It was one of three great cities including Osaka at about half a million people by the mid-1700s, and Kyoto at 350,000 by the same period. These metropolitan hubs, tied to dozens of smaller castle towns, exemplified an exceptional urban energy, with attendant cultural complexities. These factors produced challenges to the existing sumptuary regime.[28]

Fashion practice was on the rise in seventeenth-century Japan, a fact condemned by some commentators who were unsettled by these obser-vations – the opening quotation demonstrates this unease. Ihara Saikaku complained as well that 'fashions have changed from those of the past and have become increasingly ostentatious. In everything people have a liking for finery above their station. Women's clothes in particular go to extremes.'[29] City life provided the resources, inspiration and audience

[26] John Whitney Hall, *The Cambridge History of Japan: Early Modern Japan*, vol. 4 (Cambridge: Cambridge University Press, 1991), pp. 510–513.

[27] Kaoru Sugihara, 'The State and The Industrious Revolution in Tokugawa Japan' Working Paper No. 02/04, London School of Economics (2004); Kenneth Pomeranz, *The Great Divergence: China, Europe, and the Making of the Modern World Economy* (Princeton: Princeton University Press, 2000), p. 149.

[28] Constantine Nomiko Vaporis, *Tour of Duty: Samurai, Military Service in Edo and the Culture of Early Modern Japan* (Honolulu: University of Hawai'i Press, 2008), p. xxiv.

[29] Quoted in Donald Shively, 'Sumptuary Regulation and Status in Early Tokugawa Japan' *Harvard Journal of Asiatic Studies* 25 (1964/5), pp. 124–125.

for displays of self-fashioning, encouraging seemingly endless shifts in style, particularly in the 'floating worlds' or *ukiyo* of Edo, Osaka and Kyoto. Licensed prostitution formed the rationale for these floating world districts, a business that involved routine flamboyance and cavalcades of clients. These quarters attracted artists and actors, as well as teahouses, shops and theatres where the louche, the adventurous and the entrepreneurial rubbed shoulders. These neighbourhoods also drew merchants, tradesmen and visiting samurai looking for business and pleasure. One such rural samurai compared two of Japan's great cities about 1800 as he moved towards Edo: 'Entering Kyoto I saw that, as expected, the city was by far superior to Osaka; and men and women's fashion are twice as beautiful in Kyoto.'[30] The delights of Edo were yet to come. Eiko Ikegami identifies a 'series of developments in the Japanese economy and urban culture ... [that] led to a remarkable and unexpected phenomenon: the rise of popular fashion.'[31] Floating worlds were at the heart of this fashion eruption.

Ikegami argues for the vital importance of aesthetic networks, alliances of like-minded compatriots who coalesced outside regulated hierarchies. Shared interests in the theatre, the arts or the aesthetics of calligraphy, tea ceremonies or *ikebana* promulgated new social bonds. Aesthetic networks sparked fresh patterns of consumerism and new attention to style and the socially marginal groups who congregated there – artists, actors and courtesans – influenced these generative areas. Their priorities shaped these bohemian precincts. Devotees of the floating world were provided with alternate forums for self-expression, communication and even discreet defiance of the political status quo and its sumptuary laws. A walk through these neighbourhood streets offered sights and sounds to charge the senses, with parades of people to observe, some in gorgeous or outlandish attire.[32] This education in style was captured in print form by local artists, who supported themselves through the production of prints depicting city life, images that circulated throughout the country. The *ukiyo-e* genre of prints showcased beautiful courtesans wearing the latest styles, kabuki actors in costume and sumo wrestlers in action, as well as endless city scenes. Figure 3.2 is one such image, capturing an

[30] Quoted in Vaporis, *Tour of Duty*, p. 208.
[31] Eiko Ikegami, *Bonds of Civility: Aesthetic Networks and the Political Origins of Japanese Culture* (Cambridge: Cambridge University Press, 2005), p. 245.
[32] Vaporis, *Tour of Duty*, pp. 196–202.

Figure 3.2 *Plant Seller (Ueki fukujusō uri).* Kiyonaga Torii (1752–1815). FP 2 – JPD, no. 1703. Fine Prints: Japanese, pre-1915. Library of Congress, Washington, DC.

interaction between a seller of bonsai trees and two fashionably dressed women. This image offers tacit instruction in hairstyles and ensembles, and, as these printed works circulated, others learned of city fashions.[33]

Regulations sought to control innovations and troublesome innovators. Authorities focused on the commercial classes, townspeople great and small – especially ostentatious common women, including courtesans.[34] Officials banned the use of flashy gold, silver leaf or gold thread on courtesans' clothing; yet, courtesans' apparel was notoriously difficult to police; as well it was part of their professional self-promotion. In 1683, embroidery was entirely prohibited on common women's garments, including prostitutes; three years later, failing in their efforts, embroidered robes were approved for non-elite women 'if they are not especially sumptuous.'[35] In the late 1680s, women and men were threatened with arrest if found in any beautiful or stylish apparel – one can image a cat and mouse pursuit, as officials hunted out sartorial infractions. Shortly after, a woman's imprisonment was widely broadcast – her crime was wearing garments prohibited to her rank.[36] Both rank and gender figured in calculations of crime and punishment.

In 1692, 'townsmen's wives' were singled out again. Administrators complained that, 'in recent years matrons everywhere have become presumptuous, and although they do not lack clothes, they plan for the New Year silk padded robes of the latest up-to-date patterns.'[37] These denunciations reflect the tensions between the adherents of the old order and the material ambitions of creative, unruly commoners. In 1718, officials directed their attention to the fabric of undergarments, worrying that hidden fabrics might be secretly luxurious, contrary to regulation.[38] Figure 3.3 is one of innumerable prints distributed widely that featured famous courtesans. The matching hairstyles of the courtesan and her

---

[33] Allen Hockley, *The Prints of Isoda Koryūsai: Floating World Culture and Its Consumers in Eighteenth-Century Japan* (Seattle: University of Washington Press, 2003) p. 7. Courtesans were influential as well in fashion development in mid-late Qing China, 'outsider' populations that were aesthetically creative. Rachel Silberstein, 'Eight Scenes of Suzhou: Landscape Embroidery and Urban Courtesans in Nineteenth-Century China' *Late Imperial China* 36:1 (2015): 1–52.
[34] Hunt, *Governance of Consuming Passions*, p. 23.
[35] Shively, 'Sumptuary Regulation', pp. 132, 127.
[36] Shively, 'Sumptuary Regulation', p. 127.
[37] Quoted in Shively, 'Sumptuary Regulation', pp. 130–131.
[38] Shively, 'Sumptuary Regulation', pp. 127–129.

Figure 3.3 *Snow. (Yuki)* Harunobu Suzuki (1725?–1770). A courtesan walks in the snow with two female attendants and a male attendant carrying a parasol over her head. 1767–1769. FP 2 – JPD, no. 1613. Fine Prints: Japanese, pre-1915. Library of Congress, Washington, DC.

female attendants suggest a closely choreographed aesthetic unlikely to appease officials. Images like this encouraged infractions.

Cotton textiles reflected both the ready indigenization of a foreign fabric in Japan and a medium to circumvent sumptuary codes. Indian cottons were initially a costly rarity in fourteenth-century East Asia: a single painted cotton robe was worth several times the price of a silk equivalent.[39] However, increased trade in Indian cottons from the 1500s by Portuguese and then Dutch traders made these goods widely available: plain, checked, striped, patterned, painted and printed.[40] Japanese manufacturers soon imitated Indian fabrics, retaining the names and foreign ethos surrounding these textiles. Fujita Kayoko writes of 'Japan indianized' as imported and locally made fabrics reshaped tastes.[41] Cotton was also approved for non-elites, and some cities specifically authorized cotton for commoners.[42] Fujita observes, 'cotton textiles brought revolutionary changes in the material culture of non-elite Japanese [with] . . . unprecedented changes in the design of their daily clothes.'[43]

Embroidery and 'dapple tie-dye' were forbidden to ordinary women, and 'unusual weaving and dyeing' was proscribed in the clothing of all common people.[44] But a subtle sedition might escape notice in a busy city like Osaka, which was largely peopled by commoners, if cotton garments were layered with clever counterpoints of stripe and check, visible in the flutter of a hem or turned cuff, as demonstrated by the women shoppers in Figure 3.2.[45] Sumptuary regulations could be fully enforced only with draconian measures. Arrests, seizure of property and banishment from Edo were some of the harshest penalties meted out. Generally, severe punishments were few in number, and struck

---

[39] John Guy, '"One Thing Leads to Another": Indian Textiles and the Early Globalization of Style' in Amelia Peck, ed., *Interwoven Globe: The Worldwide Textile Trade, 1500–1800* (New York: Metropolitan Museum of Art, 2014), p. 14.

[40] Imports into Japan were a fraction of those carried to Europe. However, the impact of these goods was substantial.

[41] Fujita Kayoko, 'Japan Indianized: The Material Culture of Imported Textiles in Japan, 1550–1850' in Giorgio Riello and Prasannan Parthasarathi, eds., *The Spinning World: A Global History of Cotton Textiles, 1200–1850* (Oxford: Oxford University Press, 2009), pp. 181–204.

[42] Toby Slade, *Japanese Fashion: A Cultural History* (Oxford and New York: Berg Publishers, 2009), p. 53; Masayuki Tanimoto, 'Cotton and the Peasant Economy: A Foreign Fibre in Early Modern Japan' in Riello and Parthasarathi, eds., *The Spinning World*, p. 369; Yoshiko Iwamoto Wada, Mary Kellogg Rice and Jane Barton, *Shibori: The Inventive Art of Japanese Shaped Resist Dyeing* (Tokyo: Kodansha International Ltd., 1999), p. 275.

[43] Fujita, 'Japan Indianized' pp. 189–190. See also, Ikegami, *Bonds of Civility*, p. 253

[44] Shively, 'Sumptuary Regulation', p. 126.

[45] Fujita, 'Japan Indianized'; Vaporis, *Voices of Early Modern Japan*, p. xxiv.

merchants families living in visible luxury.[46] Indian cotton cloth was an important vehicle of consumer innovation and was absorbed into Japanese culture, serving as useful and inventive elements of daily wear. Despite official hostility, fashion ingenuity prevailed in many spheres.

'Anxieties about Things': Qing China and Early Modern Europe

The Qing established new dynastic dress codes reflecting Manchu authority for Chinese court and official functions, such as horseshoe cuffs on official robes (Plates 3.1 and 3.2A and 3.2B) and the rising rhetorical importance of furs. At the same time, they maintained established categorizes of dress for those above the common people; the grades of scholars, administrators and courtiers were ideally reflected in the colour of robes and assigned rank badges, worn front and back. But regulations were not universally obeyed, and Qing officialdom repeatedly revealed their 'anxieties about things',[47] itemizing what could be owned, used and displayed by different orders. However, status markers were steadily usurped by less worthy members of society, and social climbing thrived.[48] A sort of hide-and-seek took place as ambitious officials, merchants or scholars adopted restricted goods for their own use, hoping to escape detection. The eighteenth-century novelist Cao Xueqin captured the spirit of these contests in the celebrated novel *The Story of the Stone, or, The Dream of the Red Chamber*. In one scene he recounts a raid by government agents on the home of a prominent family. The agents discovered numerous cushions made of yellow satin, the signal colour of the imperial household, evidence of overreaching ambition. Furs were another focus of unlicensed extravagance, a theme doubtless familiar to readers of this novel.[49]

---

[46] Shively, 'Sumptuary Regulation', pp. 133–134.

[47] Craig Clunas, *Superfluous Things: Material Culture and Social Status in Early Modern China* (Honolulu: University of Hawai'i Press, 1991), pp. 141–160.

[48] Craig Clunas pinpointed this phenomenon for the sixteenth century, a function that continued under the Qing. 'The Art of Social Climbing in Sixteenth-Century China' *Burlington Magazine* 133:1059 (1991): 368–375.

[49] Mary M. Dusenbury, *Flowers, Dragons and Pine Trees: Asian Textiles in the Spencer Museum of Art* (Manchester, VT: Hudson Hills Press, 2004), p. 117; Schlesinger, *A World Trimmed with Fur*, pp. 42–45.

Material hierarchies were under pressure, and sumptuary laws were difficult to enforce. Furs were ranked and assigned to different social levels for winter clothes, as discussed in Chapter 2.[50] Despite these explicit commands, a court official purchased a mink-lined robe though it was not consistent with his rank, which proved a costly mistake. When he wore the garment to court, he was prosecuted, and stiff penalties were imposed, including a fine of six months' salary.[51] Plates 3.2A and 3.2B present another Qing mink-lined silk robe perhaps somewhat like the garment described above, the glossy furs sourced from distant lands. This is a globalized garment, shaped by local culture, individual taste and extended supply networks. The open lapel showcasing the mink lining offers the promise of luxury when contrasted with the more subdued exterior silk.[52] Azure silk frames the deep brown pelts on the lapel and at the interior edges of the hem and front opening, azure being another significant dynastic colour.[53] Restrained luxury emanates from this garment. But this was cost-conscious luxury, carefully crafted for appearance. Inside, the upper body of this garment was not lined with mink but with sheepskin, a much cheaper addition to this robe that would be invisible when on the body. Fur was used only where the pelts might be visible. Judicious calculation is evident throughout, with prudence taking precedence over unbridled extravagance, an exceptional example of fashion planning. We do not know who owned this robe or if it was worn in compliance with (or in defiance of) sumptuary laws. Clearly, individual calculus was fully at work, aiming for a luxurious garment within the bounds of thrift, demonstrating one consumer's negotiation with Qing fashionability.

Outside the capital, in dynamic eastern cities like Suzhou and Yangzhou, fashion was also a notable force. Rachel Silberstein observes that 'silver monetization, handicraft commercialization, and the development of a commodity economy were stimulated by an urban consumption sector.' More particularly, 'the commercialization of

---

[50] Fur use in Qing China is discussed in Chapter 2.

[51] Huimin Lai, 'The Exotic Commodities and Banner People's Daily Life in Beijing during Qianlong and Jiaqing Reign (1735–1820)' ('Qian Jia shidai Beijing de yanghuo yu qiren richang shenghuo') in Wu Jen-shu, Paul Katz and Lin May-li, eds., *The City and Chinese Modernity, (Cong chengshi kan zhongguo de xiandai xing)* (Taipei: Institute of Modern History, Academia Sinica, 2010), pp. 10–17.

[52] Patricia Bjaaland Welch, *Chinese Art: A Guide to Motifs and Visual Imagery* (North Clarendon, VT: Tuttle Pub., 2008), p. 219.

[53] Bjaaland Welch, *Chinese Art*, pp. 222–223.

handicrafts like embroidery and dressmaking' reflect the material innovations underway in mid to late Qing China.[54] Rural female embroiderers, estimated at 100,000 strong, encircled cities like Suzhou, feeding
retailers with an array of products. Analyses of contemporary garments
from this period reveal the ingredients of commoditized modish dress:
instead of deep borders of embroidery, ribbons edge robes and jackets,
and wider spaces separate embroidered motifs on fabric. Ribbons facilitated priorities of taste, while accessories like fans, embroidered fan and
needle cases encouraged stylish self-expression at a modest cost.[55] All
these innovations took place within a legal framework that seemed
increasingly toothless by the 1800s.[56] The creative styles invented,
revised and discarded in urban and suburban environments unsettled
the theoretical hierarchies of material culture.[57]

'Anxieties about things' were also widespread among officials at
the other side of Eurasia. Much of early modern Europe began this period
enmeshed in similar webs of sumptuary rules, laws that were many-sided.
Some aimed to enable specific indulgences among selected groups, deli-
neating privilege within an elastic 'license system.' In fifteenth-century
Nuremberg, for example, burghers' wives were permitted to wear bands
of silk on their cloaks, collars and sleeves after officials failed to enforce
earlier silk bans among this group.[58] Prominent commercial families
asserted their right to honourable (fashionable) dress, redefining norms.
Ulinka Rublack reminds us that

[European] Cities ... were clearly torn between their wish to use dress to
regulate expressions of gender and rank, as well as to forestall an emotional
dynamic of social competition and envy, and, on the other hand, the typical

---

[54] Silberstein, 'Eight Scenes of Suzhou', pp. 3–4, 23.
[55] For example, at the Victoria and Albert Museum, London. See https://collec
      tions.vam.ac.uk/item/O457560/fan-case-unknown/.
[56] Garrett, *Chinese Dress*, pp. 73–75.
[57] Jin-min Fan, '"Suyang", "Suyi": Ming Qing Suzhou ling chaoliu', ('Suzhou with
      Its Style and Mode as a Fashion Leader in the Ming and Qing Dynasties')
      Journal of Nanjing University (Philosophy, Humanities and Social Sciences) No.
      4 (2013): 123–141; Wu, *Pinwei shehua (Taste and Extravagance)*; Li-yueh Lin,
      'Yishang yu fengjiao: wan Ming de fushi fengshang yu fu-yao yilun', ('Costumes
      and Customs: The Vogue and Opinion on Luxury Clothes of Ordinary People in
      Late Ming China') *Xin shixue (New Historical Studies)* 10:3 (1999): 111–157.
      See Chapter 4 in this volume for additional discussion of Qing fashions and the
      role of smuggled goods in this context.
[58] Kent Roberts Greenfield, *Sumptuary Law in Nürmberg: A Study in Paternal
      Government* (Baltimore: Johns Hopkins University Press, 1918), pp. 111, 116.

Renaissance endorsement that cities were aesthetic communities, and competed not just for the elegance of their buildings … but for their inhabitants' looks as well.[59]

Regulatory regimes varied region by region, with close policing in some and lax laws in others. In rural Bohemia, far from cosmopolitan cities, church courts strictly supervised their communities and instituted punitive actions, especially against women who infringed sumptuary rules.[60] Still, even within more permissive city-states, foreign imports aroused legislators who advocated higher import duties or wholesale bans on some foreign goods. Mercantilist legislation flourished as an adjunct of sumptuary edits to protect local trades. *Local* dress was intended to sustain the *local* economy. However, many residents baulked when faced with these precepts.[61]

As the seventeenth century unfolded, European East India companies carried greater quantities of Asian fabrics and fancies to European ports. In Japan, the flood of Indian cottons and Chinese silks unsettled sartorial regimes. The reception of Asian fabrics in Europe is also noteworthy. Kenneth Pomeranz assessed the role of fashion in the expanding consumer markets of Europe, China and Japan, and in this comparison, Pomeranz notes the consumer passion for foreign manufactures in early modern Europe. China remains Pomeranz's comparative focus, and he identifies different levels of fashion-driven consumption in Europe and China, suggesting that the vogue for Asian goods in Europe 'seems attributable to a difference in the degree to which exotic goods, especially exotic *manufactured* goods, became prestigious'.[62] Research does not support this hypothesis, as with the

---

[59] Rublack, *Dressing Up*, p. 166.

[60] Sheilagh Ogilvie, 'Consumption, Social Capital, and the "Industrious Revolution" in Early Modern Germany' *Journal of Economic History* 70:2 (2010): 287–325 and '"So That Every Subject Knows How to Behave": Social Disciplining in Early Modern Bohemia' *Comparative Studies in Society and History* 48:1 (2006): 38–78.

[61] English regulations (18 and 19 Cha. II c. (1666) and 32 Cha. II c. 1 (1680)) that required the dead be buried in wool offers a case in point. Intended to support the local wool trade, many prominent families were revolted at the idea of a shroud made from such a plebeian cloth and preferred to pay the £5 fine rather than to wrap their departed in such rough fabric. *The Good-Wives Lamentation, or, The Womens Complaint on the Account of Their Being to Be Buried in Woollen*, (London, 1678), p. 6.

[62] Pomeranz, *Great Divergence*, p. 157. Original italics.

case of Indian cottons in Japan.[63] Similarly, the claim by Pomeranz that Europe embraced all foreign manufactured goods with alacrity (while Asia did not) needs revision based on individual commodities. As I show in Chapter 2, by the early 1700s the vast majority of Asian fabrics were officially barred in much of Europe. Europeans who yearned for Indian chintz or calico depended on contraband traffickers or local imitations that remained inferior for generations. These options had to suffice until local manufacturers improved.[64]

Notably, in England, all sumptuary regulations were repealed in 1604. Yet, the spirit of regulation remained strong and was enacted through powerful extralegal sanctions. Debates surrounding the presence of Asian wares were heated. In eighteenth-century Britain, women wearing chintz and calico clothing were viciously targeted – their clothes were torn from their bodies, they were beaten and burned, with acid thrown at them in hit-and-run attacks. Beginning in 1719, riots convulsed British cities month after month, reviving periodically over subsequent years. Rioters were defended at the highest levels, and the anti-calico activists harassed women for their treasonous consumer choices. All of this took place in a nation with no sumptuary legislation at all.[65] Why was there such violent resistance to Indian imports in a country with no sumptuary laws on the books?

The causes of these riots are many, including the underlying changes taking place in the British economy and the impact of global trade. Cloth workers were by this time fiercely antagonistic towards early globalism, a sentiment shared among wealthy landowners on whose land sheep were run. Present-day antipathy towards disruptive imports and foreign trade has its roots in these precedents, although female consumers today are rarely beaten for their fashion choices. The vogue for Indian cottons played a powerful role in the anti-calico riots, as

---

[63] Scholars found that unusual foreign goods attracted interest among Ming and Qing consumers in China, from Korean horsehair skirts to Mongol hats and Western clocks. Finnane, *Changing Clothes in China*, pp. 45–59 and 'Chinese Domestic Interiors and "Consumer Constraint" in Qing China: Evidence from Yangzhou' *Journal of the Economic and Social History of the Orient* 57 (2014): 112–144.

[64] Jonathan Eacott, 'Making an Imperial Compromise: The Calico Acts, the Atlantic Colonies, and the Structure of the British Empire' *William and Mary Quarterly* 69:4 (October, 2012): 731–762; Vicente, *Clothing the Spanish Empire*; Lemire, *Cotton*; Riello, *Cotton*.

[65] These events are explored in more detail in Lemire, *Cotton*, Chapter 3.

Indian goods were used by all sectors of consumers. Women's choices were visible on the streets and polemicists emphasized this fact:

all the mean People, the Servant-Maids and indifferently poor People, who would otherwise cloath themselves ... in thin Womens [wool] Stuffs made at Norwich and London ... are now cloath'd in Callicoe or Printed Linnen; ... let any one but cast Their Eyes among the Children of the meaner Sort playing in the Streets, or of the better Sort at Boarding Schools ... the Truth, is too plain to be deny'd.[66]

In the absence of regulation, a powerful alliance of landowners, wool merchants and artisans targeted the most visible and most vulnerable, aiming to stamp out this global fashion by force. Rioters enacted a vicious 'license system', encouraged and paid for by elite allies who argued that unregulated consumption would lead to 'Disorder and Confusion'.[67] One or two agnostics considered the possibility that popular fashion might increase employment, including Nicholas Barbon who asserted that 'fashion or the alteration of Dress, is the great Promoter of Trade, because it occasions the Expence of new Cloaths, before the Old ones are worn out: It is the Spirit and Life of Trade ... [and] keeps the great Body of Trade in Motion.' Yet, Barbon admitted that 'fashion' 'lyes under an ill Name amongst many Grave and Sober People.'[68] Most theorists and governments distrusted fashionable consumption, except when it could be controlled to national advantage. Faced with an influx of Asian textiles, women were assailed in grim pursuit of regulated dress.

Thus, Kenneth Pomeranz's claim that Europe embraced exotic imports wholeheartedly, while Asia did not, is not sustainable. Clearly, the potent threat of new clothing styles exercised many societies whether or not sumptuary laws were in place. Equally, where regulations abounded, commoners adopted strategies to facilitate

---

[66] Daniel Defoe, *The Just Complaint of the Poor Weavers Represented ...*, in Beverly Lemire, ed., *The British Cotton Trade*, vol. 2, (London: Pickering & Chatto, 2011), pp. 107–108.

[67] Claudius Rey, *The Weavers True Case ...* in Lemire, *The British Cotton Trade*, vol. 2, p. 190

[68] Nicholas Barbon, *A Discourse of Trade ...* (London, 1690), p. 65. This debate in Spain is discussed in Rebecca Earle, 'Luxury, Clothing and Race in Colonial Spanish America' in Maxine Berg and Elizabeth Eger, eds., *Luxury in the Eighteenth Century: Debates, Desires and Delectable Goods* (Basingstoke: Palgrave Macmillan, 2003), p. 220.

taste, sometimes in the face of great risks. World communities displayed a patchwork of aims and administrative systems, set within social hierarchies.[69] The maintenance of order was a driving force in most contexts, and material inflows from global trade upset this goal, particularly when it came to dress. Hierarchies of various sorts felt imperilled by untrammelled plebeian consumption. Imperial and colonial governments fiercely defended hierarchy, particularly where this involved definitions of race, monitoring the material boundaries expressing ethnicity and status. These contests present another defining feature of globalizing consumption.

Colonial Complexity and Creolization

The regulation of dress remained an abiding preoccupation of authorities, as people and goods intermixed in unprecedented ways. It was precisely this intermingling that sparked contention, for if Native American and enslaved Africans could redefine their status through dress, then many colonial aims were undone. Officials and wealthy settlers in the Americas endeavoured to fix a clear demarcation between Indigenous and African subjects and European and Creole settlers. To this end, missionaries, officials and others recognized the power of clothing and worked to reform or transform the dress systems of subject peoples. European slave-holding colonial regions displayed exceptional sumptuary concerns. Not only did recently landed African slaves bring their knowledge, culture and religious preferences (including preferences in dress), they were also enmeshed in a dominant European clothing culture that they in turn adapted.[70]

---

[69]   The variation in sumptuary laws is addressed in a research project and forthcoming volume, headed by Giorgio Riello and Ulinka Rublack: *The Right to Dress: Sumptuary Regulations in Comparative and Global Perspective, c. 1200–1800.*

[70]   For the sometimes-violent enforcement of African re-dressing in North and South American colonies see DuPlessis, *Material Atlantic,* Chapter 4, 'Dress Under Constraints'. Judith Carney and Richard Nicholas present Africans' contribution to the Americas' food culture. Judith Carney and Richard Nicholas, *In the Shadow of Slavery: Africa's Botanical Legacy in the Atlantic World* (Berkeley: University of California Press, 2009); and for other examples of transplanted African practices in the Americas, see Natalie Zemon Davis, 'Decentering History: Local Stories and Cultural Crossings in a Global World' *History and Theory* 50 (2011), pp. 197–202.

Africans' experiences of servitude varied markedly from dockworkers to artisans, domestic labourers to seamstresses; however, fieldwork predominated on large and small plantations and farms. When opportunity allowed, African slaves in rural and urban regions assembled resources through the sale of garden stuff, self-hiring or other strategies, using these earnings to improve their apparel. Secondhand markets offered a viable route to self-fashioning, as did the selective purchase of better, more vibrant cloth, clothing or accessories.[71] Overall, the status of slaves was illustrated by the absence of certain goods as much as the shoddy raiment of slavery. Robert DuPlessis observes that 'enslavement was also to be sartorially signalled by omissions: by what fully dressed slave bodies would lack – footwear, shaped headgear, accessories, and adornment – as well as by what garbed them.'[72] Bare feet were a defining marker of enslavement, along with ubiquitous and much treasured handkerchiefs around heads and necks. The presence of free people of African ancestry in many colonial cities tested the limits of sanctioned dress, further complicating the clothing patterns of this diasporic population.[73]

Colonial power was increasingly predicated on whiteness throughout the Americas, routinely enshrined in law and emphasized more rigidly from the later 1700s.[74] 'Whiteness' could also be inferred and

[71] Kathleen A. Staples and Madelyn C. Shaw, *Clothing through American History: The British Colonial Era* (Santa Barbara: ABC-CLIO: 2013), pp. 51–53; Sophie White, '"Wearing Three or Four Handkerchiefs around His Collar, and Elsewhere about Him": Slaves' Constructions of Masculinity and Ethnicity in French Colonial New Orleans' *Gender & History* 15:3 (2003), pp. 533–535; Ann Smart Martin, *Buying into the World of Goods: Early Consumers in Backcountry Virginia* (Baltimore: Johns Hopkins University Press, 2008), Chapter 6.

[72] DuPlessis, *Material Atlantic*, p. 131.

[73] Vincent C. Peloso, *Race and Ethnicity in Latin American History* (New York: Routledge, 2014), p. 46; Rebecca Earle, *The Body of the Conquistador: Food, Race and Colonial Experience in Spanish America, 1492–1700* (Cambridge: Cambridge University Press, 2012), p. 179 and 'Luxury, Clothing and Race in Colonial Spanish America'.

[74] The *code noir* legalized racial hierarchies in French colonies. Virginia Meacham Gould, '"A Chaos of Iniquity and Discord": Slave and Free Women of Color in the Spanish Ports of New Orleans, Mobile, and Pensacola' in Catherin Clinton and Michele Gillespie, eds., *The Devil's Lane: Sex and Race in the Early South* (Cambridge, MA: Harvard University Press, 1997), p. 235. In the slave trade of Indigenous peoples (*indios*) in Spanish America, Nancy E. van Deusen notes that 'color was one of the most significant markers of indio identity.' 'Seeing *Indios* in Sixteenth-Century Castile' *William and Mary Quarterly* 69:2 (2012), p. 209.

materialized by dress. Within Spanish colonial territories the *casta* system set out legal racial categories, including the offspring of racial mixing, or *mestizaje*. These laws were accompanied by sartorial injunctions outlining the material demarcations of race. There was serious intent behind these laws, although they were only periodically enforced. For, despite the 'fetishization of genealogies' among Spanish elites, racial categories could be surprisingly fluid, a fluidity intensified by subaltern creative dress.[75]

Visitors to Spain's American colonies marvelled at the gorgeousness of garments seen on city streets, remarking the styles among apparently ordinary labourers and servants. Red taffeta (perhaps Chinese in origin) was the choice of one Indigenous Lima woman in 1596, part of an intermixing of Andean and global material cultures.[76] Complex priorities of taste emerged from the mingling of Native American and African peoples, along with Asians and Europeans. While silk remained the preference among affluent settlers in Spanish America, others within their communities aspired to facsimiles when they could.[77] A British captain, William Betagh, wrote of Lima in the 1720s that 'of all the parts of the world, the people here are most expensive in their habit.' Spanish travellers visiting two decades later affirmed the narrow 'distinction between the several classes.' They attributed this to the fact that 'everyone wears what he can purchase. So that it is not uncommon to see a mulatto, or any other mechanic, dressed in a tissue equal to anything that can be worn by a more opulent person, they all greatly affect fine clothes.'[78]

Of course, this was not a paradise of material self-expression. The parameters of power were real and their consequences intermittently bloody. Yet, creative sartorial defiance percolated through early modern colonial landscapes. Tensions surrounding the dress of non-elite non-whites peaked at different times and in different regions of the

---

[75] Mia L. Bagneris, 'Reimagining Race, Class, and Identity in the New World' in Amelia Peck, ed., *Behind Closed Doors: Art in the Spanish American Home, 1492–1898* (New York: Metropolitan Museum of Art, 2013), p. 164; Earle, *Body of the Conquistador*, p. 179. My thanks to Michael Polushin for his insights.

[76] Karen B. Graubart, 'The Creolization of the New World: Local Forms of Identification in Urban Colonial Peru, 1560–1640' *Hispanic American Historical Review* 89:3 (2009), p. 495.

[77] DuPlessis, *Material Atlantic*, p. 205.

[78] Quoted in Earle, 'Luxury, Clothing and Race', pp. 219–220.

Americas – in general, the sartorial inventiveness of people of colour was a thorn in the side of colonial governors. In 1735, in the British colony of South Carolina, rules were ratified to quash fashion among enslaved Africans, styles unfit for servile status. Colonial officials were appalled that 'many of the slaves in the Province wear clothes much above the condition of slaves.'[79] Africans also visibly revised European garments and accessories, to the discomfort of masters and magistrates. Sophie White explores the 'significance of sartorial culture to the lives of New Orleans's slaves', a space variously administered by France and Spain in the 1700s. Clothing was one of the few items 'open to manipulation and interpretation' by slave men, women and children, even if owners supplied basic garments. The runaway slave Francisque, for example, made himself notable at a New Orleans slave dance, dressed in a 'ruffled shirt, blue waistcoat, white hat and wearing three or four handkerchiefs around his neck, and elsewhere about him.'[80] African slaves were compelled to work within the European clothing system, not least because of the garments they were assigned. White colonists, in turn, were unsettled when African slaves donned fine European clothing, or used decorative elements in innovative (African) ways. The intent of the colonial process was domination, an aim that could be bodily enforced. But, as Tim Murray observes, 'domination is never total ... [and] cultural forms arise that can both subvert that domination and transform it into new forms of colonial culture.'[81]

In fact, legislation drove some innovations. In 1789, the new Spanish governor of Louisiana instituted a '*tignon* law' directed at women of African ancestry whether free or slave, insisting that a handkerchief cover their hair. Mixed-race women were the particular target, especially those free, active and visible in urban communities.[82] Mulatto, quadroon or octoroon – slave, free or prosperous – the handkerchief would flag their subordinate standing. Or so it was hoped.[83] Legalized degradations were intended as 'symbolic whips ... woven into many areas of culture – naming, branding and clothing.'[84] Instead, this

[79] Staples and Shaw, *Clothing through American History*, p. 45.
[80] White, 'Wearing Three or Four Handkerchiefs', pp. 530, 536.
[81] Tim Murray, ed., *The Archaeology of Contact in Settler Societies* (Cambridge: Cambridge University Press, 2004), p. 10.
[82] DuPlessis, *Material Atlantic*, pp. 156–157.
[83] Meacham Gould, 'A Chaos of Iniquity and Discord', pp. 237–238.
[84] Catherine Hall, 'Gendering Property, Racing Capital' *History Workshop Journal* 78 (2014), p. 29.

headwear and its wearers became known for their élan. Urban women of African origin turned the *tignon* into a confection of dramatic height and architectural form. These women and their very visible headgear were soon seen everywhere. Their apparent lack of deference to the disciplinary intent of the law irked settlers and some visitors who identified African Caribbean women as a source of social corruption.[85] Beth Fowkes Tobin observes that 'slaves' attitudes towards clothing unnerved many British observers of the West Indian scene; perhaps this can account, in part, for the plantocrats' obsession with the topic of 'slaves' clothing.'[86]

Colonial authorities throughout the Caribbean and beyond shared this obsession. The *tignon* law in Louisiana narrowed the choices open to women of colour by forbidding silks, feathers and jewels – even among those who could afford such indulgences. Similar laws were passed in other French Caribbean colonies.[87] The ethnographic painter Agostino Brunias captured the distinctive prominence of a garment that was intended to shame (Plate 3.3), with handkerchiefs displayed in a host of millinery confections at this social event. A few heads shown at this dance were plainly wrapped. But, at celebrations and on market days, African women's patterned headwear flowered, an ornament that repudiated the intent of white legislators. Market days were important in many slave communities, offering the opportunity to dress well and socialize. Eliza Chadwick Roberts, a colonial American woman of modest means, described how enslaved Jamaicans 'deck themselves out with trinkits and other finery' on market days, goods bought from 'the profit of there [sic] Small Sales.'[88] These fashion acts

[85] Janet Schaw, *Journal of a Lady of Quality, Being a Narrative of a Journey* (Bedford, MA: Applewood Books, 1921), p. 112. This view is replicated in the writings of a French magistrate touring French Caribbean islands at the same time. Dobie, *Trading Places*, pp. 120–122.

[86] Beth Fowkes Tobin, *Picturing Imperial Power: Colonial Subjects in Eighteenth-Century British Painting* (Durham: Duke University Press, 1999), p. 161.

[87] Bagneris, 'Reimagining Race, Class and Identity in the New World', pp. 197–198; Karol K. Weaver, 'Fashioning Freedom: Slave Seamstresses in the Atlantic World' *Journal of Women's History* 24:1 (2012), pp. 51. Sartorial laws based on race were also enacted in the Cape Colony in this period. DuPlessis, *Material Atlantic*, p. 156.

[88] Quoted in Susan E. Klepp and Roderick A. McDonald, 'Inscribing Experience: An American Working Woman and an English Gentlewoman Encounter Jamaica's Slave Society, 1801–1805' *William and Mary Quarterly* 58:3 (2001), p. 655.

were claims of personhood. Though forcibly commoditized themselves and producing globalized products for world markets, they wielded materials from world trade as means of defiance and a source of pleasure.

The memoirs of the wife of a small Caribbean planter confirm the continued importance of dress into the 1820s among women of African descent – demonstrating as well the continuing distress of the planter class with these habits. The use of the 'turban', as she termed it, remained a signature style usually comprised of 'a Madras handkerchief'. So important was this headwear that women of colour with means employed a paid 'head dresser' to construct their complex turbans for celebrations, as depicted by Brunias.[89] The inspired use of handkerchiefs in Caribbean slaveholding regions transposed a humble accessory into a potent symbol of gender and racial ingenuity, 'inflecting a European style of dress with African idioms'.[90] Creativity in dress signalled tacit resistance to a servitude enforced by the law and the lash. It is ironic that the aesthetic success of *tignon* attracted the envious gaze of white colonial women, a style later copied in metropolitan Europe.[91]

Many in power wished to retain a 'license system' of consumption, though more European theorists like Nicolas Barbon argued the benefits of increased consumption by the later 1700s. Innovation in dress among non-elites undoubtedly nourished social disorder, though not necessarily in anarchic ways. But that was the threat. Defiant plebeian fashions occasionally mocked the expectation of meek compliance. Might disorderly fashions presage social disorder? That was the fear.

Large commercial ventures, directing vast cargoes of textiles, did not intend to spark social or cultural insurgency, on the contrary. Their aim was a heady income for wealthy merchants and manufacturers, with governments profiting from taxation on these cargoes. Nonetheless, unintended consequences ensued. The desire to regulate consumption remained a deeply rooted sentiment. But the capacity to constrain and

---

[89] A. C. Carmichael, *Domestic Manners and Social Condition of the White, Coloured, and Negro Population of the West Indies ... Five Years a Resident in St. Vincent and Trinidad* (London: Whitaker and Co., 1834), vol. 1, pp. 75, 146–147.

[90] Fowkes Tobin, *Picturing Imperial Power*, p. 158.

[91] Beverly Chico, *Hats and Headwear around the World: A Cultural Encyclopedia* (Santa Barbara, CA: ABC-CLIO, 2013), pp. 227–228.

enforce had limits, even within slaveholding societies.[92] Secondhand markets were another layer of this process, offering a broad avenue for the realization of consumer needs and dreams. This vitally important commerce infused a greater liveliness in the consumer market and demonstrates the difficulty of material regulation. At the same time, the burgeoning readymade sector illuminates the capacity of administrations to enact new involuntary consumption.[93] Each facet of sartorial practice marks further stages of development in a key consumer arena.

Secondhand and Readymade Clothing in Global Circulation

Systems of Value in the Secondhand Trade

Nicholas Barbon, a seventeenth-century English economic writer and real estate speculator, considered one of the benefits of fashion was that 'he Lived in a perpetual Spring; [where] he never sees the Autum of his Cloaths.'[94] This whimsical thought reflected reality for the wealthy that changed their wardrobes frequently. Certainly Giovanni Pontano subscribed to that view. The fifteenth-century humanist author wrote that 'it is not appropriate for a splendid man to let his clothes get old, because old things cannot be splendid.'[95] This perspective on virtue continued to direct elite consumption in Europe into the following centuries. However, few anywhere enjoyed pristine spring-like apparel, devoid of stains, tears and abrasions. Rather, they employed secondhand clothing as a matter of routine, hunting for apparel in its youth or middle years of life. In recent decades, studies of the secondhand clothing trade multiplied as scholars recognized the importance of this sector to economic, social and cultural practice. Its regional and international dimensions were reshaped under the pressure of global commodity flows.

---

[92] For example, Smart Martin, *Buying into the World of Goods*, Chapter 6, 'Suckey's Looking Glass: African Americans as Consumers'; White, 'Wearing Three or Four Handkerchiefs'.

[93] Styles, *Dress of the People*, pp. 247–320

[94] Barbon, *A Discourse of Trade*, p. 65.

[95] Renata Ago, *A Gusto for Things: A History of Objects in Seventeenth-Century Rome,* translated by Bradford Bouley and Corey Tazzara, with Paula Findlen (Chicago: University of Chicago Press, 2013), p. 20.

Clothing possessed dual economic value: use value (in fashion and utility) and store of value (for sale, credit or exchange). Just as textiles acted as a currency in international trade, clothing functioned as an alternate currency in textile-rich regions, valued for functional and aesthetic properties. Clothing mattered. And during the autumn years of a garment's life, it remained a useful currency of exchange, or a timely addition to someone else's wardrobe, part of a continuous recycling linking social levels and world communities. The historiography of the secondhand clothing trade began with early modern European societies, extending over time and place to address a broad range of regions, including present-day practice.[96] It is now apparent

[96] Including Donald Woodward, '"Swords into Ploughshares": Recycling in Pre-Industrial England' *Economic History Review* 38:2 (1985): 175–191; Beverly Lemire, 'Consumerism in Preindustrial and Early Industrial England: The Trade in Secondhand Clothes' *Journal of British Studies* 27:1(1988): 1–24, *Fashion's Favourite: The Cotton Trade and the Consumer in Britain, 1660–1800* (Oxford: Oxford University Press, 1991), *Dress, Culture and Commerce, Business of Everyday Life,* esp. Chapter 4 and 'The Secondhand Trade in Europe and Beyond: Stages of Development and Enterprise in a Changing Material World, c. 1600–1850' *Textile: Journal of Cloth & Culture* 10:2 (2012): 144–163; Roche, *Culture of Clothing,* esp. Chapter 12; Elizabeth Sanderson, *Women and Work in Eighteenth-Century Edinburgh* (Basingstoke: Macmillan, 1996); Susan B. Hanley, *Everyday Things in Premodern Japan: The Hidden Legacy of Material Culture* (Berkeley: University of California Press, 1997), Chapter 3; John L. Comaroff and Jean Comaroff, 'Fashioning the Colonial Subject: The Empire's Old Clothes' in John L. Comaroff and Jean Comaroff, eds., *Of Revelation and Revolution,* vol. 2, *The Dialectics of Modernity on a South African Frontier* (Chicago: University of Chicago Press, 1997), pp. 218–273; Patricia Allerston, 'Reconstructing the Secondhand Clothes Trade in Sixteenth and Seventeenth-Century Venice' *Costume* 33 (1999): 46–56; Fabio Giusberti, 'Dynamics of the Used Goods Market. Bolognese Drapers and Scrap Merchants in the Early Modern Era' in Alberta Guenzi, Paola Massa and Fausto Piola Caselli, eds., *Guilds, Markets and Work Regulations in Italy, 16th-19th Centuries* (Aldershot, UK: Ashgate, 1998); Karen Tranberg Hansen, *Salaula: the World of Secondhand Clothing and Zambia* (Chicago: University of Chicago Press, 2000); Lynne B. Milgram, 'Refashioning Commodities: Women and the Sourcing and Circulation of Secondhand Clothing in the Philippines' *Anthropologica* 46:2 (2004): 123–136; Alexandra Palmer and Hazel Clark, eds., *Old Clothes, New Looks: Secondhand Fashion* (Oxford: Berg Publishers, 2005); Danielle van den Heuvel, *Women and Entrepreneurship. Female Traders in the Northern Netherlands, c. 1580–1815* (Amsterdam: Aksant Academic Publishers, 2007); Laurence Fontaine, ed., *Alternative Exchanges: Secondhand Circulations from the Sixteenth Century to the Present* (Oxford: Berghahn Books, 2008); Bruno Blondé, ed., *Fashioning Old and New: Changing Consumer Preferences in Europe (seventeenth-nineteenth centuries)* (Tournout: Brepolis, 2009); Jon Stobart and Ilja Van Damme, eds., *Modernity and the Secondhand Trade: European*

that the old clothes trade promoted greater consumption capacity among diverse peoples.

Many textile and clothing cultures practiced reuse as a matter of necessity, a moral priority and an opportunity to profit; this honoured the value vested in cloth or clothing and its capacity for renovation.[97] Tokugawa Japan offers a case in point. The physical structure of the kimono encouraged easy exchange in secondhand markets, either of whole garments or pieces. Kimonos were readily unpicked for routine laundering, and the four panels of cloth comprising the garment often entered the old-clothes market in this unstitched state. The gowns and mantles of European women were formed of similar lengths of cloth, the selvage uncut, ready to be unmade for repair and restyling.[98] Clothing in different world communities was often made to be unmade, with the value of the cloth being most important. The mechanics of construction shaped the ways clothing was resold and recycled.

In Japan, secondhand clothing shops and stalls multiplied over the Tokugawa period, being especially numerous in Edo's Tomizawa district, where goods of better quality were sold. Trade started at dawn and continued through daylight hours. This was one of several quarters where sophisticated sorting and recycling took place, with items collected and deployed to specific markets and modes of retailing.[99] Thrift

---

Consumption Cultures and Practices, 1700–1900 (Basingstoke: Palgrave, 2012); Thomas Buchner and Philip R. Hoffmann-Rehnitz, eds., *Shadow Economies and Irregular Work in Urban Europe: 16th to Early 20th Centuries* (Vienna and Berlin: Lit Verlag, 2011); Masayuki Tanimoto, 'The Diffusion of Secondhand Cloth in the Countryside. Another Aspect of Market Formation in Tokugawa and Meiji-Taisho Japan' paper presented at the 16th World Economic History Conference, Stellenbosch, 2012; Miki Sugiura and Shinya Kobayashi, '行商と古着商 ―近世江戸とアムステルダムの都市内商業における周縁性の比較考察― 小林信也　杉浦未樹' ('Streetsellers and Secondhand Clothing Traders in Edo and Amsterdam. Marginality in Early Modern Commerce Compared'), in 行商と古着商―近世江戸とアムステルダムの都市内商業における周縁性の比較考察」 (A.Tamura, T.Kawana and H. Uchida eds.), 『国家の周縁性と近代』 (*Marginality of States and Modernity*) (Tokyo: Tosui Shobo, 2015), pp. 126–141.

[97] As discussed for eighteenth-century Damascus. Grehan, *Consumer Culture in Eighteenth-Century Damascus*, pp. 233–234.

[98] Carolyn Dowdell, 'The Fruits of Nimble Fingers: Garment Construction and the Working Lives of Eighteenth-Century English Needlewomen', unpublished MA thesis, University of Alberta.

[99] Sugiura, 'Comparative Study', pp. 14–15.

was a valued trait, esteemed by men and women of various ranks. Miyaji Umanusuke was a Confucian scholar whose family had ties to Lord Toyosuke, a noble he served on journeys to Edo in the early decades of the 1800s. Miyaji recorded his various purchases in Edo and Osaka, frequenting secondhand shops to stretch his budget.[100] It is not clear if items he bought were new or used – including silk and tie-dye fabrics, a fan and two raincoats. But this scholar did not shrink from secondhand purchases; rather he saw them as a way to satisfy his desire for quality goods at bargain prices, a sentiment shared by people of many ranks.

As in other world regions, textiles and clothing entered secondhand markets from a variety of sources, legal and illegal. Households managed their resources through the mediation of used cloth and clothing, selling and buying as required, and thieves contributed to this flow with ill-gotten stores. All neighbourhoods specializing in this trade absorbed stolen goods as a matter of course, an adjunct to popular consumerism, though troubling to victims and authorities.[101] Stolen goods slipped into capacious secondhand markets, which were essential for plebeian budgeting. In Japan, used cloth and clothing circulated well beyond the capital, as specialist dealers multiplied over the 1700s, carrying cast-off goods from Edo to the provinces. Northern regions of the country were especially keen to receive cotton goods, a fashion item less accessible there, welcomed in the form of used fabric and apparel.[102]

The significance of secondhand cloth and clothing became increasingly apparent to present-day scholars as they explored the features of pre-modern economies and economic development. To European Enlightenment *philosophes,* however, these functions remained

[100] Vaporis, *Tour of Duty,* pp. 210–217.
[101] Roche, *Culture of Clothing,* pp. 330–363; Beverly Lemire, 'The Theft of Clothes and Popular Consumerism in Eighteenth-Century England' *Journal of Social History* 24:2 (1990): 255–276; Marie Francois, 'Cloth and Silver: Pawning and Material Life in Mexico City at the Turn of the Nineteenth Century' *The Americas* 60:3 (2004): 325–362; Victoria López Barahona and José Nieto Sánchez, 'Dressing the Poor: The Provision of Clothing among the Lower Classes in Eighteenth-Century Madrid' *Textile History* 43:1 (2012): 23–42; Andrew Konove, 'On the Cheap: The Baratillo Marketplace and the Shadow Economy of Eighteenth-Century Mexico City' *The Americas* 72:2 (2015): 249–278.
[102] Hanley, *Everyday Things in Premodern Japan,* p. 72; Tanimoto, 'Diffusion of Secondhand Cloth in the Countryside' and Tanimoto, 'Cotton and the Peasant Economy'.

opaque. They typically constructed ideological models of economic life at odds with the habits and practices of the majority, blind to the activities that took place at their kitchen doors or on neighbourhood streets. Laurence Fontaine notes that these authors 'relegated all kinds of monetary circulation not strictly based on currencies to the realm of the archaic, and therefore consigned to oblivion'.[103] Unusually, Adam Smith acknowledged the agency of subjects who manipulated used attire. This was part of what Smith called a 'trucking disposition' general to most people, a trait observed in the partiality for exchange 'by treaty, by barter, and by purchase.' Smith noted how a gift of used clothing allowed a poor man to trade 'for other old clothes which suit him better, or lodging, or for food, or for money, with which he can buy either food, clothes, or lodging as he has occasion'.[104] Apparel and textiles were by far the most ubiquitous alternate currency, figuring as a material store until their liquidity was required. All those dealing with daily budgets, especially women, understood the importance of these uses. The calculus of clothing was a subject of widespread study.[105]

Street hawkers and pedlars were plentiful in urban locales, though authorities disliked their 'disorderly' ways.[106] Economic commentators might ignore their activities, but the management of households included the calculated supervision of these vital resources.[107] Importantly, women found space within this commercial realm, demonstrating their industriousness and capacity for trade, whether or not guilds or city governments approved. Street dealers of this type were vital adjuncts to fixed shops, expanding market options for the poor or those more distant from commercial centres. In many communities, guilds ordered this commerce, attempting to bring it under their monopoly control. However, this business was not easily contained. Hand-me-downs flowed from masters and mistresses to servants and might end up in second-hand markets; slaves in the colonial Americas received clothing gifts

[103] Fontaine, *Alternative Exchanges*, p. 1.

[104] Adam Smith, *An Inquiry into the Nature and Causes of the Wealth of Nations*, 3rd ed., vol. 1, (Basil: James Decker, 1801), p. 22.

[105] For discussion of the provision of clothing to English servants, see John Styles, 'Involuntary Consumers? The Eighteenth-Century Servant and Her Clothes' *Textile History* 33:1 (2002): 9–21 and *Dress of the People* .

[106] Lemire, *Dress, Culture and Commerce,* Chapter 4; Ago, *A Gusto for Things,* Chapter 4.

[107] Alexandra Shepard, 'Crediting Women in the Early Modern English Economy' *History Workshop Journal* 79 (2015): 1–24.

from their owners that they remade, reused or sold. Soldiers, sailors and pirates seized garments as booty, later directing these into commercial channels. All welcomed these interactions.[108]

The traffic in secondhand apparel encompassed every economic level including international trade, initially between proximate neighbours and ultimately spanning world markets. English merchants carried old hats, shoes, slippers and boots to France about 1600, despite protests from some Frenchmen.[109] The expanding quantities of new textiles inevitably brought greater volumes of used goods to global markets. I noted previously how worn beaver hats were traded for slaves in West Africa, carried there by Iberian merchants.[110] '*Hollandsche slae-plaecken*' (secondhand linen sheets) figured among the things offered to African merchants by the Dutch. In 1645, Dutch traders amassed 6,000 such old sheets for their business venture, beginning a routine that would see tens of thousands of old sheets shipped to West Africa for printing by local artisans and for use as apparel, part of a comingling of secondhand markets that expanded over the centuries.[111] All sophisticated, urbanized regions included commercial recycling, such as the flea markets of Istanbul and Galata – Galata being across the strait from Istanbul.[112] The well-known story of Aladdin's lamp hinged on the ubiquity of swapping old goods for new – a Middle Eastern tale originally set in China. European merchants and traders flourished by dealing in 'old' clothes in Renaissance Italy and seventeenth- and eighteenth-century France, England, the Low Countries, Netherlands, Scotland and Spain, as well as colonies and international trade

[108] Woodward, 'Swords into Ploughshares'; Brian Sandberg, '"The Magazine of All Their Pillaging": Armies as Sites of Secondhand Exchanges during the French Wars of Religion' in Laurence Fontaine, ed., *Alternate Exchanges: Secondhand Circulations from the Sixteenth Century to the Present* (Oxford: Berghahn Books, 2008), pp. 76–96; Fabio López Lázaro, *The Misfortunes of Alonso Ramíriz: The True Adventures of a Spanish American with 17th-Century Pirates* (Austin: University of Texas, 2011); Lemire, 'The Secondhand Trade in Europe and Beyond'; Shane White and Graham White, 'Slave Clothing and African-American Culture in the Eighteenth and Nineteenth Centuries' *Past & Present* 148 (1995), p. 168.

[109] Woodward, 'Swords into Ploughshares', p. 179.   [110] See Chapter 2.

[111] Henk den Heijer, 'Africans in European and Asian Clothes: Dutch Textile Trade in West Africa, 1600–1800' in Veronika Hyden-Hanscho, Renate Pieper and Werner Stangle, eds., *Cultural Exchange and Consumption Patterns in the Age of Enlightenment: Europe and the Atlantic World* (Bochum: Verlag Dr. Dieter Winkler, 2013), pp. 121–122; DuPlessis, *Material Atlantic*, p. 68.

[112] Faroqhi, 'Introduction', *Ottoman Costumes*, p. 35.

zones.[113] European colonialism stretched the channels for recycled goods further still, with cargoes of used clothing brought to Atlantic fishing ports and settlements ill-supplied with necessaries. These patterns carried into the 1800s, a labyrinth of exchange at sites as diverse as the Leipzig Fair, colonial Cape Town and imperial St Petersburg, plus centres of Christian missionary evangelism from the Pacific Islands to the Caribbean.[114] The secondhand clothing trade blended formal commercial networks with imperial and colonial systems.

Choice enlarged even for marginalized peoples, such as those who frequented the *baratillos* (bargaining or 'thieves' markets) of Madrid, Seville or Mexico City. In colonial New Spain, Indigenous women frequently coalesced around this trade, with some managing stalls in the *baratillos*.[115] Poor and middling women of all conditions valued this traffic, as it offered commercial opportunities when few options were available, one more of the market-oriented activities that increasingly occupied industrious women in vibrant economic regions. Laurence Fontaine is one of several historians who see distinctive economic practices among the generations of enterprising women

---

[113] The literature on this subject is now extensive. See, for example, Allerston, 'Clothing and Early Modern Venetian Society'; Carole Collier Frick, 'The Florentine *Rigattieri*: Second Hand Clothing Dealers and the Circulation of Goods in the Renaissance' in Alexandra Palmer and Hazel Clark, eds., *Old Clothes, New Looks: Second Hand Fashions* (Oxford: Berg Publishers, 2005), pp. 13–28; Ago, *A Gusto for Things*; Roche, *Culture of Clothing*; Lemire, 'Secondhand Trade in Europe and Beyond'; Evelyn Welch, 'New, Old and Second-Hand Culture: The Case of the Renaissance Sleeve' in Gabriele Neher and Rupert Shepherd, eds., *Revaluing the Renaissance* (Aldershot, UK: Ashgate, 2000), pp. 101–120; Harald Deceulaer, 'Secondhand Dealers in the Early Modern Low Countries: Institutions, Markets and Practices' in Laurence Fontaine, ed., *Alternate Exchanges: Secondhand Circulations from the Sixteenth Century to the Present* (Oxford: Berghahn Books, 2008), pp. 13–42; Barahona and Sánchez, 'Dressing the Poor ... in Eighteenth-Century Madrid'; Ann Matchette, 'Women, Objects, and Exchange in Early Modern Florence' *Early Modern Women* 3 (2008): 245–251; Tracy Randle, '"Consuming Identities": Patterns of Consumption at Three Eighteenth-Century Cape Auctions' in Laurence Fontaine, ed., *Alternate Exchanges: Secondhand Circulations from the Sixteenth Century to the Present* (Oxford: Berghahn Books, 2008), pp. 220–241; Francois, 'Cloth and Silver: Pawning and Material Life in Mexico City'; White, 'Geographies of Slave Consumption'.

[114] Lemire, 'Secondhand Trade in Europe and Beyond'.

[115] R. Douglas Cope, *The Limits of Racial Domination: Plebeian Society in Colonial Mexico City* (Madison, WI: University of Wisconsin Press, 1994), pp. 37–44; Elizabeth Nash, *Seville, Cordoba, and Grenada: A Cultural History* (Oxford: Oxford University Press, 2005), pp. 88–89.

interacting with the burgeoning market, including concentrated attention on secondhand markets.[116] Women seamstresses added to their income by repairing and selling secondhand and readymade items to the many urbanites desperate for bargain-priced clothes to avoid raggedness, hence expanding prospects for plebeian shoppers. Indeed, Daniel Roche states that in *ancien régime* France, 'the secondhand trade was a promoter of fashion.'[117] Even though much of the secondhand trade in Europe and Spanish America was officially in the hands of guildsmen, a substantial stream of stock circulated outside their purview. It was here where poor women thrived and survived.[118] Some worked for main-street retailers who accepted old goods in part-payment for new items and redirected worn items to likely clientele or other traders.[119] But many other labouring women animated consumer options through their work at the edge of the marketplace, enlarging consumer capacity in vital ways. Their collective activities represent an essential industriousness that must be added to the industriousness of wage-earning women and children. The latter is understood as key to the expanding consumer vibrancy in this era. The industrious commercial women of the secondhand clothing trades intensified the scope and scale of consumer markets, while sustaining themselves and their families. The industriousness of women took varied forms.

[116] Shepard, 'Crediting Women', pp. 8–10; Laurence Fontaine, *The Moral Economy: Poverty, Credit and Trust in Early Modern Europe* (Cambridge: Cambridge University Press, 2014), especially Chapters 4 and 5; Lemire, *Business of Everyday Life,* Chapter 4.

[117] Roche, *Culture of Clothing,* p. 360.

[118] Barahona and Sánchez, 'Dressing the Poor ... in Eighteenth Century Madrid', pp. 25–29; Konove, 'On the Cheap'; van den Heuvel, *Women and Entrepreneurship*; Francois, 'Cloth and Silver: Pawning and Material Life in Mexico City'; Lemire, *Dress, Culture and Commerce.*

[119] Lemire, *Dress, Culture and Commerce*; Manuel Charpy, 'The Scope and Structure of the Nineteenth-Century Secondhand Trade in the Parisian Clothes Market' in Laurence Fontaine, ed., *Alternate Exchanges: Secondhand Circulations from the Sixteenth Century to the Present* (Oxford: Berghahn Books, 2008), pp. 127–151; Clare Crowston, 'Engendering the Guilds: Seamstresses, Tailors, and the Clash of Corporate Identities in Old Regime France' *French Historical Studies* 23:2 (2000): 339–371; Marla R. Miller, 'Gender, Artisanry, and Craft Tradition in Early New England: The View through the Eye of a Needle' *William and Mary Quarterly* 60:4 (2003): 743–776.

Karen Tranberg Hansen asserts that 'consumption is hard work that has complicated implications in the realms of production.'[120] Amidst the fluidity of early modern clothing cultures another allied format appeared: readymade apparel was made in growing quantities over the seventeenth and eighteenth centuries, spilling out from imperial stockpiles, launching a new material order. The populations dressed in these garments had to learn to negotiate their attire amidst new administrative processes of involuntary consumption.

Readymade for Imperial Ventures

Wars demanded a mass of men. All needed clothing. As the size of armies and navies grew during these centuries, so too did the demands of provisioning, the full dimensions of which have yet to be traced. Charles Blount, Eighth Baron Mountjoy, tacitly acknowledged the challenges of England's lengthy war in Ireland in 1600. Among the many problems was an insufficiency of clothing for his soldiers, with only 12,000 suits of clothes for an army of 14,000. Mountjoy begged the government for garments to cover 'our naked companies'.[121] This was a savage but relatively small campaign. During the Thirty Years' War (1618–1648), Spanish forces numbered 300,000 men in 1630, a different order of challenge for supply chains.[122] Keeping fighting men adequately clothed was a task imperfectly performed, though recognized as essential. Military requirements drove readymade clothing manufacture, which surged along with martial complements and financial capacity.[123]

---

120 Hansen, *Salaula*, p. 194.
121 Lord Deputy Mountjoy to Sir G. Carew, 12 August 1600. Carew Manuscript, Lambeth Palace Library.
122 Olaf van Nimwegen, *The Dutch Army and the Military Revolutions, 1588–1688* (Woodbridge, UK: The Boydell Press, 2010), p. 11.
123 The manner of provisioning these uniforms opens important research questions. Daniel Roche notes the significance of regional French militia, 200,000 strong in the 1700s, or one in ten adult men. Too little is yet known of the production of their uniforms. Daniel Roche, 'Between a "Moral Economy" and a "Consumer Economy": Clothes and Their Function in the 17th and 18th Centuries' in Robert Fox and Anthony Turner, eds., *Luxury Trade and Consumerism in Ancien Régime Paris* (Aldershot, UK: Ashgate,1998), p. 223. The vast scale of the Chinese armies also requires a full study of the readymade clothing trade in China. Chi'en Mu, *Traditional Government in Imperial China: A Critical Analysis,* translated by Chü-tu Hsüej and George O. Totten (Hong Kong: The Chinese University of Hong Kong, 1982), p. 119.

Imperial agency directed production and consumption in many world regions, a history only beginning to be explained.

In England from the mid-1600s onwards, innovations in naval administration and the birth of the Bank of England in 1694 laid the groundwork for a dramatically expanded state-funded manufacture of men's clothing. Mariners were the principal focus, as they were among the first large communities of men to wear readymade garments routinely. Mariners were not the largest military contingent. Collectively, army regiments exceeded the total numbers of those in the navy throughout this period; but regiments were provisioned individually, usually from diverse locales, while the navy was supplied as a totality with far more centralized production. Over 40,000 naval personnel required clothing in England's Nine Years' War (1689–1697), a number that grew to over 82,000 for the Royal Navy during the American Revolutionary War (1775–1784). This was a fluid population: as men were killed, wounded or discharged, its stores were depleted or destroyed. The scale of demand grew ever larger during the French Revolutionary and Napoleonic Wars (1792–1815).[124] Readymade sailors' slops, as this wardrobe was called, represented a new concept in production: made in a range of sizes, from set patterns, ideally alike in fabric, thread and look and made by the ton. Daniel Roche argues for the power of uniforms, 'an instrument in a process designed to shape the physique and the bearing of a combative individual . . . into collective power'.[125] Slops personified naval seamen in an imperial age.

New technologies of production were devised at an unprecedented scale, with distinct systems of funding, contracting and subcontracting.[126] This system of technology linked the chancellor of the exchequer, naval administrators and wealthy merchant capitalists with networks of subcontractors and many tens of thousands of seamstresses labouring in city garrets and backrooms. As Giorgio Riello observes, 'subcontracting provided a simple means to achieve complex forms of production.'[127]

---

[124] John Brewer, *Sinews of Power: War, Money and the English State, 1688–1783* (London: Unwin Hyman, 1989), p. 30, Table 2.1.

[125] Roche, *Culture of Clothing*, p. 229.

[126] Thomas Parke Hughes defines a technological system as the combination of forces and talents of a range of occupations aimed at designing and controlling a 'human-built world'. Thomas Parke, *Human-Built World: How to Think about Technology and Culture* (Chicago: University of Chicago Press), pp. 4–5.

[127] Giorgio Riello, *One Foot in the Past: Consumers, Producers and Footwear in the Long Eighteenth Century* (Oxford: Oxford University Press, 2006), p. 179.

A largely invisible female workforce generated mountains of shirts, jackets, trousers and the like to be stored in naval warehouses before being dispatched to ships' pursers and sold to shipboard crews across the globe – a captive consumer market. The results were extraordinary. Naval crews and crews of global trading companies were offered these garments to buy; regulations required them to be kitted out in these garments, and sales of clothes on board ships were assured. Moreover, the bales of slops were as mobile as their customers.

Consider that in October 1747, during the War of the Austrian Succession, about fifteen tons of baled slop clothes were shipped from London in one season to the Royal Navy's Mediterranean headquarters at Port Mahon, Menorca.[128] In this worldwide venture, the Royal Navy dispatched essential clothing to bases along the Atlantic seaboard and Caribbean: Halifax, Nova Scotia; Boston, Massachusetts; Charleston, South Carolina; Kingston, Jamaica; and English Harbour, Antigua, the Royal Navy's base in the Caribbean.[129] This supply chain fed a consumption network stretched across the globe. The caricature of a sailor in Figure 3.4 foregrounds the products of this system, defining the rhetorical body of Britannia's defender in readymade striped canvas trousers, striped linen shirt and white waistcoat, an Indian printed cotton handkerchief around his neck, topped by a dowlas or kersey jacket and a cheap felted hat. This look defined generations of mariners, a mnemonic of imperial ventures and state-sponsored capitalist production. Slops sustained seaborne men in distant oceans, supplies carried on voyages to the Indian Ocean from the later 1600s, a practice routine within several generations.[130]

The garments worn by the eponymous mariner were not *given* in exchange for service, but were *bought* by sailors far from port from the ship's purser – part of a complex system of highly capitalized provisioning. As involuntary consumers, seamen had few options, with the cost of their clothes being subtracted from their wages at

---

[128] ADM 106/1048/312, N.A., UK.
[129] ADM 354/160/209, 234; ADM 354/161/128; ADM 106/1088/84; ADM 354/ 159/219; ADM 106/826/215; ADM 106/875/132; ADM 106/895/44, N.A., UK. ADM 354/159/219, Caird Library, The National Maritime Museum, Greenwich.
[130] ADM 106/481/64; ADM 354/164/346, N.A., UK.

Figure 3.4 *Caricature of a Sailor (One of a Set of Three), c.* 1799. John Sell Cotman, 1782–1842, British. Yale Center for British Art, Paul Mellon Collection.

the journey's end. Sailors became inescapably identified with their readymade slops, distinctive on board ship or on shore, though they pushed against intended uniformity with added shark-tooth buttons and ribboned seams on their trousers. Despite the embellishments they made, this community of men modelled clothes of corporate construction that were marked with imperial and institutional affiliation.[131]

Readymade production systems were evident in different world regions, and Indian manufacturers demonstrated their capacities in the late 1600s, making 200,000 shirts and shifts for the English East India Company (EIC). Decades later, EIC ships were stocked with Indian-made garments when refitting in Indian ports. By the mid-eighteenth-century, Indian manufacturers supplied all necessary slop clothes for Indian Ocean–based naval vessels. An official confirmed in 1761 that 'no slops have been sent to the East Indies as the commodities of that country are more proper for the wear of the seamen serving in those parts than any sent from here.'[132] Thus, a new model of readymade mass production flourished: financed by government, administered by subcontractors and powered by largely female (and Indian) labour. New forms of production were spurred by wider imperial projects. When wars abated, manufacturers and distributors looked for additional markets, and the largest, most singular population was African slaves, whose labour-powered colonial systems. Robert DuPlessis asserts that in the Atlantic world, 'the largest and most widespread non-market transfers of cloth and clothing involved slaves.'[133] Slaves' status was defined through the forcible imposition of attire with coarse shirts, or shifts, petticoat or (short) trousers, patterns enacted throughout the plantations of the Americas and beyond.[134]

Even the rudimentary apparel provided to slaves required immense investment in cloth and labour, an exceptional totality given the mass of slaves transported from Africa to the Americas. Between 1501 and 1866, over 10,700,000 African slaves were shipped to colonial destinations from Brazil to the Caribbean, mainland Spanish America to North America.[135] The economic impact of provisioning this

---

[131] Beverly Lemire, 'A Question of Trousers: Seafarers, Masculinity and Empire in the Shaping of British Male Dress, *c.* 1600–1800' *Cultural and Social History* (2016): 1–22. doi.org/10.1080/14780038.2016.1133493; Marcus Rediker, *Between the Devil and the Deep Blue Sea: Merchant Seamen, Pirates and the Anglo-American Maritime World* (Cambridge: Cambridge University Press, 1987).

[132] ADM 354/167/12, National Maritime Museum, Caird Library.

[133] DuPlessis, *Material Atlantic*, p. 80.

[134] DuPlessis, *Material Atlantic*, pp. 128–135.

[135] Eric Nellis, *Shaping the New World: African Slavery in the Americas, 1500–1888* (Toronto: University of Toronto Press, 2013), p. 31.

population was immense, and metropolitan suppliers enjoyed the profit. The British tradesman Richard Dixon specialized in 'Slops [and] Negro Cloathing etc.' directing his goods to dress often-unwilling subjects. Other plantation owners employed female slaves to make the garments required out of coarse linen, cotton guinea cloth, linsey-woolsey and coarse woollens.[136] Garments were imposed upon plantation slaves, by force if necessary, defining a vast and distinctive population of involuntary consumers who resisted the sartorial anonymity of these garments when they could.[137] 'Negro' clothes were an important sector for metropolitan contractors, part of the immense tonnage of clothing and textiles shipped to Atlantic-world destinations.[138] This dress was premised on a different sort of 'license system'; the cosmopolitanism of these garments proceeded from the origins of the goods, the global systems of supply and the mediation of the wearers themselves.

Legislation passed in Barbados and other plantation locales focused on slaves' private possessions like 'Clothes ... and other Things ... not given them by their Master'. Possession of *unlicensed* goods was seen as a threat to colonial stability.[139] Slaves worked to acquire other attire wherever possible, impelled by the dignity or expressiveness of those options. Equally, planters lobbied for legislation against slaves dressing in garments deemed unsuitable, with some masters going so far as to destroy these goods when given the chance. In the 1830s, at a gathering of Baptist slaves in Jamaica, the master burst in: 'He began to beat them with a stick, declared there should be no Baptists there, tore their clothes, took their clean linen out of the trunk and trampled

[136] Lemire, *Dress, Culture and Commerce*, p. 34; E 8/10, 23 July 1814, Hudson's Bay Company Archives, Winnipeg (my thanks to Laura Peers sharing this additional example of the trade); Weaver, 'Fashioning Freedom', pp. 47–48; See also, DuPlessis, *Material Atlantic*, pp. 130–132.

[137] Styles, *Dress of the People*, pp. 247–320.

[138] Nuala Zahedieh, 'London and the Colonial Consumer in the Late Seventeenth Century' *Economic History Review* 47:2 (1994): 248–250 and *Capital and the Colonies*, pp. 135, 263, Table 6.5; White and White, 'Slave Clothing and African-American Culture', pp. 154–155; for restocking after a slave revolt: Gordon Turnbull, *A Narrative of the Revolt and Insurrection in the Island of Grenada* (London: A. Paris, 1796), p. 12.

[139] Acts of Assembly, passed in the Island of Barbados, From 1648, to 1718 (London: 1732–39), vol. 1, pp. 120, 179; DuPlessis, *Material Atlantic*, Chapter 4; Steeve O. Buckridge, *The Language of Dress: Resistance and Accommodation in Jamaica, 1760–1890* (Kingston: University of the West Indies Press, 2004), pp. 31–33.

Figure 3.5 *A West India Sportsman*, published by William Holland, 1807. Print made by Monogrammist JF, English School. Private Collection. © Michael Graham-Stewart/Bridgeman Images.

on it – stripped the clothes of one woman.'[140] The satire 'A West India Sportsman' demonstrates the sartorial signs of slaves' intended subservience: a ragged coat, a plain one- or two-piece costume and bare feet (Figure 3.5). The enforced servitude of slaves was emphasized through the dearth of garments received, in contrast to the greater number and quality of clothing given white servants. More fearsome still, for colonial authorities, was the prospect of effective resistance. Figure 3.6 depicts one of the many African rebels in eighteenth-century Dutch Surinam, his compatriots in the distance attired in the coarse linen garments assigned by slavery. The 'Coromantyn Free Negro, or Ranger' is dressed otherwise, presented in blue breeches tied at the knee, with a white turned down waistband. The breeches look like repurposed regimental attire, visualizing the threat to colonists of mutinous slaves. Indeed, members of the regimental corps employed by the Dutch to hunt down insurgents were memorialized with identical breeches. In turn, the soldiers captured by African rebels were

[140] Quoted in Buckridge, *Language of Dress*, p. 33.

A Coromantyn Free Negro, or Ranger, armed.

London, Published Dec.r 1st 1793 by J. Johnson, S.t Pauls Church Yard.

Figure 3.6 *A Coromantyn Free Negro, or Ranger, Armed.* William Blake (1757–1827) after John Gabriel Stedman (1744–1797). *Narrative of a Five Years Expedition* copy 2, opposite p. 80. (London: J. Johnson, 1796). Huntington Library and Art Gallery.

routinely stripped of their clothes for reuse by the rebels, an upending of imperial supply chains, if only on a small scale.[141]

The global history of readymade clothing industries is incomplete. The scenario I outline predominantly treats the British Empire, with structures that are perhaps comparable to other imperial powers with similar infrastructure needs.[142] The discipline inherent in such standardized apparel directed their manufacture. Suraiya Faroqhi notes that in the Ottoman Empire, 'from the fifteenth century onwards janissaries wore standard-issue coats and underclothing delivered to them by the state authorities ... [being] put into uniforms centuries before this became customary in European armies.'[143] The particularities of this history remain opaque. The mass of involuntary consumers caught up in imperial ventures required different systems of technology to make their clothing, directing human energies and capital in new ways. During the American, French and Napoleonic Wars, the magnitude of armies and navies spread across Europe, the Americas, the Indian subcontinent and the world's oceans represented an enormous logistical challenge. James Wadham, a contractor for the Royal Navy, sent over 600,000 shirt, trousers and jackets to naval warehouses between 1780 and 1782, at the height of the American Revolutionary War.[144] As the nineteenth century opened, in the midst of a campaign against Napoleonic France, the British Navy purchased 20,000 pairs of shoes from a Sicilian contractor for their Mediterranean fleet.[145] The economic might of the British Empire impelled readymade production in a variety of world locales, while the needs of slave populations shaped manufacturing and consumption in other regions. The side effect of this production was a flow of shirts and apparel into broad colonial and metropolitan markets: as gifts for Indigenous allies, as stock at colonial

---

[141] Stedman, *Narrative of a Five Years' Expedition*, vol. 1, p. 227. The uniform of men serving the Dutch are displayed in an accompanying illustration titled 'A Private Marine of Col. Fourgeoud's Corps', facing p. 132.

[142] Roche, *Culture of Clothing*, pp. 360–1. Miki Sugiura is exploring slave clothing in the Dutch Cape Colony and Indian Ocean world and Sophie White is doing likewise for the African enslaved in the global French Empire.

[143] 'Introduction', *Ottoman Costumes*, pp. 22–23.

[144] Lemire, *Dress, Culture and Commerce*, pp. 21–22.

[145] Meaghan Walker uncovered the ever-widening impact of demand exerted by Britain's Royal Navy. I am grateful for her willingness to share this example. 'Mobilizing Clothing: British Military Dress, Culture and Economy during the French Revolutionary and Napoleonic Wars, 1793–1815', Chapter 1, unpublished PhD dissertation, University of Alberta, in progress.

trading posts, as supplies for colonial or provincial shopkeepers or as stores for travellers to the far reaches of empire.[146] Readymade garments were iconic globalized, imperial products.

My final focus is on Indigenous clothing technologies that were adopted by European traders and settlers initially wholly dependent for knowledge and supplies on Indigenous peoples – goods that also came to be made en masse. The North American climate, in the northern temperate zone, presented trials and opportunities well known to Native Americans, and their clothing technologies kept them warm, dry and mobile in summer and winter. Snowshoes and moccasins constituted critical resources dependent on alliances formalized through treaty where goods were exchanged, what Christian Anye Crouch terms 'material diplomacy.'[147] Military, missionary, settler and traveller recognized the superior qualities of locally tanned skins and local footwear, providing better footing and warmth than heavy-heeled shoes and stiff-soled boots of European design.[148] Native American women fashioned moccasins ideal for summer months and fur-lined footwear to use with or without snowshoes for the winter.[149] Footgear had military and commercial import, as immobility in winter presaged military defeat and failure in trade. French Jesuit missionaries in New France in the 1600s soon learned that, in contrast to Europe, winter was a time of easy travel, for the cold and snow '[made] all roads smooth, and the frost covering Rivers and Lakes with ice, so that one can go anywhere with safety and draft loads'.[150] The right footwear made travel possible.

[146] Timothy J. Shannon, 'Dressing for Success on the Mohawk Frontier: Hendrick, William Johnson, and the Indian Fashion' *William and Mary Quarterly* 53:1 (1996): 13–42; Richard White, *The Middle Ground: Empires, and Republics in the Great Lakes Region, 1650–1815*, 2nd ed. (Cambridge: Cambridge University Press, 2011) pp. 100, 131, 181; Lemire, *Dress, Culture and Commerce*; Margaret Maynard, *Fashioned from Penury: Dress as Cultural Practice in Colonial Australia* (Cambridge: Cambridge University Press, 1994), pp. 9–26.

[147] Christian Ayne Crouch, *Nobility Lost: French and Canadian Martial Cultures, Indians, and the End of New France* (Ithaca: Cornell University Press, 2014), p. 2.

[148] Sophie White, *Wild Frenchmen and Frenchified Indians: Material Culture and Race in Colonial Louisiana* (Philadelphia: University of Pennsylvania Press, 2013), pp. 72, 208–209.

[149] Laura Peers, '"Almost True": Peter Rindisbacher's Early Images of Rupert's Land, 1821–26' *Art History* 32:3 (2009), p. 530.

[150] Reuben Gold Thwaites, ed., *The Jesuit Relations and Allied Documents: Travels and Explorations of the Jesuit Missionaries in New France, 1610–1791 ...* with English Translation and Notes, vol. 48 (Cleveland: Burrows, 1899), p. 179.

Snowshoes and moccasins were embraced by incomers – sometimes hesitantly, sometimes quickly as they learned their merits.[151] Moccasins ultimately became ubiquitous in all of Europe's American colonies at these latitudes, usually provided by local Aboriginal communities, as with the Wendat near Quebec City on the St Laurence River. As Bruce Trigger observes, Native Americas embedded 'marketing within a framework of political and social relations'.[152] Alliances were strengthened through the timely selling of indispensable goods without which the colonial military would be vulnerable. Native Americans willingly traded to confirm commercial and diplomatic relations. Sophie White notes that 'in the Illinois Country, probate records reveal that [French] male colonists were both more thorough and more consistent in their appropriation of articles of indigenous origin.'[153] Moccasins and snowshoes were staples in this regard.[154]

Turn again to Plate 2.4, which depicts a meeting at a Red River post between a contingent of local Indigenous men and the governor and his entourage. The two men of apparent European ancestry, on the left, reflect the cultural amalgam of apparel typical of many colonial locales, especially in the choice of footwear. Indeed, moccasins are shown on every Native and non-Native man, except the governor and his staff, who are dressed according to formal European sensibilities.[155] The

[151] Linda Baumgarten, *What Clothes Reveal: The Language of Clothing in Colonial and Federal America* (New Haven: Yale University Press, 2002), pp. 64–75; Thomas Wickman, '"Winters Embittered with Hardships": Severe Cold, Wabanaki Power, and English Adjustments, 1690–1710' *William and Mary Quarterly* 72:1 (2015): 57–98.

[152] Quoted in Anne de Stecher, 'Souvenir Art, Collectable Craft, Cultural Heritage: The Wendat (Huron) of Wendake, Quebec' in Janice Helland, Beverly Lemire and Alena Buis, eds., *Craft, Community and the Material Culture of Place and Politics, 19th-20th Century* (Aldershot, UK: Ashgate, 2014), p. 43. I am deeply indebted to Anne de Stecher for her insights into this question.

[153] White, *Wild Frenchmen and Frenchified Indians*, p. 209.

[154] Beverly Lemire, 'Shirts and Snowshoes: British and French Imperial Agendas in an Early Globalizing Era, c. 1660–1800' in Miki Sugiura, Naoko Inoue, Izumi Takeda and Nao Tsunoda, eds., *Use and Value of Cloth/Clothing between the 18th and 20th Centuries: Mediators, Latecomers, and Imitators*, under review. See also, Isaac Weld, *Travels through the States of North America and the Provinces of Upper and Lower Canada during the Years 1795, 1796, and 1797*, 4th edition (London: John Stockdale, 1800), p. 232.

[155] Many elements of Peter Rindisbacher's paintings originate from a European aesthetic – gestures and groupings, for example – however, the material culture of his depictions is generally accurate and certainly in the clothing styles adopted by traders and sojourners of European origins. Peers, 'Almost True'.

need for moccasins was such that an active industry developed among the Indigenous women who resided outside the posts, some being family members of fort servants. At the Hudson's Bay Company Fort York in 1800, for example, 650 pairs were produced 'for the men's use in the summer season'.[156] As Carolyn Dean and Dana Leibsohn observe, 'in every society certain mixtures [of objects] become naturalized over time, losing their visibility and potency ... while other continue to be marked as such.'[157] Moccasins exemplify a creolized naturalized object to those in fur trade society and an Indigenous object to others, judgements dependent on place, ethnicity and rank.

The utility of moccasins spurred Euro-American businessmen to produce footwear in large quantities for local and Great Lakes markets, as well as for the more populous east coast cities. Detroit merchants replaced labour-intensive Indigenous tanning methods with more highly capitalized European style tanneries. Moccasins were among the many articles appropriated from Native American cultures and used for political as well as functional reasons. Indeed, they became a fashion in the late eighteenth and nineteenth centuries in east coast urban locales.[158] From the 1780s, advertisements appeared in eastern US newspapers announcing the arrival of 'imported moccasins' from interior manufacturing sites, the items perhaps carrying the frisson of frontier life and Indigenous culture. These were not worn on streets but repurposed, it being agreed that moccasins 'in a house [were] ... the most agreeable sort of shoe that can be imagined'.[159] This new colonial style was shaped by the interaction of cultures 'within the borderlands of the eighteenth century ... [combining] the most useful and practical elements of at least three different cultural traditions (Indian, European, and French-Canadian).'[160] Apparel of this period involved

See also Sylvia van Kirk, *Many Tender Ties: Women in Fur-trade Society, 1670–1870* (Norman: University of Oklahoma Press, 1980), pp. 54, 101–102.

[156] Van Kirk, *Many Tender Ties*, p. 54.

[157] Carolyn Dean and Dana Leibsohn, 'Hybridity and Its Discontents: Considering Visual Culture in Colonial Spanish America' *Colonial Latin American Review* 12:1 (2003), p. 5.

[158] Gillian Poulter, *Becoming Native in a Foreign Land: Sport, Visual Culture, and Identity in Montreal, 1840–1885* (Vancouver: University of British Columbia Press, 2009).

[159] Weld, *Travels*, p. 232.

[160] Catherine Cangany, 'Fashioning Moccasins: Detroit, the Manufacturing Frontier, and the Empire of Consumption, 1701–1835' *William and Mary Quarterly* 69:2 (2012), p. 275.

a distinctive cultural mixing, while readymade systems involved a wide range of participants.

Native Americans also embraced the possibilities of readymade production, building on long-run experience with military provisioning; the Wendat are a notable community that focused on this opportunity. Colonial politics offered fewer choices with the passage of time and a number of Indigenous communities turned to manufacturing as a viable option. One instance of their role as suppliers appears in a worried account from New York at the close of the Seven Years' War (1757–1763), following the British victory over the French at Quebec City in 1759. The New York writer opined that resistance was still possible from the French and their Native allies, claiming that General Vaudreuil intended 'to retake Quebec in the Winter by Storm, for which Purpose he gave Orders for 20,000 Pair of Snow Shoes to be immediately made'.[161] The scale of the supposed order is noteworthy, a measure of local Indigenous capability. After the change of colonial powers, the Wendat focused more intensively on production of crafts, embroidery arts, moccasins and snowshoes, as settler pressures increased and hunting lands were lost in the early 1800s. They produced significant quantities of goods over sustained periods for expanding markets, a subject addressed as well in Chapter 6.[162] Local leaders in Wendake adapted the putting-out system to provide employment for their people, while preserving culture capacity and advancing manufacturing skills. During the 1800s, the Wendat produced a wide range of readymade goods, including an estimated 140,000 moccasins a year, along with 7,000 pairs of

---

[161] *London Evening Post* (London, England), 24–26 January, 1760.

[162] Ruth Phillips, *Trading Identities: The Souvenir in Native North American Art from the Northeast, 1700–1900* (Washington: University of Washington Press, 1998); Anne de Stecher, 'Huron-Wendat Visual Culture: Source of Economic Autonomy and Continuity of Traditional Culture' in Pierre Anctil, André Loiselle and Christopher Rolfe, eds., *Canada Exposed / Le Canada à découverte* (Brussels: Peter Lang, 2009), pp. 131–150; Louise Vigneault and Isabelle Masse, 'Les autoreprésentations de l'artiste huron-wendat Zacharie Vincent (1815–1886): icons d'une gloire politique et sprituelle' *Canadian Journal of Art History* 32:2 (2011), p. 62 and Gordon M. Sayre, 'Self-Portraiture and Commodification in the Work of Huron/Wendat Artist Zacharie Vincent, aka 'Le Dernier Huron' *American Indian Culture and Research Journal* 39:2 (2015), pp. 19–20; Brian Gettler, 'Economic Activity and Class Formation in Wendake, 1800–1950' in Thomas Peace and Lathryn Labelle, eds., *From Huronia to Wendakes: Adversity, Migration, and Resilience, 1650–1900* (Norman, OK: University of Oklahoma Press, 2016), pp. 144–181.

snowshoes annually by the later 1800s. Production of this sort suggests the ways Native Americans responded to opportunities and constraints, with this community working to sell their readymade goods independently and through colonial retail channels.[163] Their success marked a different sort of cultural capacity, at odds with the imperial genesis of the readymade system.

Conclusion

Early modern global trade altered patterns of dress profoundly and irrevocably. This 'social skin' assumed new forms enabled by commercial expansion, hybrid influences and rising material flows. Regional fashion systems emerged in more robust forms infused with the energies of wider populations, with a new material cosmopolitanism evident in many settings. Sumptuary laws could not contain the creativity expressed through dress, despite the legislative intent in many societies. Authorities strained to enforce their laws, as was evident in Qing China, Tokugawa Japan and Europe. Colonized subjects navigated more stringent regulations intended to demarcate men and women of African and Native American ancestry. Colonized peoples lived with harsh penalties for infractions and were schooled in the serious politics of dress. Slaves flouted racialized clothing edicts in subtle ways when they could. Notably, their material innovations defined the aesthetic parameters of their societies. Some living within punitive regimes suffered for their presumptions and were shamed, beaten or imprisoned for transgressions. Racial boundaries continued to be policed in fearsome ways, even as sumptuary laws loosened or were only sporadically enforced in more places.

The secondhand clothing trade flourished throughout these centuries, and the industrious energies unleashed by this trade represent an important ingredient in consumer markets. This sector added energy to world commerce, offering an enhanced choice of considerable importance. Reuse and recycling reinforced the value of apparel in all its dimensions: as a currency, as welcome addition to wardrobes and as an important entrepreneurial space for generations of enterprising

---

163 Sayre, 'Self-Portraiture and Commodification', p. 20. See also, Montreal Editor, 'Moccasin and Indian Slipper Industry at Lorette' *Footwear in Canada* 11:12, December 1921, pp. 54–57. I am indebted to Cynthia Cooper for sharing this source with me.

women, who often collected at the margins of formal markets. Importantly, women in many regions turned their skills and energies to this market-oriented trade. Their innumerable micro-enterprises represented vital industrious additions in precincts worldwide.

The early modern global era was marked by intensive competition among competing imperial forces, across much of the globe. Dressing the men swept up in these politics drove readymade clothing production, a new imperial livery. This occasioned a different sort of 'license' system among a wider set of involuntary consumers. In this context, the linen shirt became an 'imperial commodity', stocking sailors' slop chests, covering the backs of African slaves and garbing imperial regiments.[164] A disciplined constraint now defined their clothing and status. Even as manufacturing capacity swelled, there was a controlled narrowing of choice for those engulfed in this material paradigm. The manifestation of power through uniform clothing presaged later nineteenth century institutions intent on regulating selected populations.[165] A full account of this provisioning system has not yet been made. Nonetheless, it is clear that the power of uniforms advanced inexorably, becoming a defining feature of material life. At the same time, North American Indigenous entrepreneurs directed readymade production to enable a different outcome. The survival of their communities and the preservation of their cultures depended on this productive capacity. The sum of these parts was a heightened attention to the 'social skin', which was shaped by globalizing material culture.

---

[164] Kathleen M. Brown, *Foul Bodies: Cleanliness in Early America* (New Haven: Yale University Press, 2014), p. 98; Shannon, 'Dressing for Success on the Mohawk Frontier', pp. 37–39; DuPlessis, *Material Atlantic*, pp. 125–163; Lemire, *Dress, Culture and Commerce*, pp. 11–12, 22–26; Miki Sugiura, 'Slave Clothing and Early Modern Dutch Cloth/Clothing Circulations in the Indian Ocean World' paper presented at the conference 'Dressing Global Bodies', University of Alberta, Edmonton, 7–9 July 2016.

[165] For the uniform slops enforced on men and women transported to Australia from the 1790s, see Maynard, *Fashioned from Penury*, pp. 9–26. Vivienne Richmond, *Clothing the Poor in Nineteenth-Century England* (Cambridge: Cambridge University Press, 2013); Sarah Fee, 'The King's New Clothing: "European" Dress as Political Tool in Pre-Colonial Madagascar, *c.* 1820s–1865' paper presented at the conference 'Dressing Global Bodies', University of Alberta, Edmonton, 7–9 July 2016.

4 | Smuggling, Wrecking and Scavenging

Or, the Informal Pathways to Consumption

Kichiemon of Inasa-fanazu had been involved in two previous cases of smuggling with Chinese ships. In 1721 he had engaged in smuggling as a sailor. At that time he had come to the magistrate's office and given himself up. As a result he was pardoned and permitted to continue in his former residence. The second time was in 1725 when he swam out to the number five Chinese ship. At that time, because he was known to be a previous offender, he had his nose cut off. This still did not teach him his lesson, for having acquired a letter from a certain Ch'i of the thirty-seventh Chinese boat, he waited for his chance to smuggle again.

Nagasaki, Hankach ō vol. 9, Case No. 1-B (1730).[1]

... the Hoppo[2] desired there might be a Paper fixed to your Ships Masts forbidding the Sailors to run [smuggle] any Goods on Shore, we request you will let a Paper be fixed accordingly, Intimateing that Whoever of the Sailors shall be found out to have run any Goods on Shore or on Board shall be Punished Severly ...

Letter by Captain Richard Sheppard, 19 August 1737[3]

the [French] Governor of Senegal ... inform'd us that it was the Custom of the Inhabitants of that Coast [Senegal] where the Duke of Cumberland was stranded, to consider all Shipwrecks as Gods donation to them, and that they conceived their right to be so well founded, that notwithstanding the intercourse between them and the French, they seized all french

---

[1] Hankach ō vol. 9, Case No. 1-B (1730). Quoted in Fred G. Notehelfer, 'Notes on Kyōhō Smuggling' *Princeton Papers in East Asian Studies* 1 (1972), p. 21.

[2] The English term 'Hoppo' was used to describe the Chinese imperial official responsible for customs who administered Western trade in Canton (Guangzhou).

[3] British LIbrary, India Office Records [IOR], G/12/43, p. 17.

Vessels wreck'd upon their coast with as little ceremony as the Vessels of other Nations.

> Yoff Bay, West Africa. Letter to the Directors of the English East India Company, January 1750[4]

The first Day our Ship went into Dock, I met Brown, and another; they asked me if the Sweepings of the Sugar were gone, I said no; they asked me if I would sell it, I told them it was not mine; they said you foolish Rogue, as the Ship is in Dock, you may venture to do it, so I said they might have it if they would come for it: ... Friday, November 20, I met Campbell, he asked me if he should come for the Sweepings, I told him yes, and on Sunday Night, Brown and Campbell, got a Lighter Man's Skiff, and came into the Ship.

> Testimony of Richard French in the thievery trial of Edward Brown and Alexander Campbell[5]

Goods flowed through complex circuits to their ultimate users, routes that involved legal, illicit and customary habits. While legal trade and formal corporate structures formed the backbone of global commerce, informal, extralegal or customary practices appended to these large mercantile configurations. Their influence opened markets more widely, enabling more democratic consumption among the widest diversity of people. That is the focus of this chapter. In previous chapters I traced evolving commercial systems in the cloth and clothing sectors that spanned world communities. In this chapter I assess the inventive material pathways that expanded consumption further still, channelling myriad commodities into the welcoming hands of world peoples who were increasingly familiar with globally sourced cargoes.

Extralegal systems are crucially important in explaining the penetration of these commodities to the farthest corners and least auspicious consumers. The familiarity with commodities engendered by this system disrupted the status quo. Restraints on consumptions were challenged at every turn, including the sumptuary restrictions addressed in the previous chapter. Equally, paradigms of legal commerce were widely confounded as creative and unruly schemes multiplied, maximizing material exchange and supplying heterogeneous populations (and private profits). Black

---

[4] Letter to the Court of Directors of the English East India Company, January 1750. IOR/G/12/53, British Library.

[5] 'Trial of Edward Brown and Alexander Campbell'. 8 December 1742 (t17421208-51), *Old Bailey Proceedings Online,* www.oldbaileyonline.org, version 7.2, accessed 26 November 2016.

markets, grey markets and informal interventions flourished as commodity trade expanded. Administrations struggled to enforce commercial protocols, enacting layers of legislation aimed at walling off insurgent traffic. Their failures were legion. More inventive anarchic operatives worked to opposite ends, augmenting access to consumer wares at prices unmatched by legitimate dealers. The porosity of early modern commercial systems was fundamentally important in enlarging consumerism worldwide, especially among the non-elites. This phenomenon is the focus of this chapter.

'Extralegality', Global Trade and Creative Consumption

How did those living in the wake of global trade understand new luxuries and novel commodities? Routine smuggling, sweeping of ships' holds, fishing shipwrecks or gleaning on coastlines preoccupied generations of enterprising folk, who channelled their harvests into capacious markets or bartered their stores as needed. The goods in question arose within what Igor Kopytoff terms the 'explosion of commoditization that was at the root of capitalism' where each thing was made 'exchangeable for more and more other things', while within 'the system as a whole ... more and more different things [were] more widely exchangeable'.[6] The question of exchange is key to this discussion. For this was not a fully monetized world; indeed, people across the globe relied wholly or in part on the exchangeability of things. With burgeoning capitalist trade and growing volumes of commodities, industriousness was demonstrated by involvement in exchange as well as the earning of wages – a point I emphasize in my discussion of the secondhand trade. But 'industriousness' shows itself in other scenarios as well including in legal and illegal micro-enterprise. The 'explosion of commoditization' encouraged a greater entanglement with more things, including the barter, trade and sale of commodities, steered through many conduits into consumers' hands. I explain these processes through the study of goods and systems, (local and international). Participants in these ventures secured highly unequal rewards. Nonetheless, their collective endeavours were not minor addenda to the burgeoning capitalist, globalizing market. Rather, these strategies carried significant quantities of goods more widely than

---

[6] Igor Kopytoff, 'The Cultural Biography of Things: Commoditization as Process' in Arjun Appadurai, ed., *The Social Life of Things: Commodities in Cultural Perspective* (Cambridge: Cambridge University Press, 1986), pp. 72, 73.

was possible through sanctioned channels. Of course, the initial carriage of commodities depended on the highly capitalized corporate systems that crossed cultures; from the outset, however, innumerable informal accretions affixed to these administrations, inspired by custom and opportunity. Their mediators reflect a different type of industriousness, not as described by Jan de Vries with more wages earned,[7] but through a heightened manipulation of things as they attempted to profit materially through these engagements.

Complex social relations, priorities and processes greased the passage of these things to landfall, involving those wishing to trade, wishing to buy and wishing for bargains. It is clear these were not wholly 'Smithian' cycles of exchange. How can we theorize this activity? Fernand Braudel proposed the tripartite context of early modern economic life, where, at the top 'exalted level' were the great international trading companies. Layered in the middle were the vast ranks of markets, shops and workshops, all of which rested on the deep bottom layer of shadowy material life and material exchange. Yet, these were not separate spheres, walled off one from another. Rather they showed organic interconnection, feeding off each other, reliant on like networks and alliances.[8] Innovation and tradition also wrestled for preeminence, sometimes walking hand in hand. E. P. Thompson proposed the power of custom – or moral economy – to explain certain economic priorities, as adjunct to law, sometimes accepted by authorities and the recurring habits of local people.[9] This understanding offers an invaluable context for the discussions below. Equally useful, is the concept of 'extralegality'. This term was coined by urban anthropologists Alan Smart and Filippo Zerillis to explain the economic habits and practice in contemporary developing regions, involving the active (sometimes

---

[7] Jan de Vries, *The Industrious Revolution: Consumer Behavior and the Household Economy, 1650 to the Present* (Cambridge: Cambridge University Press, 2008).

[8] For the example of mariners' enterprise and evidence of the three-part model at work within EIC trading vessels, see Beverly Lemire, '"Men of the World": British Mariners, Consumer Practice and Material Culture in an Era of Global Trade, c. 1660–1800' *Journal of British Studies*, 54:2 (2015), pp. 288–319; Huw Bowen, '"So Alarming an Evil"': Smuggling, Pilfering and the English East India Company, 1740–1810' *International Journal of Maritime History* 14 (2002): 1–13.

[9] E. P. Thompson, *Customs in Common: Studies in Traditional Popular Culture* (New York, 1993), pp. 97–98.

marginal) players in urban societies selling and consuming goods. They propose three facets of extralegality: 'the illegal; the informal; and the not-yet-(il)legal'.[10] They argue that this model avoids the 'dichotomy between legal and illegal ... [giving more] attention to fuzzy or contested boundaries'. In addition, this precept encourages us 'to resist "seeing like a state"', with an emphasis on activities according to their legal or illegal status; rather, it is imperative to assess the whole canvas of activities within economic life. Similarly, they emphasize that 'tracing illicit flows highlights the contingency of illegality'.[11]

Extralegality entwined with formal capitalist ventures, shaping and reshaping opportunities and constraints – and involving innumerable actors of every social rank in world trading zones. This was among the most vital economic sectors, extending options to the largest portion of the population, as I broached previously in the discussion of the secondhand trade in Chapter 3. The source of goods arriving in consumers' hands was a contingent affair, as commodity channels and material prospects varied enormously, within and without the letter of the law. Thus, the market economy – international trading companies and merchants of vast wealth – was as closely interlaced with the illicit shadow economy as it was with respectable markets. The routine relations of these strata fashioned transformations in the material world. As Michael Kwass notes for eighteenth-century France, 'given the vast proportions of the shadow economy, just about everyone must have known an illegal smuggler, dealer, or consumer, if they were not one themselves'.[12] The shadow economy embodied an immense material energy from smuggling networks in the Indian Ocean to routine mercantile malfeasance in the colonial Caribbean, the Canary Islands and the North Sea. Throughout, local and foreign merchants, mariners, officials and land-based citizens negotiated access to commoditized cargoes in often unaccounted ways.[13] The opening epigraphs demonstrate some of these practices.

---

[10] Alan Smart and Filippo M. Zerilli, 'Extralegality' in Donald M. Nonini, ed., *A Companion to Urban Anthropology* (John Wiley and Sons, 2014), p. 222. I thank Dr Lynne B. Milgram for generously bringing this work to my attention.
[11] Smart and Zerilli, pp. 223–224.
[12] Michael Kwass, *Contraband: Louis Mandrin and the Making of a Global Underground* (Cambridge MA: Harvard University Press, 2014), p. 87.
[13] A small fraction of the vast literature on this subject includes Anthony Disney, 'Smugglers and Smuggling in the Western Half of the *Estado Da India* in the Late Sixteenth and Early Seventeenth Centuries' *Indica* 26:1&2 (1989): 57–75;

One result is the uncertain economic statistics on which we rely.[14]
Despite a substantial and growing literature on the informal economy, too many historians wholly ignore the influence of such practice,
or proceed as if these alternative systems did not exist, as if port books
and customs ledgers constituted the full reality of commerce, as if
High Street shops and market squares constituted the sum of retailing.
Scholars are revising this view and their revisions are essential.[15] For,

Nuala Zahedieh, 'The Merchants of Port Royal Jamaica and the Spanish
Contraband Trade, 1655–1692' *William and Mary Quarterly* 43 (1986): 570–
593 and 'Trade, Plunder and Economic Development in Early English Jamaica,
1655–1689' *Economic History Review* 39 (1986): 205–222; James C. Boyajian,
Portuguese Trade in Asia under the Hapsburgs, 1580–1640 (Baltimore: John
Hopkins University Press, 1993); Paul A. Van Dyke, ed., *Americans and Macao:
Trade, Smuggling and Diplomacy on the South China Coast* (Hong Kong: Hong
Kong University Press, 2012) and Paul A. Van Dyke, *Merchants of Canton and
Macao: Politics and Strategies in Eighteenth-Century Chinese Trade* (Hong
Kong: Hong Kong University Press, 2012); Murdo J. MacLeod, *Spanish Central
America: A Socioeconomic History, 1520–1720* (Berkeley: University of
California Press, 1973, reprinted 2010), especially Chapter 20, 'The Rise of
Smuggling'; Wim Klooster, 'Jews in Surinam and Curaçao' in Paolo Bernardini
and Norman Fiering, eds., *The Jews and the Expansion of Europe to the West,
1450–1800* (New York: Berghahn Books, 2001), pp. 350–368; Robert J.
Antony, ed., *Elusive Pirates, Pervasive Smugglers: Violence and Clandestine
Trade in the Greater China Seas* (Hong Kong: Hong Kong University Press,
2010); Alan L. Karras, *Smuggling: Contraband and Corruption in World
History* (Lanham, MD: Rowman and Littlefield, 2010); Peter Andreas,
Smuggler Nation: How Illicit Trade Made America (Oxford: Oxford University
Press, 2013); Weichung Cheng, *War, Trade and Piracy in the China Seas (1622–
1683)* (Leiden: Brill, 2013); Karwan Fatah-Black, *White Lies and Black
Markets: Evading Metropolitan Authority in Colonial Suriname, 1650–1800*
(Leiden: Brill, 2015).

[14]   Some economic historians show great ambivalence towards the issue of
        smuggling, with one senior scholar advising a then junior colleague that
        smuggling should not be mentioned in his study of Atlantic and North Sea trade,
        as it made the trade figures suspect (private communication). Brian R. Mitchell
        notes that 'what is possibly a more serious defect of the external trade statistics is
        that which springs from the importance of smuggling in eighteenth-century
        Britain'. But he consoles himself with the thought that this illicit branch of trade
        was 'probably not very important'. *British Historical Statistics* (Cambridge:
        Cambridge University Press, 1988), p. 444. This conclusion was challenged by
        his contemporaries, as well as by recent scholarship. For a further discussion of
        this question and a study of a merchant-smuggler and his two sets of books, see
        Evan T. Jones, 'Accounting for Smuggling in Mid-Sixteenth-Century Bristol'
        Economic History Review 54:1 (2001): 17–38.

[15]   For example: Bruno Blondé, Natacha Coquery, Jon Stobart and Ilya Van
        Damme, eds., *Fashioning Old and New: Changing Consumer Patterns in
        Western Europe, 1650–1900* (Turnhout: Brepolis, 2009); Christian Hochmuth,

however messy and inconvenient for statistical modelling, black, grey and informal markets – and their impact on economic and material life – must be acknowledged. To do otherwise is to ignore a vibrant human endeavour, with effects that defined consumer capacity and the evolving capitalist system in this period.

At the same time, officials in imperial heartlands from Beijing to Madrid attempted to legislate in ways that would be sustainable in provincial and colonial locales. Peter Crooks and Timothy Parsons point to the tension between these imperial aims and the bureaucracies slated to enforce metropolitan rubrics. 'Bureaucracies played a role (albeit more often in aspiration than result) in providing empires with a means of articulating social power and marshalling resources in regions remote from the imperial core. In pursuit of these ends, imperial bureaucracies were authoritarian, extractive and backed by violence'.[16] Officials defined and redefined what constituted 'smuggling', and all variants from approved systems were suspect as regulators strained to control material flows, pushing and prodding cargoes into tracks favoured by economic theorists, government administrators and political incumbents. Yet, extralegality thrived, dogging imperial monopolies and regulated markets. The resulting tensions coloured consumer processes.

The unlicensed entwined with reputable traffic in ways that confounded precepts of legitimate dealing. Moreover, the authors of these laws could not rely on officials to enforce regulations. Customs agents and local officers colluded with ship commanders, seamen, boatmen,

---

'What Is Tobacco? Illicit Trade with Overseas Commodities in Early Modern Dresden' in Thomas Buchner and Philip R. Hoffmann-Rehnitz, eds., *Shadow Economies and Irregular Work in Urban Europe: 16th to Early 20th Centuries* (Vienna and Berlin: LIT Verlag, 2011), pp. 107–126; Sophie White, 'Geographies of Slave Consumption' *Winterthur Portfolio* 45:2/3 (2011): 229–248; Carol Benedict, *Golden Silk Smoke: A History of Tobacco in China, 1550–2010* (Berkeley: University of California Press, 2011), Chapter 1; Michael J. Javis, *In the Eye of All Trade: Bermuda, Bermudians, and the Maritime Atlantic* (Chapel Hill, NC: University of North Carolina Press, 2010), especially Chapter 3; Lance Raymond Grahn, *The Political Economy of Smuggling: Regional Informal Economies in Bourbon New Granada* (Boulder: Westview Press, 1997).

[16] Peter Crooks and Timothy H. Parsons, eds., *Empires and Bureaucracy in World History: From Late Antiquity to the Twentieth Century* (Cambridge: Cambridge University Press, 2016), p. 4. For an example of this tension, see William J. McCarthy, 'Between Policy and Prerogative: Malfeasance in the Inspection of the Manila Galleons at Acapulco, 1637' *Colonial Latin American Historical Review* 2/2 (1993): 163–183.

interloping traders, shopkeepers, private citizens and even members in good standing of monopoly trading companies to evade the rules whenever they could. Similarly, innumerable residents along coastlines, rivers and anchorages applied a customary sensibility to commodity flows, seeing the seasonal harvests that came in on the waves very differently than did imperial bureaucrats. This was the reality of local and long-distance commerce, as well as the hand-to-hand acquisition of goods that generated a material system of immense significance.[17] Laurence Fontaine terms these activities 'alternate exchanges', which included the extensive circulation of illegal and secondhand goods, a cornerstone of economic activity from the early modern to contemporary times. Local and illicit patterns of exchange generated a 'paradox of diversity and cohesion' that interlinked peoples and processes.[18] Extralegal practices were grafted to formally mandated commerce, sometimes pursued in the same ships. This 'explosion of commoditization',[19] when allied with extralegal circuits of exchange, magnified the effects of consumer trade. The cheapness of untaxed merchandise and its effective distribution enlarged access to new commodities and new luxuries as people smuggled, pilfered and scavenged, eluding those sent to curtail them.

Activities deemed 'economic crimes' figure centrally in the long process of what has been called the 'consumer revolution'.[20] Consumer habits and markets were buoyed by systematic and routine extralegality, manifested in the ubiquitous breach of corporate monopolies, mercantilist laws and taxation systems. A plurality of citizens saw imperial taxation as against their best interests. As a consequence, avoidance of taxes and customs duties was habitual. Regulations aimed to shape consumption choices were defied by metropolitan citizens of all nationalities, generating extraordinary levels of tax evasion for key commodities like tea, textiles and tobacco. Colonists likewise opposed distant metropolitan edicts that constrained colonial

---

[17] Laurence Fontaine, ed., *Alternative Exchanges: Second-Hand Circulations from the Sixteenth Century to the Present* (New York: Berghahn Books, 2008); see also, Beverly Lemire, *The Business of Everyday Life: Gender, Practice and Social Politics in England, 1600–1900* (Manchester: Manchester University Press, 2005), especially Chapter 4.

[18] Robert J. Antony, 'Introduction' in Antony, *Elusive Pirates, Pervasive Smugglers*, p. 5.

[19] Kopytoff, 'The Cultural Biography of Things', p. 72.

[20] Renate Bridenthal, 'Introduction' in Renate Bridenthal, ed., *The Hidden History of Crime, Corruption and the State* (New York: Berghahn Books, 2013), p. 2.

markets.[21] Alan Karras proposes that for colonial American citizens, 'smuggling was simply ... [a] vehicle for gaining leverage against a state that sought to regulate ... consumption activities and patterns'.[22] Thus, attending solely to consumer goods within the bounds of the law offers a very partial view of the extensive, inventive and unruly actions typical of that time. Bonded warehouses, courtly display and polite shopping were illusions of rectitude capturing only part of the multifarious material circuits. Consumption founded on extralegal action was essential to burgeoning consumerism and was frequently an adjunct to the seasonal fleets traversing global oceans.[23] The case of smuggled tea in

[21] W. A. Cole, 'Trends in Eighteenth-Century Smuggling' *Economic History Review* 10:3 (1958): 395–410 and 'The Arithmetic of Eighteenth-Century Smuggling: Rejoinder' *Economic History Review* 28:1 (1975): 44–49; and for the other side of this debate around the scale of smuggled goods, see Hoh-Cheung Mui and Lorna Mui, 'Smuggling and the British Tea Trade before 1784' *American Historical Review* 74:1 (1968): 44–73 and '"Trends in Eighteenth-Century Smuggling" Reconsidered' *Economic History Review* 74:1 (1975): 44–73. These latter authors accept the estimates of the deputy accountant-general of the East India Company who stated that between 1773 and 1782, more than ten million pounds of tea (pure and adulterated) were smuggled into Britain. For tobacco in Britain, see Robert C. Nash, 'The English and Scottish Tobacco Trades in the Seventeenth and Eighteenth Centuries: Legal and Illegal Trade' *Economic History Review* 35:3 (1982): 354–372. As well, see Kwass, *Contraband*; Felicia Gottmann, *Global Trade, Smuggling, and the Making of Economic Liberalism* (Basingstoke, UK: Palgrave, 2016); Hanna Hodacs, *Silk and Tea in the North: Scandinavian Trade and the Market for Asian Goods in Eighteenth-Century Europe* (Basingstoke, UK: Palgrave, 2016), Chapter 2; Chris Nierstrasz, *Rivalry for Trade in Tea and Textiles: The English and Dutch East India Companies (1700–1800)* (Basingstoke, UK: Palgrave Macmillan, 2015), Chapter 3. In world history, see Karras, *Smuggling*; and for a very useful survey of smuggling in the colonial Americas, see Wim Klooster, 'Inter-imperial Smuggling in the Americas, 1600–1800' in Bernard Bailyn and Patricia L. Denault, eds., *Soundings in Atlantic History: Latent Structures and Intellectual Currents, 1500–1830* (Cambridge, MA: Harvard University Press, 2009), pp. 141–180 and *Illicit Riches: Dutch Trade in the Caribbean, 1648–1795* (Leiden: KILTV Press, 1998).

[22] Karras, *Smuggling*, p. 131. The early (illicit) trade of tobacco in the Caribbean, discussed in Chapter 5 of this volume, exemplifies this concept.

[23] Karras, *Smuggling* and '"Custom Has the Force of Law": Local Officials and Contraband in the Bahamas and the Floridas, 1748–1779' *Florida Historical Quarterly* 80:3 (2002): 281–311; Lauren Benton, 'Legal Spaces of Empire: Piracy and the Origins of Ocean Regionalism' *Comparative Studies in Society and History* 47:4 (2005): 700–724; Charles Ludington, *The Politics of Wine in Britain: A New Cultural History* (New York: Palgrave Macmillan, 2013).

eighteenth-century Britain exemplifies the competition (and collusion) between legal distributors and illegal suppliers that 'led to a vastly
expanded market for tea'.[24] Official figures masked widespread merchant
misconduct that moved an estimated 10 million pounds, or more, of
smuggled tea between 1773 and 1782. Perhaps the best illustration of
the scope of tea smuggling comes with the changing official sales of tea
once the duty was slashed in 1784. The sale of tea at East India Company
auctions reached about 5.8 million pounds in 1783; this volume leaped to
16.3 million pounds of tea in 1785,[25] at a time when 'smuggling had been
reduced to an insignificant trickle'.[26] While it is impossible to gauge the full
volume of extralegal trade, it is clear that these practices augmented the
circulation of goods and had a tremendous impact on consumer
behaviour.

Authorities in all the major states of Eurasia developed governmental,
military and commercial bureaucracies that were transplanted to distant
settings. Official rhetoric emphasized penalties for infractions. However,
the actual capacity of regimes to enforce edicts was variable.[27] Molly
Warsh notes the wide circulation and consumption of pearls in
Venezuela and the proximate Caribbean, observing that 'the ease with
which pearls escaped official channels was a matter of great concern to the
Spanish crown'. Kent Deng argues for the inability of Ming administrators
to effectively police China's vast coastline and enforce restrictions on
foreign trade and the attendant consumerism that followed.[28] The commercial administration of Britain was also limited in its capacities, with
aims and ability that were 'often both aspirational and restricted'.[29]

[24] Mui and Mui, 'Smuggling and the British Tea Trade before 1784', p. 45.
[25] William J. Ashworth, *Customs and Excise: Trade, Production and
      Consumption in England, 1640–1845* (Oxford: Oxford University Press, 2003),
      p. 182.
[26] Mui and Mui, '"Trends in Eighteenth-Century Smuggling" Reconsidered', p. 29.
[27] For example, Notehelfer, 'Notes on Kyoho Smuggling'; James B. Lewis, *Frontier
      Contact Between Choson Korea and Tokugawa Japan* (New York: Routledge,
      2003), pp. 179–180, 184–191, 195; Crooks and Parsons, *Empires and
      Bureaucracy in World History*.
[28] Molly Warsh, 'Enslaved Pearl Divers in the Sixteenth Century Caribbean'
      Slavery and Abolition 31:3 (2010), p. 348; Kent Deng, 'Smuggling under the
      Maritime Ban in Ming China' in the panel 'Piracy, Smuggling and Black
      Markets: Rethinking Market and Consumer Practice, c. 1600s-1900s' 17th
      World Economic History Congress, Kyoto, August 2015.
[29] Philip J. Stern and Carl Wennerlind, 'Introduction' in Philip J. Stern and Carl
      Wennerlind, eds., *Mercantilism Reimagined: Political Economy in Early
      Modern Britain and Its Empire* (New York: Oxford University Press, 2013). For

Governments agonized over financial losses. They also brooded about the hazards of unfettered plebeian access to new goods. Nonetheless, the potential for profit and the unregulated cravings for 'new luxuries' sustained a complex provisioning system with extralegal channels intertwined with legal networks.[30] The following case studies explore the material routes taken by shells, wool cloth and pepper, illuminating the wide compass of extralegal practice that followed in the wake of global trade.

Shells

Learning the Value
Commodities and knowledge about their uses travelled in uneven stages. The winter of 1723 saw the unification of the English and Scottish customs boards, and in that same year an Edinburgh customs official sent a letter to the London Custom House that was redirected to the Court of Directors of the East India Company.[31] Months previously 'a parcel of Forreign Shells' was seized at the small western Scottish port of Kirkcudbright. The location of the seizure is noteworthy, it being a harbour on the River Dee open to the Irish Sea opposite the Isle of Man, a notorious haven for smugglers. A mid-century writer calculated that smuggling from that island alone cost the British government at least £300,000 annually in lost revenue and contributed as well to the destruction of 'the morals of the British subjects stretching around the said island'.[32] In 1723, writers from the Edinburgh Custom House puzzled over the shells on their hands, part of a contraband seizure and a seeming oddity of little note. They were possibly transhipped from Ostend – another fount of contraband in northwest Europe. The biggest problem for these officers was their apparent

eighteenth-century France, see Kwass, *Contraband*. The smuggling of gold and then opium into Qing China is another well-documented instance of regulatory borders falling before the demands of trade. Van Dyke, *Merchants of Canton and Macao*, p. 215.

[30] Jan de Vries defines 'new luxury' in opposition to 'old luxury', with old luxury being emblematic of fixed ranks and privileges. New luxury, in contrast, facilitated 'comfort and pleasure, [and] lent itself to multiplication and diffusion'. *Industrious Revolution*, p. 44.

[31] For the unification of the custom's administrations, Jacob M. Price, 'Glasgow, the Tobacco Trade, and the Scottish Customs, 1707–1730' *Scottish Historical Review* 175 (1984): 1–36.

[32] Malachy Postlethwayt, *Great-Britain's Commercial Interest Explained and Improved: In a Series of Dissertations on the Most Important Branches of Her Trade and Landed . . .*, 2nd ed., vol. 1 (London, 1759): 406.

ignorance of the shells' purpose and value. Smuggled goods like tea and tobacco were commonplace; smuggled shells were not. They explained as much in their second letter to London, claiming that 'few in these parts either knew the Value or Use of these shells the parcell consisting of about 14,000'.[33] The shells perplexed the Edinburgh officials.

This conundrum falls within a long history of knowledge transfer between Asia and Europe, the struggle of Europeans to understand, manage and manipulate new materials, goods integral to Asian material culture.[34] Knowledge gaps varied with local market and artisanal priorities – knowledge also varied by rank or occupation. Jan de Vries emphasizes that new consumer goods 'must be "recognizable" to the consumer' for successful market penetration.[35] Information was clearly imperfect in this instance. The fact that the goods were smuggled indicated their importance to some extent. The questions were: how important and for whom? These were not cowrie shells, shipped by the ton from the Indian Ocean, an alternate currency and source of symbolic value within the African-Eurasian world. If the Edinburgh customs officers served in the African slave trade, they would have known cowrie shells.[36] Rather, these were mother-of-pearl shells with a shining, translucent multicoloured interior surface, employed by artisans from Japan to Asia Minor in furnishings, jewellery and accessories. European artisans learned their worth over time. In 1723, Edinburgh officials claimed bafflement.

Shellwork trickled into Europe from 1500, eliciting wonderment. European artisans only gradually mastered the tricks of handling this substance. Fans are a case in point. Delicately carved fan sticks (often using mother-of-pearl) showed the exceptional dexterity of Japanese and Chinese artisans, crafting objects of broad cultural resonance. Folding fans, a Japanese invention, were exported from Japan to China from the tenth century, and the fashion spread. Long a symbol of elegance in Asia, fans became an essential transcultural prop. In 1671, the English seaman, Edward Barlow, recalled his first sighting of fans in China, observing that

---

[33] British Library, IOR, E/1/14/100f, (April 1723).
[34] See, for example, Maxine Berg, *Luxury and Pleasure in Eighteenth-Century Britain* (Oxford: Oxford University Press, 2005), pp. 46–72; Giorgio Riello, *Cotton: The Fabric That Made the Modern World* (Cambridge: Cambridge University Press, 2013), pp. 160–186.
[35] De Vries, *Industrious Revolution*, p. 155.
[36] Bin Yang, 'The Rise and Fall of Cowrie Shells: The Asian Story' *Journal of World History* 22:1 (2011): 1–25.

Figure 4.1 Brisé fan, made of mother-of-pearl, pierced, carved and gilded. Made in France, mid-1700s. CIRC. 248–1953. © Victoria and Albert Museum, London.

'the better sort of them, both men and women carry ffanes'.[37] Plate 4.1, the portrait of *Pieter Cnoll and his Family* (1665), displays the way fan use crossed cultures. Cnoll was senior merchant of the Dutch East India Company (VOC) in Batavia at the time of the painting's creation and was a powerful and wealthy man married to Cornelia Van Neyenrode, a Eurasian woman born in Japan.[38] The use of fans in cultural and sexualized displays intrigued foreign observers and these exquisite notions travelled back to Europe as souvenirs or private cargo. Fans were one of many items readily transferred to European markets, and in the 1500s they were the preferred gift of European monarchs. Thereafter they became a coveted accessory for all manner of European and colonial women.[39]

French artisans ultimately crafted the most delicate brisé fans comprised entirely of mother-of-pearl, an enviable object inspired by Asian invention (Figure 4.1). Maxine Berg explores the mercantilist ideals that drove

---

[37] Basil Lubbock, *Barlow's Journal of his Life at Sea in King's Ships, East and West Indiamen and Other Merchantmen from 1659 to 1703* (London: Hurst and Blackett, Ltd., 1934), vol. 1, p. 222.

[38] Jean Gelman Taylor, 'Meditations on a Portrait from Seventeenth-Century Batavia' *Journal of Southeast Asian Studies* 37:1 (2006): 23–41. Further analysis of this portrait and its significance can be found in Chapter 6.

[39] Yu Zhao, 'Huai xiu ya wu: Suzhou zheshan liubai nian (shang)', ('Elegance in the Sleeves: Six Hundred Years of Folding Fans of Suzhou (I))', *Collectors*, vol. 10 (2010): 71–78; Andrew Sofer, *The Stage Life of Props* (Ann Arbor: University of Michigan Press, 2003), pp. 121–127.

European import-substitution when 'imitation was considered to be part of the inventive process'.[40] Mastering the manipulation of shells from distant oceans challenged European artisans to carve, inlay, pierce and sculpt in new media. Their successes were celebrated, as with the out-standing works of Dutch goldsmith Dirck van Rijswijck, whose memor-able mother-of-pearl fans were commemorated in verse, in 1660: 'From now on, one does not have to travel to China, to cross so many seas ... to search for the court of the sun ... full splendour [can be found] in Van Rijswijck's house nearby'. Van Rijswijck fashioned breathtaking objects using shells, including the still-life image on black marble (Figure 4.2). His was a novel iteration of the iconic vase and floral still life, typifying the international commerce of the age. Peonies, tulips and porcelain circulated as global trade goods, along with the shells employed in this picture. This was 'worldly art',[41] attracting streams of sophisticated and prominent buyers from across Europe.[42]

Mother-of-pearl was increasingly treasured and was not unknown in Scotland. John Clerk, a Scottish merchant based in Paris in the mid-seventeenth century, sent a mother-of-pearl item to a wealthy client in Edinburgh.[43] However, such dealings involved a select few, something that would change only gradually. Should we be surprised that Edinburgh Custom officials claimed ignorance of the shells they seized eighty years after Clerk's shipment? Capital cities of Europe hosted innumerable shopkeepers who understood the quality and cost of various goods. But connoisseurship circulated first among skilled confederates and fashionable retailers, who educated discern-ing clients about the best accoutrements for their homes and bodies.[44] By 1700, skilled hands in capital cities transposed shells

[40] Maxine Berg, 'From Imitation to Invention: Creating Commodities in
      Eighteenth-Century Britain' *Economic History Review* 55:1 (2002), p. 2.
[41] The Dutch redefined still-life paintings with the proliferation of the floral genre
      during the Golden Age, celebrating commerce, domesticity and materialism
      with equal vigour. Mariët Westermann, *A Worldly Art: The Dutch Republic
      1585–1718* (New Haven: Yale University Press, 1996); Simon Schama, *The
      Embarrassment of Riches: An Interpretation of Dutch Culture in the Golden
      Age* (Berkeley: University of California Press, 1988).
[42] Daniëlle Kisluk-Grosheide, 'Dirck van Rijswijck (1596–1679), A Master of
      Mother-of-Pearl' *Oud Holland* 111:2 (1997), pp. 77, 84–85.
[43] I thank Ashley Sims for this timely reference.
[44] Ilja Van Damme, 'Middlemen and the Creation of a "Fashion Revolution": The
      Experience of Antwerp in the Late Seventeenth and Eighteenth Centuries' in
      Beverly Lemire, ed., *The Force of Fashion in Politics and Society: Global*

Figure 4.2 Black marble inlaid with engraved mother-of-pearl, in an ebony frame, 1662. Dirck van Rijswijck (1596–1679), Amsterdam. Purchase, The Howard Bayne and Rogers Fund, 1986. 1986.21. Metropolitan Museum of Art, New York.

from their virgin state into everything from fan sticks and jewellery, buttons and boxes, to furniture inlay, knife handles, game boards

Perspectives from Early Modern to Contemporary Times (Aldershot, UK: Ashgate, 2010), pp. 21–40; Jon Stobart, 'Selling (through) Politeness: Advertising Provincial Shops in Eighteenth-Century England' *Cultural and Social History* 5 (2008): 309–328; Natacha Coquery, 'The Semi-Luxury Market, Shopkeepers and Social Diffusion: Marketing Chinoiseries in Eighteenth-Century Paris' in Bruno Blondé, Natacha Coquery, Jon Stobart and Ilya Van Damme, eds., *Fashioning Old and New: Changing Consumer Patterns in Western Europe, 1650–1900* (Turnhout: Brepolis, 2009), pp. 121–132.

and gambling chips.[45] Manufacturers sought out raw materials and judged these on the basis of quality and price, doubtless including smuggled goods in their calculations. Toys and notions, sold to discerning clientele, were then deployed in the poetics of politeness wherein 'good manners, good sense and good nature [were] ... constituent parts'.[46] The task of fashionable retailers and artisans was to provide props for polite performance, or aspirational activities.[47]

Importantly, definitions of tastefulness were not set solely in capital cities, but were conceived as well in provincial settings, with implications for the circulation of goods and knowledge.[48] Stana Nenadic considers the regional tastes in eighteenth-century Glasgow and Edinburgh, where 'custom and the traditions of family associations remained an important force in the construction of patterns of consumption'. Further, she notes that 'the middle-rank appropriation of elite goods in this part of Britain was highly selective, and founded in a cultural agenda that was distinct to the groups concerned'.[49] Perhaps mother-of-pearl held little appeal in this precinct at this time. It took almost six months for Scottish officials to set the final price on their 'parcell of shells'. They reappraised these from a scant £59 in the early

[45] Alden Gordon and Maurice Déchery, 'The Marquis de Marigny's Purchases of English Furniture and Objects' *Furniture History* 25 (1989): 98; Frances Collard, 'A Catalogue of the Furniture in Sir John Soan's Museum' *Furniture History* 44 (2008): 12. For examples, in the collection of the Victoria and Albert Museum, see T.177–1920; T.87–1956; T.365:1, A.2–1922; 2–1995; M.148–1917; 584–1854; Gilbert. 392–2008; 1111–1882; W.22–1962; 1048–1902; 861–1907.

[46] Mr. Addison, *Interesting Anecdotes, Memoirs, Allegories, Essays, and Poetical Fragments, Tending to Amuse the Fancy, and Inculcate Morality*, vol. 8 (London, 1795), p. 58.

[47] Natacha Coquery, 'The Language of Success: Marketing and Distributing Semi-Luxury Goods in Eighteenth-Century Paris' *Journal of Design History* 17:1 (2004): 71–89. On fashionable taste see Amanda Vickery, '"Neat and Not too Showy": Words and Wallpaper in Regency England' in John Styles and Amanda Vickery, eds., *Gender, Taste, and Material Culture in Britain and North America, 1700–1830* (New Haven, CT: Yale University Press, 2006), pp. 201–224; and Hannah Greig, 'Leading the Fashion: The Material Culture of London's *Beau Monde*' in John Styles and Amanda Vickery, eds., *Gender, Taste, and Material Culture in Britain and North America, 1700–1830* (New Haven, CT: Yale University Press, 2006), pp. 293–314.

[48] Helen Berry, 'Promoting Taste in the Provincial Press: National and Local Culture in Eighteenth-Century Newcastle-upon-Tyne' *British Journal for Eighteenth-Century Studies* 25 (2002): 1–17.

[49] Stana Nenadic, 'Middle-Rank Consumers and Domestic Culture in Edinburgh and Glasgow 1720–1840' *Past and Present* 145 (1994): 125.

winter of 1722 for over 14,000 shells to £514 by the spring of 1723, even as hundreds of shells vanished from the bundle. Only when the EIC posted samples to Scotland, with precise rates for each size and quality, were the Edinburgh officials able to account fully for their captured prize.[50]

Smuggling Networks and Negotiations

Price, alone, does not reveal the full significance of these shells. Attempts to recover this freight from the customs warehouse laid bare the smugglers' network. The shells were landed in Kirkcudbright by design, to circumvent the charges assigned by the government and the East India Company. In this case, smugglers planned to move the shells from Kirkcudbright to Edinburgh and then on to London, where there were dealers and artisans aplenty to process them and sell the finished goods. Nameless men at sea managed the initial landing, liaising with a local smuggler, who had allies on shore including the 'collector' of customs in Kirkcudbright plus a London agent. An 'intercepted Letter' revealed the full intrigue. Officials in Edinburgh learned that a local man, R. Lesley, and the unnamed collector of customs in Kirkcudbright were co-conspirators, 'concerned in this Collusive Seizure of the Mother-of-pearl Shells ... and for Running Tea etc Imported from Ostend'.[51]

In many respects this network looks little different from any legal partnership, with men setting contracts and directing goods to appropriate markets. In accordance with Lesley's plan, the smuggled tea was sent to Edinburgh with an agent to follow 'with presents' for their business associates – a China punch bowl and arrack, a South Asian liquor, for a celebratory punch. The shells, on the other hand, were meant for London, where artisans waited to produce low-cost populuxe goods for countless customers.[52] Once the contraband was seized, Lesley had a problem. He began negotiations with the local customs collector, looking for a way to recover the shells, by bribery if necessary. But he needed Gregg, his London partner, for help in these talks. Edward Gregg was well established in the commercial and maritime

---

[50] British Library, IOR/E/1/14/33–34, 98, 100ff.
[51] British Library, IOR/E/1/14/118, 24 June 1723.
[52] The term 'populuxe' was coined by Cissie Fairchilds, meaning a cheaper copy of elite fashionable wares. 'The Production and Marketing of Populuxe Goods in Eighteenth-Century Paris' in John Brewer and Roy Porter, eds., *Consumption and the World of Goods* (London: Routledge, 1993), pp. 228–248.

world of the capital and he was asked to find a place on a merchant ship for the Kirkcudbright collector's son, who needed work. A mutually beneficial solution was agreed: if the smugglers found a place for this young man 'going on a long Voyage', then the grateful father/customs man would return the shells to R. Lesley.[53] The anatomy of this commercial accord became clear.

Smugglers and their allies spanned geography and social rank. By the later 1500s, northern European markets received goods from the Indies through robust smugglers' networks, including the notable French port of La Rochelle. In the 1570s, an English author reported that as 'all the pirates of Fraunce doe discharge here ... You shall have manye thinges of the Indews [Indies] of portingall [Portugal], Better cheape then in portingall'.[54] The foundational relationship between extralegality and 'new luxuries' continued in the following centuries, with actors spanning the gamut from pirates to princelings. Michael Kwass finds clergy and nobles involved in the eighteenth-century French black market.[55] Such social elites, who would offer space to store or distribute smuggled goods, were always fewer in number in extralegal trade than plebeian irregulars. However, the social breadth of those engrossed in this traffic is noteworthy. Storage space proximate to large urban markets was essential for illegal traders, who routinely used inns when offloading their wares. But other options were also available. British customs officials were concerned about 'Foreign Ministers house[s] ... [especially] any Foreign Minister's having protected any Persons concerned in the practice of Smuggling'.[56]

By 'Foreign Minister' they meant diplomats, the distinctive coterie of overseas residents prominent in all major metropoles and renowned for their webs of informants. In 1772, the eye of British officialdom fell on the Count de Haslang, Envoy Extraordinary and Minister Plenipotentiary of His Most Serene Electoral Highness, the Duke of Bavaria. The elderly count had come to Britain in 1739 and was a long-time resident of Golden Square, an address centrally located in the chic West End of London. De Haslang possessed exceptional social connections in diplomatic and

---

[53] British Library, IOR/E/1/14/119.
[54] 'A speciall direction for divers trades of marchaundize to be used for soundrie placis unpon adverticements, as well for the chusing of the time and wares for every of those placis.' Transcribed in Conyers Read, 'English Foreign Trade under Elizabeth' *English Historical Review* 29 (1914), p. 521.
[55] Kwass, *Contraband*, pp. 97–98.
[56] National Archives, UK, T/1/489/116, 10 July 1772.

fashionable circles, was a favourite of George II and a long-time friend of smugglers. His extralegal allies provided vital subventions on which he relied.[57] In turn, de Haslang offered storage space – which he had aplenty, with two houses on Golden Square, a chapel and outbuildings at his disposal – along with his protection.[58] Informants described night-time deliveries whereby 'Nine Horses were unloaded at his Door' in one instance and seven horses unpacked on another, with 'the Avenues to the square ... [being] stopt up to prevent Persons going into it' during the offloading.[59] The Count's housekeeper issued tickets to the cognoscenti to enable genteel purchasers to buy tea at a discount, or to send their servants to shop. He was one of numerous envoys whose position allowed them to move everything from French gloves to tea or mother-of-pearl fans. Horace Walpole commented on the routine venality among diplomats while noting de Haslang's prowess at dancing even at age sixty-five and his capacity to charm. In his private journal Walpole wrote as well that 'Haslang, the Bavarian Minister ... maintained himself for above thirty years by gaming, smuggling, and selling protections against arrests'. Walpole thought it exceptional for European diplomats *not* to smuggle, as 'Ministers of smaller foreign courts, whose pay is scanty, taking advantage of their sacred character, were turned notorious smugglers, and, without paying duties, kept warehouses of contraband commodities'.[60] We may wonder about the contents of these warehouses. Equivalent alliances involving governors and senior colonial officials, and ministers in the Qing court thrived elsewhere, remarkable only in the ubiquity of these pacts.[61]

---

[57] Frederick Teague Cansick, *A Collection of Curious and Interesting Epitaphs ... in the Ancient Church and Burial Grounds of Saint Pancras, Middlesex* (London: J. Russell Smith, 1869), p. 55; Horace Walpole, *The Letters of Horace Walpole, Earl of Orford*, vol. 2, ed. Peter Cunningham (London: William G. Bohn, 1861), p. 426; Horace Walpole, *The Correspondence of Horace Walpole with George Montagu, Esq.* vol 1 (London: Henry Colburn, 1837), p. 333.

[58] F. H. W. Sheppard (General Editor), 'Golden Square Area: Warwick Street' *Survey of London*, vols. 31 and 32: St James Westminster, Part 2, British History Online, www.britishhistory.ac.uk/report.aspx?compid=41468.

[59] National Archives, UK, T/1/489/116, 10 July 1772.

[60] Horace Walpole, *Journal of the Reign of King George the Third, from the Year 1771 to 1783*, ed. Dr Doran, vol. 1 (London: Richard Bentley, 1859), p. 112.

[61] McCarthy, 'Between Policy and Prerogative'; Linda M. Rupert, *Creolization and Contraband: Curaçao in the Early Modern Atlantic World* (Athens, GA: University of Georgia Press, 2012), pp. 4–12, 87–90, 163–211; Karras, 'Custom

The fruits of illicit trade, such as the parcel of shells, extended fashionable pleasures well beyond court circles. This was a malleable material and mother-of-pearl was used judiciously in lower quality wares, decorating the rivet on a fan or otherwise dressing it up with modest touches of a distinctive substance. This ingredient elevated items otherwise made of cheap components, ornaments appealing to plebeian females.[62] A 1746 English-made fan is a case in point. Wood and paper, with a touch of iridescent mother-of-pearl, became a pleasing fitment with the deft labour of artisans. Smuggled shells offered cheaper costs to makers and, ultimately, cheaper prices to buyers. By 1700, the fan trade claimed importance not simply in Spain, France or the Netherlands, but also in England.[63] Little wonder, then, that smugglers laboured to supply this market. English fan makers described their craft as employing 'multitudes of Men, Women and Children in the making', with fixings coming from global sources, whereby they prepared 'abundance of Materials for Fanns, by which there is a great Consumption'.[64] Fans were apparently essential accessories by this date for all manner of women: 'The Worst of Trulls must have their Fann', moaned Daniel Defoe in 1725, in the tone of a misogynistic moralist.[65] Though Defoe deplored this popular female indulgence, it is easy to draw a connection between the trove of shells that landed in Kirkcudbright and the common women who 'must have their Fann'.[66] Cheaper shells allowed cheap and pretty trappings.

Has the Force of Law'; British Library, IOR/E/1/15, 38, Miscellaneous Letters, 1723/4, regarding illicit trade to Barbados; and below.

[62] The cheapest fans seldom survive and were less often collected by major museums. For examples of eighteenth-century European-made folding fans with mother-of-pearl used as rivets, pivots, thumb-guard or as similar minor ingredients in this accessory, see 99.823; 1976.308; 48.1010; 1997.122; 1976.213; 1976.327 at the Museum of Fine Arts Boston.

[63] Nancy Armstrong, *Fans in Spain* (London: Philip Wilson Publisher, 2004), pp. 59–61.

[64] 'The Fann-Makers Grievance, by the Importation of Fanns from the East-Indies' in Beverly Lemire, ed, *The British Cotton Trade*, vol. 1 (London: Pickering and Chatto), p. 135.

[65] Daniel Defoe, 'London Ladies Dressing-Room: Or the Shop-keepers Wives Inventory' in Beverly Lemire, ed, *The British Cotton Trade*, vol. 2 (London: Pickering and Chatto, 2009), p. 264.

[66] Fan-making developed into another of the adopted crafts among European artisans and mother-of-pearl was one of many elements translated by master craftsmen. S. W. A. Drossaers and Th. H. Lunsingh Scheurleer, *Inventory of the Household Effects/Items in the Residences of the Oranges Relating the Pieces*

New-style luxuries and consumables shaped and reshaped habits, industry and social meanings, often leaving only evanescent traces; they were nonetheless part of the 'explosion of commoditization that was at the root of capitalism'.[67] The shadow economy contributed mightily to this genesis. Millions of pounds of tea were illegally landed on British shores and dispersed along extralegal arteries, like Count de Haslang's network. This tea has long since been steeped and sipped, deployed in ceremonies of comfort and politeness. If tea drinking is temporal and the tea itself long degraded, we may think again about the scale and meanings of smuggling when considering historic mother-of-pearl artefacts (Figures 4.1 and 4.2). We cannot know how the makers of these objects acquired their raw materials. But we know that shine and luminescence were vital fashion traits in societies that valued reflection and refraction in a candlelit age.[68] However dazzling these materials, they cannot distract us from the knowledge that 'corruption and the toleration of smuggling' were at the heart of consumer practice in these centuries, at all social levels.[69] Meditation on a mother-of-pearl fan or knife handle, gambling chip or game board, reminds us of the varied players invested in consumption, supplying props for the theatrics of pleasure that filled genteel and commercial calendars.

Cloth[70]

Scholars now focus with increased intensity on the histories of consumption in China itself, including the patterns of fashionable

1567–1795, vol. 1 (1974): 143, 160–162, 182, 187, 190; Vilhelm Slomann, 'The Indian Period of European Furniture – I' *Burlington Magazine* 65:378 (1934): 112–126. For uses of 'pearl' or mother-of-pearl in English trades, see 'Pear – Pekoe tea', Dictionary of Traded Goods and Commodities, 1550–1820 (2007), www.british-history.ac.uk/report.aspx?compid=58837andstrquery= mother+of+pearl, accessed 11 March 2014

[67] Kopytoff, 'The Cultural Biography of Things', p. 72.

[68] An exhibition by Ann Smart Martin explores questions of luminosity and material culture. 'Reflections: Furniture, Silver, and Paintings in Early America', Elvehjern Museum of Art, University of Wisconsin-Madison, 2003 and 'Lustrous Things: Luminosity and Reflection before the Light Bulb' in Anne Gerritsen and Giorgio Riello, eds., *Writing Material Culture History* (London: Bloomsbury Academic, 2015), pp. 157–164.

[69] Karras, *Smuggling*, 124.

[70] The term 'cloth' refers to wool fabrics in this time period. Wool fabrics may include both heavy goods and the range of new lighter fabrics made of worsted thread – long-staple wool, finer and more tightly spun – sometimes mixed with

consumerism in the Ming and Qing that energized long-distance trade.[71] Antonia Finnane recently observed that in the study of consumerism, 'there is a marked imbalance between the bodies of relevant empirical research available in China and the West'.[72] Yet, despite the disparity, historians can demonstrate the material dynamism of urban China from the late Ming era through the Qing. These regimes were notable for 'extravagant dress and rapid change in fashion, wide distribution of specialized food products, and the consumption of food, rice wine and tea in restaurants and tea shops [as] a vital part of social life'.[73] The seagoing cargoes passing through Chinese ports, plus the Chinese commercial networks in Southeast Asia, represented important material vitality where custom and creativity contended.[74] Ming

other threads such as silk or linen to produce more fashionable wares. Worsted wool textiles became the most popular cloth in Qing markets.

[71] Among the most influential English language works in this field are Craig Clunas, 'The Art of Social Climbing in Sixteenth-Century China' *Burlington Magazine* 133 1059 (1991): 368–375, *Superfluous Things: Material Culture and Social Status in Early Modern China* (Cambridge: Polity Press, 1991) and 'Things in Between: Splendour and Excess in Ming China' in Frank Trentmann, ed., *The Oxford Handbook of the History of Consumption* (Oxford: Oxford University Press, 2012), pp. 47–63; Timothy Brook, *The Confusions of Pleasure: Commerce and Culture in Ming China* (Berkeley: University of California Press, 1998); and more recently Sarah Dauncey, 'Illusions of Grandeur: Perceptions of Status and Wealth in Late-Ming Female Clothing and Ornamentation' *East Asian History* 25/26 (2003): 43–68 and 'Sartorial Modesty and Genteel Ideals in the late Ming' in Daria Berg and Chloe Starr, eds., *The Quest for Gentility in China: Negotiations Beyond Gender and Class* (London: Routledge, 2007), pp. 134–154; Antonia Finnane, *Changing Clothes in China: Fashion, History, Nation* (New York: Columbia University Press, 2008); Jin-min Fan, 'Suzhou with Its Style and Mode as a Fashion Leader in the Ming and Qing Dynasties', ('"Suyang", "Suyi"': Ming Qing Suzhou ling chaoliu') *Journal of Nanjing University (Philosophy, Humanities and Social Sciences)* 4 (2013): 123–141; Wu Jen-shu, *Pinwei shehua: wanming de xiaofei shehui yu shi dafu (Taste and Extravagance: Late Ming Consumer Society and the Gentry)*, (Beijing: Zhonghua Book Company, 2008); Rachel Silberstein, 'Eight Scenes of Suzhou: Landscape Embroidery and Urban Courtesans in Nineteenth-Century China' *Late Imperial China* 36:1 (2015): 1–52.

[72] Antonia Finnane, 'Chinese Domestic Interiors and "Consumer Constraint" in Qing China: Evidence from Yangzhou' *Journal of the Economic and Social History of the Orient* 57 (2014), p. 128.

[73] John E. Wills Jr. 'European Consumption and Asian Production in the Seventeenth and Eighteenth Centuries' in John Brewer and Roy Porter, eds., *Consumption and the World of Goods* (London: Routledge, 1993), p. 134.

[74] Yangwen Zheng, *China on the Sea: How the Maritime World Shaped Modern China* (Leiden: Brill, 2012); Craig Lockard, '"The Sea Common to All": Maritime Frontiers, Port Cities, and Chinese Traders in the Southeast Asian Age

officials noted that 'powerful families traded overseas with large ships. Scoundrels secretly profited from it'.[75] Despite the equivocal response of officials in Beijing, Chinese demand for goods created a dense mesh of commercial links. The history of global trade reveals contacts and alliances, competition and conciliation, as well as subversion and subterfuge. An English vessel carrying various wool fabrics as well as cotton, pepper and ivory attempted a commercial venture to Taiwan in 1675. Well received by local merchants, the English left several agents in Taiwan to assess local commerce; Dutch competitors quickly captured these men.[76] Imperial politics shaped the context of commercial adventures. European trading companies worked to secure an agreed presence in the port of Canton, from the late 1680s, becoming routinized in the 1700s, adding new elements to an environment celebrated for material plenty.[77] These connections offered ample opportunity for extralegal coalitions serving China's urban middle ranks and elites. One commodity that gained increased attention in Qing China was wool cloth.

In this section I examine a counterflow commodity set amidst the main East-to-West currents of Eurasian commodity exchange. It was long acknowledged that Europe had a seemingly boundless appetite for Asian wares that drove oceanic trade after 1500, while Asian polities were largely indifferent to most European manufactures. However, European-made wool fabrics eventually developed a niche appeal among the urbane shoppers in China. This mode marked a new cosmopolitan style that did not rely on the development of new habits, as with tobacco. Rather, imported wool fabrics further animated the fashion markets in eastern Chinese cities. The flourishing extralegal trade that ensued relied on the conjunction of three elements: first, the developing fashion for worsted cloth; next, a robust transnational

of Commerce, *ca.* 1400–1750' *Journal of World History* 21:2 (2010): 219–247; Leonard Blussé, 'Chinese Century. The Eighteenth Century in the China Sea Region' *Archipel* 58 (1999): 107–129; Reid, 'An 'Age of Commerce' in Southeast Asian History'.

[75] Lockard, 'The Sea Common to All', p. 225.
[76] Yoneo Ishii, ed., *The Junk Trade from Southeast Asia: Translations from the Tôsen fusetsu-gaki, 1674–1723*, (Singapore: Institute of Southeast Asian Studies, 1998), pp. 197–198.
[77] Leonard Blussé, *Visible Cities: Canton, Nagasaki, and Batavia and the Coming of the Americas* (Cambridge, MA: Harvard University Press, 2008), pp. 50–55; Van Dyke, *Merchants of Canton and Macao*.

fraternity of black marketeers; and, finally, enterprising individuals feeding worsted cloth through extralegal channels. This is the scenario I explore. Extralegal traffic provided Chinese clients with more and perhaps cheaper fabrics that they now desired.

Nicholas Thomas observes that 'objects were not what they were made to be but what they have become'.[78] This statement is particularly true in cross-cultural exchange. Lighter, worsted wool cloth intended for European suiting, genteel gowns or curtaining became something else when received in China, a fashionable exotic valued by sophisticates. Their esteem for these fabrics explains the attention it received from smugglers. A highly politicized commodity in Britain, EIC merchants long despaired of marketing this stuff in India and their failure led to heated invectives and laws to end the importation of Asian textiles in Britain – all to protect native woollen and worsted manufacturing. But, if attempts to vend woollen cloth in India yielded little, trade with China held promise.

British merchants were not the only ones attempting to sell wool fabric to this significant, demanding set of buyers. Once the fad became known, every commercial player from Europe worked to augment their trade as and when they could. However, the introduction of worsted wool fabrics to China was a gradual process requiring education and calculation among Chinese merchants and consumers, with many intermediaries involved. In 1683, Dutch VOC ships were reportedly headed to a coastal port near Shanghai, with cargo including 'large amounts of woollen cloth, camphor, pepper, sappanwood and other things', with the intent to trade with 'the Great Qing', according to Chinese informants in Nagasaki.[79] A few years later in 1685, English EIC agents gave a full piece of violet-coloured worsted cloth as a gift to 'the Chief Mandarin', to demonstrate the fine dyeing and finishing of these goods and encourage a taste for this fabric.[80] In time, worsteds like camlet became a prominent import in China, a fine, lustrous fabric, figured on the surface with a hot press; and calamancos, a glossy

---

[78] Nicholas Thomas, *Entangled Objects: Exchange, Material Culture, and Colonialism in the Pacific* (Cambridge, MA: Harvard University Press, 1991), p. 4.

[79] Ishii, *Junk Trade from Southeast Asia*, p. 206.

[80] British Library, IOR/G/12/16, China Factory Records, Supercargoes (Ship's) Diary, China Merchant, 1685, p. 227 v. The wool cloths discussed here were among worsted fabrics discussed in note 70 above. See Chapter 2 of this volume for further discussion.

worsted textile with a patterned face, were also favoured. Both were redolent of silk but outside the sumptuary constraints assigned those fabrics. Chinese aesthetic tradition favoured textiles with a gleaming burnished surface and European worsted fabrics offered this indulgence with less cost or concern associated with exquisite silks.[81] In 1719, 300 pieces of calamanco and twenty-five of camlet were dispatched to Canton, as several EIC Directors believed 'they may sell well ... [and] Money may be got by them'. This was still a speculative venture; but these merchants hoped they would learn by this 'the real worth of our Woollen Goods in the Chineeses opinion'.[82]

The Chinese approved these goods and the timing was auspicious. Many Chinese cities were replete with aspiring men and women: "the lower elite and relatively wealthy but non-elite merchant and artisan families' that closeted around southern cities'.[83] Courtesans were another set of important consumers, for though they were officially marginalized, some were very well connected and highly influential in setting fashions. They joined with those seeking out more innovative and attractive commodities, with artisans pushed to produce endless novelties at manageable prices. The commoditization of consumer products is one of the key attributes of the Chinese market at this time. Cities like Suzhou, on the Yangtze River Delta west of Shanghai, were renowned for the exquisite style of their goods and the elegance of their distinguished citizens.[84] Wool cloth arrived at a point when cultured buyers had multiple aspirations. They looked for new-style materials to express a fashionable sensibility and hoped to fit themselves for a winter climate in goods of note. Sumptuary restrictions seemed to be an equivocal issue, sliding to the back of mind until brought to the fore. Patterned, glossy and brightly dyed worsted wool fabrics met all concerns.

Worsteds were employed with increasing frequency in a variety of furnishings and apparel, from the court at Beijing to the cities of

---

[81] I note Rachel Silberstein's observation on the tradition of fabric made from peacock feathers, a storied commodity, commemorated in a major literary text. Also, Paulo Zamperini, 'For the Love of a Peacock: Affect and Fashion in Late Imperial Chinese Fiction', unpublished paper presented at the conference 'Dressing Global Bodies', University of Alberta, Edmonton, July 2016.

[82] British Library, IOR/E/3/100, p. 34 – Directors to the supercargoes of the Carnarvon, 1719.

[83] Silberstein, 'Eight Scenes of Suzhou', p. 3.

[84] Silberstein, 'Eight Scenes of Suzhou', p. 23.

Suzhou, Yangzhou and beyond. By the mid-eighteenth century, there was a highly competitive market for these fabrics, evident in the complaints by a British supercargo on the late arrival of his EIC vessel in Canton: 'we found (our arrival here being so very late) the [Chinese] Merch.ts had already bought great quantities of Woollen goods and India Commoditys br[ough]t By Forreign Ships, as well as there being a great quantity in private Trade, which we believe they would have given [a better price to us] had we arrived earlier in the Season'.[85] The fact that European officers carried worsted textiles as private trade confirms its recognized profitability, for these men were wholly committed to their personal advancement. Wool cloth of this type remained a major commodity carried by the Dutch to Canton, with the VOC purchasing between 50 and 100 per cent of Leiden's output after 1742.[86] The Dutch and British competed fiercely for advantage, with the British claiming superior finishing techniques and the Dutch cheaper and more effective dyeing. In 1750, an EIC supercargo noted the Chinese preference for 'a piece of Dutch Stuff very like our Hairbine, but better manufactured'. But he also remarked on the success of certain English calamancos: 'The Striped and Flow'd one were greatly liked ... [and] the flowered with Stripes, but the former they gave the preference to greatly, desiring that what should come in future might be all of that Sort'.[87] The Chinese market was a prize worth winning.

The 1763 sample book of striped and figured calamancos from an English worsted manufacturer in Norwich suggests some of the many colours and patterns available (Plate 4.2). A contemporary noted that in the mid to late Qing era 'all tastes in clothing are determined by the brothels' and courtesans'', which self-advertising included innovative coloured clothing: 'brightly shaded woolen fabrics and printed cottons, subverting traditional color associations like marital red'.[88] The colours and patterns pushed the boundaries of style. When Chinese

---

[85] British Library, IOR/G/12/53, China Factory Records, Supercargoes (Ship's) Diary, Grantham and York, 1750, p. 64.

[86] Yong Liu, *The Dutch East India Company's Tea Trade with China, 1757–1781* (Leiden: Brill, 2007), pp. xix–xx, 37–38.

[87] David Ormrod, *The Rise of Commercial Empires: England and the Netherlands in the Age of Mercantilism, 1650–1770* (Cambridge: Cambridge University Press, 2003), pp. 111–121. British Library, IOR/G/12/54, Ship's Diary, 27 September 1750, p. 28.

[88] Quoted in Silberstein, 'Eight Scenes of Suzhou', p. 34.

consumers wore these goods they demonstrated sophisticated knowledge of foreign commodities and proved their access to these wares. Beijing elites and court officials also employed a growing range of wool fabrics for clothing and accessories, a fashion that spread into the 1800s.[89] He Shen, the Qianlong emperor's favourite minister and a notoriously corrupt official, amassed vast stocks of the most desirable merchandise for his personal use, for gifts and judicious exchange. In 1799, at the time of his fall from grace with the arrival of a new emperor, He's private warehouses were crammed with foreign commodities including over 1,800 bolts of selected wool fabrics.[90]

Retailers and embroiderers laboured to produce the range of goods demanded by their clientele, including embroidered clothing and accessories. The immense number of female embroiderers residing outside Suzhou supplied urban retailers with myriad accessories, garments and furnishings.[91] The application of embroidery to wool cloth combined two fashionable elements, evidence of which survives in museum collections (Plates 4.3 and 4.4). The embellished parts of the garment pieces in Plate 4.3 reveal the processes of manufacture, with embroidery applied separately to individual parts. The Victoria and Albert Museum holds four comparable examples, all constructed of dark blue wool cloth, all embroidered with like motifs. These artefacts raise the curtain on a workshop scene where shopkeeper and workers prepared multiple garments for fashion conscious shoppers out of stocks of imported cloth – or where a merchant collects embroidered goods completed by rural women.[92] Another example survives in a nineteenth-century skirt panel of vivid yellow wool broadcloth, heavily overlain with an embroidered naturalist landscape (Plate 4.4). The subversive colour choice in the broadcloth confirms fashionable incursions into formerly privileged material culture, as this colour was intended for the imperial family alone. It was now worn by

[89] Huimin Lai, 'Exotic Commodities and Banner People's Daily Life in Beijing during Qianlong and Jiaqing Reign (1735–1820)' ('Qian Jia shidai Beijing de yanghuo yu qiren richang shenghuo') in Wu Jen-shu, Paul Katz, and Lin May-li, eds., *Cong chengshi kan zhongguo de xiandai xing (The City and Chinese Modernity)* (Taipei: Institute of Modern History, Academia Sinica, 2010), pp. 1–35

[90] Zheng, *China on the Sea*, pp. 235–236.

[91] Silberstein, 'Eight Scenes of Suzhou', p. 23.

[92] T.150–1948; T.150A-1948; T.150B-1948; T.150C-1948, Victoria and Albert Museum, London.

adventurous urbanites using imported wool cloth to best advantage. The weight and drape of these clothes fit the calculus of appearance articulated by Zhou Sheng in the 1840s: 'Undergarments should be soft ... [and] outer garments should be hard, as they define the shape of the body'.[93] Wool broadcloth, camlet and calamancos offered new means to decorate and delimit the body. This review of Qing fashion sets the scene for the smuggling that helped buoy this style. Once market certainty was established for specific goods – like wool cloth in China – the benefits of extralegal trade became more evident, encouraging a plethora of inventive supply chains that evaded taxes and duties. When appetites are strong, stores would be sought from those happy to deal outside approved channels, initiating supplementary conduits of supply with perhaps lower prices for eager consumers.

Asian Smuggling Networks and Extralegal Channels

During the eighteenth and nineteenth centuries wool fabrics entered the established smuggling networks that knit together Eurasian commerce. The seas and oceans abutting the eastern coast of Asia sustained an array of extralegal players, balancing regional opportunities. The demand for Chinese silk thread and fabric in Japan (and Japanese copper in China), for example, encouraged creative commercial practices among Chinese, Japanese and Dutch merchants and mariners, regularly sidestepping the Tokugawa regulatory apparatus. The granting of monopolies to prominent Japanese traders emboldened unsanctioned Japanese competitors, despite the capital punishment promised those convicted of crimes.[94] As in other world precincts, some of the wealthiest merchants in Nagasaki directed extensive smuggling ventures, partnering with foreign operatives. Their pacts followed the dictates of local and distant markets, employing wily strategies as required.[95]

The Pearl River Delta was embedded in the same extralegal culture. As Robert Antony explains, 'the entire Pearl River delta ... encompassed a single huge trading system that involved Western trade at Macao and Canton, as well as coastal and Southeast Asian junk trade. ... the vast shadow economy of pirates, smugglers, and Triads had fully

[93] Quotes in Finnane, *Changing Clothes in China*, pp. 63–64.
[94] John E. Wills, *1688: A Global History* (New York: W. W. Norton and Co., 2001), pp. 156–157.
[95] Notehelfer, 'Notes on Kyoho Smuggling', pp. 1–32.

integrated into the regular legitimate economy'.[96] Coalitions evolved, with Europeans added to the mix of commercial and nautical men. The Portuguese colony of Macao, on the southern mouth of the Pearl River, was a lading site for Portuguese vessels, as was Whampoa for other European ships on the north. Once anchored, cargo and ships' officers travelled up the Pearl River to the company factories in Canton (Guangzhou). Macao and Whampoa were the two most active smuggling sites, from which goods were moved to Canton. Collusion was routine, ensuring mutual profit.[97] At the same time, regulations intended to regiment the mechanics of trade were issued on all sides, beginning with the court at Beijing and administered locally by the emperor's appointed supervisor of trade and customs, who was termed 'the Hoppo' by Europeans. The opening excerpt exemplifies the intended authority of the imperial representative and the lawless forces he faced. Every European trading company delivered lists of rules to their employees, trying to limit planned or improvised misadventures that might imperil company standing. Distant officials back in Europe feared angering Chinese authorities and losing privileges; they equally dreaded the rapaciousness of the men they employed. The EIC issued 'strict' orders time and again: 'We positively forbid you, the Captain and all the Officers and Ship's Company running [smuggling] any Goods whatsoever'.[98] Extralegal enterprise was ubiquitous and took many forms: random pilferage; organized pilferage; small-scale smuggling to and from Asia; and large-scale, coordinated and systematic extralegal commerce.[99]

As Europeans over-wintered or returned seasonally to Macau, Whampoa and Canton, liaisons and business relationships were struck, providing the social context for inventive gambits. The portrayal of river traffic and shore-based buildings and pedestrians captures the proximity of commercial actors in Canton, Europeans and Chinese of every rank (Figure 4.3); this closeness among all parties was intensified on waterways that were less easily policed. One of the commonest ploys was for officers of European merchant companies to smuggle

[96] Antony, *Elusive Pirates, Pervasive Smugglers,* p. 111.
[97] Van Dyke, *Merchants of Canton and Macao,* pp. 15–16, 28–29.
[98] British Library, IOR/E/3/106, Miscellaneous Letter Book 1733–1736, p. 6.
[99] Van Dyke, *Merchants of Canton and Macao,* pp. 28–29, 125. Yoneo Ishii speculates on the prevalence of smuggling into Nagasaki and environs by Chinese junks, but determines the scope of any such traffic may be unknowable. *Junk Trade from Southeast,* note 36, p. 226.

Figure 4.3 *Fort Opposite the Factory*, Canton, 1793. William Alexander (1767–1816), British. Yale Center for British Art, Paul Mellon Collection.

goods upriver claiming their chests held personal belongings, as Chinese customs officials did not inspect such luggage. Despite regulations to the contrary, this trick was widely practiced by officers, who would then pass on their stocks of wool and other goods to Chinese intermediaries. Pilferage of official cargoes heading up river was another risk and wool cloth was notable among the pilfered wares. To prevent such felonies required that 'the most trusty Men of the Ships Crew ... watch the Goods'. Officers were urged to check that 'there [was] no communication between the Cabin where the Chinese live [on board the boat], and that part of the Vessel where the Goods are stowed'.[100] Repeated directions from supercargoes to ships' officers suggest the opportunities in play and the insubordination at work: 'you are required to send up to Canton all the Bales of Woollen Goods, and

---

[100] British Library, IOR/E/3/106, Letter Book 1733–36, p. 97; similarly, IOR/G/ 12/57, China Factory Records, Supercargoes (Ship's) Diary, Royal Duke, 1753, p. 22.

the Lead which you have on board – and that you will order some trusty Persons to come in each Boat to prevent pilferage'.[101] 'Roguerys' on the Pearl River were deplored by EIC directors, who knew well that 'great Frauds have been Committed in the Boats which they lay along side the Ships in Canton River occasioned by the Seamens deserting from them in the Night whereby the Chinese have Opportunityes to Pilfer Goods out the Chests'.[102] Wool cloth seemed to evaporate from the heaps of cargo, despite all precautions. Thievery required cross-cultural connivance from shore-based allies able to pass along secreted goods. Supercargoes feared this collusion and demanded seamen keep 'the doors in the sterns of the Boats … fixed with Tape, or Paper and sealed', with no contact allowed within the vessel or with the shoreline. Guards were tasked to enforce this order. Sleep at inopportune moments was also proscribed.[103] These scenarios were ripe with potential for malfeasance.

Coalitions ensued between Chinese boatmen and shore-based traders, as well as between European and Chinese partners. Language facility was rarely a barrier to communication, as noted by the English mariner Edward Barlow, who spent months in China in 1671 and again in the 1680s, 'an indifferent cold climate' in winter. Barlow kept careful note of all of the commodities on offer when 'the China people came on board with commodities to sell' and plotted ways he could profit even as a humble seaman. He planned that on his return trip to China, 'if I carried a small venture in some sort of goods I might gain a little money by it'.[104] European sailors had regular interactions with Chinese stall keepers on the quay as well as vendors on Danes Island, an area set aside for their recreation. Mariners were entrepreneurial by nature, learning the value of trade first-hand, and could arrange their own introductions to resident dealers keen to take any oddments offered them.[105] In this way, parcels of wool cloth slipped into the vast markets of Canton. Large-scale extralegal shipments required greater capital and

---

[101] British Library, IOR/G/12/55, China Factory Records, Supercargoes (Ship's) Diary, Essex and Caesar, 1751, p. 9.
[102] British Library, IOR/E/1/206, Miscellaneous Letters, 1746.
[103] British Library, IOR/G/55, China Factory Records, Supercargoes (Ship's) Diary, Essex and Caesar, 1751, p. 17.
[104] Lubbock, *Barlow's Journal*, vol. 1, pp. 204–221, vol. 2, pp. 394–397.
[105] British Library, IOR/G/12/60, Letter Book, 1777, p. 5, Letter 26. For discussion of sailors' attachment to private trade and smuggling, see Lemire, 'Men of the World'.

capacity. The packages and bales handled by poor boatmen and mariners contrast with the smoothly devised plots that moved cloth by the ton along extralegal circuits.[106]

One important strategy was to stow goods unlawfully on EIC ships sailing from Europe to Asia. Extralegal carriage of wool cloth began early in the 1700s, as the commercial possibility of this commodity became clear. In 1715, an EIC surveyor in London sent a note to the Court of Directors in the middle of his search of a vessel, telling of his discoveries: 'found in the shipes hold and bredroum [bread room] 34 small Bailes of Cloth and we do believe ther is mor onder the bred: ... we opened two of them one Is Red and one is blue'.[107] By the mid-1700s, 'Woollen Goods' were among the most popular articles concealed on Asia-bound ships as mariners of all ranks schemed to profit from this fad.[108] Industrious players hid bales, boxes and parcels on board the craft, like Third Mate Thomas Powney, who 'Clandestinely Shipt [wool] Cloth and Lead on board' and lost his position when discovered. The chief mate on the Carnarvon likewise attempted to carry 'One Bale and two small Boxes of Cloth', and his deception was undone.[109] Larger illicit ventures involved the meeting of ships far from watching eyes, either off the coast of Europe, or in the Canary Islands, Madeira or the Cape Verde Islands. This was a cat and mouse game played on a global scale, relying on luck as well as careful planning. European companies often forbade their crewmen from private trade in the most desirable goods, like wool cloth. But crew risked their jobs to conduct this trade, even as officials policed their actions.

In 1758, EIC bureaucrats noted that one of their vessels stopped at Pondicherry, a French colonial settlement on the east coast of India, and picked up 120 pieces of scarlet wool cloth 'consigned to a French Gentleman at Canton'. An edict was issued as a consequence, stating that 'If any of our own Servants shall appear to be concerned in a Trade of this Clandestine nature they may depend upon incurring our highest displeasure'.[110] Corporations relied on informants and quizzed ship

---

[106] British Library, IOR/G/12/60, Letter Book, 1777, Letter 26.

[107] British Library, IOR/E/1/6/125b, Miscellaneous Letters, 16 November 1715.

[108] British Library, IOR/E/4/618 Correspondence with India, 1765, p. 75. Cloth is the common term used for wool goods in this time period.

[109] British Library, IOR/E/1/206, Miscellaneous Letters, 1746, pp. 56; E/4/618, Correspondence with India, 1765, p. 79.

[110] British Library, IOR/E/4/862, Correspondence with India 1759–1763, pp. 20–21; IOR/E/1/206, Miscellaneous Letters, 1746, pp. 79–80.

passengers or others who happened upon suspicious vessels. A 'Secret Committee' was established by the Court of Directors to address this mercantile threat. The occasional discovery of offenders illuminates the high resolve of extralegal traders with the greatest opportunity for gain.[111] In February 1766, EIC authorities in London reported to Fort William, Calcutta, on another large-scale smuggling scheme.

We are now to acquaint you that having received certain Information that very large Quantities of Unlicensed Goods had been put aboard the Ships Anson and London in Madeira Road in their late Voyages, Upon their return We entered into a strict Examination as to the truth thereof, And although for some time the Captains and Officers absolutely denied their Concern in or knowledge of any such unlicensed Trade, at last Cap. Edward Lord Chick of the said Ship Anson, and Capt. John Webb of the London owned to us that they had taken in at Madeira … a Large Quantity of Lead, Iron, Cannon Shot and Copper amounting to the Sum of £1164. … also Cloth and Long Ells [wool cloth] amounting together to £6859.10.[112]

Mariners in major Atlantic ports were periodically interrogated about the illicit carriage of cargo, and some confirmed the wholesale lading of goods on to Asia-bound EIC vessels. Such was the case for the ship Pigot, captained by George Richardson. About thirty-five bales 'believed to be Cloth' were seen being loaded on the Pigot in the port of Tenerife, destined for Canton. London instructed its administrators in India to cross-examine and discharge Richardson and another suspect captain, 'which we look upon in the same aggravating light'. The authorities ultimately accepted Richardson's smooth denial of the suspect 'bales' and the severe reprimand he received left him free to sin again, should chance allow.[113]

Unlucky men, including captains and other officers, were dismissed from the company's service when their entrepreneurial infractions were confirmed; such was the fate of Captain Richard Lewin, who arranged to carry 'Military Stores, Cloth and other Illicit Articles' on his eastward voyage. In these ambitious schemes, partner vessels set off intending to meet up with the Asia-bound East Indiaman at a rendezvous. When the ships met the extralegal merchandise was loaded on the EIC

---

[111] Bowen, 'So Alarming an Evil'.
[112] British Library, IOR/E/1/618, Correspondence with India, p. 181.
[113] British Library, IOR/E/1/618, Correspondence with India, pp. 311–312, 893; IOR/E/1/618, Correspondence with India, 1765, p. 80.

ship on the captains' orders. The large investments in goods and the hiring of sloops, mimicked the care and capital devoted to sanctioned trade.[114] Some of these stores might be covertly offloaded on the Indian coast, as illicit networks were fully developed there as well. In all cases, a robust black market economy was ready to receive the goods at the Pearl River Delta and shunt them to the fashion markets of China.[115]

Handling wool cloth did not carry the risks of trading in more dangerous illicit commodities and the influx of extralegal stores of cloth continued to feed the vogue in China.[116] There is abundant evidence of the fashion driving these shipments; the routes taken by these fabrics are more opaque. Every discovery of smuggled worsted cloth marks a point in the wider geography of commerce. These textiles were a staple of global commercial circuits (legal and extralegal). Details of these money-making partnerships are rarely revealed, as with the shell smugglers discussed above. But the anatomy of this traffic is clear. We can also be sure of their diligent intent to disperse these attractive materials within dynamic Chinese markets, materials ready to be cut, embroidered and tailored as required. Modish urbanites enjoyed less costly garment as a result of this illicit flow. This veiled feature of global trade was an essential facet of the commercial and consumer practice that defined the age.

Pepper

Scavenging Coasts and Harbours: Custom, Enterprise and Regulation

My last case study explores the material politics of coastal scavenging or 'wrecking' and its affiliated practices. These have a long and inglorious history, notable for their noisome and dangerous traits. This was another measure of the globalizing age. No source of

---

[114] British Library, IOR/E/4/618 Correspondence with India, 1765, pp. 75–77, 79–81; IOR/E/4/621 Correspondence with Fort William, 1772, p. 323. For Dutch instances of this and other practices, see Japp. R. Bruijn, *Commanders of Dutch East India Ships in the Eighteenth Century,* translated by R. L. Robson-McKillop and R. W. Unger (Woodbridge, UK: Boydell Press, 2011), especially Chapters 11 and 12.

[115] British Library, IOR/E/4/616 Correspondence with Fort William, 1755, pp. 361–362, 857–858; IOR/E/4/618 Correspondence with Fort William, 1765, pp. 75–79.

[116] British Library, IOR/E/1/71/3, Miscellaneous Letters, 8 July 1782.

material wealth was more varied and no results more capricious than the scavenging of shipwrecks. Yet, this harvest was more and more routinized. The heightened number of passages and greater numbers of ships at sea brought more vessels crashing to shore due to storms, poor seamanship and ill fortune. The recurring calamities documented from the 1500s spawned new literary and artistic genres, highlighting the terror, pity and possibilities of such events. Chronicles of these disasters emerged as a powerful genre of the age, with scenes of fatal wrecks and the pitiless waves presented by writers and artists.[117] The dreaded prospect of ships wrecked on rocky shores was matched by the pathos of mariners marooned for years. Within this maritime culture, people proximate to sea routes learned the value of scanning the coast during and after a storm to see what washed up.[118] These harvests were uncertain and only a fraction of worldwide trade. Yet they became consistent enough to justify close attention to coastlines and passing vessels. In Southeast Asian waters, 'salvage, even sabotage, by island and coastal dwellers along all the sea lanes important to European trade was very common. Shipwrecks provided welcome windfalls'.[119]

Wrecks preoccupied travellers and bureaucrats and appear in many memoirs including that of the Portuguese diplomat Tomé Pires. He recounted the fate of a Portuguese ship lost in 1512 on the coast of Sumatra, where a leader of that country 'recovered everything water could not spoil, wherefore they say he is very rich. ... No one lives on

---

[117] For the new genre of Portuguese shipwreck narratives, see James Duffy, *Shipwreck and Empire: Being an Account of Portuguese Maritime Disasters In a Century of Decline* (Cambridge, MA: Harvard University Press, 1955); also for Spain: William J. McCarthy, 'A Spectacle of Misfortune: Wreck, Salvage and Loss in the Spanish Pacific' *The Great Circle* 17:2 (1995): 95–108. Among the many other tales of shipwreck, see Daniel Defoe, *The Life and Strange Surprizing Adventures of Robinson Crusoe of York, Mariner ...* (London, 1719); Pierre Vlaud and Elizabeth Friffith, *The Shipwreck and Adventures of Monsieur Pierre Vlaud, a Native of Bordeaux, and Captain of a Ship ...* (London: T. Davies, 1771); *Shipwrecks and Disasters at Sea; Or Historical Narratives of the Most Notable Calamities ...* (Edinburgh: George Ramsey and Co, 1812). Museum collections are replete with painting, prints and ceramics depicting shipwrecks of various sorts, including the Rijksmuseum, the British Museum, the National Maritime Museum and the Museum of Fine Arts, Boston, commemorating disasters on the world's oceans.

[118] The wreck of the York in the River Shannon, Ireland is recorded in British Library, IOR/E/4/861, p. 991, among the many records of EIC ships lost.

[119] McCarthy, 'A Spectacle of Misfortune', p. 98.

the coast except watches to see who goes by'.[120] A Spanish Jesuit, Adriano de Las Cortes, wrote of his fearsome journey in the winter of 1625 between Macao and Manila, during which his ship grounded on the coast of China. Local fishermen claimed jewellery from survivors, plus the chests and barrels driven on shore. They were determined foragers, collecting whatever came to hand.[121] A British sailor in the 1720s, shipwrecked on Madagascar, complained of the treatment by locals who used the lead 'procur'd from the Wreck of our Ship'. Perhaps they considered this their due, as these same people risked their lives to pull storm-tossed wretches from the crashing surf.[122] Figure 4.4 offers a fictionalize scenario of the survivors stranded on the coast of Africa circa 1814, with notable assistance provided by the men and women on shore. The earlier 1720s ship was laden with goods from Bengal, and the excitement of the event drew two or three hundred people to the beach 'picking up Pieces of Silk and fine Callico', a common response to such events.[123] Locals offered assistance, but also collected whatever they could – the contents of most commercial vessels were well known to Malagasy people, who had been long invested in the Indian Ocean trading system.[124]

Tokugawa Japan was intentionally buffered from foreign influences by imperial policy, with regulations directing the ports and places where foreigners could anchor. But, imperial dictates could not direct the wind and waves and the ships driven at their will. As global shipping expanded, the oceans that encircled the island empire carried myriad ships ashore in whole or in part, bringing provincial Japanese villagers in touch with foreign people and products. An estimated

[120] Quoted in McCarthy, 'A Spectacle of Misfortune', p. 98. See also Rhys Richards, 'A "Lost Galleon?" The Spanish Wreck at Taumako' *The Journal of Pacific History* 34:1 (1999): 123–128.

[121] Timothy Brook, *Vermeer's Hat: The Seventeenth Century and the Dawn of the Global World* (London: Profile Books Ltd., 2008), pp. 87–94. A large 2,000-ton Manila-built vessel on the Manila-Acapulco run, *Nuestra Senora de la Concepcion*, laden with silks, furnishings, porcelain, spices and lacquer ware, went aground on an island in the Northern Marianas, the cargo scattered on the sands. Shirley Fish, *The Manila-Acapulco Galleons: The Treasure Ships of the Pacific* (Central Milton Keynes: AuthorHouse, 2011), pp. 3–4.

[122] *Madagascar: or, Robert Drury's Journal, during Fifteen Years Captivity on That Island. ... Written by Himself ...* (London, 1729), pp. 12–13.

[123] *Madagascar: or, Robert Drury's Journal*, p. 14.

[124] *Madagascar: or, Robert Drury's Journal*, pp. 263, 27; British Library, IOR/G/12/53, pp. 4–5, 7.

Figure 4.4 *African Hospitality.* John Raphael Smith (1751–1812), after George Morland (1763–1804). RP-P-1969–82. Rijksmuseum, Amsterdam.

1,500 shipwrecks foundered on Japan's coastline during the Tokugawa era, a number likely to rise as scholars continue their search through local archives. Spanish, Chinese, Ryukyuan, Korean, Dutch and Russian ships are counted in this list. And while regulations prohibited local and foreign interactions in the provinces, these contacts occurred as a matter of course. One accidental encounter swept 'a wooden chest . . . filled with Chinese goods, including a mirror, coins, a fan and paper' onto the shore of the southern Japanese Island of Tosa. All these items were commoditized goods, common cargo or part of personal luggage with market origins. Strange buttons and handkerchiefs found their way onshore in the early 1800s, evidence of interactions with passing whalers. Luke Roberts concludes that 'finding such flotsam was common enough for Tosa fishermen and coastal villagers, and it is easy to imagine that many objects of value escaped being reported at all'.[125] Maritime wreckage of all sorts was prized across cultures and these providential discoveries became more common across this era.

[125] Luke S. Roberts, 'Shipwrecks and Flotsam: The Foreign World in Edo-Period Tosa' *Monumenta Nipponica* 70:1 (2015), p. 111.

From the China Seas to the African coastlines, spoils were hotly defended as the property of coastal rulers and residents. Shoals, currents, rocks and reefs offered hazards to seafarers, when charts were too few and inadequate for safe passage. An Englishman, Philip Dormer Stanhope, discovered this to his cost during an unfortunate coastal voyage from Calcutta to Madras in 1775, a journey of nearly 900 nautical miles that ended in shipwreck. Having survived the powerful breakers, he and his companions encountered well-armed gangs of men who began 'stripping us of every thing valuable we had about us ... with as much avidity and as little ceremony as if we had been cast away on the western coast of England'.[126]

Narratives of such catastrophes typically reflect the views of beleaguered captains, traumatized seafarers or despairing investors. Much less is written of the coastal folk whose lives were entangled with the heightened tempo of trade. They too were ineluctably linked to ocean-going shipping – some as fishermen, some as mariners, some as captured cargo – but all coastal residents witnessed and participated in the material circuits of seaborne commerce.[127] This included, of course, riches carried onshore by the waves. Generations learned the measure of large-scale and small-scale shipping, the size, shape and (possible) cargo of vessels glimpsed on the horizon or lying close at anchor. And they learned to hunt for treasure that followed a gale. Wherever winds and tides brought ships close to the coast, wherever strong currents and fierce storms flung them on the strand, locals scavenged and valued the commodities they recovered.[128] Such was the case among Cape Colony slaves, who routinely combed the beaches near Cape Town after a storm, hoping to augment their meagre rations with the detritus of shipwrecks.[129] Like their Malagasy brethren, they looked for advantage

---

[126] Philip Dormer Stanhope, *Genuine memoirs of Asiaticus, in a Series of Letters to a Friend, during Five Years Residence in Different Parts of India* ... (London: 1784), pp. 62–63. I thank Meaghan Walker for kindly bringing this tale of shipwreck to my attention. The western coast of England had a notable history of wrecking.

[127] Lockard, 'The Sea Common to All'; Roberts, 'Shipwrecks and Flotsam'.

[128] For a description of the currents contesting at the Cape of Good Hope, see *The History of a Ship from Her Cradle to Her Grave* (London: George Rutledge and Sons, 1882), pp. 131–132.

[129] Robert S. DuPlessis, *The Material Atlantic: Clothing, Commerce, and Colonization in the Atlantic World, 1650–1800* (Cambridge: Cambridge University Press, 2016), p. 136.

Plate 2.1 *Portrait of a Woman of the Slosgin Family of Cologne*, 1557.
Barthel Bruyn the Younger (*c.* 1530–1607/1610?). 32.100.50. The Friedsam
Collection, Bequest of Michael Friedsam, 1931. Metropolitan Museum of Art,
New York.

Plate 2.2 *Portrait of the Russian Ambassador, Prince Andrey Priklonskiy,* Folio from the Davis Album, 1673–1674. Ali Quli Jabbadar. 30.95.174.5. Theodore M. Davis Collection, Bequest of Theodore M. Davis, 1915. Metropolitan Museum of Art.

Plate 2.3 *Portrait of a Chinese Man.* Chinese man portrayed . . . in a long fur-coat and cap and smoking a long pipe, with a tobacco bag on the left . . . William Alexander (1767–1816), British. British Library, London, UK. © British Library Board. All Rights Reserved/Bridgeman Images.

THE RED LAKE CHIEF with some of his FOLLOWERS Arriving at the RED RIVER and Visiting the GOVERNOR

Plate 2.4 *The Red Lake Chief with Some of His Followers Arriving at the Red River and Visiting the Governor,* 1821–1834. Peter Rindisbacher (1806–1834). M977.51. © McCord Museum, Montreal.

Plate 2.5 *Colcha,* coverlet or hanging. Silk embroidery on silk ground, made in Bengal, India for the European market. 2013.9. Denver Art Museum.

Plate 2.6 *Colcha*, bedcover or hanging. 1775–1825. Wool (*sabinilla*) ground with cotton crewel embroidery. Made in Mexico. 1956.54. Denver Art Museum.

Plate 3.1 *A Mandarin in His Court Dress*, undated. William Alexander, (1767–1816), British. Yale Center for British Art, Paul Mellon Collection.

(a)

(b)

Plate 3.2 A and B Two views of a blue silk robe lined with mink and lambskin for a man. Mactaggart Art Collection (2010.20.3), University of Alberta, Edmonton, Canada.

THIS PLATE (representing a NEGROES DANCE in the ISLAND of DOMINICA) is humbly dedicated to the Hon.ble Charles O'Hara Brigadier GENERAL of their Majestys Army in America.

Plate 3.3 *A Negroes Dance in the Island of Dominica*, 1779. Print made by Agostino Brunias (1728–1796), Italian, active in Britain (1758–70; 1777–80s). B1981.25.1958. Yale Center for British Art, Paul Mellon Collection.

Plate 4.1 *The Batavian Senior Merchant Pieter Cnoll and His Family*, 1665. Jacob Coeman (c. 1632–1676). SK-A-4062. Rijksmuseum, Amsterdam.

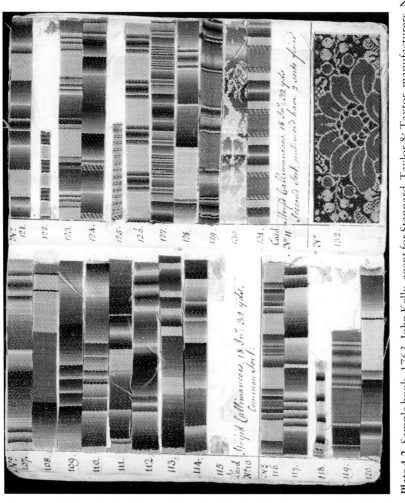

Plate 4.2 Sample book, 1763. John Kelly, agent for Stannard, Taylor & Taxtor, manufacturers, Norwich, England. © Victoria and Albert Museum, London.

Plate 4.3 Polychrome silk embroidery on blue wool fabric, eighteenth to nineteenth century. Intended to be used as decoration for a dress part. T.150–1948. © Victoria and Albert Museum.

Plate 4.4 Fragment of an embroidered skirt panel. Wool broadcloth, embroidered with peonies, rocks and butterflies on yellow wool ground, 1870–1880. 15.559. Denman Waldo Ross Collection. Museum of Fine Arts, Boston.

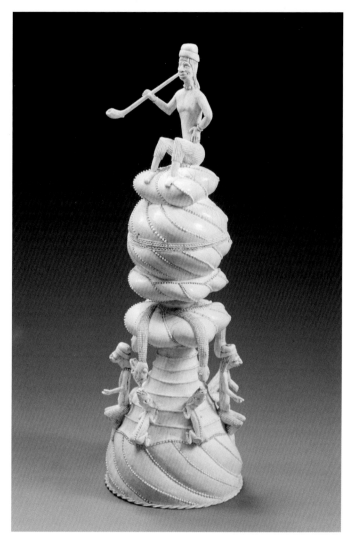

Plate 5.1 Sapi-Portuguese ivory saltcellar, made in Sierra Leon, early sixteenth century. Weltmuseum, Vienna, inv.no. 63.468.

Plate 5.2 *Lady by a Lake Smoking a Hookah, surrounded by a Female Entourage, c.* 1745. Guler, India. IS.32.1949. P.C. Manuk and Miss G. M. Coles Bequest through The Art Fund. © Victoria and Albert Museum.

Plate 5.3 *A Raja Smoking a Hookah, c.* 1690-1710, India, Rajasthan, Kota. 1981.371.2. Gift of Wendy Findlay, 1981. Metropolitan Museum of Art, New York.

Plate 5.4 *A Slave in Harbour, c.* 1630–1660. Unknown (Flemish artist).
Accession No. 823. Purchased 1914. National Gallery of Canada, Ottawa.
Photo: NGC.

Plate 5.5 Glazed earthenware spittoon, *c.* 1715–1725, one of a pair, showing genteel European smokers and African slaves harvesting and rolling tobacco. BK-NM-12400-403. Gift of the heirs of J.F. Loudon, The Hague. Rijksmuseum, Amsterdam.

Plate 5.6 A snuffbox, with inner picture of a mistress and her black servant, *c.* 1740, (silver), London. Private Collection. © Michael Graham-Stewart / Bridgeman Images.

Plate 6.1 Painted cotton chintz palampore or bed cover, mordant and resist dyed and painted, early 1700s, made on the Coromandel Coast, India. IS.182–1965. Given by Miss H. Lowenthal. © Victoria and Albert Museum, London.

Plate 6.2 Palampore, cotton chintz made in India, *c*. 1725–1750. Inv. BK-1971–118. Rijksmuseum, Amsterdam.

Plate 6.3 Embroidered quilt, silk thread in pinks, yellows, blues and greens on a linen ground, *c.* 1700. Castelo Branco, Portugal. T.67–1927. © Victoria and Albert Museum, London.

Plate 6.4 Woman's crewel wool needlework pocket, *c.* 1740–1760. Cotton and linen cloth embroidered with wool. American. Acc. No. 1958–180. The Colonial Williamsburg Foundation. Gift of Mr. Ernest LoNano.

Plate 6.5 A and B Front and back views of a Red River Firebag, or Octopus Bag, made in the Red River Style, *c.* 1850s. Anonymous. Royal Alberta Museum, Edmonton, Canada.

Plate 6.5 A and B (Cont.)

Plate 6.6 Black broadcloth wool jacket with moose hair and quill embroidery, 1860s–1870s. M7417. © McCord Museum, Montreal.

Plate 6.7 Pumps, red wool, leather-covered heels, with moose hair embroidery, 1850–1875. Huron Wendat maker(s). T.10–1929. © Victoria and Albert Museum, London.

when it was offered. In 1722, an edict from local Dutch VOC officials condemned those Cape slaves 'more inclined to undertake expeditions along the beaches and elsewhere to carry off jetsam' than to give aid to formal salvage efforts.[130] Conflicts simmered between customary habits and new institutional priorities, as common folk claimed the refuse from international trade.

In the winter of 1750, the East India Company ship the *Cumberland* beached on the coast of West Africa, in Yoff Bay, in what is now Senegal. The ship wallowed on shore 'all her Masts overboard' and their companion ship, the Grantham, could do nothing with 'the Surfs being so high'. The ship, its crew and cargo were quickly claimed by the local ruler, his people ensuring survivors were 'striped of all the valuables they had upon their backs'. Delicate negotiations ensued among the interested parties: the French Governor of Gorée, the EIC captains, the local West African sovereign and Mr. Horner from the near-by English slaving centre, Fort James, a 'free Merchant of that place ... who speaks the language'. The intent of the EIC officers was to free the captured crew and 'if possible to save part of the Cargoe'.[131] They proposed to hire African divers, directed by the enterprising Mr. Horner, to work the wreck while paying off the local ruler. Diving for salvage was routinely attempted in world oceans.[132] But this plan came to naught, for, as the French Governor explained,

it was the Custom of the Inhabitants of that Coast where the Duke of Cumberland was stranded, to consider all Shipwrecks as Gods donation to them, and that they conceived their right to be so well founded, that notwithstanding the intercourse between them and the French, they seized all french Vessels wreck'd upon their coast with as little ceremony as the Vessels of other Nations.[133]

The tide of goods washed ashore might be assessed differently from region to region, within different cultural systems. But coastal peoples shared a sense of entitlement to storm-tossed cargoes, a perspective

---

[130] Karel Schoeman, *Early Slavery at the Cape of Good Hope, 1652–1717* (Pretoria: Protea Book House, 2007), p. 230.
[131] British Library, IOR/G/12/53, p. 5.
[132] For examples from the Spanish Empire see McCarthy, 'A Spectacle of Misfortune', pp. 98–104; Richards, 'A "Lost Galleon"'. An example of an English endeavour 'to bring from the coast of Africa the contents of a wreck' in 1797 can be found in National Archives, UK, HO/42/41/91.
[133] British Library, IOR/G/12/53, pp. 7, 20–27, 36.

very much at odds with the commercial precepts of capitalist corporations and imperial administrations. The loss of a ship and its cargo was a perennial anxiety to these companies, captains and insurers. During the two and a half centuries of the Manila trade, forty galleons were lost; the size and capacity of these vessels was enormous and the losses similarly great.[134] The English East India Company lost thirty-nine ships between 1747 and 1788, East Indiamen being among the largest cargo carriers of the age.[135] The stretch of water along the southern tip of the African coast accounted for 21 per cent of VOC shipwrecks from 1602 to 1796, with a total loss of 244 ships in all waters.[136] The toll on British shipping from shipwrecks amounted to between three to five per cent annually from the seventeenth to nineteenth centuries, with the southern counties of Kent and Cornwall accounting for approximately 4,000 wrecks each since records were kept.[137] The number of ships alone does not reflect the totality of the costs, for the greater the size of cargo ship, the higher the relative loss. Sailors understood the sea's dangers intimately and the predatory interests of those scanning a sinking vessel.

Edward Barlow described in painful detail the storm in 1675 that dashed his ship on the Goodwin Sands, a ten-mile long sandbank off the southeast coast of Kent. Its hazards are magnified by wind and tide at a point where less than twenty miles separates the shores of England and France. Sailors from the port of Deal, 'the Deal men' as Barlow termed them, swarmed Barlow's crippled craft and pillaged the sailors' sea chests, taking 'all the best things out' before they left the broken ship.[138] The infamous Goodwin Sands brought ruin to many merchant vessels over the years.[139] Folks on shore profited as best they could

---

[134]   The estimated cost of these losses was 60,000,000 pesos' worth of property. McCarthy, 'A Spectacle of Misfortune', p. 99.

[135]   www2.warwick.ac.uk/fac/arts/history/ghcc/research/eicah/houses/valentines mansion/shipwrecks/, accessed 8 May 2017.

[136]   Alexis Catsambis, Ben Ford and Donny L. Hamilton, eds., *The Oxford Handbook of Maritime Archaeology* (Oxford: Oxford University Press, 2011), p. 481.

[137]   Peter Earle, *Sailors: English Merchant Seamen, 1650–1775* (London: Methuen, 1998), p. 110; Cathryn Pearce, *Cornish Wrecking, 1700–1860: Reality and Popular Myth* (Woodbridge, UK: Boydell Press, 2010), pp. 21–22.

[138]   Lubbock, *Barlow's Journal*, p. 264. Deal boats were singled out for their prominence among English smugglers. *Methods to Prevent Smuggling in Great Britain* (London, 1780), p. 2.

[139]   The EIC ship Dolphin (1764), Admiral Gardner (1809) and Britannia (1809) all struck the Goodwin Sands, as did a Dutch VOC ship Rooswijk (1739) and

Figure 4.5 *The Wreck of* Nympha Americana, *a Spanish Corsair, near Beachy Head. 29 November 1747.* Printed by John Henry Hurdis (1800–1857). Royal Pavilion & Museums, Brighton & Hove.

from the wealth travelling by sea. 'The Wreck of the Nympha Americana, a Spanish Corsair near Beachy Head', Figure 4.5, shows the ant-like industry of local men and women picking over the carcass of the broken craft, coordinating the hauling of barrels and unpacking of chests. Her British prize crew was escorting this rich Spanish privateer to London when she came aground, a windfall that electrified the district. The wreck attracted many hundreds whereby 'great quantities of her cargo were carried off by people from different parts, 60 of whom perish'd on the Beach, Downs, and other places; one was shot, and one broke his thigh'.[140] Similar histories are recounted in innumerable seafaring towns and villages, along global sea-lanes, with souvenirs of these events incorporated into family and community lore.[141] Governments looked with hostility on the customary practices of coastal communities already

HMS Northumberland and HMS Stirling Castle both in 1703; see www.eic ships.info/voyages/lostships/lostshiplistA.asp and www.en.wikipedia.org/wik i/List_of_shipwrecks_of_England#Goodwin_Sands.

[140] Henry Martin, *The History of Brighton and Environs* ... (Brighton: John Beal, 1871), p. 257.

[141] The 1707 sinking of a Danish East India Company ship, *Norske Løve*, off the Faroe Islands, is a case in point. The ship's bell was recovered and installed in

viewed with suspicion as smugglers. To the authorities, wrecking represented unaccountable opportunism in the face of commercial disaster, as well as defiance of imperial regulation.

A British official opined that 'the spirit for plunder seemed to pervade all ranks living near the shore, and all other labour ceased the day following a gale of wind. Men, women, and children, were on the shore, looking out for articles, which they deemed their own property as soon as they touched or moved them'.[142] The term 'plunder' is a contentious word, revealing a fully capitalist conceptualization of the cargo in the mind of this writer. Little wonder, as this fellow was employed by Lloyds underwriters to assess the loss of a ship about 1800 on the Kent Coast, a craft he found 'sadly plundered by boats of all descriptions' from every port along the coastline. He secured warrants to search the surrounding houses, uncovering 'liquors of every description, cheeses, hams, haberdashery in great abundance, and variety of broad cloths, linen-drapery, hardware of all sorts, hosiery, hats ... with articles of almost every kind'.[143] This extralegal bounty infused consumer markets all along the shore and well inland, windfalls that coincided with shipping, tides and tempests.

Peppercorn Harvests

Pepper is not as rhetorically prominent as tea, sugar or tobacco in early modern histories of taste, although its heritage of regional and long-distance trade was ancient and celebrated and ultimately underpinned early modern globalism.[144] This spice became more commonplace as oceanic trade networks expanded, opening new flavour horizons to formerly un-peppered populations, with new cultural constructs transforming the 'ordered pattern' of foods and ingredients.[145]

---

the local cathedral. Wrecks on Pacific Islands also left tangible histories. Richards, 'A "Lost Galleon"'; Roberts, 'Shipwrecks and Flotsam'.

[142] John Harriott, *Struggles through Life, Exemplified in the Various Travels and Adventures in Europe, Asia, Africa, and America, of Lieut. John Harriott*, 2nd ed., vol. 1 (London, 1808), pp. 90–91.

[143] Harriott, *Struggles through Life*, pp. 89, 90.

[144] C. W. Brouwer, 'Pepper Merchants in the Booming Port of al-Mukha: Dutch Evidence for an Oceanwide Trading Network' *Die Welt des Islams* 44:2 (2004): 214–280.

[145] For a discussion of Mary Douglas's theorizing of food, see Stephen Mennell, *All Manner of Food: Easting and Taste in England and France from the Middle Ages to the Present* (Chicago: University of Chicago Press, 1985), p. 10

Pepper penetrated new markets in Europe and its colonies gradually, with Portugal shunting stocks of pepper to northern European ports like Antwerp over the 1500s.[146] The momentum of pepper penetration increased over the 1600s, with the VOC by far the dominant importer by the later 1600s given its base in the Spice Islands; pepper comprised 29 per cent of its cargoes 1668–1670. The English East India Company acquired the stocks that it could, though it was of decreasing importance over time.[147] By the 1670s, the cost of pepper dropped as imports soared, with the price in England falling to about 7 pence a pound. Imports ebbed and flowed in response to Asian politics and company priorities, rising again to over two million pounds weight in 1743, in officially registered cargoes.[148] But pepper long circulated untaxed, landed illegally or as a result of a random shipwrecks. Indeed, a British pamphleteer complained in 1720 that 'pepper is publickly and generally Sold for a less Sum than the Duty'.[149] In time it became a very common culinary addition, aligned with salt as a necessary element of cookery.

Was pepper a luxury good by the mid-1700s? It was certainly a luxury presence when displayed in silver pepperboxes or pepper casters on banquet boards, the sharp scent of the freshly ground corns ready for attending guests.[150] But the pickling of herring now needed the addition of peppercorns to suit most northern European tastes. And the commonest pea soup or hog's feet and ears were thought better with a

---

[146] M. A. Ebben, 'Portuguese Financiers and the Spanish Crown in the North Sea Area in the First Half of the Seventeenth Century' in Juliette Roding, Lex Heema van Voss eds., *The North Sea and Culture (1550–1800)* (Hilversum: Verloren, 1996), p. 204; Margaret Spufford, *The Great Reclothing of Rural England: Petty Chapmen and their Wares in the Seventeenth Century* (London: Hambledon Press, 1984), pp. 62, 64, 66, 178–179, 193.

[147] Ormrod, *Rise of Commercial Empires*, p. 190, Table 6.3.

[148] K. N. Chaudhuri, *The Trading World of Asia and the English East India Company, 1660–1760* (Cambridge: Cambridge University Press, 1978), pp. 320, 527.

[149] Robert Loggin, *The Case Fully and Truly Stated representing Great Frauds, Committed in His Most Sacred Majesty's Customs, in Relation to the Duty on Pepper and Tobacco* ... (London, 1720), p. 2.

[150] Silver pepper boxes and pepper casters, made in Europe and colonial America, can be found in the collection of the Metropolitan Museum of Art, New York, including 33.120.215a, b; 24.109.30a, b; 48.187.114a–c; 48.187.378.379; 68.141.71–73.

little sprinkling of pepper in Britain by this date. While peppering a mutton chop for grilling was routine for cooks who wanted more than mustard for zest.[151] For chophouse cooks and street vendors who fed hungry labourers, cheap pepper gave a fillip to inferior meats or common makings.[152] Pepper was a nicety by this time, savoured as well by commoners who knew its bite and understood its value.

In June 1744 a customs officer based in South London stopped 'two Sacks of Pepper' shipped up from Kent on a carrier wagon. The amount of pepper was substantial at three hundredweight (over 152 kilos) and the officer justified his seizure on the grounds the pepper was probably smuggled. In fact, the bags of pepper were the result of the long tradition of wrecking along the Kent coast.[153] As the carrier recounted, 'the said Pepper was pickt up out of the sands on the Coast of Kent, by the Poor People in the Country, which they presume come from some Wreck Vessel'.[154] The East India Company had recently lost two ships in the channel, and the investigation revealed that the spice likely came from one 'cast away at Folkstone'.[155] The carrier explained, 'there being no body to Appear for it, [the poor people] thought it their own Property and sold it'.[156] We can imagine the scene as women and children scoured the sands with each incoming tide, backs bent,

---

[151] Many cookbooks compiled in the 1600s and 1700s record the habit of peppering meat and other vitals, suggesting a chronology of use that long preceded its formal recording. Eliza Smith, *The Compleat Housewife: or Accomplish'd Gentlewoman's Companion* ... (London, 1753), p. 390; Walter, Bayley, *A Short Discourse of the Three Kinds of Pepper in Common Use* (London, 1588); Kristine Kowalchuk, *Preserving on Paper: Seventeenth-Century Englishwomen's Receipt Books* (Toronto: University of Toronto Press, 2017); *The Court and Country Cook: Giving New and Plain Directions* ... (London, 1702), p. 56; Mary Kettilby, *A Collection of Above Three Hundred Receipts in Cookery, Physick, and Surgery; for the Use of All Good Wives, Tender Mothers, and Careful Nurses. By Several Hands. The Fifth Edition* ... (London, 1731), pp. 11, 28; Hannah Glasse, *The Art of Cookery, Made Plain and Easy* ... (London, 1745); *Madam Johnson's Present: Or, Every Young Woman's Companion, in Useful and Universal Knowledge* ... (London, 1759), p. 105; *The Frugal House-Keeper, or, The Compleat Cook* ... (London, 1778), p. 56.

[152] *Verses, Addressed to Sally, at a Chop-House, in London; and Left by the Author on the Table* (London, 1790?).

[153] John G. Rule, 'Wrecking and Coastal Plunder' in Douglas Hay, Peter Linebaugh, John G. Rule, E.P. Thompson and Cal Winslow, eds., *Albion's Fatal Tree* (London: Allen Lane, 1975), pp. 167–188.

[154] British Library, IOR/E/1/32/164.   [155] British Library, IOR/E/1/32/165.

[156] British Library, IOR/E/1/32/166.

hands picking the peppercorns from the strand or raking and sifting out the corns. Hours of backbreaking work were needed until enough was amassed to send to market. Each step in the laborious process leading to London was coordinated: the pepper was collectively harvested, bagged and weighed; a market was identified, and the carrier bought the fruits of this harvest to London. He knew the ropes. At this date, legislation had not yet been passed by Parliament to make the collecting and resale of scavenged materials illegal. That would come mid-century, as authorities worked to limit plebeian access to storm-tossed goods.[157] For the moment, the pepper might be suspect, but the harvesters of this exotic crop were not yet criminalized for their enterprising ways.

There were structural forces at work in this extralegal network, channelling the pepper to South London, joining a flow of other cargo moving towards shopkeepers and retailers.[158] Folkestone, the largest local town, was deeply entrenched in the smuggling trade and was notorious to officialdom. A local grocer once calculated that '20 or 30 cargoes were run in a week' with the collaboration of local smugglers plus French and Dutch compatriots. Shipments were then conveyed to inland retailers and distributors.[159] Residents of the region were enmeshed in the stream of 'new luxuries'. Women and children knew and assisted in these

---

[157] *A Bill for Enforcing the Laws against Persons, Who Shall Steal or detain Shipwrecked Goods; and for the Relief of Persons Suffering Losses Thereby.* (London, 1753). When passed, the legislation became 26 Geo. II c. 19. An analysis of the rich Cornish history of 'wrecking' and scavenging is provided by Pearce, *Cornish Wrecking.*

[158] The Lancashire shopkeeper, William Stout, regularly bought untaxed tobacco from sailors who took small quantities as their 'privilege' or 'portage', getting this at a much lower rate than would be possible is buying tobacco paying full duties. J. D. Marshall, ed., *The Autobiography of William Stout of Lancaster, 1665–1752* (Manchester: Manchester University Press, 1967): 95, 105–106, 161. There is an extensive literature on smuggling in the tobacco trade, including *The Report of the Committee of the House of Commons Appointed to Enquire into Frauds and Abuses in the Customs* (London, 1733); Alfred Rive, 'A Short History of Tobacco Smuggling' *Economic History* 1 (1929): 554–569; T. C. Baker, 'Smuggling in the Eighteenth Century: The Evidence of the Scottish Tobacco Trade' *Virginia Magazine of History and Biography* 62 (1954): 387–99; Nash, 'English and Scottish Tobacco Trade'; Peter Linebaugh, *The London Hanged: Crime and Civil Society in the Eighteenth Century* (London: Allen Lane, 1991), Chapter 5, 'Socking, the Hogshead and Excise'.

[159] Cal Winslow, 'Sussex Smugglers' in Douglas Hay, Peter Linebaugh, John G. Rule, E. P. Thompson and Cal Winslow, eds., *Albion's Fatal Tree* (London: Allen Lane, 1975), p. 123.

schemes, learning as well the value of combing the beaches after storms. Their involvement with commoditized exchange is typical of this period, an apprenticeship in new luxuries. Kentish towns like Hawkhurst and Cranbrook were inland transit points for storage and break of bulk. The Cranbrook carrier who brought the pepper to London understood this circuit and likely connived in the transport of run goods. It was no coincidence that a customs agent stopped him at a South London inn, as many such hostelries were deeply implicated in the distribution of smuggled wares.[160] Large-scale smugglers and small-scale scavengers alike served networks of provincial and metropolitan retailers, pedlars and carriers, such was the demand for these products.

The sea provided with abundance, on occasion. Recovered goods were then used, bartered or sold through the extensive retailing networks that criss-crossed region and nation. The pepper harvest epitomizes the place of custom in extralegal traffic. The livelihood of the men, women and children depended on yields from the ocean commons – the beaches and shoreline were essential parts of these commons, part of 'the informal rural economy'.[161] Regional practice sanctioned all goods that came in on the waves, whether kelp or timber, porpoise or pepper. There were uncertainties within the evolving moral economy of many societies and custom conflicted with increasingly strict legal embargoes on gathering flotsam, jetsam and mercantile waste, with new edicts aimed at protecting capitalist traffic.[162] In the late eighteenth century, clerics denounced coastal gleanings and constables hurried to catch residents working a wreck, terming them 'Vultures'.[163]

---

[160] Winslow, 'Sussex Smugglers', pp. 124–127.

[161] Rosemary Ommer and Nancy J. Turner, 'Informal Rural Economies in History' *Labour / Le Travail* 53 (2004): 127–157.

[162] Common law stipulated the rights of owners and the king in varying circumstances. Theodore Barlow, *The Justice of Peace – A Treatise Containing the Power and Duty of That Magistrate* ... (London 1745), p. 591. See also, Rule, 'Wrecking and Coastal Plunder', pp. 167–168.

[163] Thomas Francklyn, *Serious Advice and Fair Warning to All That Live upon the Sea-Coast of England and Wales, Particularly to Those in the Neighbourhood of Weymouth and Portland ... on Occasion of Several Shipwrecks at That Time upon the Coast of England* (London, 1756), p. 57; *Cheap Repository. The Wreck* (London, 1795); *Sunday Reading. The Shipwreck. To Which Is Added, The Execution of Wild Robert* (Dublin, 1795). These clerics shared common sentiment with late seventeenth-century Catholic missionaries who despised the natives of the Marianas Islands they encountered in the 1680s. The natives were wearing jewellery from a Spanish galleon lost there a generation earlier. McCarthy, 'A Spectacle of Misfortune', pp. 101–102.

The bountiful seas brought a greater current of these wrecks with each generation, and gleaning from these hulks added to the extralegal circulation of commodities in distinctive ways.

Historians of past generations examined British wrecking or scavenging as part of the criminalization of custom, one of the new 'social crimes' of the 1700s. These scholars focused on clashes between tradition and the more stringent legal apparatus of eighteenth-century Britain. Little attention was paid to the actual goods garnered from the shore, the cultural context of these harvests and importance of their use by plebeian populations.[164] Previous historians characterized these people as living within the 'narrow horizons of village life'. In fact, generations of local men set out to sea, sent home gifts and circulated luxuries; they crewed ships of all sorts and built deep links to transnational maritime trade. Wreckers showed product knowledge, information likely shared by coastal people of all ranks. They knew and understood the cargoes freighted in vessels, pilfering when they could.[165] Sailors and their families displayed a hard-won cosmopolitanism that was earned through pain and toil, including intimate familiarity with 'new luxuries'.[166] This knowledge shaped the practice of wrecking and scavenging as peppercorn harvesting makes clear.

The diligence of the coastal families scavenging the sands must be acknowledged; they invested in arduous labour for a purpose, much like their coastal compatriots on the West African shore. This toilsome work speaks to the value assigned even sandy peppercorns. They made this effort because this was a known commodity, because there was a system in place to realize its value and because they had easy access to a distribution network. They could profit from their pains. Beachcombers were not alone in their industry, as those focused on ships' holds during unlading were similarly attentive. In this case, I refer to sweepings, which were noted in an opening excerpt. Figure 4.6 captures some of the industry of those serving ships moored in the Thames and the range of

---

164 For a discussion of 'social crime' and 'wrecking', see John G. Rule and Roger Wells, *Crime, Protest and Popular Politics in Southern England, 1740–1850* (London: Hambledon Press, 1997), pp. 153–168.

165 Rule and Wells, *Crime, Protest and Popular Politics*, pp. 155, 157.

166 This was a widely held phenomenon, demonstrated as well in the Dutch fishing village of Maassluis. Hester Dibbits, 'Pronken as Practice: Material Culture in the Netherlands, 1650–1800' in Rengenier C. Rittersma, ed., *Luxury in the Low Countries: Miscellaneous Reflections on Netherlandish Material Culture, 1500 to the Present* (Brussels: Pharo, 2010), 135–158.

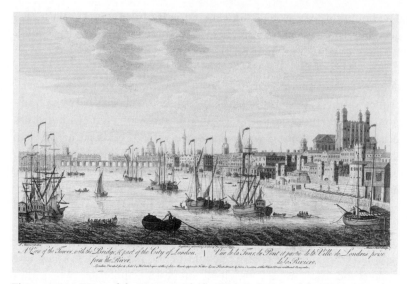

Figure 4.6 *A View of the Tower with the Bridge, & Part of the City of London, from the River,* 1753. Robert Sayer (1725–1794), after Jacob Maurer (1737–1780). RP-P-1932–465. Rijksmuseum, Amsterdam.

craft plying the waters. The people on the water served legal and extra-legal ends, scenes that were replicated in worldwide anchorages. Once anchored, vessels were laboriously unloaded, a sometimes contentious affair, as many manoeuvred to secure the pickings from long-distance trade. Outright theft was commonplace and risky, as were efforts by crew to run goods ashore.[167] But more subtle manoeuvres could also yield results, with pacts made between those on ship and on shore – a relationship addressed in two of the opening quotations for Nagasaki and London. In June 1718, Thomas Berry of Deptford, styling himself a 'Tobacconist', denounced Mr. Spencer to the East India Company Court of Directors. Spencer worked for the EIC as a 'Surveyor of the River' and was responsible for oversight of ships' cargoes, including full unlading. Berry insisted Spencer was an unfaithful servant, open to

---

[167] For example, see *Old Bailey Proceedings Online* (www.oldbaileyonline.org, version 7.0, 18 March 2014), October 1729, trial of Francis Skinner John Barden, alias Barton (t17291015-73); *Old Bailey Proceedings Online* (www.oldbaileyonline.org, version 7.0, 18 March 2014), October 1743, trial of Joseph Joyner (t17431012-22); British Library, IOR IOR/E/1/8/160; E/1/28/66,107; E/1/32/204, 205a; E/1/49/54.

inducements, and had left large quantities of pepper on board for the sweepers in return for payments and 'severall expensive Treats'. Berry charged that Mr. Spencer knowingly left as much as 600 weight of loose pepper in the hold of 'the Ship Borneo', implying this haul was then secreted ashore untaxed.[168]

These allegations open another window into the other ways damaged, broken and damp wares entered the market. Sweepings of all sorts were prized by labouring Londoners and other *porteños,* for the debris from a sea voyage had worth. As a ship's master explained, 'after the cargoe is deliver'd, that which is left, trod under foot, we call sweepings', and these flowed to petty dealers embedded in seafaring and port societies.[169] Berry called himself a tobacconist, but he also ran a public house in Deptford where he handled a variety of goods likely extracted from ships' cargoes, exchanged with a wink and a nod. Berry was assiduous in courting the men working the river who could give him advantage, offering Spencer a cask of wine on one occasion.[170] Reciprocity was standard, as was the circulation of gifts among partners, commodities 'exchangeable for more and more other things'.[171] Mr. Spencer hotly denied wrong-doing, insisting that he fulfilled his duties and 'took care to get up what Pepper I could'. He explained that some pepper had dropped into the iron ballast and 'was run between and underneath ... breaking ye Corns of Pepper and Damp of ye Bottom of ye Ship ... however I took it all up'. On the night in question, Berry circled round the anchored ship in a small rowboat, looking for the chance to buy the ship's sweepings. Spencer insisted that the allegations against him were inspired more because he took care in 'Sweeping the Ships (as they call it) *too* clean'.[172]

---

[168] British Library, IOR/E/1/9/114.

[169] *Old Bailey Proceedings Online* (www.oldbaileyonline.org, version 7.0, 18 March 2014), January 1759, trial of Richard Ford Connell Neal (t17590117-35); (Camel hair swept up in a warehouse) *Old Bailey Proceedings Online* (www.oldbaileyonline.org, version 7.0, 18 March 2014), April 1722, trial of Thomas Cross (t17220404-38); (sugar swept from ships' holds) *Old Bailey Proceedings Online* (www.oldbaileyonline.org, version 7.0, 18 March 2014), December 1742, trial of Edward Brown Alexander Campbell (t17421208-51); *Old Bailey Proceedings Online* (www.oldbaileyonline.org, version 7.0, 18 March 2014), September 1766, trial of Anthony Barber John Merryjohn (t17660903-31).

[170] British Library, IOR/E/1/9/119b and *Old Bailey Proceedings Online* (www.oldbaileyonline.org, version 7.0, 18 March 2014), December 1766, trial of Robert Brewster (t17661217-19).

[171] Kopytoff, 'The Cultural Biography of Things', p. 73.

[172] British Library, IOR/E/1/9/119c. My emphasis.

Pepper habitually found its way off anchored ships, bagged as sweepings, bought at places like the 'house in Fleet-lane' known to take these leavings. Enterprising women like Cecelia Barton of East London were also 'reputed for dealing with Hoymen and others who get Goods on Shore without payment of duty'.[173] Inferior goods entered capacious consumer markets where innumerable pedlars, tavern keepers, cookshop-keepers, victuallers and lodging housekeepers would buy, sell or use a commodity they valued. Pepper added piquancy, altering the well-known tastes of meats and soups. Its heat was deemed an acceptable addition to foods, a taste that spread from elites to wider populations, one of the new flavours of empire. Cosmopolitan cuisine characterized many parts of the globe by this date, gustatory innovations enacted by slave and free, sailor and cook's servant, scavenger and ship's sweeper.[174]

The 'Poor People of Folkstone', who laboriously collected bags of pepper, enjoyed a happier ending than some, as did the carrier. The directors of the East India Company deliberated and decided in their favour. The fruits of this 'wrecking' were deemed to be lawful – not by right, but as an act of charity. The Court of Directors replied to the head of the London Custom House on 13 June 1744, a week after the initial seizure, writing that 'as the Value of the Pepper is but Small The Court don't think it worth their while to Claim the same'.[175] The bags of gritty pepper were returned to the carrier to find their place in the market. We can be sure they found a buyer unfazed by their condition. Though 'much Damaged and full of Sand', the peppercorns entered an inexhaustible arena for imperial groceries, goods that circulated globally in ever-greater quantities.[176] The movement of pepper as sweepings from ships' holds or gleanings from the shore exemplifies the messy 'material civilization' described by Fernand Braudel, a phenomenon that he struggled to define, writing that, 'a proper term will one day be found to describe the infra-economy, the informal other half

---

[173] British Library, IOR E/1/30/41 (1741); *Old Bailey Proceedings Online* (www.ol dbaileyonline.org, version 7.0, 18 March 2014), October 1789, trial of Thomas Rumbald (t17891028-22).

[174] Judith Carney and Richard Nicholas Rosomoff, *In the Shadow of Slavery: Africa's Botanical Legacy in the Atlantic World* (Berkeley: University of California Press, 2009); Shannon Lee Dawdy, '"A Wild Taste": Food and Colonialism in Eighteenth-Century Louisiana' *Ethnohistory* 57:3 (2010): 389–414; Troy Bickham, 'Eating the Empire: Intersections of Food, Cookery and Imperialism in Eighteenth-Century Britain' *Past and Present* (2008), pp. 73, 106.

[175] British Library, IOR/E/1/205, p. 289.   [176] British Library, IOR/E/1/32/166.

of economic activity'. The self-sufficient barter he described was indeed robust and sustaining; but this barter intersected with extralegal networks extending far beyond the 'very small radius' Braudel proposed.[177] Whether coastal gleanings by Cape Colony slaves, a box washed ashore in southern Japan or flotsam on a Kent beach, global commodities permeated coastal communities of all kinds.[178] People in these locales – and many others – launched myriad modest enterprises to capture this bounty, securing a measure of the fruits of global trade with cycles that repeated season after season. The possibility of barter, profit and pleasure from globalized wares animated generations of those on the coast and in harbours. Thus, material civilization in this era included extraordinary connections to commodities at all levels of society, as the stuff of international commerce moved through many hands.

Conclusion

I began this chapter by emphasizing the 'explosion of commoditization' that defined burgeoning capitalism, 'making more and more different things more widely exchangeable'.[179] Commoditization brought more 'things' to the marketplace and engaged more people and more labour in creative exchange. Allied to this 'explosion' were inventive and extractive activities that redirected goods from sanctioned to extralegal channels, making cheaper commodities more widely available. There was an unwitting symbiosis between formal capitalized commerce and the many schemes siphoning its stock. Governments and corporations undoubtedly lost as a result of extralegal incursions, with lower revenues for both. But consumers won. The goods extracted in these processes did not disappear from markets; rather they followed other pathways to willing buyers whose material lives were enriched. Smuggling certainly reflected the largest part of this extralegal traffic. But we must also take note of other customary systems that shaped material flows, including the

---

[177] Fernand Braudel, *Civilization and Capitalism, 15th to 18th Century, The Structures of Everyday Life*, vol. 1 translated by Siân Reynolds (New York: Harper and Row, 1985), pp. 23–24.

[178] Schoeman, *Early Slavery at the Cape of Good Hope*, p. 230; Cheryl Ward and Uzi Baram, ' Global Markets, Local Practice: Ottoman-period Clay Pipes and Smoking Paraphernalia from the Red Sea Shipwreck at Sadana Island, Egypt' *International Journal of Historical Archaeology* 10:2 (2006): 135–158; Roberts, 'Shipwrecks and Flotsam', p. 111.

[179] Kopytoff, 'The Cultural Biography of Things', pp. 72, 73.

scavenging of coastlines, the fishing of shipwrecks and the sweeping of cargo holds. Cosmopolitanism advanced through the diffusion of these materials and the development of new cultural formats. Cosmopolitan tastes, once established, affected markets more generally, augmenting the scope and scale of commodity traffic through legal as well as extralegal efforts.

Scavengers and wreckers in developing economies may seem the least propitious part of this assembly, asserting customary rights in a variety of locales, to the consternation of commercial and imperial officials. Wrecking challenged increasingly restrictive laws enacted by national governments and international corporate bodies. Wreckers' opportunities were irregular. But harvests were sufficiently routine to justify the placing of watchers on the Malacca Straits 'to see who goes by', or for coastal folk to scan stormy seas and pace the coastline to see what washed ashore after a blow.[180] The increased passage of ships and the windfalls from shipwrecks drew material worlds more closely together, broadcasting commodities to people who knew, learned or invented uses for these gleanings.

Governments and corporations advocated regulations that were ineffective in quashing the legions of conspiratorial customs agents, interloping sea captains and cunning merchants at the heart of extralegal affairs.[181]

---

[180] McCarthy, 'A Spectacle of Misfortune', p. 98; Richards, 'A "Lost Galleon"'. Beachcombing after a storm extended as well to at least one educated English cleric, who collected beans washed up from wrecks, growing them to see what they were and how they may assist in feeding the local poor. Joan Thirsk, *Food in Early Modern England: Phases, Fads, Fashions 1500–1760* (London: Hambledon, 2007).

[181] For example, Virginia Benitez Licuanan and José Llavador Mira, eds., *The Philippines under Spain*, Book VI (1594–102), (Manila: National Trust for Historical and Cultural Preservation of the Philippines, 1996), pp. 140–142; Disney, 'Smugglers and Smuggling in the Western Half of the *Estado Da India*'; Van Dyke, *Americans and Macao: Trade, Smuggling and Diplomacy on the South China Coast*; Yosaburō Takekoshi, *The Economic Aspects of the History of the Civilization of Japan*, vol. 2 (London: Routledge, 1930), pp. 182–188; Notehelfer, 'Notes on Kyoho Smuggling'; Zahedieh, 'The Merchants of Port Royal Jamaica and the Spanish Contraband Trade'; Pilar Nogues-Marco, 'Bullionism, Specie-Point Mechanism and Bullion Flows in Early 18th Century Europe', unpublished dissertation, Institut d'Etudes Politiques de Paris (2010); Klooster, 'Inter-Imperial Smuggling'; Thomas C. Barrow, *Trade and Empire: The British Customs Service in Colonial America, 1660–1775* (Cambridge, MA: Harvard University Press, 1967); Richard Pares, *War and Trade in the West Indies 1739–1763* (London: 1963); William Smith McClellan, *Smuggling in the American Colonial at the Outbreak of the Revolution: With Special Reference to the West Indies Trade* (1912, reprinted

Commercial alliances across borders and ethnicities were the order of the day, yielding coalitions that gave a more malleable shape to consumer channels and augmented the practice of fashion.[182] The material dynamics assessed in this chapter encompassed all manner of communities, some nominally marginalized. But, clearly, the new geographies of consumption extended well beyond metropolitan salons and imperial centres.[183] Smugglers and beachcombers handled luxuries, necessities and novelties as constituents of global trade, giving economic life a more heterogeneous pattern. Each season of winds and storms brought new takings. Each landing of untaxed goods materialized fertile links in this globalizing world.

Westminster, MD: Heritage Books, 2007); British Library, IOR/H/399, pp. 2, 7, 55; IOR/H/495/875; IOR/H/496/1, pp. 4–10, 11–17, 21–25, 907, 911, 922.

[182] British Library, IOR/H/496/922, 28 March 1799 and IOR/H/495/1–4 and 875, 1798.

[183] White, 'Geographies of Slave Consumption'.

5 | Tobacco and the Politics of Consumption

There is besides a very fine little seed resembling seed of marjoram, which produces quite a large plant. This plant is highly prized and they dry it in the sun after collecting heaps of it. They wear it around their neck in little pouches ... [using] a kind of cylinder with a hole in the end in which they stick a piece of this dried plant which, having rolled it between their hands, they set fire to it and take the smoke of it into their mouth by the other end of the cylinder. They take in in such quantities that it comes out of their eyes and nose. Thus they perfume themselves at all hours of the day.

> André Thevet, *Les singularitez de la France antarctique* ... (1558)[1]

The Moores of Sierra Leona feed on Rice ... But Tobacco is planted about every mans house, which seemeth half their food: the boll of their Tobacco-pipe is very large, and stands right upward, made of clay well burnt in the fire. In the lower end thereof they thrust in a small hollow cane, a foot and a halfe long, thorow which they suck it, both men and women drinking the most part down [of the smoke], each man carrying ... a small purse ... full of Tobacco, and his Pipe. The women doe the like in their wrappers, carrying the Pipe in their hands.

> William Finch, *Observations of William Finch, Merchant* ... (1607)[2]

The samurai took him along to the mouth of the cave, sat down on the edge of a smooth rock, pulled out a flint and began stuffing a short-stemmed pipe with tobacco. Although it seemed a bit vulgar, he appeared to be a great lover of tobacco, and Bagyū thought the smell of the smoke was surely that of

---

[1] *André Thevet's North America: A Sixteenth-Century View*, translation, with notes and introduction by Roger Schlesinger and Arthur P. Stabler (Kingston and Montreal: McGill-Queen's University Press, 1986), pp. 10–11.

[2] *Observations of William Finch, Merchant, Taken Out of His Large Journall. I. Remembrances Touching Sierra Leona, in August 1607.* In *Purchas His Pilgrimes. In Five Bookes* (London, 1625), p. 415.

Maidome [tobacco grown near Kyoto]. 'It's a fine tobacco, with a pleasant smell'.

Jōkanbō Kōa, *'The Spirit of Kudō Suketsune Criticizes the Theatre'* (1752)[3]

Tobacco illuminates the politics and practice of early modern global consumption in unique ways. First, this substance arises from the culture and technology of Native Americans and was central to their spiritual and social lives. This era was defined by the integration of the Americas into the burgeoning global system, marking it off from all previous periods, a benchmark in human history. Tobacco's diffusion exemplifies this seminal chronology and is one of the unforeseen legacies that Indigenous Americans provided to the world. This history, alone, justifies close attention to this extraordinary substance, a plant whose use and meanings added dramatically to new global commodities, habits and routines. This plant was embraced first by agents of early modern globalization, newcomers to the Americas – merchants, missionaries and mariners – and through them imparted to the world. Knowledge of this plant shaped new material manners. It was adapted and mediated by people who learned the many Native American modes of ingesting this leaf. I chart this journey as a new product added to the stockpile of goods that fuelled the 'explosion of commoditization' that defined this period, with men, women and children producing, selling and using this leaf across the globe.[4] The adaptations that ensued are revealed through the material culture of consumption. I explore these innovations through geographic case studies and artefact analyses. The wholesale commercialization of tobacco utterly transformed the context of this crop from its original status, even as ceremonial use of tobacco persists among Native Americans to this day. Overall, the increased employment of this herb marked rising cosmopolitanism among world peoples.

Expansive systems of production and distribution followed colonial contact and land seizure. Consumer markets were often sustained through bloody imperial contests and the mass enslavement of labour,

---

[3] Referencing a mid-eighteenth-century edition of a popular ancient revenge story. Jōkanbō Kōa, 'The Spirit of Kudō Suketsune Criticizes the Theatre in *Modern-Style Lousy Sermons* (1752)' in Haruo Shirane, ed., *Early Modern Japanese Literature: An Anthology 1600–1900* (New York: Columbia University Press, 2002), p. 456.

[4] Igor Kopytoff, 'The Cultural Biography of Things: Commoditization as Process' in Arjun Appadurai, ed., *The Social Life of Things: Commodities in Cultural Perspective* (Cambridge: Cambridge University Press, 1986), p. 72.

while widespread networks of tobacco smuggling flourished as offshoots of commercial, state and military structures. Tobacco became the focus of intensive imperial interest in many world communities. Governments tried (and largely failed) to control this trade, looking for new sources of revenue premised on consumption. I briefly consider aspects of 'extra-legal' commerce in the context of the previous chapter and the nature of this substance.[5]

Labour practices were altered profoundly in response to the commoditization of tobacco, particularly those tied to Western capitalist slave production and commodity transportation, the next theme addressed in this chapter. I study tobacco's exceptional uses in systems involving slave and free, fixed and peripatetic workers. Labourers in these circumstances shared elements of constraint, the manipulation of tobacco supplies and a limited access to open markets. The provision of tobacco to these populations became part of a new-style labour discipline focused on the amplification of labour output. Working people resisted these controls as they could. The dynamics of this disciplinary consumption are unmatched by any other of the new consumables of this era such as coffee, tea or sugar. The use of tobacco in regulated labour regimes realigns our understanding of this era as providing an expansion of choice; regimes of coercive consumption also emerged, demanding new analysis.

The commoditization of tobacco in Western societies also involved the construction of racially coded media specific to this crop, which is the final subject of this chapter. New racialized stereotypes, in the service of imperial agendas, were allied to popular consumption, providing tacit instruction on the ranking of peoples and the new signification of skin colour. Historians of European empires explore various cultural practices through which racial identities were fashioned, including the growing metaphoric power of goods. Sugar is widely addressed as one of the pivotal commodities through which fortunes were made, consumption was transformed and racial categories were redefined.[6] Tobacco also emerged as a coded

---

[5] This term is defined as 'the illegal; the informal; and the not-yet-(il)legal'. Alan Smart and Filippo M. Zerilli, 'Extralegality' in Donald M. Nonini, ed., *A Companion to Urban Anthropology* (John Wiley and Sons, 2014), p. 222.

[6] For example, Sidney Mintz, *Sweetness and Power: The Place of Sugar in Modern History* (New York: Viking, 1985); Elborg Forster and Robert Foster, eds., *Sugar and Slavery, Family and Race: The Letters and Diary of Pierre Dessalles, Planter in Martinique, 1808–1856* (Baltimore: Johns Hopkins University Press, 1996); Moon-Ho Jung, *Coolies and Cane: Race, Labor, and Sugar in the Age of Emancipation* (Baltimore: Johns Hopkins University Press, 2006); Elizabeth Abbott,

commodity in European imperial spheres, shaping the understanding of race through consumption and its representations. The concept of racial 'whiteness' was created over a long time frame in European metropoles and colonial settings, a status intended to culturally contain, colonize and subjugate peoples of colour, a repositioning enacted over centuries.[7] Cultural constructs reinforced legal edicts.[8] I demonstrate the foundational role of racial stereotypes in tobacco advertising and material culture that helped delineate the colonized and colonizer. Thereafter, social categories were reinforced in daily cycles of buying, smoking, snuffing and chewing – 'an identity instituted through a *stylized repetition of acts* '.[9] Visual and material cultures were adroitly employed in these recitals; new facets of gender, rank and race resulted. I trace the coding of this commodity, as consumption strengthened the privilege of whiteness. Throughout, this leaf acquired consequential new meanings that were seminal to the more globalized, capitalized and racialized period that emerged.

From Strange Encounters to Colonial Commodity

Tobacco was entwined with Native American spiritual practice, medicament and exchange throughout the Americas from the lands of the Bering Strait through North, Central and South America, with different

Sugar: A Bittersweet History (Toronto: Penguin Group, 2008); Ivy Ken, *Digesting Race, Class, and Gender: Sugar as Metaphor* (New York: Palgrave Macmillan, 2010); Stefanie Affeldt, *Consuming Whiteness: Australian Racism and the 'White Sugar' Campaign* (Vienna: LIT Verlag GmbH and Co., 2014); Vincent C. Peloso, *Race and Ethnicity in Latin American History* (New York: Routledge, 2014).

7   The burgeoning field of 'whiteness studies' includes seminal historical studies such as David R. Roediger, *The Wages of Whiteness: Race and the Making of the American Working Class* (New York: Verso, 1991); Matthew Frye Jacobson, *Whiteness of a Different Color: European Immigrants and the Alchemy of Race* (Cambridge, MA: Harvard University Press, 1998). And for a review of foundational questions, see Peter Kolchin, 'Whiteness Studies: The New History of Race in America' *Journal of American History* 89:1 (2002): 154–173 and the Australian journal *Critical Race and Whiteness Studies*.

8   Kathleen Brown, 'Native Americans and Early Modern Concepts of Race' in Martin Daunton and Rick Halpern, eds., *Empire and Others: British Encounters with Indigenous Peoples, 1600–1850* (Philadelphia: University of Pennsylvania Press, 1999), pp. 79–100; Katherine Ellinghaus, Jane Carey and Leigh Boucher, eds., *Re-Orienting Whiteness* (New York: Palgrave Macmillan, 2009); Ann Twinam, *Purchasing Whiteness: Pardos, Mulattos, and the Quest for Social Mobility in the Spanish Indies* (Stanford: Stanford University Press, 2015).

9   Judith Butler, 'Performative Acts and Gender Constitution: An Essay in Phenomenology and Feminist Theory' *Theatre Journal* 40:4 (1988), p. 519. Original italicization.

Figure 5.1 Pipestone pipe, 100 BCE–400 CE from the Hopewellian culture, Ohio. 2011.154.144. Ralph T. Coe Collection, Gift of Ralph T. Coe Foundation for the Arts, 2011. Metropolitan Museum of Art, New York.

forms of ingestion and ceremonies evolving over millennia. Tobacco from several species was a cherished trade good, and seed development suited to diverse climates was patiently advanced, domesticating the *nicotiana* plants that grew wild. Seeds as well as leaf tobacco were widely traded, so treasured was this plant for sacred and social use.[10] The environmental adaptability of domesticated *nicotiana* presaged its later spread worldwide.

The sophisticated pre-Columbian history of tobacco is exemplified in artefacts amassed in major museums, acquired and displayed for very different ends.[11] Figure 5.1 shows a carved pipestone tobacco pipe from

[10] Joseph C. Winter, 'Traditional Uses of Tobacco by Native Americans' in Joseph C. Winter, ed., *Tobacco Use by Native North Americans: Sacred Smoke and Silent Killer* (Norman: University of Oklahoma Press, 2000), pp. 9–58; Emory Dean Keoke and Kay Marie Porterfield, *Encyclopedia of American Indian Contributions to the World: 15,000 Years of Inventions and Innovations* (New York: Checkmark Books, 2003), pp. 204–205.

[11] Forrest D. Colburn, 'From Pre-Columbian Artifact to Pre-Columbian Art' *Record of the Art Museum, Princeton University* 64 (2005): 36–41; Cecelia F. Klein, 'Not Like Us and All the Same: Pre-Columbian Art History and the Construction of the Nonwest' *Anthropology and Aesthetics* 42 (2002): 131–138.

peu plus long. Celuy qui veult faire feu mettra le plus

Figure 5.2 André Thevet, (1502–1590) *Les singularitez de la France Antarctique*, ... Paris: For the heirs of Maurice de la Porte, 1558, p. 101. Library of Congress, Washington, DC.

the Ohio region of North America, removed from a burial mound by an enthusiastic collector. Its origins between 100 BCE and 400 CE denote the antiquity of ceremonial tobacco use and the attention paid to ingestion vessels by Indigenous societies. This pipe figures among countless pre-Columbian artefacts, and later artistic renderings of Indigenous tobacco smoking, that emerged following contact and colonial expansion. André Thevet, a sixteenth-century Franciscan priest and cosmographer, sketched Indigenous Americans from what is now Brazil, perhaps during his sojourn there between 1555 and 1556.[12] Among the notable elements in this scene is the large, smoking cigar held by the lead male (Figure 5.2). Images such as this reveal Europeans' imaginative portrayal of Indigenous

---

[12] Marcel Trudel, 'Thevet, André' in *Dictionary of Canadian Biography*, vol. 1, University of Toronto/Université Laval, 2003– www.biographi.ca/en/bio/thevet_andre_1E.html, accessed 29 February 2016.

peoples and the material culture they employed. But, Europeans' first response to this herb was confusion, as they observed the esteem awarded this plant among innumerable Native Americans and the manner of its use.

Marcy Norton presents a telling account of the puzzled Spaniards who first observed tobacco following the 1492 landing of Christopher Columbus in the Caribbean. Having no knowledge of the local flora, they at first discounted its significance, the 'firebrands of weeds' used by men and women who revelled in its 'fragrant smoke'. They took greater notice with each incursion, it being so vital in all interactions. Diplomatic and social ceremonies routinely included the sharing of 'black smoking tubes', and instruction followed as local people schooled the newcomers.[13] Some Spaniards were bemused at this seeming outlandish antic that was so utterly outside their experience. But, smoking remained a staple of diplomacy and relaxation, and Spaniards soon adopted Indigenous tobacco ingestion in all its forms: cigars, cigarettes, pipes, snuff and chewing.[14]

Norton offers an important reassessment of the diffusion of tobacco beyond the Americas, and the concept of contact zones is especially apposite in this history. In contact zones throughout the Americas, local Indigenous knowledge was decisive in shaping tobacco's reception among Europeans and other wayfarers. Meanings were transmitted in coves, beaches and harbours where the 'improvisational dimensions of imperial encounters' scripted new scenarios.[15] Impromptu interactions prevailed as men and women traded, shared, drank and fought, with exchanges mediated by the materials at hand. Tobacco was sold or communally enjoyed, smoked or chewed for the benefits ascribed to this substance by Indigenous Americans steeped in its uses. These leaves were not devoid of meaning until 'medicalized' by European writers in the later 1500s, as some historians previously argued.[16] On the contrary, Norton demonstrates the robust Native

[13] Marcy Norton, *Sacred Gifts, Profane Pleasures: A History of Tobacco and Chocolate in the Atlantic World* (Ithaca: Cornell University Press, 2010), pp. 44–50.

[14] Francis Robicsek, 'Ritual Smoking in Central America' in Sander L. Gilman and Zhou Xun, eds., *Smoke: A Global of Smoking* (London: Reaktion Books, 2004), pp. 30–37.

[15] Mary Louise Pratt, *Imperial Eyes: Travel Writing and Transculturation*, 2nd ed. (New York: Routledge, 1992), p. 8.

[16] Norton argues for the significance of tobacco and chocolate 'beyond biological determinism or cultural relativism'. *Sacred Gifts, Profane Pleasures*, pp. 7–9.

American social, medicinal and spiritual meanings, and these, Norton argues, were transmitted to new arrivals. The routine ingestion of tobacco through smoke or saliva developed within the 'trans-Atlantic communities of habituated consumers encompassing elite networks of colonial officials, well-travelled missionaries, and merchants, and plebeian networks of mariners'.[17] Jean de Léry, a Protestant missionary, was one of this fraternity who studied the tobacco culture of the Native Americans he encountered. In his case he established a mission among the Tupinambas in present-day Brazil, noting their processes of growing and drying the leaf. He was particularly intrigued by its sustaining use during war, when 'they [would] go three or four days without nourishing themselves on anything else'.[18] The power of this herb boded large for these newcomers.

European written accounts of the Americas multiplied, sometimes with the help of literati who relied on facts provided by seasoned navigators. Such was the case with André Thevet, whose 1557 description of northern North America depended on the first-hand accounts of other voyagers.[19] Thevet produced a detailed description (which opens this chapter) of tobacco use among the Haudenosaunee (Iroquois) near what is now Montreal, on the St Lawrence River. His description suggests both curiosity and familiarity with tobacco by the mid-sixteenth century, describing the seed, plant and the smoking process in terms comprehensible to his readers. Importantly, he employs the term 'perfume' in describing the practice of smoking: 'Thus they perfume themselves at all hours of the day'.[20]

The use of this word is instructive, providing a recognizable context for tobacco smoke, as perfuming smoke was very familiar to early modern Europeans. Incense was burned in religious ceremonies from ancient times, and these fumes held mystic purposes and were integral to Catholic and Judaic sacred practice. Thevet, a French court almoner for Catherine de Medici and later cosmographer to the king, was certainly accustomed to the uses of smoke for medicinal and domestic uses that were routine features of life.[21] Tobacco was one of numerous

---

[17] Norton, *Sacred Gifts, Profane Pleasures*, p. 11.
[18] Peter C. Mancall, 'Tales Tobacco Told in Sixteenth-Century Europe' *Environmental History* 9:4 (2004), p. 653.
[19] Trudel, 'Thevet, André'.   [20] *André Thevet's North America*, pp. 10–11.
[21] Jonathan Reinarz, *Past Scents: Historical Perspectives on Smell* (Champaign, IL: University of Illinois Press, 2014), pp. 25–64; Holly Dugan, *The Ephemeral*

American botanical novelties that initially puzzled Europeans, botanicals whose powers and potential profitability were the focus of intensive experimentation and debate.[22] Their circulation in court circles was also a feature of the era, perhaps encouraging Thevet to claim he introduced tobacco to France.[23] Though his assertion was refuted, he made tobacco smoke intelligible to elite readers who were far from its source communities in America. The men who crewed the ships that visited these lands were not among his audience; they secured knowledge at a personal level, season by season, decade by decade, along the margins and waterways of the American landmass. In the late 1500s and early 1600s, the St Lawrence River on the northeast American coast drew 350 to 380 ships annually – French, Spanish, Portuguese, English and Basque. Accordingly, the Europeans who frequented these and other anchorages received instruction in tobacco and broadcast their knowledge with the trade winds to a wide multi-ethnic audience.

Caribbean ports in the late 1500s and 1600s also pulled in voyagers, an unregulated mix of peoples – Indigenous, slave, creole and European freebooters – defying Spanish monopoly claims.[24] An estimated 300 voyages to the Caribbean were made by English ships alone between 1550 and 1624, involving an approximate 25,000 sailors and 900 ships.[25] Lengthy, hazardous trans-Atlantic crossings were followed by periods at anchor as vessels were repaired and refitted, and crews refreshed after long deprivation. Needs of many sorts were expressed and met, including the desire for respite from hard labour. Seamen epitomized a distinctive early modern fraternity, whose arduous

History of Perfume: Scent and Sense in Early Modern England (Baltimore, MD: Johns Hopkins University Press, 2011); Alain Corbin, *The Foul and the Fragrant: Odor and the French Social Imagination,* translated by Aubier Montaigne (Cambridge, MA: Harvard University Press, 1986).

[22] The commercial potential of balsam was another focus of interest in the early 1500s. Antonia Barrera, 'Local Herbs, Global Medicine: Commerce, Knowledge, and Commodities in Spanish America' in Pamela H. Smith and Paula Findlen, eds., *Merchants and Marvels: Commerce, Science, and Art in Early Modern Europe* (New York: Routledge, 2002), pp. 163–181.

[23] André Thevet, *Portraits from the French Renaissance and the Wars of Religion,* translated by Edward Benson, ed. Roger Schlensinger (Kirksville, MO: Truman State University Press, 2010), p. xvii.

[24] For a further example of the mingling of peoples and illicit trade in defiance of Spanish injunctions, see Molly Warsh, 'Enslaved Pearl Divers in the Sixteenth Century Caribbean', *Slavery and Abolition* 31 (2010), 345–362.

[25] Joyce Lorimer, ed., *Sir Walter Ralegh's Discoverie of Guiana* (Aldershot, UK: Ashgate, 2006), p. lix.

oceanic travels served 'unprecedented imperial ventures'.[26] The new-style masculinity that emerged incorporated telling signs and symbols, including the tobacco pipe. A Spanish physician reported in the 1570s that the 'Indian for their pastime, do take the smoke of the Tobacco, for to make themselves drunk withal'. Newcomers willingly experimented, feeling the pains of heavy toil and searching for relief.[27] Tobacco eased fatigue, reduced hunger, lifted spirits and restored stamina.[28] Sailors habitually binged when opportunity allowed, and they tested new foods and intoxicants with alacrity, encouraging cultural blending and an intermixing of people, practice and goods.[29] The new social character of tobacco took root within a distinctive mobile maritime community that was instrumental in new imperial and global contests. The tobacco pipe and the tobacco quid were soon emblematic of nautical men, a curiosity they passed along to inquisitive patrons, investors and connoisseurs, defining cosmopolitanism of a new sort. A contemporary Spanish author claimed that tobacco flourished as a direct result of seamen's habits, which were shared by 'all of the people who travel by sea'.[30] Mariners of all ranks served as a 'bridge between consumers and distributors', translating this routine in new cultural contexts with each port of call.[31]

A passion for tobacco infected all manner of European mariners and merchants, including the Portuguese, who profited before 1550 from local species found in Brazil, carrying it back to Iberia and then globally.[32] Competitive Dutch merchants financed a series of voyages to Guyana in the late 1500s, leaving a factor on the coast to continue trade with Indigenous peoples, with a particular emphasis on locally grown tobacco. Dutch captains toured the coast of Venezuela in search of pearls, gold and tobacco, with some success, resulting in a passion for

[26] R. W. Connell, *Masculinities* (Cambridge: Polity Press, 2005), p. 187.

[27] Gibson, *Empire's Crossroads*, pp. 50–51.

[28] Edmund Gardiner, *The Trial of Tobacco, Wherein His Worth Is Most Worthily Expressed . . .*, (London, 1610), 5–7.

[29] For a fuller discussion of sailors' role in material culture, see Beverly Lemire, '"Men of the World": British Mariners, Consumer Practice and Material Culture in an Era of Global Trade, *c.* 1660–1800' *Journal of British Studies* 54:2 (2015): 288–319.

[30] Norton, *Sacred Gifts, Profane Pleasures*, 157.

[31] Norton, *Sacred Gifts, Profane Pleasures*, p. 157.

[32] Peter Bakewell and Jacqueline Holler, *A History of Latin America to 1825*, 3rd ed. (Oxford: Wiley Blackwell, 2010), p. 441.

Cracostabak [Caracas tobacco] back in the Netherlands. In 1607, Spain banned tobacco growing by Venezuelan settlers in a desperate bid to quash their illegal contact with the Dutch, who bought up a whole year's crop under the nose of imperial agents. In defiance, Indigenous farmers delivered to the Dutch what the Spanish settlers could not.[33] Piratical sojourners dogged Spanish shipping and colonies in the late 1500s and early 1600s, especially in the Caribbean, picking off craft stuffed with colonial wares like sugar, pearls and tobacco.[34] Colonial competition among European powers drove the diffusion of tobacco culture to new and wider realms.

Thomas Hariot, a mathematician, geographer and student of Native American languages, set out on the ill-fated first attempt to plant an English colony in Roanoke Island, Virginia in 1585. His later 1588 account included a telling description of the use of this dried herb by the East Coast Native Americans and by the colonists themselves. One of the successful features of that expedition was their further education in tobacco, a stuff now known and celebrated by the cognoscenti. Writing of his time in Roanoke, Hariot observed that

The leaves thereof being dried and brought into powder: they [Native Americans] use to take the fume or smoke thereof by sucking it through pipes made of claie into their stomacke and heade; from whence it purgeth superfluous fleame & other grosse humors, openeth all the pores & passages of the body ... We ourselves during the time we were there used to suck it after their maner, as also since our returne, & have found manie rare and wonderful experiments of the vertues thereof; ... the use of it by so manie of late, men & women of great calling as else, and some learned Phisitions also, is sufficient witnes'.[35]

In 1596, Lawrence Kemys, a contemporary of Hariot and member of Raleigh's 1595 expedition to Guiana, recounted the leisured diplomacy

---

[33] Jonathan I. Israel, *Dutch Primacy in World Trade, 1585–1740* (Oxford: Clarendon Press, 1989), pp. 64–66; Ed C. de Jesus, *The Tobacco Monopoly in the Philippines: Bureaucratic Enterprise and Social Change, 1766–1880* (Manila: Ateneo de Manila University Press, 1980), p. 7.

[34] Kenneth R. Andrews, *Trade, Plunder and Settlement: Maritime Enterprise and the Genesis of the British Empire, 1480–1630* (Cambridge: Cambridge University Press, 1984), p. 283. For the politics of pearls, see Molly Warsh, 'A Political Ecology in the Early Spanish Caribbean'. *William and Mary Quarterly* 71:4 (October 2014): 517–548.

[35] Thomas Hariot, *A Brief and True Report of the New Found Land of Virginia ...* (London, 1588), n.p.

over pipes that took place between local chiefs and the expedition leadership: 'some two howrs, until their pipes bee all spent'. Indeed, as this party traversed the coastal lands of South America, they judged each region by its tobacco, whether it was 'good' or 'no good'.[36] There were profits to be made from this knowledge.

Tobacco plantations were launched in 1589 in Trinidad, a Spanish venture. Smuggling followed in tandem. Indeed, extralegality was an integral facet of tobacco commoditization, and its traffic via capacious illicit channels moved this crop more rapidly and more broadly than those narrow avenues approved by Spanish imperial administration.[37] The taste for tobacco was set by 1600, with Brazil becoming the first large-scale producer of this commodity. The profit potential in this plant was clear to metropolitan merchants, governments and colonists who dreamed of wealth as the new century dawned, with tobacco plantations spreading across Brazil, the Caribbean, Virginia and globally.[38] Consumers' boundless appetites encouraged the commercialized cultivation of tobacco, reaching ever-wider communities.[39]

[36] Lawrence Kemys, *A Relation of the Second Voyage to Guiana. Perfourmed and Written in the Yeare 1596* (London, 1596), n.p.

[37] Andrews, *Trade, Plunder and Settlement,* pp. 295–296. For extralegality see Chapter 4, and Alan Smart and Filippo M. Zerilli, 'Extralegality' in Donald M. Nonini, ed., *A Companion to Urban Anthropology* (John Wiley and Sons, 2014), p. 222. I thank Dr Lynne B. Milgram for generously bringing this work to my attention.

[38] Marcy Norton and Daviken Studnicki-Gizbert, 'The Multinational Commodification of Tobacco, 1492–1650' in Peter C. Mancall, ed., *The Atlantic World and Virginia, 1550–1624* (Chapel Hill, NC: University of North Carolina Press, 2007), pp. 251–253; Bakewell and Holler, *A History of Latin America,* p. 441. Settlers, such as the Dutch in New Amsterdam, also traded with local Indigenous peoples for tobacco, as in the 1630s with the Mohawk. Gail D. MacLeitch, *Imperial Entanglement: Iroquois Change and Persistence on the Frontiers of Empire* (Philadelphia: University of Pennsylvania Press, 2011), p. 39. For an instance of the circulation of Trinidad tobacco from Amsterdam to London 1608–1609, see National Archives, UK (hereafter N.A., UK), E 134/7Jas1/East14.

[39] For the growth of this trade among European nations, see Antonio Gutiérez Escudero, 'Hispaniola's Turn to Tobacco: Products from Santo Domingo in Atlantic Commerce' in Bethany Aram and Bartolomé Yun-Casalilla, eds., *Global Goods and the Spanish Empire, 1492–1824: Circulation, Resistance and Diversity* (London: Palgrave, 2014), pp. 216–229, www.palgraveconnect.com/pc/doifinder/10.1057/9781137324054.0001, accessed: 15 March 2016; Nuala Zahedieh, *The Capital and the Colonies: London and the Atlantic Economy 1660–1700* (Cambridge: Cambridge University Press, 2010), pp. 197–210; Norton and Studnicki-Gizbert, 'The Multinational Commodification of

Bound Together by Smoke: A New Global Taste

Early Diffusion: West Africa

Few substances spread as quickly and comprehensively as did tobacco, one of the most distinctive consumables of this era. Global trade provided vector populations in sailors, merchants and missionaries, moving through world communities. Those introduced to this leaf quickly adopted the herb and commoditized its production and distribution, augmenting their cultural habits, sociable practices and mercantile ventures.[40] Throughout, the customary forms of tobacco devised in the Americas remained in place, even as the equipment, accessories and meanings evolved.

West Africa was among the earliest regions introduced to tobacco outside the Americas, likely the work of Iberian mariners. Iberians were well known in this region as, long before 1500, they had colonized the islands of the eastern Atlantic and pushed ever farther south along the West African coast. Their seamen frequented both sides of the Atlantic: the fishing grounds off Newfoundland as well as the trading ports in North and West Africa. But the urgent desire for colonial labour changed their commercial priorities after 1500. African slave labour was formalized in Brazil and Spanish America, and Portuguese voyages increased between West Africa and colonial America, as the Portuguese were licensed to supply slaves to Spanish colonies. Human cargo formed the bulk of their trans-Atlantic cargoes, and tobacco shadowed these relations.[41]

Tobacco', pp. 251–273; James Pritchard, *In Search of Empire: France in the Americas, 1670–1730* (Cambridge: Cambridge University Press, 2004), pp. 130–139; James Lang, *Portuguese Brazil: The King's Planation* (New York: Academic Press, 1979); Jacob M. Price, *France and the Chesapeake: A History of the French Tobacco Monopoly, 1674–1794, and Its Relationship to the British and American Tobacco Trade*, 2 vols. (Ann Arbor: University of Michigan Press, 1973); Jacob M. Price, *The Tobacco Adventure to Russia: Enterprise, Politics, and Diplomacy in the Quest for the Northern Market for English Colonial Tobacco, 1676–1722* (Philadelphia: American Philosophical Society, 1961); Matthew P. Romaniello and Tricia Starks, eds., *Tobacco in Russian History and Culture: From the Seventeenth Century to the Present* (New York: Routledge, 2009).

40 Sander L. Gilman and Zhou Xun, eds., *Smoke: A Global History of Smoking* (London: Reaktion Books, 2004); Carol Benedict, *Golden Silk Smoke: A History of Tobacco in China, 1550–2010* (Berkeley, CA: University of California Press, 2011);

41 Geoffrey V. Scammel, *The First Imperial Age: European Overseas Expansion, c. 1400–1715* (London: Routledge, 2004), pp. 38–40; Linda A. Newson and Susie Minchin, *From Capture to Sale: The Portuguese Slave Trade to Spanish South*

Plate 5.1 symbolizes cross-cultural exchange in tobacco use and representation. This carved ivory saltcellar emerged out of an established fifteenth-century Portuguese commerce in Sapi ivory carvings from what is now Sierra Leone.[42] Sierra Leone was one of several West African regions noted for the high quality of these arts, which were often sought as gifts for noble patrons who underwrote Portuguese voyages. Works such as this ultimately accrued in courtly cabinets of curiosities with other relics of imperial exploits. Scholars now recognize the importance of these arts in presenting African views of the Portuguese. This ivory saltcellar, made in the early sixteenth century, eventually entered the collection of the Habsburg Archduke Ferdinand II, ruler of Further Austria. This was one of many ornaments he acquired from his Habsburg kin, whose commercial and military networks encircled the world.

The largest figure on top of this saltcellar is shown with distinctive striped trousers as might be worn by a working sailor, plus a cap and straight hair suggestive of a Portuguese mariner. The large tobacco pipe in his hand is diagnostic of the time and place and seafaring population. The bead or pearl necklace circling his throat also hints at the riches sailors displayed when times were good. The three men around the base are shown in identical loose-fitting striped trousers, with straight hair, caps and necklaces. The long-stemmed tobacco pipe marks a mobile fraternity whose habits were known in West Africa and this carver likely witnessed the smoking phenomenon, if he was not already a smoker himself – he was certainly deft in drafting this distinctive smoking device and modelling the physical posture of pipe-holders.[43] West Africa was enmeshed in Atlantic and global commercial networks, as materialized in this carving.

America in the Early Seventeenth Century (Leiden: Brill, 2007), pp. 1–17; Ivan Elbl, 'The Volume of the Early Atlantic Slave Trade, 1450–1521' *Journal of African History* 38:1 (1997): 31–75. The role of tobacco in the disciplining of slaves is addressed below.

[42] My thanks to Prof. Renate Piper for bringing this object to my attention. Thanks also to Dr Barbara Plankensteiner, Curator, Weltmuseum, Vienna, for allowing me to study this artefact. See also, Barbara Plankensteiner, 'Salt-Cellar' in Helmut Trnek and Nuno Vassallo e Silva, eds., *Exotica: The Portuguese Discoveries and the Renaissance Kunstkammer* (Lisbon: Calouste Gulbenkian Museum, 2001), pp. 93–94.

[43] Plankensteiner, 'Salt-Cellar', pp. 94–96.

Some Africans might encounter tobacco only after their capture, enslavement and perilous crossing to America. A contemporary writer asserted that African slaves in the region of Santo Domingo had 'habituated themselves to the use of tobacco' by 1535 on the plantations where they laboured.[44] This plant developed special meanings for Caribbean labourers 'who smoke tobacco because they say that when they stop working and inhale the tobacco they are no longer fatigued'.[45] The quotation that opens this chapter leaves no doubt about the broad penetration of tobacco over the 1500s in vibrant trading regions like Sierra Leone, a pattern that continued into the next century with local tobacco pipes 'a foot and a halfe long'.[46]

The movement of tobacco through Africa resulted from oceanic connections and land-based circulation, not all of which are catalogued. The use of baked clay pipes with a large elbow-shaped bowl has been closely studied as a means to unravel the date and diffusion of tobacco from the Americas to West Africa. Comparable pipes in this style were found by archaeologists in both 'the hinterland of the northern coast of the Gulf of Mexico' and the Dawu region of Ghana, inland from the coastal port of Accra. John Hawkins' involvement in the slave trade in the 1560s and his sojourn on the coast of Florida in 1564 offers one possible transmission route. Botanical evidence also suggests the flow of tobacco and tobacco seed to West Africa from eastern North America, regions of British, Dutch and French colonial engagement.[47] Generations of seamen conveyed ships to and from African and American ports, often with multi-ethnic crews, carrying personal goods to barter or share on shore. The sailor atop the ivory saltcellar attests to the cultural translation of American tobacco in this region by the early 1500s. There were few parts of the continent that did not receive and adopt this product by century's end, with tobacco arriving in Uganda about 1600.[48]

Similarly, Islamic trading networks diffused novel goods like tobacco throughout North and West Africa, the Mediterranean and Middle

[44] E. R. Billings, *Tobacco: Its History, Varieties, Culture, Manufacture and Commerce* ... (Hartford, CN: American Publishing Company, 1875), p. 33.
[45] Gutiérez Escudero, 'Hispaniola's Turn to Tobacco', p. 222.
[46] *Observations of William Finch, Merchant, Taken Out of His Large Journall. I. Remembrances Touching Sierra Leona, in August 1607* .... In *Purchas His Pilgrimes. In Five Bookes* (London, 1625), p. 415.
[47] Philips, 'African Smoking and Pipes'.
[48] Snuff-taking also became a staple of tobacco ingestion in western and southern Africa. Philips, 'African Smoking and Pipes'.

East, with Syria enjoying its pleasures by 1570.[49] An English merchant off the Horn of Africa in about 1600 recorded that locals 'love Tobacco'; but he grumbled that they were 'loth to give any thing for it'.[50] The captain of an English East India Company (EIC) ship socialized with Gujarati merchants encountered in 1608 when both awaited favourable winds while anchored at Socotra, an island in the Indian Ocean southeast of Yemen. After one of many friendly dinners he gave the senior Guajarati merchant 'smale parcells of Tobacco' as a token of their amity.[51] By this date tobacco was embedded in a range of social and economic contexts. To expand their profitable trade, both Dutch and Portuguese moved tobacco from Brazilian plantations to West Africa as a matter of priority over the 1600s, expanding the market for this leaf and paying for slaves with this currency. Tobacco leaf soaked in molasses, in the Bahian style, became a favourite along the length of the African Atlantic coast, a source of enormous profit for the Portuguese empire.[52] The exchange of slaves for tobacco from the Americas was another significant facet of this commerce, a product of slave labour directed to the procurement of new generations of slaves.

About 1700, the French missionary Godefroy Loyer confirmed tobacco's ubiquity in present-day Ivory Coast. The dimensions of local pipes astonished Loyer as well, along with the prevalence of this habit among women as they worked and men as they lounged 'pipe in mouth'. Loyer's subsequent publication included a frontispiece on this theme: the king and his entourage are seated on an elevated platform draped with leopard skins and the king's outsized long-stemmed pipe signals his pre-eminence

---

[49] Rudolph P. Matthee, *The Pursuit of Pleasure: Drugs and Stimulants in Iranian History, 1500–1900* (Princeton: Princeton University Press, 2005), p. 119. A 1676 account of entertainment of ships' officers at a Turkish man's house in Aleppo notes the trifecta of new stimulants on offer, as the group was 'courteously entertained with tobacco and coffee and chocolate'. G. E. Manwaring, ed., *The Diary of Henry Teonge Chaplain on Board H.M.'s Ships Assistance, Bristol and Royal Oak 1675–1679* (London: Routledge, 1927), p. 152.

[50] *Observations of William Finch*, p. 418.

[51] Richmond Barbour, 'The East India Company Journal of Anthony Marlowe, 1607–1608' *Huntington Library Quarterly* 71:2 (2008): 299.

[52] Pierluigi Valsecchi, *Power and State Formation in West Africa: Appolonia from the Sixteenth to the Eighteenth Century* (New York: Palgrave Macmillan, 2011), p. 180; Bakewell and Holler, *History of Latin America*, p. 441; James Walvin, *Slavery in Small Things: Slavery and Modern Cultural Habits* (Chichester, UK: John Wiley and Sons, 2017), pp. 59–60.

to the assembled Europeans. This ruler kept the trade in imported tobacco firmly in his grasp as a vital source of revenue, organizing its sale within his territory.[53] He was among the prominent African leaders who augmented their wealth and power through access to high-quality, plantation-grown tobacco, applying taxes and building distribution networks throughout the hinterlands. The globalized web spread further as a consequence.

Over the following century this commodity became normalized among a host of African societies, most particularly in coastal regions, where locally grown crops and imported supplies from American plantations ensured a plentiful stock. The dhow traffic that knitted together Indian Ocean communities also carried tobacco along its routes. It is little wonder that Francis Roger, an English traveller en route to India, encountered well-established tobacco knowledge on the Comoros Island of Johanna (Anjouan) in 1702. On that date, a sultan of that region was entertaining Roger and some shipmates. During their host's brief absence, 'we exceeded the bounds of civility a little ... by looking into the Womens apartment ... they begg'd some tobacco of us wch: we gave them'. Further north, when docked at Aden, Roger noted the distinctive material culture of tobacco during visits at the houses of 'black Merch'ts' [merchants] who 'entertain'd us wth. Tobacco in the long pipes of a Yard & ½ long, & Coffee, setting cross-d legg'd on th/e matts on ye floor as we likewise did'.[54] The impact of plantation production extended as well to world markets in Asia, flowing along Portuguese imperial trade routes. The vast and diverse territories of Asia steadily embraced tobacco in ways specific to their cultures.

Oceanic Connections, Public Performance: Asia

Tobacco arrived in Japan by at least the late 1500s.[55] The Atlantic, Indian and Pacific oceans were fully linked by the 1570s, forging the first fully global complex, with new mercantile pathways intersecting

---

[53] Godefroy Loyer, *Relation du voyage du Royaume d'Issyny, Cote d'Or, Païs de Guinee, en Afrique. La description du païs, les inclinations, les moeurs, and la religion des habitans* ... (Paris: Arnoul Seneuze et Jean-Raoul Morel, 1714), pp. 86, 130–131, note 190. My translation.

[54] IGR/18, Journal of Francis Roger to the East Indies in the Arabia Merchant, 1701–1705, Caird Library, National Maritime Museum, Greenwich.

[55] Norton, *Sacred Gifts, Profane Pleasures,* 44–45. See also, Joyce Lorimer, 'The English Contraband Tobacco Trade in Trinidad and Guiana, 1590–1617' in K. Andrews, N. P. Canny and P. E. H. Hair, eds., *The Westward Enterprise:*

long-established channels. Silver was the driving force that forged the trans-Pacific link in this chain, impelling Spanish fleets from Acapulco to Manila. Tobacco attended these travels.[56] Despite tobacco's initial distance from Asia, the new and old commercial labyrinths were so robust and so dynamic that the rapid circulation of this substance is no surprise. K. N. Chaudhuri writes of New World crops 'invading' Asia: 'The spread of tobacco, maize, and potatoes followed the lines of transoceanic trade'.[57] The arrival of Portuguese seamen on the south coast of China from the 1520s and in Japan from 1543 presaged the rising presence of extra-Asian traders, long-distance crews and their habits. Archaeologists debate the purpose of clay pipes, dated 1549, found in a Ming kiln in Guangxi, southern China; some contend these were for tobacco smoking, while others demur. Nonetheless, the pipes hint at the circulation of this herb undocumented by written records.[58] Whether or not these were among the first locally made Chinese tobacco pipes, later documentation confirms the spread of similar devises. Here, too, sailors, merchants and missionaries were mediators. In the 1570s, a Japanese merchant of Nagasaki, perhaps instructed in the art of smoking by Portuguese travellers, passed along the trick to Chinese Fujian merchants visiting the port city. Or, were these Fujian merchants already familiar with this herb and looking for suppliers? Certainly, tobacco seeds were previously brought to Fujian, most probably from Manila.[59]

Manila drew the largest number of Chinese ships of any Asian port after the 1570s, where the annual arrival of the galleons from Acapulco

English Activities in Ireland, the Atlantic, and America, 1480–1650 (Liverpool: Liverpool University Press, 1978), pp. 124–150. Finch, '*Observations of William Finch*'; François Caron and Joost Schouten, *A True Description of the Mighty Kingdoms of Japan and Siam*. Reprinted from the English edition of 1663, with Introduction, Notes and Appendixes by C. R. Boxer. (London: Argonaut Press, 1935), p. 46; David T. Courtwright, *Forces of Habit: Drugs and the Making of the Modern World* (Cambridge, MA: Harvard University Press, 2001), pp. 14–15.

[56] Dennis O. Flynn and Arturo Giráldez, 'Born with a "Silver Spoon": The Origin of World Trade in 1571' *Journal of World History* 6:2 (1995): 201–221.

[57] K. N. Chaudhuri, *Trade and Civilization in the Indian Ocean: An Economic History from the Rise of Islam to 1750* (Cambridge: Cambridge University Press, 1985), p. 31.

[58] Benedict, *Golden Silk Smoke*, p. 257, note 5. Lucie Olivova accepts the premise these were tobacco pipes. Lucie Olivova, 'Smoking in Qing China' *Asia Major* 18:1 (2005), p. 226.

[59] Benedict, *Golden Silk Smoke*, p. 19.

offered not only masses of silver, but the prospect of American crops like chilli, papaya, corn and tobacco, reshaping regional habits within decades.[60] Hand to hand, pipe by pipe, tobacco trickled through networks of interest. 'In short', as Carol Benedict observes, 'any one of the European or Asian agents moving between the ports of East and Southeast Asia in the vibrant Nanyang maritime arena could well have been the first to bring tobacco to the Southeast Coast [of China]'.[61]

Once in Asia, tobacco spread by land and sea. The trails linking Burma to Yunnan, for example, were vital corridors serving Western China and Central Asia. Though few written records survive, the domestication of American agricultural crops in western Yunnan by the late 1500s confirms the adaptability and vitality of these links.[62] Zen Yuwang (b. *circa* 1610) traced the advent of tobacco in his region outside Shanghai, noting that in his youth 'only the Fujianese used it'. By 1644 the transformation was complete and 'there is not an official or soldier who does not smoke. It has even extended to the common folk; eight out of ten is the proportion for the past twenty years'.[63] Further north, across the Sea of Japan, Japanese merchants, smugglers and sailors learned its merits, sometimes through chance meetings. Though foreigners were directed to Nagasaki, the assigned single port of entry into Japan, storms and nautical accidents brought unexpected contacts. Accounts of eighteenth-century events suggest the ways improvisational meetings could occur. On an island in the southeast of Japan, locals recorded chance encounters with distressed vessels including a western ship in need of food and water. After an amicable exchange of goods, local men were invited on board and given strong drink followed by a substance (snuff) 'put ... in our noses'. In another instance grateful western seamen tossed bundles of tobacco on to the deck of a fishing boat that towed them out of danger.[64] The rising tide

---

[60] Anthony Reid, *A History of Southeast Asia: Critical Crossroads* (London: Wiley Blackwell, 2015), p. 73.

[61] Benedict, *Golden Silk Smoke*, p. 19.

[62] The land route from Burma to Yunnan was an extremely important and well-used conduit for the critical cowrie shell trade, a vital part of land-based routes essential for the dispersal of key commodities. Bin Yang, 'The Rise and Fall of Cowrie Shells: The Asian Story' *Journal of World History* 22:1 (2011): 1–25; Benedict, *Golden-Silk Smoke*, pp. 27–28.

[63] Quoted in Benedict, *Golden-Silk Smoke*, p. 20.

[64] Luke S. Roberts, 'Shipwrecks and Flotsam: The Foreign World in Edo-Period Tosa' *Monumenta Nipponica* 70:1 (2015), pp. 96–99.

of tobacco production propelled it into new territories even in the face of official resistance.

Japan

Tobacco was often greeted with suspicion by authorities, as early adherents of this substance were often lowly men, women and foreigners, including a smattering of merchants, a caste not highly regarded in East Asia. Indeed, tobacco's foreignness sparked concerns in many regions, as it was outside the sumptuary apparatus of Eurasian states, an unfamiliar and potentially disruptive commodity.[65] The newly established Tokugawa regime (1603–1868) was consolidating its power as tobacco arrived, following a period of increased commercial pressure from the Portuguese and then the Dutch. The word *tabako* in Japanese was inherited from the Portuguese *tabaco*, a translation across cultures that took root.[66] Farmers experimented with this new crop and artisans attempted new-style accoutrements. A small-scale tobacco grower documented in the 1570s on the east coast of Honshu, the main island of Japan, possibly supplied foreigners based in the port of Nagasaki. Apprentices in Japanese cities were observed smoking tobacco with 'instruments' by 1608.[67] By the 1630s it was one of the welcome commodities circulating through the China Seas, with widespread regional cultivation and sale.[68] Thereafter, regional tobacco culture evolved with élan.

Tobacco won adherents among the Japanese military: prominent samurai and their male servants as well as low-ranked samurai discovered its restorative benefits. However, following a period of military and social disorder, the Shogun instituted stringent social regulations

---

[65] James Grehan, 'Smoking and "Early Modern" Sociability: The Great Tobacco Debate in the Ottoman Middle East (Seventeenth to Eighteenth Centuries)' *American Historical Review* 111:5 (2006): 1352–1377; Carol Benedict, 'Between State Power and Popular Desire: Tobacco in Pre-Conquest Manchuria, 1600–1644' *Late Imperial China* 32:1 (2011), pp. 13–17; Matthee, *Pursuit of Pleasure*, p. 119.

[66] Constantine Nomikos Vaporis, *Voices of Early Modern Japan: Contemporary Accounts of Daily Life during the Age of the Shoguns* (Santa Barbara, CA: Greenwood, 2012), pp. xxvi, 99.

[67] Barnabas Tatsuya Suzuki, 'Tobacco Culture in Japan' in Sander L. Gilman, Xun Zhou, eds., *Smoke: A Global History of Smoking* (London: Reaktion Books, 2004), p. 77.

[68] Benedict, *Golden-Silk Smoke,* pp. 18–21; Olivova, 'Smoking in Qing China', pp. 227–228.

for dress and deportment, directed particularly at young military-trained men, the servants of samurai or masterless samurai on the fringe of society. Smoking was a publically subversive indulgence – an option officially forbidden them after a 1615 edict. Pacification left these fighting men fewer avenues for advancement and some turned their energies to material inventions devising outlandish dress, hairstyles and habits. Such men, *kabuki-mono*, 'crooked', bizarre men, were ordered not to smoke or loiter in public, not to talk loudly, gesticulate wildly or show off their unsightly hair, clothes and gestures. In fact, the later theatrical tradition of *Kabuki* dramatized the looks and tastes of this extraordinary collective in a theatrical form that eventually thrived in the licensed courtesan districts called *ukiyo*, or 'floating world', of Japan's major cities. The 'floating world' embraced new aesthetic traditions and consumer practices, like smoking. In 1649, another law forbade tobacco smoking among rural non-elites – to no avail. Tobacco took root in the cities and countryside of Japan, while a strange new subculture further popularized the evolving material culture of this habit.[69] The 'floating world' provided a fertile venue for inventive accoutrements, elaborate tobacco containers and hugely long-stemmed pipes, evocative, suggestive and performative objects involving an increasingly essential indulgence.[70]

There was soon a variety of tobacco at hand, as described in the opening excerpt, with the finest quality for discriminating palates. As noted in Chapter 3, the floating world districts attracted a constant flow of provincially based *daimyo* or lords and their retainers, temporarily resident in the capital.[71] Licensed brothels, plus teahouses, theatres, shops and restaurants offered a host of distractions with relaxation augmented through tobacco.[72] Courtesans, like the one

---

[69] Eiko Ikegami, *Bonds of Civility: Aesthetic Networks and the Political Origins of Japanese Culture* (Cambridge: Cambridge University Press, 2005), pp. 260–271.

[70] Timon Screech, 'Tobacco in Edo Period Japan' in Sander L. Gilman and Zhou Xun, eds., *Smoke: A Global History of Smoking* (London: Reaktion Books, 2004), pp. 95–99; Donald H. Shively, 'Sumptuary Regulation and Status in Early Tokugawa Japan' *Harvard Journal of Asiatic Studies* 25 (1964–1965), p. 154.

[71] Constantine Vaporis, *Tour of Duty: Samurai, Military Service in Edo and the Culture of Early Modern Japan* (Honolulu, University of Hawaii Press, 2008).

[72] Jurgis Elisonas, 'Notorious Places' in James L. McClain, John M. Merriman and Kaoru Ugawa, eds., *Edo and Paris: Urban Life and the State in the Early Modern Era* (Ithica: Cornell University Press, 1994), pp. 253–291.

Figure 5.3 Man and woman smoking, for a room screen. Okumura Masanobu (1686–1764), (attributed to), *c.* 1690–1715. RR-P-2000–351. Purchased with the support of F. G. Waller-Fonds. Rijksmuseum, Amsterdam.

portrayed (Figure 5.3), offered entertainment and instruction of many sorts, including in the brandishing of tobacco pipes for those unskilled in their handling. The pipe shown in here is a *kiseru,* usually four to twelve inches long. Smoking offered expressive potential in the manipulation of smoke or placement of accoutrements. The gracefully placed tobacco pipe reflected a courtesan's artistry, the fruit of long training. These women and their acolytes were provisioned by local shops that sold a variety of pipes, sporting the long stem and small bowl of this region, embellished with costly or affordable materials as budgets allowed. These accessories were yet another source of anxiety for authorities, concerned about fitments that blurred social lines, including outrageous spending on tobacco pouches by common townsmen.[73] Tobacco became normalized as a medium of sociability, notable in the mid-1600s among the mercantile trading classes. When François Caron, a Dutch East India Company (VOC) servant, was asked to

[73] Shively, 'Sumptuary Regulation', p. 135.

describe routine hospitality among this community he observed that 'the Japanese are very hospitable and civil to such as visit them, they treat them with Tobacco and with *Tsia* [tea]'.[74] Thus, a new ingredient was incorporated into pleasurable routines of daily life.

Ukiyo-e, woodblock prints furthered the fashion for tobacco.[75] In Figure 5.4 a Sumo wrestler holds a larger, heavier pipe typically ornamented with metalwork and used by these massive men.[76] Samurai and commoners who lived on the fringe of society might employ weighty pipes, such as *kenka-kiseru*, as 'fight pipes' or 'brawl pipes' that were useful for smoking as well as for attacks. Common folk were forbidden weapons; but objects of daily use could be modified to suit the purpose, skirting the law.[77] These pipes exemplify the specialized accessories that developed over time, to the point that in 1822, a noted Edo artist published a book containing 150 designs for the metal fittings on tobacco pipes, intended for discerning shoppers with a variety of needs.[78] By the late Tokugawa period, large merchant houses instructed their staff on the etiquette of greeting customers: 'When a customer enters the shop, you must bow first, and offer tea and tobacco'.[79] Tobacco's infinite malleability suited the most extravagant formalities and the simplest everyday ceremonies, a commodity that punctuated daily interactions.

[74] Caron and Schouten, *A True Description of the Mighty Kingdoms of Japan and Siam,* p. 46.

[75] Mary Elizabeth Berry, *Japan in Print: Information and Nation in the Early Modern Period* (Berkeley: University of California Press, 2006).

[76] For other examples of Sumo wrestlers and these distinctive tobacco pipes, see *The Sumo Wrestler Musashino Monta* (1848–1854), www.loc.gov/pictures/col lection/jpd/item/2008660066/ Library of Congress Digital Collections; and in the Museum of Fine Arts Boston, *Parody of the Heroes of the Three Kingdoms* (1830s) and *Station 24 ... Sumo Wrestler Koyanagi Being Carried across the Oi River* (1845–1846) http://www.mfa.org/collections/object/parody-of-heroes-o f-the-three-kingdoms-eiy%C3%BB-mitate-sangokushi-sum%C3%B4-wres tlers-inazuma-raigor%C3%B4-r-%C3%B4nomatsu-midorinosuke-c-and-hido shi-rikiya-l-464874; www.mfa.org/collections/object/shimada-station-the-%C 3%B4i-river-shimada-no-eki-%C3%B4igawa-from-the-series-fifty-three-pair ings-for-the-t%C3%B4kaid%C3%B4-road-t%C3%B4kaid%C3%B4-goj%C 3%BBsan-tsui-215010

[77] Serge Mol, *Classical Weaponry of Japan: Special Weapons and Tactics of the Martial Arts* (Tokyo: Kodansha International, 2003), pp. 88–89.

[78] Matsunosuke Nishiyama, *Edo Culture: Daily Life and Diversions in Urban Japan, 1600–1868,* translated and edited by Gerald Groemer (Honolulu: University of Hawai'i Press, 1997), p. 15.

[79] Ikegami, *Bonds of Civility,* p. 350.

Figure 5.4 *Sumo Wrestlers Tanikaze and Daidozan Bungoro*, about 1794. Utagawa Toyokuni I (1769–1825). 49.1281. Gift of Porter Sargent. Museum of Fine Arts, Boston.

Indian Ocean World

The adaptability of tobacco is evident in every world region, including the Indian subcontinent and the Islamic world. Here, too, the Portuguese were instrumental. Goa was seized in 1510 and became Portugal's major colonial holding on the southwest coast of the subcontinent, an important conduit for the passage of tobacco inland. Portuguese tobacco from colonial Brazil travelled from Bahia to Goa, via Lisbon. And the response was rapid, including a rise in local growers and attempted taxation of the crop.[80] This plant created a sufficient stir to be included in Ottoman physicians' manuals by the late sixteenth century.[81] By the century's close, the passion for smoking was evident even to literary commentators, including the use of the hookah or water pipe.

This refined means of smoking cooled the fumes by passing the smoking tube through water before reaching the mouthpiece.[82] By 1604, tobacco drew the attention of the nobleman Asad Beg recently returned from the Deccan, where tobacco was well known. Beg aimed to promote this curiosity in the northern India court and he commissioned a water pipe as a gift for Emperor Akbar (1542–1605),: 'decorated with jewels. Its neck was three cubits long; it was dried and dyed, and both ends were decorated with precious stones and enamel work ... The mouthpiece was an oval Yemeni carnelian. A golden burner was used to light it'.[83] Unfortunately, the emperor declined the smoking experiment on the advice of his physician, though courtiers concurred that tobacco was well known in Mecca and Medina. But Asad Beg was

---

[80] A. J. R. Russell-Wood, *The Portuguese Empire, 1415–1808: A World on the Move* (Baltimore: Johns Hopkins University Press, 1992, 1998), p. 141; Philomena Sequeira Antony, 'Hindu Dominance in the Goa-Based Long-Distance Trade During the Eighteenth Century' in S. Jeyasella Stephen, ed., *The Indian Trade at the Asian Frontier* (New Delhi: Gyan Publishing House, 2008), pp. 214–215.

[81] Tim Insoll, *The Archaeology of Islam in Sub-Saharan Africa* (Cambridge: Cambridge University Press, 2003), p. 344–345; Grehan, 'Smoking and "Early Modern" Sociability', p. 1354.

[82] A Persian invention, this technology adapted an earlier Ethiopian manner of smoking cannabis. Matthee, *Pursuit of Pleasure*, p. 124–127.

[83] Annemarie Schimmel, *The Empire of the Great Mughals: History, Art and Culture*, translated by Corinne Attwood (London: Reaktion, 2004), p. 194; B. G. Gokhale, 'Tobacco in Seventeenth-Century India' *Agricultural History* 48:4 (1974), pp. 486–487; Kumkum Chatterjee and Clement Hawes, *Europe Observed: Multiple Gazes in Early Modern Encounters* (Cranbury, NJ: Associated University Presses, 2008), p. 52.

determined to encourage this novelty among other courtiers, as he had 'bought a large supply of tobacco and pipes, [so he] sent some to several of the nobles, while others sent to ask for some, and the practice was introduced'.[84]

The emperor's endorsement would have raised the value of Beg's tobacco stock. Still, his connections added a cachet to this novelty, and the leisurely ingestion of smoke through the hookah became an elegant pastime embraced by elites. Artisans quickly turned their hands to crafting exquisite implements, though cheaper everyday hookahs were soon plentiful in the marketplace. These devices came to epitomize a new masculine sociability throughout Mughal India, Safavid Persia and the Ottoman Empire. Pleasure was now defined in the early modern Ottoman Islamic state, argues James Grehan, through the auspices of the water pipe and the leisurely, sociable ingestion of tobacco smoke. Masculine sociability acquired distinct public dimensions through shared smoking in Ottoman coffeehouses, where men might bring their own mouthpieces for use with the hookahs supplied. Smoking also became a domestic indulgence that was acceptable for women as well as men with the means and time to revel in private pleasures.[85]

Across the Indian subcontinent, official esteem for this plant was matched by its rapid spread. An anonymous Persian author summarized the trajectory of this habit since the time Prince Khurram ascended the throne (1628–1658) as Shah Jahan:

the practice of Smoking pervaded all Ranks and Classes within the Empire. Nobles and Beggars, Pious and Wicked, Devotees and Free-Thinkers, poets, historians, rhetoricians, doctors and patients, high and low, rich and poor, all! all seemed intoxicated with a decided preference over every other luxury, nay even often over the necessities of life.[86]

Indian artists from the Mughal and later periods captured this fashionable pastime among rulers and elites, with innumerable portraits of relaxed indulgence with a hookah. A number of the women of the

---

[84] Gokhale, 'Tobacco in Seventeenth-Century India', p. 487.
[85] Grehan, 'Smoking and "Early Modern" Sociability'.
[86] Henry Yule and A. C. Burnell, eds., *Hobson-Jobson. A Glossary of Colloquial Anglo-Indian Words and Phrases, and of Kindred Terms* (London: John Murray, 1903), p. 705. The editors calculated that this document was part of a collection of manuscripts written by a Persian scholar.

Mughal court were innovative in their fashion practice, influencing elite Hindu and Rajput women's styles as they mingled at select social events.[87] The image in Plate 5.2 was painted in the hill state of Guler in the Lower Himalayas where tobacco culture readily took root, its material form commemorated among local elites.[88] Accompanied by her attendants, this pampered young woman demonstrates her aesthetic through accoutrements, gesture and pose, incorporating the delights of the hookah with her other indulgences. This is an idealized scene in keeping with this lady's status, one of many similar images crafted in courts throughout the subcontinent, demonstrating the breadth of this fad. High-caste women in India were permitted to relish tobacco in approved private spaces, an additional sensory pleasure added to their repertoire.

A Rajasthan artist painted a complementary work shown in Plate 5.3, with a raja at his ease set against a more open panorama and a wider claim of significance. This raja enjoys both the gratification of the tobacco pipe, with the box for betel at his knee, another established psychotropic indulgence. Expressions of elite Mughal manliness now required a gracious use of tobacco, including the correct ways to share the pleasures of smoking with dinner guests. An allotted time with the hookah marked the unhurried conclusion of a banquet, part of the dignified sociability prescribed for Mughal hosts.[89] The hookah habit spread as well among European commercial and corporate men, visitors or residents on the subcontinent. A long-serving functionary with the EIC recounted in 1783 that 'in thirty years' residence, I never could find out one single luxury of the East, so much talked of here, except sitting in an arm-chair, smoking a hooka'.[90] Far from the courts and palaces of Mughal India, diamond miners labouring in the Kollur mine, the source of the finest diamonds in the empire, were routinely heartened with supplies of tobacco and betel.[91] These two substances – one of ancient heritage and the other an innovation – were deemed essential to their labours.

---

[87] Soma Mukherjee, *Royal Mughal Ladies and Their Contribution* (New Delhi: Gyan Publishing House, 2001), pp. 81–82.

[88] John Robert Alderman, 'Bidar' in Navina Najat Haidar and Marika Sardar, eds., *Sultans of Deccan India 1500–1700, Opulence and Fantasy* (New York: Metropolitan Museum of Art, 2015), pp. 180, 186.

[89] Rosalind O'Hanlon, 'Manliness and Imperial Service in Mughal North India' *Journal of the Economic and Social History of the Orient* 42:1 (1999), p. 82.

[90] Yule and Burnell, *Hobson-Jobson*.

[91] Karin Hofmeester, 'Diamonds as a Global Luxury Commodity' presented at the European Social Science History Conference, Vienna, April 2014.

In South and Southeast Asia, tobacco was linked with or became a substitute for betel, a widely used mind-altering substance. Betel leaves form the wrapper of a quid commonly chewed throughout this region, containing the seed of the areca palm and a dollop of lime, typically crushed shells. The bundle was then chewed until the benefits expired, a custom in parts of the Indian subcontinent and Southeast Asia. In 1521, Antonio Pigafetta opined that 'all the people in those parts of the world use it, for it is very cooling to the heart, and if they ceased to use it they would die'.[92] Like tobacco, betel offered succour from the trials of life, physical and social. Labours were hard, and food sometimes scarce: betel was a relief. The sharing of betel, the offering of betel and the ritual enjoyment of betel were integral to these societies. Tobacco fit readily within this regime. Members of the Islamic Mataram court on Java accepted smoking and chewing tobacco as agreeable innovations, offering guests their choice of betel or tobacco at banquets by the early 1600s. Locals added tobacco to their quid, perhaps in imitation of chewing tobacco used by globalized mariners.[93] And some European sojourners added betel leaf to their pipe tobacco. Betel and tobacco were sympathetic pairings distinct to this region.

Tobacco developed as a social *lingua franca* within the Asian seafaring world, the American leaf melding into betel-chewing cultures. This use also marked imperial encounters and colonial agendas. Batavia, the cynosure of Dutch authority and the Asian capital of the VOC, drew people from many parts of Asia and Europe.[94] Ethnic strife sparked from time to time among the residents of Batavia, amidst the many interracial partnerships forged in business, households and families. Material culture expressed allegiances as well as divisions within this multi-ethnic colony, with residents not so easily controlled as officials might wish.[95] Some VOC officials denounced this mixing, with one new

[92] Anthony Reid, 'From Betel-Chewing to Tobacco-Smoking in Indonesia' *Journal of Asian Studies* 44:3 (1985), p. 530.
[93] Reid, 'From Betel-Chewing to Tobacco-Smoking in Indonesia'; Gokhale, 'Tobacco in Seventeenth-Century India', p. 486.
[94] Leonard Blussé, *Visible Cities: Canton, Nagasaki, and Batavia and the Coming of the Americans* (Cambridge, MA: Harvard University Press, 2008), p. 5.
[95] Michael North, 'Production and Reception of Art through European Company Channels in Asia' in Michael North, ed., *Artistic and Cultural Exchange between Europe and Asia, 1400–1900* (Aldershot, UK: Ashgate, 2010), pp. 89–108 and 'Art and Material Culture in the Cape Colony and Batavia in the seventeenth and eighteenth Centuries' in Thomas Da Costa Kaufmann and

arrival condemning the 'scandalous living' of Batavia's Dutch residents, particularly with interracial unions.[96] Perceptions of tobacco use illuminate colonial tensions. Nicolaas de Graaf was a ship's doctor serving VOC crews, first arriving in 1640. He was clearly unsettled by his encounters with Batavian families, most particularly '*Mestiço* and *Kastiço* as also the *Batavian* children who are born of a Dutch father and mother'. His condemnation focused on apparently privileged children, Dutch as well as Eurasian, raised in circumstances de Graaf apparently despised.

these [youth] know nothing of anything, neither are they fit for aught else but to preen themselves a little, chew betel, smoke cigarettes, drink tea, or lie on a carpet or mat; thus they sit all day long, idle and vain, without doing a hand's turn, and that mostly squatting on their heels like an ape on its arse.[97]

The hybrid uses of betel and cigarettes by a group of young Batavians upset his conception of suitable behaviour. Local Asian-style deportment was abhorrent in his eyes, testament to a dangerous creolization at odds with developing European colonial ideals. In de Graaf's view, the colonial setting, as much as the intermingling of peoples, foreshadowed dire consequences. Tobacco figures here as an emblem of the global, an emblem of the creole, interpreted within the particular dynamics of an unequal colonial regime.

Extralegality and Tobacco Consumption

The elevation of tobacco to a global commodity brought profound changes in sociability as well as worldwide fiscal administrations, only some of which I address here. 'They sow tobacco in abundance', reported Edward Terry to the EIC, on a journey about 1616 from the

Michael North, eds., *Mediating Netherlandish Art and Material Culture in Asia* (Amsterdam: Amsterdam University Press, 2014), pp. 111–128; Jean Gelman Taylor, *The Social World of Batavia: Europeans and Eurasians in Colonial Indonesia,* 2nd ed. (Madison, WI: University of Wisconsin Press, 2009), Chapter 1.

[96] Gelman Taylor, *The Social World of Batavia,* p. 15.

[97] Nicolaas de Graaff, *Oost-Indise Spiegel,* edited by J. C. M. Warnsinck, (The Hague, 1930), translated by C. R. Boxer in François Caron and Joost Schouten, *A True Description of the Mighty Kingdoms of Japan and Siam.* Reprinted from the English edition of 1663, with Introduction, Notes and Appendixes by C. R. Boxer (London: The Argonaut Press, 1935), p. 15.

west coast city of Surat to the northern inland city of Agra, then capital of the Mughal Empire. Between 1600 and 1650, Indian peasants across Mughal India quickly accepted this crop, recognizing its potential.[98] Indeed, tobacco's profitability was acknowledged at all strata, including by Prince Khurram (1592–1666), later successor to Emperor Akbar. When the Prince was governor of the western province of Gujarat, he carried on his own trade in tobacco through to the Red Sea, continuing this venture even when he ascended to the Mughal throne, despite the EIC grumbles.[99] Tobacco developed into a major export from Gujarat into the eighteenth century, and, as in other world regions, officials soon recognized the taxation potential. The Mughal Empire successfully secured an estimated 'millions of rupees' in taxes by the late 1600s.[100] But despite this tax harvest, every administrative system lived with the reality of tax evasion and strived to fend off this threat.

Prominent Indian families profited from the tax system, acting as tax farmers personally or through their agents, as in the French-controlled region of Pondicherry. Hindu contractors dominated the tobacco-related trade and taxation activity in Goa from 1675 through the 1700s.[101] Smuggling was always a major concern. The English East India Company calculated how best to raise their revenue through taxes on tobacco entering their trading forts and, later, the territories they controlled. In 1758, EIC London administrators worked to consolidate control of Bombay's taxable trade – proposing a more rigorous system that would eliminate 'those pitiful [tax] Farms of Tobacco Shops, Bang Shops etc. now existing' – and proposed steep new taxes. The author of this scheme wrote with glee that in Bombay they might 'farm out the Tobacco [tax] at 31,000 Rupees Pr. Annum though hardly a Blade of Tobacco grows upon the

---

[98] John F. Richards, 'The Seventeenth-Century Crisis in South Asia' *Modern Asian Studies* 24:4 (1990), p. 631.

[99] Mukherjee, *Royal Mughal Ladies and Their Contributions*, pp. 235–236; Gokhale, 'Tobacco in Seventeenth-Century India', pp. 488–491.

[100] Chaudhuri, *Trade and Civilisation*, p. 186; Gokhale, 'Tobacco in Seventeenth-Century India', pp. 487–488.

[101] B. Krishnamurthy, 'Indian Commercial Intermediaries and the French East India Company in Coromandel during the Seventeenth and Eighteenth Centuries' in S. Jeyaseela Stephen, ed., *The Indian Trade at the Asian Frontier* (New Delhi: Gyan Publishing House, 2008), pp. 182–183 and Antony, 'Hindu Dominance in the Goa-Based Long-Distance Trade', pp. 214–216.

Island'.[102] EIC officials calculated the ways tax farmers could profit from their monopoly of taxation and sale, whereby 'no person whatever is suffered to vend Tobacco [except the tax farmer]'. Additionally, they proposed that anyone caught planting tobacco would be 'deeply Taxed or ... a Certain proportion of their Produce is thrown to the [tax] Farmers'. The challenge was to quash extralegal practice, a daunting prospect that they acknowledged, advising the 'necessity to enclosing your Town, to prevent Clandestine Practices'.[103] They hoped that walls and policing would suffice, but 'clandestine practices' flourished in every precinct.

Imperial administrations strived to control the circulation of tobacco as with other consumer goods.[104] This substance in particular offered an enticing new source of revenue the scale of which became apparent as demand soared. I mentioned above the frustration of Spanish authorities that failed to contain colonial supplies within the designated supply chains. This illicit redirection of crops was one of many stratagems aimed at facilitating private profit at the expense of monopoly capitalist or state coffers. As the tobacco trade soared, large-scale and small-scale schemes designed to avoid tax payments emerged. In Britain, the collusion of merchants and customs officers was commonplace with false listings of import weights, false declarations of damaged stocks and false statements on the re-export of tobacco. Extralegality prevailed. Sailors predominated among the small-scale dealers. Indeed, in 1768, an Edinburgh Custom House official described the long-established practice among Scottish sailors where 'the Tea, Spirits, India Goods, and Tobacco, [were] continually brought home by them in small Parcells on their own Account ... and their Wives and Children being interested therein are all anxious for the Successful Smuggling of the Cargo'.[105]

---

[102]   British Library, India Office Records [thereafter BL, IOR], E/4/616, 3 March
        1758. The consolidation of EIC tax system for inland Bengal was complete by
        1765, based on taxes on the sale of salt, betel and tobacco.
[103]   For discussion of the tobacco trade in Bengal, India, British Library (hereafter
        BL), IOR/L/PARL/2/6/4, Inland Trade in Salt, Betel-Nut, and Tobacco, and for
        smuggling, see BL, IOR/Z/E/4/1/T46, 1753–1771, smuggling in Malabar,
        1817–1818, BL, IOR/F/4/626/17002, prevention of smuggling in Madras,
        1818–1924, BL, IOR/Z/E/4/41/T285. BL, IOR E/4/616, pp. 729, 731.
[104]   See Chapter 4 for a wider discussion of the capacities of imperial
        administrations and the challenges they faced policing access to consumer
        goods.
[105]   T 1/466/243 (1768), NA, UK.

Large-scale ventures required planning on a par with legitimate trade, and tobacco smuggling was big business. Trade statistics show an annual high of 36,350,000 pounds of tobacco imported into England in 1686–1688, a number that dropped sharply to about 26,000,000 until the 1730s. As demand remained high, extralegal strategies were clearly at work. Provincial ports were the main hubs of extralegal finagling, from which supposed re-exports were shipped to smuggling hubs like Dunkirk and Ostend. After that, perhaps half these official 're-exports' returned to England through commercial connivance, and the rest poured into France and other parts of Europe. The flow of tobacco to the Low Countries grew 'fivefold in the first half of the eighteenth century reaching a peak of 3,700,000 lb. in the 1740s'.[106] Arriving at the full volume of smuggling is impossible. Best estimates conclude that the scale of smuggling in England was arguably close to that of tea, the most notorious, intractable and voluminous of smuggled wares.[107]

In France, tobacco smuggling was legendary.[108] Michael Kwass sees this eighteenth-century phenomenon as a demonstration of the globalized ties enfolding France, with the result that a rare luxury became a plebeian necessity and a sovereign source of revenue. 'Fiscalized' consumption policies put high taxes on consumables, bringing in nearly 57 per cent of the French national budget in 1788, a policy that rubbed against the inclination of French men and women. A set of wealthy financiers or tax farmers as they were called, undertook to collect these taxes for the French state. They operated a massive enterprise dedicated to processing and selling tobacco and collecting consumption taxes, with vast centralized manufactories and distribution networks down to the smallest village. 'A colossus, it dwarfed every other institution in France, public or private, except for the royal army'.[109] This fiscal behemoth was teased and provoked relentlessly by the machinations of smugglers in every region and every sector. High walls and guard

---

[106] Robert C. Nash, 'The English and Scottish Tobacco Trades in the Seventeenth and Eighteenth Centuries: Legal and Illegal Trade' *Economic History Review* 35 (1982), pp. 355–356, 361.

[107] Nash, 'The English and Scottish Tobacco Trades', p. 362.

[108] For the trials of containing smuggling and the tobacco tax farming in France see Michael Kwass, *Contraband: Louis Mandrin and the Making of a Global Underground* (Cambridge, MA: Harvard University Press, 2014).

[109] Kwass, *Contraband*, p. 47.

posts could not keep smuggled tobacco out of Paris, nor could border guards keep it out of France more generally.

This trade was riddled with chicaneries from the colonial origins of this leaf to the shop counter. Kwass charts the major artery of large-scale smugglers along the eastern margins of France, from the northern coastlines of the Low Countries down through Alsace and Switzerland.[110] Land borders were infinitely permeable and regional folk were long skilled in negotiating the passage of goods untaxed. Furthermore, though growing this crop was banned, tobacco was widely planted in alpine valleys and prepared in Rhineland cities and when mixed with colonial leaf it provided a decent product agreeable to many. Pedlars turned smuggler as required, moving unsanctioned goods to market.[111] At the same time, large bands of specialist *contrebandier* roamed the borderlands, lauded as heroes by many, funnelling tobacco over the border. A contemporary French economist calculated that a staggering 40 per cent of the tobacco consumed in France in 1770 came from extralegal sources.[112] Regardless of the veracity of such estimations, one thing is clear: early modern governments on every continent strived to sustain imperial agendas through the taxation of a now essential commodity.[113] Paradoxically, extralegal circulation might assist in this process on occasion, as cheaper tobacco encouraged the growth of consumption more generally. If smuggled supplies dried up for a time, those with a habit turned reluctantly to legal sources for their weed, adding their collective mite to government coffers as officials intended. Tobacco was a necessity for states and populations.[114]

The power of tobacco is evident in the wholesale reorganization of taxation systems to try to profit from the craving for this commodity. Equally, the creative interventions of extralegal communities confirm

---

[110] Kwass, *Contraband*, pp. 58–61.
[111] Laurence Fontaine, *History of Pedlars in Europe,* translated by Vicki Whittaker (Cambridge: Polity Press, 1996), p. 32.
[112] Kwass, *Contraband*, pp. 58–63.
[113] Patrick K. O'Brien, 'The Political Economy of British Taxation, 1660–1815' *Economic History Review* 41 (1988): 1–32; Robert M. Kozub, 'Evolution of Taxation in England, 1700–1815. A Period of War and Industrialization' *Journal of European Economic History* 32 (2003): 363–388.
[114] Colin Jones and Rebecca Sprang, 'San-culottes, *san café, sans tabac*: Shifting Realms of Necessity and Luxury in Eighteenth-Century France' in Maxine Berg and Helen Clifford, eds., *Consumers and Luxury: Consumer Culture in Europe, 1650–1850* (Manchester: Manchester University Press, 1999), pp. 37–62.

its broad and growing constituency. Globalized tobacco changed practices in many institutional settings, altering social contracts and social constructs in the process. I move next to consider the impact of tobacco in labour practices and racial meanings, two more areas touched by this leaf.

Shaping Labour and Race through Western Consumer Practice

Tobacco, Labour and Coercive Consumption

Tobacco supplies surged in Western imperial environs as a result of vast capitalist investment, including in plantations and slaves, large-scale transport and processing. At the same time, new styles of consumption arose among populations symbolic of this era: plantation slaves, long-distance sailors and the voyageurs of North America. Tobacco proved its value as a means to discipline these workers and augment labour output among men and women enmeshed in these burgeoning capitalist institutions. This new coercive consumption reflected the priorities of capitalist entities and their representative captains, overseers and administrators who used the psychotropic effects of this leaf to private advantage. Labourers in different settings were habituated to this substance – voluntarily and involuntarily – and found some comfort in this habit. Hard, relentless strain was eased by tobacco.[115] To this end, tobacco was supplied to wage earners and contracted labourers, enslaved and half-free, who were entangled in new-style systems of work. I explore this very different pattern of consumption, seeing a new model in play. The rise of early modern consumerism has been conceived as an expanded banquet of choices including for the industrious classes of women, men and children who worked more assiduously for access to new goods.[116] The disciplinary consumption I describe involved the systematic constraint of choice in distinctive labour environments.

One of the striking features of tobacco was its pervasive use among those whose blood, sweat and toil made this globalizing world possible. An early

---

[115] For a discussion of the physiological effects, see Jordan Goodman, *Tobacco in History: The Cultures of Dependence* (London: Routledge, 1993), pp. 3–6.

[116] Jan de Vries, *The Industrious Revolution: Consumer Behavior and the Household Economy 1650 to the Present* (Cambridge: Cambridge University Press, 2008).

example of tobacco's role among slave labourers was mentioned above; in sixteenth-century Hispaniola a shortage of tobacco might presage unrest among the 25,000 slaves on the island. They needed its consolation, for even after hard labour when they 'inhale the tobacco they are no longer fatigued'.[117] Habituation to tobacco came early in a captive's life.

Slave traders and slaveholders mastered the calculated distribution of tobacco to their captives from the sixteenth century, practices routinized thereafter. Such approaches took root in all regions where European imperial powers wielded authority. In southern Africa, the Dutch introduced these procedures from their arrival at Table Bay, paying local people for labour with tobacco as well as food and drink.[118] Slave owners at the Cape of Good Hope employed tobacco as a strategic investment. The Cape Colony was a treasured way station serving long distances fleets, from which the VOC extended its territorial reach year by year after 1652. The Dutch were knowledgeable about tobacco and traded it with the local Khoikhoi population from the outset. Slaves seized from this group, or carried in from afar, were offered the solace of tobacco for their travails, and slaves shipped in from Madagascar were introduced to the use of tobacco even before they reached the Cape. The VOC instructed slave traders in the treatment of their human cargo, wanting to receive a quiescent troop of slaves in good physical shape. They required captains to issue captives 'three to four leaves to each of them per week', along with essential clay pipes.[119]

Supplying tobacco, whether in pipes or snuff, to slaves on board slaving ships became a general practice among European captains as they aimed for a biddable human payload.[120] These supplies were routinely stocked on slave ships, in preparation for the Middle

---

[117] Gutiérez Escudero, 'Hispaniola's Turn to Tobacco', p. 222.

[118] Julia C. Wells, 'Eva's Men: Gender and Power at the Cape of Good Hope' in Tony Ballantyne and Antoinette Burton, eds., *Bodies in Contact: Rethinking Colonial Encounters in World History* (Durham, NC: Duke University Press, 2005), p. 86.

[119] Karel Schoeman, *Early Slavery at the Cape of Good Hope, 1652–1717* (Pretoria: Protea Book House, 2007), pp. 57, 121.

[120] *Report of the Lords of the Committee of Council appointed for the Consideration of all Matters relating to Trade and Foreign Plantations … dated the 11th of February 1788, concerning the present State of the Trade to Africa, and particularly the Trade in Slaves,* part 2, pp. 117, 123, parlipapers. proquest.com.login.ezproxy.library.ualberta.ca/parlipapers/docview/t70.d75. hcsp-001563?accountid=14474; Marcus Rediker, *The Slave Ship: A Human History* (New York: Viking, 2007), pp. 31–32, 58, 238, 269; Robert Harms,

Passage. In addition to rolls of cheap tobacco, slave ships such as the mid-eighteenth-century *Fredensborg* from Copenhagen stocked barrels of 'slave or Negro pipes', another material adjunct of the global trading system. Commonly, the launch of a vessel from Guinea to the Americas was marked by the captain's order to supply 'pipes and tobacco to all the slaves'.[121] Leaving the coast of Africa was a critical point in the voyage, when African captives felt the greatest despair or impulse to revolt. Tobacco might mollify these reactions. Slave traders were schooled in the techniques of controlling their human cargo, by force or by enticement; and during the trans-Atlantic run, conditions were often fraught, a time when the leaf served an important role.[122] Tobacco was also dispensed on arrival at their destination, to support slaves' spirits prior to public auction after their perilous voyage. Captain Peter Blake gave his human cargo 'Fresh water to wash & palme oyle & tobacco and Pipes'.[123] Extra labours performed by slaves on board might also be rewarded with more tobacco, while, once on land, slave owners offered it in a selective manner to facilitate their aims. In the case of the Dutch Cape Colony, newly arrived slaves were tempted with extra tobacco 'to encourage' them in Christian schooling[124]

Procuring compliance through tobacco was a common ploy in the Cape Colony, as in other locales. Of course, only the cheapest stock was used. Thus, on New Year's Day of 1674 in Cape Colony, it was reported that 'to encourage slaves, each was presented with a small present ... as well as a piece of almost spoilt tobacco, which generosity made these poor menials very cheerful and happy'. Tobacco became a weekly dole in many localities, though serendipity might augment slaves' access. In 1686, when local VOC officials received a particularly bad lot of tobacco from Mauritius, it was decided to 'distribute it thriftily to the Hon. Company's slaves'.[125] More tobacco, however poor in quality, was clearly preferable to less (or none at all), and discipline was enforced through the gifting or withholding of leaf. The lack of tobacco and clothes drove one slave to flee his

---

The Diligent: A Voyage Through the Worlds of the Slave Trade (New York: Basic Books, 2002), p. 380.

[121] Leif Svalesen, *The Slave Ship Fredensborg,* translated by Pat Shaw and Selena Winsnes (Indianapolis: Indiana University Press, 2000), pp. 33, 112–114.
[122] Harms, *The Diligent,* p. 300.
[123] Stephanie E. Smallwood, *Saltwater Slavery: A Middle Passage from Africa to American Diaspora* (Cambridge, MA: Harvard University Press, 2007), p. 160.
[124] Rediker, *Slave Ship,* pp. 216, 269.
[125] Schoeman, *Early Slavery at the Cape,* pp. 143, 187.

master in 1705; the old man hoped to get both from his sister in Cape Town.[126] For slaves, the measure of tobacco they received determined in part the severity of their conditions, a fact well known to those managing the capture, trade and oversight of this constituency. In 1727, British Captain William Snelgrove wrote instructions for his first mate: 'when in the road att Whydah (Benin)'. Security was his foremost concern, and among the policies he advised was the issuing of tobacco once a week.[127] The merchants financing these slaving ventures were entwined in Europe's commercial labyrinths, and some of them were experienced in the tobacco trade itself; all of them were attuned to the techniques of maximizing profits.[128] Once enslaved men and women were disbursed to plantation settings in the Americas, they soon discovered how they could secure tobacco, whether through the aegis of owners and overseers or by growing their own supplies in small gardens. Some Africans were experienced tobacco farmers, and every opportunity to ensure self-sufficiency of supply would be cherished, to try to mitigate the control of their overseers.[129]

A *Slave in Harbour* (Plate 5.4) mirrors tobacco's trajectory after 1500. This extraordinary seventeenth-century portrait demonstrates the pervasive awareness of the slave/pipe allegiance, a phenomenon rendered by an anonymous Flemish artist in an evocation of international trade. A manacled African slave is centre stage holding a long-stemmed white clay tobacco pipe. This pipe was likely one of the millions exported from the Netherlands and used routinely on Dutch or other European vessels. In the mid-1600s one of the largest centres of clay pipe production was in Gouda, where pipe makers produced an estimated 1,000–1,500 pipes daily from each workshop. There were 80 members of the pipe-makers' guild in Gouda in 1665, 223 in 1686 and an estimated 611 in 1730, feeding vast national and international markets with cheap tobacco trappings for a variety of smokers.[130] The juxtaposition of the African and his

126 Schoeman, *Early Slavery at the Cape*, pp. 191, 263–264.
127 Rediker, *Slave Ship*, p. 58.
128 William Andrew Pettigrew, *Freedom's Debt: The Royal African Company and the Politics of the Atlantic Slave Trade* (Chapel Hill, NC: University of North Carolina Press, 2013), pp. 51–52, 64–65.
129 Ann Smart Martin, *Buying into the World of Goods: Early Consumers in Backcountry Virginia* (Baltimore: Johns Hopkins University Press, 2008), p. 181.
130 Jan De Vries and A. M. van der Woude, *The First Modern Economy: Success, Failure and Perseverance of the Dutch Economy 1500–1815* (Cambridge, 1997), pp. 309–310; G. L. Apperson, *The Social History of Smoking*

(Dutch?) clay pipe recalls the strategic ways slave traders seasoned their human cargo in the hopes of compliance. The figure's relaxed handling of the pipe shows his familiarity with this ritual. Dried fish, bread and cheese suggest the staples of a well-stocked ship. The knife at his foot sounds the only discordant note, not meant to reverse his state of enslavement, but perhaps a warning of slaves' rebellious potential though chained ever so tightly. Tobacco was intended to mitigate rebellious sentiments. His red robe hints at the embers walled in the pipe's bowl.

Habituating enslaved Africans to tobacco was a calculated investment aimed at securing a more quiescent and productive population during transit and on land. Policies of this type recurred as well in other labour environments, where influence could be exerted on critically important workers with limited or irregular market access, such as long-distance sailors. Mariners were among the first communities to adopt North American tobacco, whether manning cargo or slave ships, and they were dependent on this leaf and vulnerable to the manipulation of this commodity by those in command.

Capitalist commercial bodies like the EIC directed tobacco access during long voyages, often through a profit driven supply system. This format accorded with the slop system on naval and large commercial vessels, selling goods at inflated prices to a captive seaborne workforce. Mariners bought what they needed, covering the cost of their purchases when paid out at the journey's end. As early as the 1620s, Directors of the EIC approved the carrying of hogsheads of 'low-priced' tobacco 'which may be sold to the mariners at 8s. per lb. and not above'. The wording of this instruction suggests earlier attempts to finagle even more money from crewmen, so desperate might they be for a pipe or a chew.[131] The price per pound was likely well beyond the means of a common seaman if he did not have a nest egg, as eight shillings exceeded the weekly wages of all but skilled craftsmen.[132] But many would indulge, in the hopes of a good

(Middlesex, UK: Echo Library, 2006), p. 35; Jerome E. Brooks, *The Mighty Leaf: Tobacco through the Centuries* (New York: Little Brown, 1952), p. 62.

[131] The seventeenth-century sailor Jan Struys knew the pain of tobacco scarcity, recounting an encounter during a northern voyage to Russia with a 'tobacco starved Russian guide'. Kees Boterbloem, *The Fiction and Reality of Jan Struys: A Seventeenth-Century Dutch Globetrotter* (Basingstoke, UK: Palgrave Macmillan, 2008), p. 68.

[132] Clive Emsley, Time Hitchcock and Robert Shoemaker, 'London History – Currency, Coinage and the Cost of Living' *Old Bailey Proceedings Online* (www.oldbaileyonline.org, version 7.0) accessed 24 March 2016.

payout at the end of the voyage. Certainly, 'tobacco for the use of the mariners' remained a staple on EIC and naval vessels over these centuries, hedged round with regulations.[133] At the same time, some captains routinely squeezed their crews when at sea, making exorbitant profits from the needs of their men.

Sea captains acknowledged that 'its usual for Masters of Ships to make profit of[f] what goods they sell to their Marriners'. Alternately, they might offer tobacco as a treat to seamen during particularly onerous crossings to assuage anger or unrest, recognizing the sustaining effects of tobacco on exhausted bodies.[134] Canny captains also dispensed tobacco and spirits to their crews from time to time to foster loyalty and get the best work from these hands. This was a particularly valuable strategy for passages with high mortality rates or notorious brutality, as in the slave trade with Africa.[135] James Clemens, a Liverpool merchant and slave trader, followed this plan and instructed the captain who served him to do likewise, serving out tobacco and spirits 'prudently', which he promised would 'attach them [the crew] . . . both to you and the Ship'.[136]

Mariners enjoyed their treats when they could. Tobacco became a lodestone in their working lives, a measure of their quality of life, however briefly enjoyed. Seamen, who could, carried rolls of tobacco for future use or sale, and Edward Barlow attempted this in 1675, ultimately losing half his stock in a shipwreck. In the melee Barlow saved only 'four rolls of tobacco out of nine which I had on board'.[137] Private stores diminished the monopoly enjoyed by captains and ships' pursers. Yet if dependent on ships' stores, a sailor's payout could be meagre indeed, once the cost of on-board supplies was subtracted.[138] Repeated complaints led the British Parliament to question slave trade

---

[133] *Court Minute Book of the East India Company,* VII, 'East Indies: September 1624, 1–10, 13–20', *Calendar of State Papers Colonial, East Indies, China and Japan, Volume 4: 1622–1624* (1878), pp. 382–410. www.british-history.ac.uk/report.aspx?compid=69785andstrquery=mariners, accessed 1 March 2013; W.G. Perrin, 'Documents: Seamen's Clothes' *Mariner's Mirror,* vol. 3–4, pp. 150, 281.

[134] Marcus Rediker, *Between the Devil and the Deep Blue Sea: Merchants, Seamen, Pirates and the Anglo-American Maritime World, 1700–1750* (Cambridge: Cambridge University Press, 1987), p. 143.

[135] Rediker, *Slave Ship,* pp. 321–322.   [136] Rediker, *Slave Ship,* p. 195.

[137] Lubbock, *Barlow's Journal,* vol. 1, p. 264.

[138] Stephen F. Gradish, 'Wages and Manning: The Navy Act of 1758' *English Historical Review* 93:366 (1978), p. 55, note 1.

captains in particular, resulting in the introduction of a Bill to protect seamen from the clutches of grasping commanders. It was proposed that ships' captains be forbidden from selling their crew tobacco and other necessaries amounting to more than a quarter of their monthly wages.[139] This attempted regulation illuminates the tensions surrounding seafarers' tobacco consumption. Although it made them subject to exploitation, it was a necessity – however it might be obtained.[140]

Voyageurs were another vital waterborne labour force, essential for moving massive cargoes of furs and trade goods along North America's rivers and lakes, on hazardous journeys of long duration. Here, too, fur trade merchants used tobacco as a lure and a goad in their effort to attract canoe men for these travels and manage their labour while en route.[141] Extra rations of tobacco might be pledged for special occasions, but not all promises were met. All parties recognized that tobacco provided voyageurs with the impetus to power the flotillas of large trade canoes, loaded with trade goods in one direction and furs on the return. Hazards and drudgery came in equal measure, as with an ocean-going passage. Voyageurs navigated thundering rapids where the mastery of a canoe was a matter of life and death, while portages meant carrying backbreaking loads between waterways. Miles travelled on rivers were gauged by the renewal of their pipes; 'twenty-five miles . . . or 'eighteen pipes' against the current' – one pipe per hour. Tobacco comforted and sustained. But, in a familiar scenario, some officials, like those in the North West Company, encouraged 'poor men' on lengthy journeys to spend excessively on tobacco when this was not supplied as a perquisite, taking the cost of these purchases out of future wages. Like many sailors, such expenditures left working men with little to show for their pains.[142]

---

[139] 'A Bill, Intituled An Act to continue, for a limited Time, several Acts of Parliament for regulating the shipping and carrying Slaves in British Vessels from the Coast of Africa', *House of Lords Sessional Papers*, 1791, pp. 11–12.

[140] Described in ballads and poems as well as visual culture. C. S. In his Majesty's Sea-Service, *Poems, on Several Occasions* (London, 1768), pp. 34, 35, 37, 39, 50, 90.

[141] Sophie White, *Wild Frenchmen and Frenchified Indians: Material Culture and Race in Colonial Louisiana* (Philadelphia: University of Pennsylvania Press, 2013), p. 177. The term 'voyageur' was given to men contracted by fur trading companies to paddle canoes through river networks to distant trading posts. Unsanctioned, independent traders, of which there were many, were termed by French authorities *coureur de bois*, or 'runner of the woods'.

[142] Carolyn Podruchny, 'Unfair Masters and Rascally Servants? Labour Relations among Bourgeois, Clerks and Voyageurs in the Montreal Fur

Tobacco figured importantly in fur trade culture at all levels and was often a focus of intense negotiation. In the later 1700s, the Hudson's Bay Company (HBC) included tobacco as part of wage compensation for all who worked at their inland trading forts, from the most skilled factor to unskilled labourers. It was a spur and reward for heavy strain.[143] Alexander Henry, a British fur trader with the North West Company, described his winter use of tobacco when living with the Anishinaabeg (Ojibwa) in 1763–1764, terming it 'my principal recreation, after returning from the chase'.[144] To gauge its importance, consider the fleet of forty canoes dispatched by the HBC in 1816, with 10,000 lbs. of tobacco both for trade and for its labourers, a mark of its singular consequence.[145]

Capitalist transactions set many of the parameters for tobacco consumption in world communities, with the growing supplies of this commodity measuring their success. Capitalist institutions likewise initiated new norms of consumption for enslaved Africans and itinerant male workforces tasked with transporting commodities from point to point across the globe. Discipline was at the heart of these consumer routines, regulation aimed at the effective functioning of slave ships and plantations, and driving the relentless transit of cargo in ocean-going and riverine fleets. Access to tobacco was policed in new ways. Yet, despite the disciplinary intent of these policies, tobacco retained a diversity of meanings among some constituencies.

Corporate priorities alone did not fully shape the valuation of tobacco within fur trade society, and Native Americans' beliefs surrounding this substance persisted. Indigenous peoples were integral to the fur trade system at many levels, as partners in trade, as sexual partners of voyageurs and fur traders, as trading post

Trade, 1780–1821' *Labour/Le Travail* 43 (1999), p. 65; Jennifer S. Brown, 'A Partial Truth: A Closer Look at Fur Trade Marriage' in Theodore Binnema, Gerhard J. Ens and R.C. MacLeod, eds., *From Rupert's Land to Canada* (Edmonton: University of Alberta Press, 2001), p. 63.

143 Jim Warren and Kathleen Carlisle, *On the Side of the People: A History of Labour in Saskatchewan* (Regina: Coteau Books, 2006), pp. 5, 8.

144 Alexander Henry, *Travels and Adventures in Canada and the Indian Territories between the Years 1760 and 1776* (New York: Riley, 1809), p. 156.

145 Jan Grabowski and Nicole St-Onge, 'Montreal Iroquois *engagés* in the Western Fur Trade, 1800–1821' in Theodore Binnema, Gerhard J. Ens and R.C. MacLeod, eds., *From Rupert's Land to Canada* (Edmonton: University of Alberta Press, 2001), p. 40.

residents and as fellow paddlers. This fact is illustrated in the over 1,000 Haudenosaunee (Iroquois) from the St Lawrence River Valley who signed up as *engagés* or contract paddlers for up to three years around 1800 – men who were being pushed out of their traditional lands. Merchants competed for tested voyageurs in these years. These men, along with the many other Métis embedded in fur trade culture, added yet another layer of Indigeneity to a commerce steeped in their traditions.[146] Voyageurs respected the spirituality vested in tobacco, as exemplified by Joseph Labrie in 1802. During his journey, as the convoy of canoes navigated the vastness of Lake Superior, Labrie offered a prayer to the '*mere des vents* ' (Mother of the Winds), offering the water a twist of tobacco, a penny and a piece of flint steel in a petition for safe travel.[147] Lake Superior, called the Great Sea by Anishinaabeg, daunted all but the brave. Such shared rituals were of long standing among Europeans embedded or adopted into Native American societies. Indigenous beliefs persisted amongst this multi-ethnic workforce alongside the growing capitalist management of tobacco.[148] The Native American esteem given to tobacco continues as an alternate understanding of this plant, one entirely different from that accounted in ledgers.

Overall, however, the power of commodity tobacco produced an inequitable framework for labourers on land and water. Access to this leaf affected populations with limited market options that performed essential labour in capitalist ventures: whether slaves, voyageurs or long-distance mariners.[149] These men and women worked within labour structures where their employers/owners determined their conditions of consumption and the price they would pay.

---

[146] Grabowski and St-Onge, 'Montreal Iroquois *engagés*', pp. 23–58.

[147] Carolyn Podruchny, *Making the Voyageur World: Travellers and Traders in the North American Fur Trade* (Lincoln, NE: University of Nebraska Press, 2006), pp. 72–73.

[148] Daniel A. Scalberg, 'The French-Amerindian Religious Encounter in Seventeenth and Early Eighteenth-Century New France' *French Colonial History* 1 (2002), pp. 106–107; Henry, *Travels and Adventures in Canada*, pp. 64–65, 178.

[149] Tobacco's manipulation among martial populations remains to be explored. Tobacco was 'distributed gratis to serving soldiers [in the French army] from the time of Louis XIV, the substance was thorough-going masculine'. Jones and Sprang, 'San-cullottes, *san café, sans tabac*', p. 55.

Labourers with wider options fared better. In South India, in comparison, weavers enjoyed better labour conditions and relished tobacco and betel as a matter of course.[150] These weavers acknowledged their dependence on these substances, noting in their petition denouncing price increases that 'if we have not or can't be permitted by reason of a hurry of Business which sometimes happens to get our victuals We can cheerfully bear it if we have but Beetle and Tobacco'. Between 1701 and 1733 the EIC repeatedly raised taxes on these stimulants, and weavers reacted assertively, relocating to French and Danish territories where they could be assured of these necessities at cheaper cost. They would not be coerced into paying higher prices.[151] Heavy toil was made endurable through new consumer habits and routines, including the soaring use of sugar among industrial labourers, what Sydney Mintz termed 'one of the people's opiates'.[152] The new consumption scenarios that evolved were distinct to this period.

Jan de Vries defined the 'industrious revolution' as a crucial period before western industrialization, with a marked increase in waged labour in preference to leisure, especially among women and children of northwest Europe and colonial North America. This population took up waged work in greater numbers, often in new trades, to acquire the decencies and small luxuries characteristic of this era, making their choices from increasingly capacious options.[153] Among free labourers, the vast itinerant male workforce that transported cargoes over long distances by water (mariner and voyageur) represented another 'industrious' set. However, they endured a different pattern of consumption. As workforces were shaped by capitalist paradigms (slave and free), so too were their consuming cultures. The role of tobacco in coercive consumption marked a new stage of economic and cultural practice.[154]

---

[150] For the comparative advantages enjoyed by South Indian weavers, compared to British weavers, see Prasannan Parthasarathi, 'Rethinking Wages and Competitiveness in the Eighteenth Century: Britain and South India' *Past and Present* 158:1 (1998): 79–109.

[151] Prasannan Parthasarathi, *The Transition to a Colonial Economy: Weavers, Merchants and Kings in South India, 1720–1800* (Cambridge: Cambridge University Press, 2001), p. 15. I thank Prasannan Parthasarathi for bringing this example to my attention.

[152] Mintz, *Sweetness and Power*, p. 174.

[153] De Vries, *Industrious Revolution*, especially Chapters 2 and 4.

[154] I note the use of tobacco within the truck system in particular. Simon Stevens, 'A Social Tyranny: The Truck System in Colonial Western Australia, 1829–99' *Labour History* 80 (2001): 83–98; Karin Lurvink, *Beyond Racism and*

Creating Racialized Consumption

Tobacco was commoditized as part of European imperial and colonial policy, and the culture that grew up around this staple helped generate a racialized colonial consciousness in Western societies, shaped through everyday habits. The visual and material culture of tobacco developed unique racial tropes premised on the inseparable pairing of tobacco consumption and stereotypical racial representations of colonialism. Cultural theorist Stuart Hall noted the important work of the late twentieth and early twenty-first centuries, which included 'interrogating stereotypes [which] makes them uninhabitable. It destroys their naturalness and normality'. A parallel project is to uncover the gestational trajectory of racial stereotypes, a process that can also 'destroy their naturalness and normality'.[155] I take on this task in the last section of this chapter.

I examine the political culture of tobacco consumption in specific Atlantic-based communities, with a concentration on the British Atlantic world. The power of European imperialism and colonialism was forcefully expressed and integral to burgeoning capitalism. In this context, African slaves and Native Americans were incorporated into representations of racial hierarchies as part of everyday consumption.[156] The other part of this equation was the gradual enactment of whiteness in opposition to the colonized and the enslaved. Habits of thinking were created in the course of habits of use, and tobacco was seminally important as a result of the imagery and advertising shaping its use. It was culturally coded through images of its two generative communities: Native American and African, with the occasional European figure standing as overseer or master. New hierarchies of race were being constructed through reiterative visual instruction. New stereotypes emerged as a diagnostic of tobacco, a mnemonic for smoking, a discourse founded on a burgeoning racial order. For retailers, the

---

Poverty: The Truck System on Louisiana Plantations and Dutch Peateries, 1865–1920, PhD dissertation, Vrije Universiteit Amsterdam, 2016.

[155] Stuart Hall, Sut Jhally, Sanjay Talreja and Mary Patierno, *Representation and the Media* (Northampton, MA: Media Education Foundation, 1997), n.p.

[156] The question of consumption in foods and empire is addressed in Troy Bickham, 'Easting the Empire: Intersections of Food, Cookery and Imperialism in Eighteenth-Century Britain' *Past and Present* 198 (2008): 71–109; Rebecca Earle, *The Body of the Conquistador: Food, Race and the Colonial Experience in Spanish America, 1492–1700* (Cambridge: Cambridge University Press, 2012).

use of these images seemingly guaranteed tobacco's quality, as consumption grew in colonies and metropoles.

Not all European colonial regions relied on intensive slave labour for tobacco production, although Portuguese planters adopted slavery almost instantly in Brazil. In Cuba free Indigenous and non-Indigenous labourers worked small tobacco farms for generations. Slave-based plantations came in the eighteenth century in this precinct.[157] Other colonies turned to slave labour more quickly, as in the Chesapeake Bay region of North America, which became fully dependent on slave-grown tobacco over the 1600s. Throughout, the violence and inequities embedded in colonization reshaped metropolitan people as fully as those in distant settlements, in ways of thinking and routines of representation.[158] The systems unleashed in colonial locales were mirrored in commercial and cultural media, shaping the consumption dynamics that evolved. Tim Murray observes that

[157] Bakewell and Holler, *A History of Latin America*, p. 441; Eric Williams, *Capitalism and Slavery* (Chapel Hill, NC: University of North Carolina Press, 1944, 1994), p. 21; Laura Náter, 'The Spanish Empire and Cuban Tobacco during the Seventeenth and Eighteenth Centuries' in Peter A. Coclanis, ed., *The Atlantic Economy during the Seventeenth and Eighteenth Centuries: Organization, Operation, Practice, and Personnel* (Chapel Hill, NC: University of North Carolina Press, 2005), pp. 252–276; Josep M. Fradera and Christopher Schmidt-Nowara, 'Introduction: Colonial Pioneer and Plantation Latecomer' in Josep M. Fradera, Christopher Schmidt-Nowara, eds., *Slavery and Antislavery in Spain's Atlantic Empire* (New York: Berghahn Books, 2013), pp. 3–6.

[158] The charge that slave-grown sugar was a pollutant poisoning the body politic was made emphatically by eighteenth- and nineteenth-century abolitionists. Consumer politics were a dynamic part of the marketplace after the 1750s, with sugar as their focus, not tobacco. See, for example, Clare Midgley, *Women Against Slavery: The British Campaign, 1790–1870* (London: Routledge, 1992) and 'Slave Sugar Boycotts, Female Activism and the Domestic Base of British Anti-Slavery Culture' *Slavery and Abolition* 17:3 (1996): 137–162; Elizabeth Kowaleski-Wallace, *Consuming Subjects: Women, Shopping, and Business in the Eighteenth Century* (New York: Columbia University Press, 1997), pp. 37–51; Charlotte Sussman, *Consuming Anxieties: Consumer Protest, Gender and British Slavery, 1713–1833* (Stanford: Stanford University Press, 2000); Julie L. Holcomb, 'Blood-Stained Sugar: Gender, Commerce and the British Slave-Trade Debates' *Slavery and Abolition* 35:4 (2014): 611–628. For contemporary sources, see William Fox, *An Address to the People of Great Britain on the Utility of Refraining from the Use of West India Sugar and Rum*, 5th ed. (London: M. Gurney and W. Darton, 1791); Anna Letitia Barbauld, *Epistle to William Wilberforce, Esq. on the Rejection of the Bill for Abolishing the Slave Trade* (London: T. Johnson, 1791).

Colonialism is not domination but the effort to produce relations of dominance, to produce social orders that have not previously existed. . . .it is oriented toward incorporation, exploitation, assimilation and reform; however these operations are understood, they are transformative ones, ones that typically entail not only new forms of government and economic exchange but . . . new habits and new modes of embodiment as well.[159]

Chesapeake Bay leapt to the forefront of Atlantic tobacco producing regions, along with Portuguese Brazil.[160] In England, tobacco prices dropped sharply as Virginia supplies came on stream in the 1630s, a source that grew in importance.[161] Owners of large plantations competed for the best slaves and, by the mid-1600s, sought out those with experience in tobacco cultivation in Africa, skills that could augment output in America. A Virginia official championed the slave system in 1683, stating that the 'low price of Tobacco requires it should bee made as cheap as possible, and the Blacks can make it cheaper than Whites'.[162] Tobacco production soared thereafter, with British and Dutch merchants competing fiercely for new markets. These pre-eminent mercantile powers drove the sale of this commodity and defined its features. Colonial imports represented immense sources of wealth from both domestic consumption and re-export (legal or extralegal). Colonial tobacco and the smaller domestic-grown European crops reached an estimated 35 million kg in 1700, rising to 60 million kg by 1790, with colonial imports vastly

---

[159] Tim Murray, *The Archaeology of Contact in Settler Societies* (Cambridge: Cambridge University Press, 2004), pp. 9–10.

[160] Goodman, *Tobacco in History,* pp. 142–144; C. Knick Harley, 'Trade: Discovery, Mercantilism and Technology' in Roderick Flour and Paul Johnson, eds., *The Cambridge Economic History of Modern Britain* vol. 1 (Cambridge: Cambridge University Press, 2004), pp. 182–183; Kwass, *Contraband,* pp. 30–31; Vitorino Magalhães Godinho, 'Portugal and the Making of the Atlantic World' *Review: A Journal of the Fernand Braudel Center* 28:4 (2005): 313–337.

[161] Goodman, *Tobacco in History,* p. 61. Anglo-Chesapeake trade in this leaf grew from 365,000 pounds annually over the years 1628 to 1631, rising to 17.6 million pounds in 1672. Jacob M. Price, *Tobacco in Atlantic Trade: the Chesapeake, London and Glasgow* (Aldershot, UK: Valorium, 1995), p. iii

[162] Anthony S. Parent Jr., *Foul Means: The Formation of a Slave Society in Virginia, 1660–1740* (Chapel Hill, NC: University of North Carolina Press, 2003), pp. 61–66; Goodman, *Tobacco in History,* pp. 164–189.

exceeding leaf grown in Europe.[163] Both African slaves and Native Americans were implicated in this colonial production.

Coll Thrush explores the recurring presence of Indigenous North Americans in London 'at the Heart of Empire', from the telltale rise of tobacco smoke in dockside taverns to the steps of moccasin-shod Native American travellers on city streets. Thrush observes that 'London had to learn to be colonial'.[164] This telling observation fits as well for other centres of empire in Europe. The celebrated and anonymous presence of Native Americans at the heart of empire was part of this instruction, as were other cultural and political forces. Indeed, the intentions of settler colonialism, the priorities of imperial powers, were fostered as resolutely in the heart of empire as in the lands of conquest. Thrush writes of the processes this entailed, noting that

settler colonialism required both the physical and narrative removal of Indigenous populations ... practices of dispossession [that] ultimately had their origins in political, military, and ideological proclivities and prerogatives that were born in London.[165]

---

[163] For a statistical assessment of European consumption trends see Goodman, *Tobacco in History*, Chapter 4. Despite the Spanish aim to be self-sufficient in tobacco, demand was so high that Britain was able to export 1.2 million pounds of tobacco to Spain between 1729 and 1730, remaining an intermittent but important source of supply through the remainder of the century. France, too, had an inexhaustible appetite for Virginia tobacco. Paul Butel, *The Atlantic*, translated by Iain Hamilton Grant (London: Routledge, 1999), pp. 139–141; John R. Fisher, *The Economic Aspects of Spanish Imperialism in America, 1492–1810* (Liverpool: University of Liverpool Press, 1997). The Dutch specialized in blending, which involved mixing cheap locally grown tobacco with Virginian, Brazilian and Caribbean varieties. They dominated this trade with twenty-three blending establishments in Amsterdam in 1700, pushing to expand their tobacco sales in Germany and Scandinavia. Israel, *Dutch Primacy in World Trade*, pp. 265–266, 397. For figures on the legitimate trade in tobacco, see Carole Shammas, *The Pre-Industrial Consumer in England and America* (Oxford: Clarendon Press, 1990), Chapter 4 and Jon Stobart, *Sugar and Spice: Grocers and Groceries in Provincial England 1650–1830* (Oxford: Oxford University Press, 2013), pp. 30–39 for the significance of colonial groceries such as tobacco; for the Netherlands, de Vries and van der Woude, *First Modern Economy*; de Vries, *Industrious* Revolution, pp. 157–158.

[164] Coll Thrush, *Indigenous London: Native Travelers at the Heart of Empire* (New Haven: Yale University Press, 2016), p. 36.

[165] Thrush, *Indigenous London*, p. 16.

Figure 5.5 Tin-glazed Delft Tobacco Jar produced by De Drie Klokken (The Three Bells Factory), The Netherlands, *c.* 1750–1820. C. 65 & A-1997. Given by G. H. W. Rylands in memory of his mother, Betha Wolferstan Rylands. © Fitzwilliam Museum, Cambridge.

Tobacco media provided unique tutorials in the politics of empire, reaching wide audiences with lessons readily learned.[166] The Dutch-made tobacco jar in Figure 5.5 illustrates the sorts of tuition that ensued, one of innumerable containers of this sort now populating museum collections and auction sites. The decorative imagery encapsulates the colonial context of tobacco production and distribution: the European trader sits at his ease in front of a large ship used for the carriage of this crop, rhetorically claiming the colonial lands with his presence. The Native American man facing him carries his tobacco pipe, a mnemonic of the ritual transfer of knowledge that underpinned this global trade. The Angolan town of Macuba, noted on the bottom of the jar, acknowledges

---

[166] Troy Bickman, "'A Conviction of the Reality of Things": Material Culture, North American Indians and Empire in Eighteenth-Century Britain' *Eighteenth-Century Studies* 39:1 (2005), pp. 30–31.

the source of African labour that now powers the production of this commodity and denotes as well a distinctive type of premium tobacco grown in Martinique.[167] This object was crafted in Delft to celebrate the colonial capacities of European conquerors and the riches that flowed from their work.[168] But, it was a rather sedentary propaganda tool ensconced on a shop shelf; its visual and ritual impact was limited to those who saw, used and relied on the contents of this jar. The impact of such emblems was vastly augmented when applied to mobile and ubiquitous paper paraphernalia allied to the tobacco trade.

Illustrated trade cards, billheads and tobacco wrappers reveal mainstream European thinking about tobacco and its imperial context, imparted to customers over generations. This printed ephemera was among the most prolific and significant advertising of the eighteenth century, linking image, print and commodity in innovative ways: the vizualization of colonial policies. Indeed, trade cards are argued to be 'more central to pre-nineteenth century advertising than were newspapers and newssheets'.[169] The British Museum holds perhaps the largest trade card collection in Britain at 15,000 items. A survey of these trade cards and other online sites confirms the distinctiveness of tobacco advertising, for African slaves are not presented in trade cards or tokens in conjunction with sugar retailing, despite their seminal role in production. Sugar loaves decorated the trade cards of sugar bakers and sugar sellers, a neutral insignia, with slave labour veiled from public eye. Likewise, grocers' trade cards advertising tea as well as sugar typically obfuscate the context of sugar making. The rare exception underlines a preference for robed Chinese men, rather than toiling

---

[167] Billings, *Tobacco*, p. 387.

[168] Another Delft tobacco jar displaying this popular theme is held in the Cooper Hewitt Smithsonian Institution, Jar (Netherlands), *ca.* 1735–1765; Manufactured by Vergulde Bloempot [de] (the Golden Flowerpot); tin-glazed earthenware; 26 x 21 x 21 cm (10 1/4 x 8 1/4 x 8 1/4 in.); Bequest of Walter Phelps Warren; 1986–61-71. And a twin of Figure 5.9, by the same maker, noting 'Havana' tobacco on its label, is held at the Fitzwilliam Museum, Cambridge, C.64 and A-1997. Online auction sites are replete with similar objects.

[169] Maxine Berg and Helen Clifford, 'Selling Consumption in the Eighteenth Century: Advertising and the Trade Card in Britain and France' *Cultural and Social History* 4:2 (2007), p. 146; see also, Maxine Berg, *Luxury and Pleasure in Eighteenth-Century Britain* (Oxford: Oxford University Press, 2005), pp. 270–277.

Africans, as the emblem for this commercial sector.[170] This contrasts dramatically with tobacco retailing.[171]

From the 1600s onwards, tobacco advertisements consistently show-cased Native Americans and African slaves, as metonyms for imperial conquest and the products that ensued. A mid-seventeenth-century trade token, from a business in Pancras Lane, London, reflects the colonial imagery that persisted through time: a man in a feathered headdress, with a large pipe in his mouth, carrying a tobacco leaf, emblems aligned with a business called the 'New Virginia'.[172] Such imagery references not only the culture from which tobacco emerged, but suggests as well the attempted control of these people, lands and products. A hierarchy of peoples was gradually being set in place, one that over time developed into the racial stereotypes addressed by Stuart Hall, stereotypes that were ultimately naturalized, normalized and embedded in European culture.[173]

Pipes, tobacco rolls and tobacco leaves joined with Indigenous Americans and enslaved Africans as ubiquitous eighteenth-century commercial iconography, celebrating a violent land usurpation, plantation production and its adjunct metropolitan consumption. These paper media were widely known and widely viewed: 'distributed on the street, door-to-door, or at sales'.[174] The dark-skinned men inscribed on these sources could be seen as sacrifices, if you will, to the power of imperial consumer appetites. Dark-skinned colonized men appear in

---

[170] One example from the John Johnson Collection (Trade Cards 11(33), Bodleian Library, Oxford) shows a black youth rolling a hogshead of tobacco ashore, with a Chinese man seated on a case of tea. Chandler and Newsom, Tea Dealers and Grocers, Bristol. For examples of trade tokens of sugar sellers: T.2314, London, 1649–1672; 1847,0304.542, London, 1649–1672; T.1189, Chipping Campden, 1667; T.1044, Essex, 1668; T.1043, Essex, 1669; T.802, Colchester, 1649–1672; T.4548, Blackley, 1671; 1992,0103.2, Manchester, 1649–1672, British Museum, London. For examples of grocers' trade cards, see George Farr, Heal, 68.99, *c.* 1750s; R. Brunsden, Heal, 68.45, 1750–1760; John Richardson, Heal, 68.248, 1756; John Reece, D, 2.2367, 1760–1818; Richard Orchard, D,2.2333, 1760–1818; D. Barrett, Heal, 68.19, n.d.; H. P. Gurner, Heal, 68.125, n.d.; M. Jones, Heal, 68.167, n.d. This pattern of commercial imagery is confirmed in the English provincial trade cards published in Stobart, *Sugar and Spice.*

[171] Catherine Molineux, 'Pleasures of the Smoke: "Black Virginians" in Georgian London's Tobacco Shops' *William and Mary Quarterly* 64:2 (2007): 327–376.

[172] Trade token, N2090, 1648–1673, Museum of London.

[173] Hall, Jhally, Talreja and Patierno, *Representation and the Media*, n.p.

[174] Molineux, 'Pleasures of the Smoke', p. 343.

half of the 400 trade cards of tobacconists held in the British Museum, with some figures clearly African, others Indigenous American and still others a fictive pastiche.[175] This mobile media offered popular instructions in the politics of colonial production. Circulating from hand to hand, trade cards and tobacco wrapping paper presented images of conquered and enslaved peoples as mimetic for this commodity. The control of these bodies is made explicit, as a precondition for the consumption of tobacco products by the presumably white-skinned imperial subjects. The use of 'Indians' as shop signs and store markers further exemplifies the racial ordering under way.[176] The power of colonialism was not obfuscated or vaguely referenced. The violence underlying the production of tobacco was often overt, as in Figure 5.6, an eighteenth-century tobacco wrapper or trade card, crudely printed with a stark message of power. It is a simplified rendering of an illustration from the 1626 *Generall Historie of Virginia* that lauded Captain Smith's defeat of the Paspahegh, rhetorically claiming tobacco and the land on which it grows.[177] British settlers now controlled this territory and its precious crop, a patriotic point designed to appeal to customers who benefitted from the colonial system.

Advertisements of this type travelled widely through Britain, Europe and beyond. The illustrations on tobacco trade cards such as Figure 5.7 were examined, exchanged and saved, presenting clear narratives of imperial hierarchies from the white overseer and his black slaves, to the ships beyond that carried them to their new setting and transported tobacco to eager buyers; this image is a variant of that on the Dutch tobacco jar in Figure 5.5. Viewers absorbed the stereotypes that ordered these new racial categories, adding them to an evolving legal

---

[175] The British Museum's Heal and Banks Collection contains one of the largest collections of trade cards in Britain. Molineux, 'Pleasures of the Smoke', p. 330, note 5. Note also, the trade card for 'Stansfield & Co.s Super-Fine Tobacco, Castle-Street, Bristol', showcasing two Native American men in feather headwear, one with a pipe, backed by a hogshead of tobacco. Bristol Museums and Art Gallery, Bristol, UK.

[176] Painted wooden representation of a Native American woman (Pocahontas?), n. d. A8067, Museum of London; the second figure is of a Native American male, *circa* 1780, A6481; while the third figure wears a skirt of tobacco leaves and a feathered headdress. But his skin tone reflects the more hybrid conceptions of racial categories that emerged from plantation systems – A5881, Museum of London. See also Colonial Williamsburg's collection online. These images continued through the 1800s.

[177] Molineux, 'Pleasures of the Smoke', pp. 340–341.

Figure 5.6 Tobacco wrapper or trade card, 1700–1799, PLA2001. © PLA Collection/Museum of London.

and cultural framework that might include direct personal experience of racialized hierarchies. Marcus Rediker notes how sailors learned their whiteness as they served aboard slave ships, in a context of brutally enforced racial gradients of power. These men 'would, on the ship and coast of Africa, become "white", at least for a time, as

Figure 5.7 Tobacco dealer's trade cards. New York Public Library Digital Collections. George Arents Collection, The New York Public Library.

the "vast machine" helped to produce racial categories and identities'.[178] Instruction in these newly defined racial orders took many forms. This was a cumulative process of instruction, whether through direct colonial knowledge, the reports of settler relatives, the political discourse of legislators, the enactment of laws, the advocacy of slave traders, the experiences of soldiers and sailors or the repeated routine depiction of a stereotypical servitude of dark-skinned peoples before white masters. These scenarios underpinned the colonial context of tobacco consumption, demonstrating the might of imperial systems, the ubiquity of colonial enslavement and the fruits of colonial trade. The sweep of this iconography was wide-ranging. Figure 5.8 is a tobacconist's trade card, in Dutch, from Kreuznach in the south Rhineland, a German region that lacked colonies of its own but was ready to embrace this now essential product and the racial tropes that enveloped this commodity. Similar motifs circulated widely in more

---

[178]   Rediker, *Slave Ship*, p. 260.

august circles, crafted by artisans well aware of the benefits of lauding the power of imperialism over the dark-skinned subjects held in thrall. Slavery and colonial conquest were memorialized, along with the goods now so essential to comfort and conviviality.

Materials of many sorts reinforced the racialism entwined with the consumption of this commodity, including domestic furnishings. This ceramic spittoon from about 1715 (Plate 5.5) offers a rich juxtaposition of images: the harvesting of tobacco by African slaves and the processing of the leaves, in the presence of bewigged European men who are revelling in their smoke and are being served by domestic slaves. The racial order is wholly naturalized and normalized in this colourful jug, with tobacco once again the medium of instruction, another of the many primers on the working of the new racialized order. The expectoration of tobacco-laced spittle is implicitly sanctioned in polite society with the use of this vibrant container and its affecting vignettes. These were popular themes for artisans and artists of the day. Tableaux with settlers, African slaves and smoking Native Americans embellished innumerable maps and atlases, as well as other accoutrements of European life.[179] Colonial culture was constructed with the aid of these everyday items, where reductive motifs affirmed new normative hierarchies.

My final example of instructive material culture is a silver-gilt snuffbox from the 1740s. It demonstrates the intimate as well as the public use of racial stereotypes in the theatrics of consumption (Plate 5.6). This English-made trinket houses an interior painting on ivory portraying the sexualized image of a white woman, perhaps a courtesan, with a young black slave standing behind her. The boy's livery and the silver collar around his neck suggests his menial state, a slave in a wealthy household, his raised open hand perhaps a sign of compliance. This male accessory allowed the owner a private or shared titillation along with a pinch of snuff. When the indulgence was over and the snuffbox closed, the woman and boy were sealed inside. Both the woman and the African boy represent aspirational elements of eighteenth-century elite male authority, symbolically deployed. Tobacco consumption

---

[179] For example, image detail, *Quaker Tobacco Planters, Barbados,* 1680. Maps C.24 e23, no. 88. British Library; detail of *A Map of the Western Parts of the Colony of Virginia,* 1754, London, J. Gibson, Yale University Ancient Map Collections Online, www.library.yale.edu/MapColl/oldsite/map/amer.html, accessed 11 February 2016.

Figure 5.8 Unknown, label for Americanischer Tobacco sold by Karcher & Jung, 1750–1800 {nd}; Waddesdon (National Trust) Bequest of James de Rothschild, 1957; acc. no. 3686.4.39.67. Photo: University of Central England Digital Services © National Trust, Waddesdon Manor.

presented a key opportunity to consolidate priorities of many sorts. Perhaps the owner of this toy was invested in the tobacco trade, a plantation owner, or just a gentleman who delighted in the fashionable pleasure of snuff and the symbolic control of subordinates as a statement of elite imperial masculinity.[180] Snuffboxes marked genteel refinement in seventeenth and eighteenth century Europe, with gestures, etiquette and trappings fitting a privileged standing. Tobacco offered a medium through which to explore displays of consumption, where authority and race were now clearly defined. This snuffbox was a less public example of the 'Picturing of Imperial Power'. As Beth Fowkes Tobin asserts, 'Paintings, as is the case with all cultural production, are not merely reflections of larger social and economic forces; they participate in the production of meaning ... [where] Imperial power was asserted, redeployed, and negotiated in what seem to be relatively benign, even mundane paintings'.[181]

In sum, a combination of media redefined tobacco and its consumption, as well as the peoples engulfed in its production and use. Tobacco schooled Europeans in colonial politics and a new racial order, features both constructed and enforced in that age. Catherine Hall observes the impact of Caribbean colonial ties, insisting that 'the links between Jamaica and England were not neutral, not simply a chain of connection. The relations between colony and metropole were relations of power. More significantly, they were relations which were mutually constitutive, in which both coloniser and colonised were made'.[182] Consumer practices of this period involved not simply new supply chains, but a new calculus of power and practice; instruction in these politics came with smoke and snuff.[183]

---

[180] Karen Harvey, 'The History of Masculinity, circa 1650–1800' *Journal of British Studies* 44:2 (2005): 296–311.

[181] Beth Fowkes Tobin, *Picturing Imperial Power: Colonial Subjects in Eighteenth-Century British Painting* (Durham, NC: Duke University Press, 1999), pp. 1, 2.

[182] Catherine Hall, *Civilizing Subjects: Metropole and Colony in the English Imagination, 1830–1867* (Chicago: University of Chicago Press, 2002), p. 8.

[183] For a discussion of colonialism and consumption of a later period, see Joanna de Groot, 'Metropolitan Desires and Colonial Connections: Reflections on Consumption and Empire' in Catherine Hall and Sonya Rose, eds., *At Home with the Empire: Metropolitan Culture and the Imperial World* (Cambridge: Cambridge University Press, 2006), pp. 166–190.

Conclusion

Tobacco took a tangled path on its global circuit. As it spread, it wholly recast habits of relaxation and challenged notional sumptuary orders, gradually becoming integral to economies and cultures in countless global communities from West Africa to Japan. The spread of this commodity marked the age of globalization as perhaps no other and its presence in ever more polities offers a new gauge of cosmopolitan material culture.

It was a measure of the ways men and women interacted with the fruits of global trade. Peasants quickly took up the task of growing this crop, sure of their markets, as this plant offered relaxation or consolation for those constrained by poverty or position, as well as income for small farmers. But it was the ambitions of plantation owners, government administrators and corporations that most profoundly affected this leaf. Markets across the globe were soon flush with this commodity, a fact so routine that both high ranked Mandarin and more humble Chinese subjects were painted with their ubiquitous pipes on hand for their pleasure.[184] But this was only part of the story. This leaf opened possibilities for new coercive consumption and was soon used to control and direct African slaves who learned to find solace in its use. Hard-driven seamen initially championed its benefits, spurring its geographic diffusion along global sea-lanes. Yet they, too, were faced with inequitable options. Their reliance on this weed made them vulnerable to abuse, for they worked within a system designed to profit from their needs. Voyageur shared this vulnerability. The labour of slaves, seamen and voyageurs fuelled the new global system and controlling their labour was crucial to the success of intersecting ventures. I demonstrate the power of coercive consumption to regulate and restraint choice for a defined constituency, even as commodity production soared. Tobacco offered a disciplinary tool for the task.

States bureaucracies across the globe aspired to tax and control tobacco, sparking another form of addiction to this wealth-generating commodity. The literature addressing their efforts is copious, as are the studies revealing the frustration of administrators as extralegal traffic thrived. The expanding taste for new luxuries like tobacco, modestly priced, previously unknown outside the Americas, drove its global

---

[184] See Plates 2.3 and 3.1, painted by William Alexander in 1793.

cultivation and a shared indulgence. And the sociability fostered by tobacco changed material life, whether in Mughal courts or Edo cities. Native Americans initially facilitated this spread, through diplomacy and trade. Slave labour in the Americas drove production and politicized its use. Both groups, in turn, were reified as emblems of this commodity in western cultures. New racial stereotypes and new forms of racialized consumption became part of imperial infrastructure, conveyed to new generations through various media, naturalizing the hierarchies of race being set in place. The repercussions echoed through the centuries ahead. The plant that was a gift from Native Americans to European newcomers, a sacred 'healing, numbing and pain-relieving plant', was commoditized, secularized and racialized, reinforcing new imperial agendas.[185]

---

[185] Norton, *Sacred Gifts, Profane Pleasure*, p. 15.

6 | Stitching the Global

Contact, Connection and Translation in Needlework Arts in the Sixteenth through Nineteenth Centuries

The inhabitants [of Bengal], both men and women, are wonderously adroit in all manufactures, such as of cotton cloth and silks, and in needlework, such as embroideries, which are worked so skilfully, down to the smallest stitches, that nothing prettier is to be seen anywhere ...

François Pyrard, *Voyage ... to the East Indies* (1619)[1]

The squaws are very ingenious in many of their handiworks. We find their birch-bark baskets very convenient for a number of purposes. My bread-basket, knife-tray, sugar-basket, are all of this humble material. When ornamented and wrought in patterns with dyed quills, I can assure you, they are by no means inelegant.... The Indians are acquainted with a variety of dyes, with which they stain the more elegant fancy-baskets and porcupine-quills. Our parlour is ornamented with several very pretty specimens of their ingenuity in this way, which answer the purpose of note and letter-cases, flower-stands, and work-baskets.... Many of the young girls can sew very neatly.

Catherine Parr Traill, *The Backwoods of Canada ...* (1836)[2]

Asia was the source of richly decorative commodities such as porcelain and textiles that carried hybrid designs, some devised through cross-cultural contact over centuries. After 1500, these goods captured a global audience of consumers and sparked new needs and wants, as discussed in previous chapters. But they also triggered translations that were a tribute to the potency of the decorative merchandise itself. Asian wares served as primers for a more globalized aesthetic with motifs amenable to wide cultural interpretation, inspiring artisans and amateurs alike. Recent studies of Asian-sourced products emphasize the reach of these goods and

---

[1] François Pyrard, *The Voyage of François Pyrard of Laval to the East Indies, ...* Translated into English from the third French edition of 1619 ..., vol. 1 (London, Hakluyt Society, 1887), p. 329.

[2] Catherine Parr Traill, *The Backwoods of Canada: Being Letters from the Wife of an Emigrant Officer Illustrative of the Domestic Economy of British America ....* (London: C. Knight, 1836), pp. 168, 169, 170.

their adaptability to different tastes and purposes, including extensive imitations.[3] Samuel Johnson, the noted eighteenth-century British lexicographer, defined imitation as 'a method of translating looser than paraphrase, in which modern examples and illustrations are used for ancient, or domestick for foreign'.[4] The wider flow of Asian and Asianized wares offered models suited to innumerable imitations. Professional and amateur needleworkers outside Asia were among the first to reorient their designs in light of these products and venture new-style renditions. I track that history in this chapter. Worldwide ties hastened material mixing, generating a more globalized vocabulary of design that crossed space and time – a new visual *lingua franca* emerged from this mixing. This language of design employed floral motifs more generally in discursive processes, modeled on Asian exemplars. As well, emblems of material globalism figured as a shorthand of shared connection – the vase with floral bouquet is one such motif, employed for centuries on furniture, ceramics, printed textiles and soft furnishings. Embroidery was an early and persistent translational technology, responding to new globalizing forces. The genesis of this *lingua franca* was not a top-down progression directed from on high, dominated by corporate urgency. Rather the flow of goods engendered new idioms that were grafted on local design stock, yielding a variable but recognizable lineage that marked this era.

Asian floral patterns were among the most powerful emblems of early globalization, speaking to different communities and encouraging a rhetorical exchange. Corporate entities did not intend this communication in signs, though they drove commercial circuits. Rather, I will show

---

[3] John Guy, *Woven Cargoes: Indian Textiles in the East* (London: Thames and Hudson, 1998); Maxine Berg, 'From Imitation to Invention: Creating Commodities in Eighteenth-Century Britain' *Economic History Review* 45 (2002): 1–30 and *Luxury & Pleasure in Eighteenth-Century Britain* (Oxford: Oxford University Press, 2005), especially Chapter 2 'Goods from the East'; Giorgio Riello and Prasannan Parthasarathi, eds., *The Spinning World: A Global History of Cotton Textiles, 1200–1850* (Oxford: Oxford University Press, 2009); Beverly Lemire, *Cotton* (Oxford: Berg, 2011); Amelia Peck, ed., *Interwoven Globe: The Worldwide Textile Trade, 1500–1800* (New York: Metropolitan Museum of Art, 2013); Robert Finlay, 'The Pilgrim Art: The Culture of Porcelain in World History', *Journal of World History* 9:2 (1998) and *The Pilgrim Art: Cultures of Porcelain in World History* (Berkeley: University of California Press, 2010).

[4] 'imitation, n'. OED Online. December 2016. Oxford University Press. www.oed .com.login.ezproxy.library.ualberta.ca/view/Entry/91777?redirectedFrom=imit ation, accessed 23 January, 2017.

how the movement of cargoes, the movement of people, and the needlework of countless hands gave voice to usually voiceless populations
living through these events. I chart the history of this globalizing process
from a material perspective, with contributions from many communities: slave and free, colonizer and colonized. As Asian goods circulated
to new locales, those with sharp eyes and deft fingers deciphered these
objects with needles and fibres, wrestling with – and playing with – the
challenge of translation. These renderings were crafted by a mass of
largely *unlettered* women and men, whose embellished works furnished
homes, dressed bodies and stocked storehouses. Although unlettered,
they were deeply *literate* in signs and symbols. This distinction is key,
foregrounding the interpretive capacities of needleworkers increasingly
touched by globalized objects.

Women in many societies were urged to 'write with their needles',
often restrained from other chronicles. In this era, skills in symbolic
literacy were sharply honed and artfully deployed, thereby revealing
the maker's ties to wider worlds and her picturing of geopolitics.[5]
This responsive stitchery charts the impact of early globalism, as
needleworkers fashioned loose paraphrases time and again or
instructed others in these forms. The importance of ornamented
wares encouraged the movement of people as well as products, transplanting specialist skills to worldwide locales along with imported
cargoes.[6] I track these processes in this chapter. Embroiderers themselves are usually less visible than their work and we must attend to the
fruits of their lives and labours.[7] I focus on embroidery for the malleability and visuality of this art, for the mobility of this technology and
adaptability of its practitioners.

---

[5]   Ann Rosalind Jones and Peter Stallybrass, *Renaissance Clothing and the
       Materials of Memory* (Cambridge: Cambridge University Press, 2000), 134;
       Peck, *Interwoven Globe*, pp. 9, 36–37, 50, 86, 97, 148, 150–153, 161, 167, 176,
       189, 218, 232, 237.
[6]   This could apply as well to skilled Africans who were enslaved and whose
       movement by the millions defined this period. In this case, however, I address
       populations less studied from Asia.
[7]   Distinct traditions and trajectories remained in regional needle arts, even with a
       rising cosmopolitanism. For example, Rachel Silberstein, 'Eight Scenes of
       Suzhou: Landscape Embroidery, Urban Courtesans, and 19th-Century Women's
       Fashions' *Late Imperial China* 36:1 (2015): 1–52; Talia Schaffer, 'Berlin Wool'
       Victorian Review 34:1 (2008): 38–43; Anna Lana, 'Through the Needle's Eye:
       Embroidered Pictures on the Threshold of Modernity' *Eighteenth-Century
       Studies* 31:4 (1998): 503–510.

The global and the colonial were often parallel forces, the cargoes of one used to materialize the relationships of the other, including through the intersection of stitchery and people.[8] The concept of 'entangled objects' fits the events in this chapter.[9] Object study forms the core of my analysis in this chapter, as a careful reading of artefacts enriches chronologies of this era. The 'Social Life of Things', pursued singly or in groups, is now recasting historical understanding of this period, revising a once dominant Eurocentric stance, addressing the circulation of knowledge and the lives of people and things.[10] I explore the transportation of needleworkers as well as freight, linking Asia, Europe and the Americas. Asian women and men, among others, moved (or were moved) as a result of their skills, intensifying the processes of *métissage*. Case studies in these regions are capped by a singular analysis outside the broad timeline of this volume. In my final case study, I survey the needlework fashioned by Native Americans, including the Wendat (Huron) of northeast North America. Their needle wares offer seminal examples of the impact of globalized design, the growth of cosmopolitan material culture and the ways a colonized people secured a position in the marketplace. Catherine Parr Traill, in the opening excerpt, offered her qualified approval of some embellished goods crafted by Anishinaabeg (Ojibwa) women, observing the 'very pretty specimens of their ingenuity'. She remarked as well that 'many of the young girls can sew very neatly'.[11] Importantly, the works they made found space

---

[8] For a discussion of intimacy, the colonial and the global, see Tony Ballantyne and Antoinette M. Burton, 'Introduction: The Politics of Intimacy in the Age of Empire' in Tony Ballantyne and Antoinette M. Burton, eds., *Moving Subjects: Gender, Mobility, and Intimacy in an Age of Global Empire* (Urbana, IL: University of Illinois Press, 2009), pp. 1–30.

[9] Nicholas Thomas, *Entangled Objects: Exchange, Material Culture, and Colonialism in the Pacific* (Cambridge, MA: Harvard University Press, 1991).

[10] Arjun Appadurai, ed., *The Social Life of Things: Commodities in Cultural Perspective* (Cambridge: Cambridge University Press, 1986); Marcy Norton, *Sacred Gifts, Profane Pleasure: A History of Tobacco and Chocolate in the Atlantic World* (Ithaca: Cornell University Press, 2008); Molly Warsh, 'Adorning Empire: A History of the Early Modern Pearl Trade, 1492-1688', unpublished PhD, Johns Hopkins University, 2009); Anne Gerritsen and Giorgio Riello, eds., *The Global Lives of Things: The Material Culture of Connections in the Early Modern World* (Abingdon, UK: Routledge, 2016); Beverly Lemire, 'A Question of Trousers: Seafarers, Masculinity and Empire in the Shaping of British Male Dress, *c.* 1600–1800' *Cultural and Social History* 31:1 (2016): 1–23.

[11] Parr Traill, *The Backwoods of Canada*, pp. 168–170.

within a fully cosmopolitan market distinct to this time, despite the increasingly hostile colonial circumstances. This history is a critical capstone to the process I explore.[12]

Cross-Cultural Flows, Material Translation

K. N. Chaudhuri notes that 'long-distance trade subsumes an exchange of information on cultural values and interpretations, social systems, technology, and artistic sensibilities'. He adds that global connections are 'instrumental in the creation of a language of signs with an immense range of significance'.[13] No formal enrolment was required to learn from these goods and the boundaries of knowledge could not be policed. The women, men, and children who loaded, unloaded and sailed the trading ships, washed linens and bartered goods, traded or were traded themselves, also bought, used, repaired, cleaned and adapted these wares. They (re)interpreted objects in diverse contexts, employing varied spiritual and cultural criteria demonstrated in object use. Laurier Turgeon observes that 'objects like cultures are not immutable ... they change as they move through time and space. Instead of viewing objects simply as products of established social and cultural worlds, recent theories of material culture have demonstrated that the object participates actively in the construction and transformation of these worlds'.[14]

We must first recognize the *layered* categories of Asian wares circling the globe: ceramic, textile, lacquer ware, furniture and metalwork. Contacts with these media, often patterned and designed, magnified

---

[12] For examples of craft among both the Māori and the Andamanese peoples, see Conal McCarthy, '"To Foster and Encourage the Study and Practice of Māori Arts and Crafts": Indigenous Material Culture, Colonial Arts and Crafts and New Zealand Museums'; and Claire Wintle, 'Negotiating the Colonial Encounter: Making Objects for Export in the Andaman Islands, 1858–1920' in Janice Helland, Beverly Lemire and Alena Buis, eds., *Craft, Community and the Material Culture of Place and Politics, 19th–20th Century* (Aldershot, UK: Ashgate, 2014), pp. 59–82, 143–160.

[13] K. N. Chaudhuri, 'Trade as a Cultural Phenomenon' in Jens Christian V. Johansen, Erling Ladewig Petersen and Henrik Stevnborg, eds., *Clashes of Cultures: Essays in Honour of Niels Steensgaard* (Odense: Odense University Press, 1992), p. 210

[14] Laurier Turgeon, 'Material Culture and Cross-Cultural Consumption: French Beads in North American, 1500–1700' *Studies in the Decorative Arts* 9:1 (2001–2002), p. 86.

and intensified their combined impact. These items touched different facets of life, reached diverse social and ethnic populations, amending sociable pastimes and redefining comforts as well as aesthetic possibilities. Reiterative contact and use amplified their affect. For change did not depend on a single influential media or a fleeting conjunction. Powerful influences were achieved through the unremitting impact of complementary material systems and routine layered interactions of material culture, sustained through global trade. Imitations and translations followed. The importance of commercial traffic is clear, in its aggregate spread as well as the paths taken by objects.[15] In this respect, the agency of these goods must be taken into account for their catalyst effects.[16]

Nowhere were goods and people more densely layered than in Batavia, a port that boasted numerous multi-ethnic households, permanent or semi-permanent, where cultural mixing took place and material innovation followed. This exceptional city was headquarters of the Dutch East India Company (VOC) in Asia and attracted a continuous flow of people from Europe and the polities abutting the Indian Ocean and China Seas, being 'a magnetic international emporium'.[17] Alliances of various sorts flourished, sometimes briefly, sometimes over long duration, creating new-style multicultural expressions evident in material culture. Laura Peers describes the *intimate* contact zone within multi-ethnic households in the mid-nineteenth-century Red River settlement in America's northern plains. Her insights are instructive for the many regions that experienced a similar mixing, a contact zone that was 'not a place, or an abstract concept or a space to experience strangeness, but something which existed within themselves, in the marriages of their parents'.[18] Affective scenarios such as this recurred countless times, as suggested in the 1665

---

[15] For the globalized Atlantic, see Robert S. DuPlessis, *The Material Atlantic: Clothing, Commerce and Colonization in the Atlantic World, 1650–1800* (Cambridge: Cambridge University Press, 2016).

[16] Chris Gosden, 'What Do Objects Want?' *Journal of Archaeological Method and Theory* 12:3 (2005), p. 196. See Chapter 1 for additional discussion of the agency of things.

[17] Leonard Blussé, *Visible Cities: Canton, Nagasaki and Batavia and the Coming of the Americans* (Cambridge, MA: Harvard University Press, 2008), p. 37.

[18] Laura Peers, '"Many Tender Ties": The Shifting Contexts and Meanings of the S BLACK Bag' *World Archaeology* 31:2 (1999), p. 291. For the theory of 'contact zone' see Mary Louise Pratt, *Imperial Eyes: Travel Writing and Transculturation* (London: Routledge, 1992).

family portrait of Pieter Cnoll, senior merchant of the VOC in Batavia, his wife Cornelia, two daughters and two domestic slaves (see Plate 4.1). At first glance, this portrait appears to sustain the concept of a unique European mobility, with travel 'the property of colonizers, and stasis the preternatural condition of the indigene'.[19] In fact, travel was a common experience of colonized people adapting to ruptures in their life course, transitions sometimes captured by the needle. This portrait also hints at the dependence of Dutch colonizers on the knowledge and resources of their multi-ethnic household in crafting comfort and conjugality.[20] The densely layered objects and meanings in this family vignette evoke the transformational relationship of people and things that typified this age.

Cornelia was born in Hirado, Japan, in the 1620s to a Japanese mother and a Dutch VOC father. She spent years in her natal land, trained as a female child whose expectations lay between two cultures. Her life demanded practical as well as polished skills.[21] Symbolic references to the power of trade are everywhere in this portrait, a force that fashioned Cornelia's life. Merchant ships anchor on the far horizon. The floral displays in porcelain vases are a trope of this period that was rehearsed in many forms.[22] The Cnoll portrait emphasizes the material politics of Batavian life with fans, dogs, pearls, peonies and accoutrements, the person-to-person, family-to-family mixing of goods and people that accompanied globalizing processes. Forces that shaped Cornelia's life path also shaped the lives of many others, lives figured in material culture.

The dexterity with which women navigated the global is a phenomenon of the age and should not be neglected.[23] Cornelia arrived in Batavia

[19] Ballantyne and Burton, 'Introduction: The Politics of Intimacy in the Age of Empire', p. 5.

[20] Marcy Norton emphasizes the dependence of Spanish colonists in New Spain on Indigenous people, being so numerically outnumbered by Native Americans and Africans. Formal and informal familial relations intensified processes of acculturation of many kinds. Marcy Norton, 'Tasting Empire: Chocolate and the European Internalization of Mesoamerican Aesthetics' *American Historical Review* 111:3 (2006), pp. 670–679.

[21] For a synopsis of the life of Cornelia van Nijenroode (1629–1692?), see resour ces.huygens.knaw.nl/vrouwenlexicon/lemmata/data/Nijenroode, accessed 24 May 2016; Jean Gelman Taylor, 'Meditations on a Portrait from Seventeenth-Century Batavia' *Journal of Southeast Asian Studies* 37:1 (2006): 23–41.

[22] For example, Figure 4.2.

[23] For the voluntary and involuntary travels of Native American children, women and men in the sixteenth and seventeenth centuries, see Coll Thrush, *Indigenous London: Native Travelers at the Heart of Empire* (New Haven: Yale University Press, 2016), Chapter 2.

from Japan, perhaps on a junk or a VOC vessel, and later boarded another ship to journey to the Netherlands. She joined streams of female wayfarers, few as well documented or materially comfortable as she.[24] The majority of the women making this voyage were of multi-ethnic origin, steeped in cosmopolitanism and in search of opportunities.[25] They brought their histories, their goods and their talents on these travels, further evidence of what Natalie Zemon Davis terms 'cultural crossings'.[26]

Sojourners' Tales

Many Asian and Eurasian women journeyed between cultures, either on one-time missions or in cyclical travels that were a matter of routine. They conveyed their skills and aesthetic sensibilities in their person, their tastes and their pastimes. Traces survive of these 'cultural crossings' that demonstrate the creative intermixing appending people and cargoes. Embroidery was a skill that increased the value of women and men, slave or free, and their voyages are sometimes documented on this account. In the sixteenth and early seventeenth centuries, artisans with these talents were shunted from place to place in Asia and sometimes carried further afield with the aim of improving the quality of local embroidery. In 1511, a large Portuguese vessel loaded with 'rich spoils' ran aground on the coast of Sumatra. Besides the luxury cargo, Portuguese authorities bemoaned the loss of 'many women that did embroidery'. Needleworkers of this sort also formed part of the booty seized from the major commercial port of Malacca (Melaka). Other 'embroidresses' from Southeast Asia landed successfully in Lisbon, enriching the pool of talent in the workshop at the Portuguese Royal Palace and becoming famed for their artistry.[27] On other occasions Lisbon received more Asian needleworkers: Japanese and Chinese men,

---

[24] Cornelia was fighting her second husband's predations on her inheritance from her first husband and travelled to the Netherlands to bring her case to court. Her son died during the voyage. Gelman Taylor, 'Meditations', p. 36; Leonard Blussé and Diane Webb, *Bitter Bonds: A Colonial Divorce Drama of the Seventeenth Century* (Princeton, NJ: Markus Wiener, 2002), p. 158.

[25] Gelman Taylor, 'Meditations', pp. 29–35.

[26] Natalie Zemon Davis, 'Decentering History: Local Stories and Cultural Crossings in a Global World' *History and Theory* 50 (2011), p. 197.

[27] Maria Jose de Mendonça, 'Some Kinds of Indo-Portuguese Quilts in the Collection of the Museu de Arte Antiga' in *Embroidered Quilts From the Museu*

plus women embroiderers from the Philippines. Filipino women were noted embroidery specialists. In this period, skills were most easily transferred in the body of the person herself. Improving European embroidery required the physical presence of Asian embroiderers, in addition to richly varied examples of artistry found in imported cargoes. The transplanting of Asian embroiderers played a critical role in the formal transmission of aesthetics, augmenting the impact of freighted goods.[28]

Embroidery is a plastic art, malleable and able to absorb and modify designs without significant economic investment. Rank, gender and ethnicity shaped the education and inspiration that were expressed in aesthetic practice, skills touched as well by geography and time period. Needlework pattern books were few in Europe in the 1600s, becoming more commonplace as parts of lady's journals from the later 1700s. Schoolrooms and workshops were routine sites of instruction for those with access to these institutions, while households served as another educational site for generations of women and girls: kin, servants or slaves. We must likewise keep in mind the direct educational spur of Asian goods themselves as these were observed, handled and studied. This was another component of what Alfred Gell called 'the agency of things', the 'effects that things have on people'.[29] Needleworkers could respond quickly to new stimuli through methods that requiring limited financial input. The introduction of new motifs and new materials demanded imagination from needleworkers. But exquisite talents were not obligatory in the translation process, as amateurs also attempted variants, a trend evident in less celebrated artefacts.[30] Costs could also be relatively modest, requiring needles, thread, ribbon, beads and basic

Nacional de Arte Antiga, Lisboa (London: Kensington Palace, 1978), pp. 13–14.

[28] Edward R. Slack, 'The *Chinos* in New Spain: A Corrective Lens for a Distorted Image' *Journal of World History* 20:1 (2009), p. 42; Maria Joao Pacheco Ferreira, 'Chinese Textiles for Portuguese Tastes' in Amelia Peck, ed., *Interwoven Globe: The Worldwide Textile Trade, 1500–1800* (New York: Metropolitan Museum of Art, 2013) pp. 54–55.

[29] Gosden, 'What Do Objects Want?', p. 193. Alfred Gell, *Art and Agency: An Anthropological Theory* (Oxford: Clarendon Press, 1998).

[30] I present several examples of less than excellent embroideries later in the chapter. My favourite example of enthusiastic but imperfect stitchery is the workbag made by two English sisters, Elizabeth and Anne Batten, 1747, Victoria and Albert Museum, London. These makers wrestled with their interpretation of Asian-inspired motifs.

cloth or other media to be adorned – very moderate outlays compared to the fixed capital investment required for mills, kilns or elaborate looms where other systematic adaptions would be tried.[31] The needle-powered unique elaborations.

In 1847, Mary Margaret, Countess of Wilton, denounced the neglect of 'the needle and its beautiful and useful creations [that] hitherto remained without their due meed of praise and record'.[32] She noted scornfully the preference of historians for the 'false prestige' of 'the scathing and destroying sword'. Since issuing her indictment, Wilton's concerns have been addressed by many scholars, confirming the utility of studying the needlework made by women and men for insights into cultural value and the politics of making. Rozsika Parker launched a contemporary feminist critique of historical Western embroidery almost a century and a half after Wilton's account. Parker challenged those who would ignore women-made needle arts, assigning them marginal status. She insisted that embroidery was 'art', a defiant repositioning in the 1980s, now more widely accepted. She emphasized as well the underlying intent of those engaged in this work, those who 'transform material to produce sense – whole ranges of meanings'.[33] I attend to these meanings, positioning these works within global narratives, signalling the contributions of these arts, artists and amateurs within the confluence of world events.[34]

Asian patterning included many forms: densely flowered borders, the sinuous twining of flowered vines; distinctive trees of life, the scattered

---

[31] Maxine Berg, 'In Pursuit of Luxury: Global History and British Consumer Goods in the Eighteenth Century' *Past and Present* 182:1 (2004): 85–142; Giorgio Riello, *Cotton: The Fabric That Made the Modern World* (Cambridge: Cambridge University Press, 2013).

[32] Although the author is stated as being Mrs. Owen, internal and other evidence indicates that this history is the work of Mary Margaret Stanley Egerton, Countess of Wilton (1801–1858). *The Illuminated Book of Needlework ... Including An Account of the Ancient Historical Tapestries ...* (London: Henry G. Bohn, 1847), p. v.

[33] Rozsika Parker, *The Subversive Stitch: Embroidery and the Making of the Feminine* (London: The Women's Press Ltd., 1984), p. 6. Male guild members often performed the highest quality embroidery; however, women's needlework remained a persistent facet of female religious communities and household employment at all social classes, as well as a part of paid female labour.

[34] Laurel Thatcher Ulrich pointed to needlework as a vital scholarly source to uncover the history of women, as 'far more women were accustomed to using needles than pens'. 'Of Pens and Needles: Sources in Early American Women's History' *Journal of American History* 77:1 (1990), p. 205.

placement of flora, insects and birds; or the important positioning of vases overflowing with botanic wealth (Plates 6.1 and 6.2). The impact of these themes was felt in many settings, including among the women embroiderers in Castelo Branco, Portugal. Embroidered quilts from the Indian subcontinent were a notable fashion from the 1500s onwards, as were printed and painted Indian cotton palampores (bedcoverings and hangings), a subject addressed in Chapter 2. These vibrant furnishings revised the look of bedrooms, an increasingly important domestic space, and the Bengal embroidered hanging illustrates the visual richness of this media (Plate 2.5). Portugal, as an early importer of these wares, was likewise a site of early imitations and innovations. Indian quilts were revered throughout Iberia, and in the town of Castelo Branco such quilts appeared routinely in women's dowries.[35] These draperies (Plates 6.1 and 6.2) demonstrate some of the appeal of Indian fittings. Porcelain vases – sources of verdant vines or lavish bouquets – anchor each corner of the exterior border and mark the interior corners as well in the palampore (Plate 6.1). The tree of life motif is rendered in several variations, demonstrating imaginative versions of a seminal subject. Goods like these offered active tuition, heightened further if combined with a tutor skilled in the arts of reproduction. Imports and information flowed to the border town of Castelo Branco, perhaps including foreign embroiderers themselves. We cannot trace all the routes taken by migrants. But it is clear that the agency of goods encouraged imitations. Thereafter, women in this region of Portugal developed a speciality in embroidered quilts based on Indian models, products renowned in Lusitanian circles (Plate 6.3).

The tree of life motif possessed ancient cultural and religious resonance shared in many traditions, including Hinduism, Buddhism, Islam, Judaism and Christianity, the tree being a metaphor for life, fecundity and spirituality.[36] Asian forms encouraged Europeans to address decorative priorities from new vantage points, looking for the

---

[35] Barbara Karl, '"Marvellous Things Are Made with Needles": Bengal *Colchas* in European Inventories, c. 1580–1630' *Journal of the History of Collections* 23:2 (2011), p. 310.

[36] George Lechler, 'The Tree of Life in Indo-European and Islamic Cultures' *Islamica* 4 (1937): 369–419; Zofja Ameisenowa and W. F. Mainland, 'The Tree of Life in Jewish Iconography' *Journal of the Warburg Institute* 2:4 (1939): 326–345; E. O. James, 'The Tree of Life' *Folklore* 79:4 (1968): 241–249.

familiar in a different decorative vernacular. Plate 6.2 in particular demonstrates the breadth of Indian botanic forms, including densely patterned borders. Those who owned or saw these goods had much to consider.[37] Imitations followed. Castelo Branco embroiderers turned to plain linen, which cost a fraction of the outlay for richly decorated Indian palampores. Locally made linen was then patterned in silk thread, often following the tree of life motif (Plate 6.3). Work on such projects could take place in formal and informal settings, in workshops or in homes, involving journeywomen and -men, or domestic servants and slaves. With or without Asians as instructors, the women of Castelo Branco launched an effective facsimile of this globalized style. This was one of many to take root in Iberia and its colonies, where embroidered quilts, or *colcha*, became a byword of local needlework arts.[38] The Mexican *colcha* presented in Plate 2.6 offers another restatement of this style.

'Translation' is a useful word for describing a global material environment in flux. We need to be attentive to connections and the translations that ensued as each culture assessed and digested the patterns and precepts found in imported wares. Peter Burke discusses *textual* translation in a way that may apply to *textiles*, noting that 'translations were often made indirectly, at second hand'. Such can be the case with copies recopied in turn. Burke writes further that 'whether translators follow the strategy of domestication or that of foreignizing, whether they understand or misunderstand the text they are turning into another language, the activity of translation necessarily involves both decontextualization and recontextualization'.[39] Stitches visualized knowledge systems. Asian wares intruded into aesthetic, spiritual and functional systems to be 'decontextualized' and 'recontextualized' in a myriad of world locales, not all of which I discuss here. Stitching was performative, learned and

---

[37] Lemire, *Cotton*, Chapter 5; Maria João Ferreira, 'Asian Textiles in the Carreira da Índia: Portuguese Trade, Consumption and Taste, 1500–1700' *Textile History* 46:2 (2015), p. 158; Jack Goody, *The Culture of Flowers* (Cambridge: Cambridge University Press, 1993).

[38] Mary Montaño, *Tradiciones Neuvomexicanas: Hispano Arts and Culture of New Mexico* (Albuquerque: University of New Mexico Press, 2001), pp. 111–112. See Chapter 2 for further discussion of embroidered *colcha* in Spanish America.

[39] Peter Burke, 'Cultures of Translation in Early Modern Europe' in Peter Burke and R. Po-Chia Hsia, eds., *Cultural Translation in Early Modern Europe* (Cambridge: Cambridge University Press, 2007), pp. 27, 38.

articulated, denoting traits of gender, rank and ethnicity. We cannot essentialize the sites of stitchery or the agents in these generative processes. What marks this period were the diffusion of new models and the absorption of new motifs that blended with local idioms to develop a new *lingua franca* in design. Translation was the critical intermediate step, and women were essential arbiters in this practice.

How many embroiderers travelled the world's oceans? There were no muster lists of needlewomen as there were for the crews on merchant ships. Many women, though lacking a formal designation of 'embroiderer', also possessed skills in stitchery as one of their talents – the embellishment and repair of fabrics being ubiquitous training for women of many cultures. Domestic service and workshop life demanded capacities of this sort. Other sources suggest the ways 'cultural crossings' were routinized, with aesthetic translations as a part of relocation. Michael H. Fisher writes of the 'counterflows' of labour that characterized British East India Company ventures. He notes that 'more Indian seamen than any other class went to Britain', essential labour for ships' crews.[40] Less celebrated and less visible, generations of Asian domestics accompanied European travellers on these passages, servant and slave, women and men. Europeans resident in Asia depended on local labour for their comforts, with households defined by their ceaseless domestic industry, including the intimate care of a lady's or gentleman's clothing and person. Deftness with a needle was critical to the care and making of fashions and fittings.[41] The colonial process included the routinized toil of Indigenous women and men in countless homes, an intimate site of labour and essential as a mechanism of colonial settlement and expansion.[42] These women and men instructed Europeans in the sensory facets of Asian life, including aesthetics denoted in textile forms.

[40] Michael H. Fisher, *Counterflows to Colonialism: Indian Travellers and Settlers in Britain 1600–1857* (Delhi: Permanent Black, 2004), p. 32.

[41] For expectations of British servants by their employers, see Amy M. Froide, *Never Married: Singlewomen in Early Modern England* (Oxford: Oxford University Press, 2005), pp. 89, 174.

[42] Victoria K. Haskins and Claire Lowrie, 'Introduction' in Victoria K. Haskins and Claire Lowrie, eds., *Colonization and Domestic Service: Historical and Contemporary Perspectives* (New York: Routledge, 2015), pp. 1–18 and B. W. Higman, 'An Historical Perspective: Colonial Continuities in the Global Geography of Domestic Service' in Haskins and Lowrie, *Colonization and Domestic Service*, pp. 19–40.

Figure 6.1 *Room with Son, Johnny, and Slave, Flora*, Ceylon, 1784. Jan Brandes (1743–1808). NG-1985-7-2-4. Rijksmuseum, Amsterdam.

The watercolour scene of Johnny and the domestic slave Flora suggests the relationships, proximities and material complexity that defined colonial family life (Figure 6.1). Flora was likely a constant presence for the Dutch boy and a contributor to colonial material life in many ways.[43]

---

[43] For domestic slavery in Anglo-Indian households, see Margot Finn, 'Slaves Out of Context: Domestic Slavery and the Anglo-Indian Family, c. 1780–1830' *Transactions of the Royal Historical Society* 19 (2009): 181–203.

The naming of this woman breaks the bounds of anonymity, a state that was all too common for many Asian domestics. Here, Flora demonstrates her textile capacities, certainly one of many talents at her command.[44] This vignette by Jan Brandes, a Lutheran pastor in the employ of the VOC, was crafted as a memento of a particular time and place – and of relationships that stretched across oceans – depicting everyday intimacy in a scene where the female slave holds a pivotal space.[45]

When journeys arose, Asian servants and slaves travelled with their charges, linking world ports and world communities. They cared for babes and children; they accompanied officers and gentlewomen on long journeys. Some spent years in Europe as their employers settled into new abodes and new domestic routines were established. How was the collective and individual influence of these Asian sojourners expressed? Tony Bickham talks of food as being 'at the heart of the British imperial experience', noting changing culinary tastes over the eighteenth century. The appetite for curries can be tracked in published cookbooks of that era, echoing cravings learned in Asia that were now satisfied in British households.[46] Europe's corporate connections with Asia predicated many changes in habit, with Asian domestics reinforcing the tastes acquired in Asia while living conjointly with families throughout the metropole.

Patterns in needlework were touched not only by imports or by the travels of embroiderers to European workshop, but also by the steady stream of Asian servants whose needle skills expressed their cultural capital. Importantly, the journeys and sojourns of these Indian domestics model similar travels linking Manila and Acapulco, whereby Asian servants and slaves, many with fine textile skills, settled in New Spain with their masters and mistresses. Their origins varied, coming from 'Timor, Ternate, Makassar, Burma, Ceylon, and India'. The women, in particular, were noted as 'excellent seamstresses . . . and neat and clean

---

44 For a nineteenth-century example of food service as part of the interaction between Indian servants and colonists, see Cecilia Leong-Salobir, *Food Culture in Colonial Asia: A Taste of Empire* (Abingdon, UK: Routledge, 2011), pp. 60–87.

45 Max de Bruijn and Remco Raben, eds., *The World of Jan Brandes, 1743–1808: Drawings of a Dutch Traveller in Batavia, Ceylon and Southern Africa* (Amsterdam: Waanders Publishers-Rijksmuseum, 2004).

46 Troy Bickham, 'Easting the Empire: Intersections of Food, Cookery and Imperialism in Eighteenth-Century Britain' *Past and Present* 198 (February 2008), pp. 103–107.

in service'.[47] Female Asian domestics were tasked to sew as matter of course.[48] And while their acknowledged work has receded into obscurity, their contributions are certain. In 1769, the EIC mandated that Britons returning from India with Indian servants place a bond, which would be refunded upon the servants' return. Throughout, the numbers of Indian domestics arriving (and settling) in Britain grew steadily.[49] Hundreds of letters were written to the EIC Directorate requesting permission to bring servants to and from India, with costs covered by the employer. These journeys involved an enforced closeness in small spaces, where routine dependency defined relationships between employer and attendant.[50] Reading between the lines, a pattern becomes clear of Indian servants cycled to and from the subcontinent, staying for indeterminate lengths of time, shaping metropolitan culture in important ways.

Margot Finn has explored the innumerable connections forged between Britain and India through family lives, micro-histories that trace reciprocal relationships. The life stories and the material traces uncovered in this project reflect the profound changes underway in the colonial metropole, including its material life.[51] The Indian servants disembarking in Britain add another dimension to this history.[52] One request letter sent to the EIC in 1712 noted the 'two black servants who have been sometime in England & their Masters having no farther Occasion for them, & they Desirous to return to

---

[47] Slack, 'The *Chinos* in New Spain', p. 41.

[48] For the Caribbean and African slaves, see Karol K. Weaver, 'Fashioning Freedom: Slave Seamstresses in the Atlantic World' *Journal of Women's History* 24:1 (2012), pp. 44–59.

[49] Michael H. Fisher, 'Excluding and Including "Natives of India": Early Nineteenth-Century British-Indian Race Relations in Britain' *Comparative Studies of South Asia, Africa and the Middle East* 27:2 (2007), p. 307.

[50] Mss/77/178.0, Journal of a Voyage to Bengal on the Sea Horse East Indiaman 1777, p. 253. Caird Library, National Maritime Museum, Greenwich.

[51] See the website East India Company at Home, 1757–1857, for its case studies at blogs.ucl.ac.uk/eicah/home/, accessed 5 June 2016. Also, Kate Smith, 'Empire and the Country House in Early Nineteenth-Century Britain: The Amherts of Montreal Park, Kent' *Journal of Colonialism and Colonial History* 16:3 (2015). *Project MUSE,* doi:10.1353/cch.2015.0042.

[52] British anxiety about the intimacy that developed between their children and Indian servants is considered in Dara Rossman Regaignon, 'Intimacy's Empire: Children, Servants, and Missionaries in Mary Martha Sherwood's "Little Henry and his Bearer"' *Children's Literature Association Quarterly* 26:2 (2001): 84–95.

their own Country'.[53] A similar appeal was made to repatriate a servant named Lucretia to Fort St George in 1713.[54] The seasonal arrival and departure of EIC vessels was accompanied by a flurry of correspondence concerned with the disposition of Indian women and men. In 1733, return passage was arranged for a married Indian couple that resided in Britain for an unspecified period of time; following the birth of their child in Britain, they wished to return to Bombay, a request that was granted. Rosa stayed with Mrs. Jane Snow for some months after sailing from India to England in 1734, most likely keeping her clothes in order, perhaps helping curate Indian novelties for friends and family, or completing small needlework projects.[55] East Indiamen sailed according to assigned seasons, with many months between arrivals and departures and Indian servants could expect a minimum six-month stay in Britain. Documentation is suggestive, outlining the multilayered, sustained, domestic interactions in Asia and Europe during which new translations marked household material culture.

An eighteenth-century traveller, Johanna Kellett, noted the 'Black Woman Servant that İ brought over with me in the Wilmington in August last' when writing to the EIC in late February 1736, requesting the woman's return passage. When large, wealthy families traversed the oceans, their entourage included numbers of Indian attendants. In one case, three 'Black Women' were deemed necessary 'to attend to my family' on a journey from Bengal in 1716. Some years later, three other servants named 'Susan, Susan, & Taliciana ... Attended Mrs Watson [and] her Children, and Master Russell to England'. Catherina, termed a 'black servant', cared for a child on the voyage to London over months in 1767, before being sent back to India. Another woman named Soubina, 'a Black Nurse' cared for another child on a journey to England in 1768, perhaps being a member of the household in Bengal long before this journey.[56] Britons leaving for India also hired Indian servants in the metropole, confirming the routine presence of this population in London and major ports, women and men available for long-distance journeys as

[53] BL, IOR/E/1/4/199, 16 January 1712.
[54] BL, IOR/E/1/4/374, 23 December 1713.
[55] BL, IOR/ E/1/24/25, 12 January 1733; IOR E/1/26/2, 9 January 1735.
[56] BL, IOR/E/1/7/50, 5 September 1716; IOR/E/1/29/155, 19 December 1740;
      IOR, E/1/24/25, 6 February 1733; E/1/26/2, 9 January 1735; E/1/27/82, 25
      February 1736; E/1/50/103, 11 February 1768; E/1/50/123 19 February 1768.

well as employment *in situ.*[57] Passing reference to the duration of Indians' residency in Britain includes phrases like 'some Years since', 'Seven Years Agoe', or 'last Year', bolstering the important fact of Indians in European households, hinting at their cumulative impact. Like the travellers from Batavia absorbed into Dutch society, these residents from the subcontinent seeded their new British homes with skills and capacities acquired in Asia, now reinterpreted in new terrain.[58]

Emma Rothschild terms this relational pattern 'the inner life of empires' founded on family and individuals, where surviving documentation is 'extraordinarily diverse and disproportionate'.[59] The Johnstone family, the subject of Rothschild's study, returned to England in circumstances like those I describe, in the care of Belinda, a Bengali servant well known to them. Belinda lived four years with the Johnstone family in London, on their return from India about 1771, before moving with them to Scotland and ultimately being transported to America.[60]

Domestic slavery also figured in these relationships, shaping household structure and service. Indeed, some of the embroiderers mentioned above were enslaved and served in both commercial and domestic settings. Margot Finn emphasizes the pervasiveness of domestic slavery in Asia, particularly in households of EIC staff in India. Slavery in the Indian Ocean world involved a majority female constituency, who were assigned a higher value than males. Their roles were primarily domestic, and they employed talents from cleaning and cooking to concubinage, as well as the production and care of clothing and furnishings. Stitchery was among their aptitudes.[61] The intimate contact zone is iterated here in another context including the enslaved children of enslaved concubines who might learn practical skills essential for girls.[62] Young female slaves were also shipped from India to Europe as gifts, including to at least one royal household, as arranged

---

57   BL, IOR/E/1/15/48, 6 March 1724; IOR/E/1/55, 3 April 1771, IOR/E/1/55, 5 April 1771.
58   BL, IOR/E/1/50/124, 19 February 1768; IOR/E/1/55, 8 April 1771; IOR/E/1/40/35, 9 February 1757; IOR/E/1/24/11, 12 January 1732.
59   Emma Rothschild, *The Inner Life of Empires: An Eighteenth-Century History* (Princeton: Princeton University Press, 2011), p. 5.
60   Rothschild, *Inner Life of Empires*, pp. 87–91.
61   Finn, 'Slaves Out of Context'.
62   Peers, 'S BLACK Bag'; Sophie White, *Wild Frenchmen and Frenchified Indians: Material Culture and Race in Colonial Louisiana* (Philadelphia: University of Pennsylvania Press, 2013).

by the Danish East India Company in the 1740s.[63] This systematic movement of people compels us to think about the sustained influence of human travellers in combination with the flow of commodities, the sum of which was transformative.

These countless connections denote other ways in which the material culture of one world region was transposed and translated in another, moving across shipping routes and invested in family settings. Did Asian slaves and sojourners teach stitchery in households as well as workshops? Almost certainly. Did they help with collective embroidery projects within the family, guiding young hands or assisting mistresses? Again, this is probable. Documentation is slight but suggestive, outlining the multilayered interactions in Asia, Europe and other colonial settings. The presence and contributions of these sojourners cannot be ignored. Practices evolved and tastes changed, shaped by (and shaping) slave and free, colonial and metropolitan subjects. The passage of goods, the passage of people and the revision of material culture mark globalizing systems, systems that were expressed in new floral design and the varied translations of these forms.

Floral Exchange: Europe and Beyond

How did European women respond to the flood of patterned textiles and ceramics from Asia? There is a large literature on the dramatic influences of Asian imports on European industry, commerce and fashion, some of which I have addressed in previous chapters. Investors and industrialists attempted imitations of various sorts, efforts that advanced only gradually until the eighteenth century. It is also useful to consider the question in a new way, examining botanical motifs in light of European custom and popular culture, as new interpretations of botanic aesthetics flowed into the region. Natalie Zemon Davis, E. P. Thompson and others demonstrate the persistence of long-standing 'rites, pageants, and ceremonies' in a Europe steeped in tradition.[64] I consider the floriated

---

[63] K. Struwe, *Vore gamle Tropekolonier*, ed. Johannes Brøndsted, vol. 6 (Copenhagen: SAXO, 1967).

[64] Quoted in E.P. Thompson, *Customs in Common: Studies in Traditional Popular Culture* (New York: The New Press, 1993), p. 50; Natalie Zemon Davis, *Society and Culture in Early Modern France: Eight Essays* (Stanford: Stanford University Press, 1975), pp. 114, n. 141; Robert Darnton, *The Great Cat Massacre: And Other Episodes in French Culture History* (New York: Basic Books, 1984), p. 133.

imports from Asia not just for their qualities as determined by account books and fashionable shoppers, but also for the ways this imagery melded with traditional beliefs and values.[65] Popular folk culture included vibrant botanic knowledge and traditions, some of which authorities approved and others they disparaged as disruptive or worse.[66] Flora of many kinds were planted or collected for medicinal, gustatory and social uses, with some plants holding particular resonance.[67] Flowers and fruits marked calendars and life passage.[68] Priests in France customarily blessed flowers and herbs during the Catholic holy day of the Assumption of the Virgin and heaps were scattered in the marketplaces on which celebrants danced. The connection between the botanic and female fecundity is clear. Even in England, in the heart of the northern Reformation, traditions held sway, as with maypoles in the spring as women were crowned Queen of May with wreaths of posies.[69] Floral folk customs were sustained with purpose, like the 'Old Maypole' dressed with garlands in a Somerset town. When a new landowner cut it down in the spring of 1724, two local men felled an elm to make another maypole despite promised punishment.[70] Floral culture mattered and was resilient in many areas of life, part of a persistent magical or occult practice found throughout Enlightenment Europe.[71] Thus, another way to

---

[65] Riello, *Cotton*, pp. 148–150.

[66] Early modern European physicians who attempted to systematize customary knowledge captured traditional and elite botanic wisdom – as did Nicholas Culpeper (1616–1654), whose 1652 volume was reprinted for generations. *Culpeper's English Physician and Complete Herbal* ... (London: Lewis and Roden, 1805).

[67] For discussion of the habitual use of flowers as culinary and medicinal additions in common and elite English households, as well as those in Europe, see Joan Thirsk, *Food in Early Modern England: Phases, Fads, Fashions 1500–1760* (London: Hambledon Continuum, 2007), pp. 50–52, 71, 82 and Joan Thirsk, *Alternative Agriculture: A History from the Black Death to the Present Day* (Oxford: Oxford University Press, 1997), pp. 39–40; Amy Gazin-Schwartz, 'Archaeology and Folklore of Material Culture, Ritual, and Everyday Life' *International Journal of Historical Archaeology* 5:4 (2001): 263–280.

[68] Natalie Zemon Davis, *The Gift in Sixteenth-Century France* (Oxford: Oxford University Press, 2000), pp. 45–46.

[69] Edward Muir, *Ritual in Early Modern Europe*, 2nd ed. (Cambridge: Cambridge University Press, 2005), pp. 101–102, 204.

[70] Thompson, *Customs in Common*, pp. 16–97; Goody, *Culture of Flowers*, p. 283.

[71] Jacqueline van Gent, *Magic, Body, and Self in Eighteenth-Century Sweden* (Leiden: Brill, 2009).

measure the penetration of globalized floral motifs is to assess their uses in private and customary forms, seeing whether tradition and innovation allied.

Flora should be recognized for the functional and affective purposes they served: vital physic, esteemed flavouring, sign of life-cycle stage and general source of female power. No motif was more affiliated with female arts than the botanic.[72] 'Gathered my Balm flowers', wrote Martha Ballard in July 1801; this midwife was a valued resident of her colonial community in Maine and was noted for her healing skills.[73] Like women before her, the botanic knowledge she employed took many shapes, enhancing her reputation. That being so, we might expect that floral decoration devised by women and girls would always be visible: a claim for prestige and a source of pride, as with the quilts described above. However, my first case study combines customary use and globalized flora in a private garment never publically displayed: the tie-on pocket. Pockets were hidden from the public eye beneath flowing petticoats or gowns, a practice followed by women of all social classes in northwest Europe and their colonies from the seventeenth through the nineteenth centuries. Pockets, attached to tape or ribbon, were cinched around the waist over the shift and accessed through side slits made in the outer garment. Barbara Burman argues for the pocket's sexualized meaning, with a 'uterine symbolism in both its shape and its function', secured at the centre of the female body.[74] This garment allowed a unique material privacy and a unique management of self-selected goods to facilitate private and domestic life. This secreted garment was also commonly embroidered in floral stitchery in variations of the globalized style. The girls and women crafting these symbolic and functional objects were apparently comfortable with these

---

[72] Barbara Ehrenreich and Deirdre English, *Witches, Midwives, and Nurses: A History of Women Healers*, 2nd ed. (New York: Feminist Press, 2010), pp. xiv–xv, 19.

[73] Laurel Thatcher Ulrich, *A Midwife's Tale: The Life of Martha Ballard, Based on Her Diary, 1785–1812* (New York: Vintage Books, 1990), p. 354. Ulrich notes Ballard's deep dependence on traditional English herbal knowledge, typically passed from mother to daughter. In colonial settings herbal cures were also learned from Native Americans and Africans, augmenting botanic possibilities.

[74] Barbara Burman, 'Pocketing the Difference: Gender and Pockets in Nineteenth-Century Britain' *Gender & History* 14:3 (2002), p. 452; see also, Ariane Fennetaux, 'Women's Pockets and the Construction of Privacy in the Long Eighteenth Century' *Eighteenth-Century Fiction* 20:3 (2008): 307–334.

Figure 6.2 Pair of white linen pockets embroidered with wool thread in a floral design, 1770–1780. 001078. © Museum of London.

expressions, while keeping true to the usage and meaning of their pockets. Figure 6.2 and Plate 6.4 are two examples of the many floral embroidered pockets in museum collections. Other instances of popular culture offer parallel illustrations of concealment and the power of the botanic.

Custom still held sway in many aspects of European life. The custom of deliberately concealing garments in house walls flourished in Scandinavia, central and northwest Europe, and their colonies in the Americas and Australia from the sixteenth through the nineteenth centuries. Hidden objects could hold particular power.[75] In such cases, garments were ritually sacrificed and hidden in walls by house openings. The items themselves were typically worn and commonplace,

---

[75] Hidden knots, for example, were believed to impede fertility and their discovery near a crib could lead to charges of witchcraft. Van Gent, *Magic, Body and the Self,* pp. 148, 183.

the used garments seen to hold spiritual force to protect the homes' inhabitants once in place. The phenomenon confirms the importance of careful attention to material signs, for this practice is recorded only through physical evidence. There is no contemporary written documentation of this widespread, long-lived practice. These objects signal a persistent customary, non-Christian belief that paralleled the Age of Enlightenment, rising commercial capitalism and colonial conquests.[76]

Was there a similar symbolic intent with hidden embroidered pockets, given their shape and placement? In fact, a mid-eighteenth-century pear-shaped pocket was recovered from its domestic hiding place in an attic wall of an eighteenth-century house in Oxfordshire. Before it was put between the walls, this homemade accessory was stuffed with a baby's cap, hop seeds and coins, elements rich in symbolic significance. And although this object was not embroidered, it was made of cloth printed with a tendril vine bedecked with deep-pink flower buds.[77] This deliberately concealed pocket is rife with allusions to women's generative powers, with intentionality apparent in the choice of fabric. This echoes the choice of floriated designs on so many pockets. Embroidered pockets reference botanic knowledge as well as being an exercise in feminine forms. The embroidered pockets in museums collections are similarly suggestive, and several scholars consider floral embroidered pockets to be the norm, an important observation.[78] Early modern globalization shaped the imagery employed and altered the vocabulary of design, while holding true to the female alignment with traditional wisdom. There seems to be a seamless dedication in these embellishments to customary gender power allied to the female body and botanic culture. These pockets evince the continued power of the botanic amidst aesthetic change. Yet they also confirm the deep penetration of globalized floral idioms, comfortably integrated into customary rites or

---

[76] Dinah Eastop, 'Outside In: Making Sense of the Deliberate Concealment of Garments within Buildings' *Textile* 4:3 (2006): 238–255; Sarah Randles, 'Material Magic: The Deliberate Concealment of Footwear and Other Clothing' *Parergon* 30:2 (2013): 109–128; www.concealedgarments.org, accessed 5 June 2016.

[77] www.concealedgarments.org/cache/28558/, accessed 23 June 2016. Fennetaux, 'Pockets', pp. 332–333; Anna Harrison and Kathryn Gill, 'An Eighteenth-Century Detachable Pocket and Baby's Cap, Found Concealed in a Wall Cavity: Conservation and Research' *Textile History* 33:2 (2002): 177–194.

[78] Harrison and Gill, 'An Eighteenth-Century Detachable Pocket', p. 182.

gendered garments, corroborating the adaptability of the new floral lexis.

Samplers, cushion covers and chimneypieces were some of the many stitchery exercises for *public* display, along with large collaborative projects such as embroidered quilts, bed curtains and hangings.[79] Numerous examples of this type denote the important public recitation of floral themes. I am intrigued by the countless humble efforts archived in museum storerooms, demonstrating the priorities of those wielding their needles in domestic or schoolroom settings. Their compositions narrate the aesthetic translations underway in Europe and its colonies, recounted through needle and thread. Figure 6.3, completed in 1686, confirms the powerful visual impact of Asian ceramics and textiles on European and Euro-American audiences and the interpretations that ensued. A cotton/linen fabric provides the base for this blue and white composition, a colour choice saluting the renowned blue and white ceramics of Asian origin. The author of this work adopts the iconic motif of the porcelain vase filled with domestic and trans-planted blooms: roses, carnations, tulips and an iris. Two birds anchor the bottom corners, the parrot a mnemonic of distant shores. She edges this still life with a version of the foaming wave motif that was typical of Chinese ceramics and their imitators in this period. This may be a case where translation was attempted 'indirectly, at second hand', with the seamstress never having seen Chinese wares.[80] Yet the interpretation proves the power of the originating media. The initials R. H. show her pride in this artistry, a hybrid confection marking the wider forces within which personal projects were performed.

Philadelphia resident Elizabeth Jefferis left a later record of her skills in a crewelwork piece dated 1777 (Figure 6.4). Laurel Thatcher Ulrich observes that 'needlework education was a form of consumption, but it was not frivolous. Bending over their embroidery frames, little girls added value to themselves as well as to the silks their parents pur-chased'.[81] The materials for this project were less costly than silk, the

---

[79] Laurel Thatcher Ulrich, *The Age of Homespun: Objects and Stories in the Creation of an American Myth* (New York: Knopf, 2001), Chapter 4 and 6; and for older women's floral patterned embroidery, see Aimee E. Newell, *A Stitch in Time: The Needlework of Aging Women in Antebellum America* (Athens, OH: Ohio University Press, 2014), Chapters 5 and 7.

[80] Burke, 'Cultures of Translation in Early Modern Europe', p. 27.

[81] Ulrich, *Age of Homespun*, p. 147.

Figure 6.3 Blue wool embroidery on twill cotton / linen cloth, made by R.H., 1686. 34.2. Gift of Mrs. Edward R. Warren. Museum of Fine Arts, Boston.

dexterity of the maker determining its worth. Jefferis was another in the long line of females trained to these tasks, sometimes as an ornament of genteel womanhood, at other times as a way to earn a living. Her familiarity with worldly commodities can be expected, as Philadelphia was a major Atlantic port. The palampore lineage is fully apparent in this work with a stylized tree of life, but Jefferis' is a simplified paraphrase with two

Figure 6.4 Linen ground embroidered with crewel wool, 1777, Philadelphia, Pennsylvania, made by Elizabeth Jefferis. 59.20. Rogers Fund, 1959. Metropolitan Museum of Art, New York.

branches hanging in mid-air as perches for parrots, amidst carnations, roses and tulip. Too small to be a hanging or bed cover, the truncated scale of Jefferis' piece (86 x 80 cm) nevertheless required planning and adjustments. The results are imperfect. But perfection is not my focus. Rather, I consider the intention of the maker and the ornamentation employed. Elizabeth Jefferis shows fluency in the vocabulary of design that originated in Asia and coursed through European and colonial realms. She mastered its idioms and domesticated its phrasing. In this respect Jefferis joined Asian, Eurasian, European, colonial and Indigenous women who deployed variants of these signs and designs, though different life

circumstances defined their condition: 'transform[ing] material to produce sense – whole ranges of meanings'.[82] Native American women
added to this material conversation.

Indigenous North American Art in a Globalizing World

Ruth Phillips is at the forefront of cultural analyses of Native American
art, including her influential work on the embroidery arts of Indigenous
peoples from northeast North America. Given that pre-contact
Indigenous design was predominantly geometric, Phillips identifies the
rhetorical power of 'the floral' as a major problematic, asserting that 'the
ubiquity of the floral within Euro-North American art and material
culture must itself be examined to develop a more adequate explanation
of its successful incorporation into Aboriginal art'.[83] That is my purpose
here. The floral culture Phillips notes arose within a wide set of globalizing forces, with European colonizers mediating multivocal designs.
Indigenous needlework was another vital element in the genesis of a
new cosmopolitan material culture, with needleworkers responding to
objects and discursive systems percolating along trade routes over
centuries.

Europeans connected Native Americans more fully to globally sourced
floriated commodities, with different chronologies of interaction at different points on the continents. My focus is northern North America,
where Native Americans saw and used Asian wares such as printed and
painted Indian cottons and interpreted these forms.[84] I begin with the
painted calico shirts that entered the northern Great Plains through the
Hudson's Bay Company posts: nearly 900 calico shirts were shipped in
1678, with another 500 in 1679. Chintz shirts with printed designs, along
with more costly 'painted' calico shirts and 'fine' calico decorated in
designs that typified the Indian subcontinent, were dispatched to HBC
trading sites in James Bay and Hudson's Bay over the 1670s and 1680s.[85]

---

[82] Parker, *The Subversive Stitch*, p. 6.
[83] Ruth Phillips, *Trading Identities: The Souvenir in Native North American Art
       from the Northeast, 1700–1900* (Seattle and London: University of Washington
       Press, 1998), p. 158; see also 'Reading and Writing between the Lines'
       Winterthur Portfolio 45:2/3 (2011): 107–124.
[84] The histories of Indigenous arts in Spanish and Portuguese colonies in the
       Americas follow a different chronology.
[85] A 15/1 Grand Journal 1676–1682, Hudson's Bay Company Archives, Archives
       of Manitoba.

Between 1689 and 1690, 241 additional vibrant shirts were added to the trade goods at the HBC's Fort York, along with over 230 silk and herba sashes of unspecified style.[86] Population levels in this region were such that this number of objects would have wide-ranging effects. Once they arrived in Indigenous communities, Indian fabrics took on new meanings, for, as Nicholas Thomas observes, 'objects change in defiance of their material stability … [for example] What was English or French, in becoming Inuit, is reconstituted socially through Indigenous categorization'. In this case, what was Indian of the subcontinent (made for European markets) became Native American by virtue of trade and use, and by Indigenous value systems. We may discern some of the meaning changes that ensued through later Indigenous-made floral wares. For, 'objects were not what they were made to be but what they have become'.[87]

Fort York, ultimately one of several HBC posts, lay on the western coast of Hudson's Bay between two navigable rivers that ran far inland (Map 2.3). The floral-patterned commodities traded there augmented the range of visual idioms available to Native Americans, populations long steeped in medicinal, symbolic and spiritual botanic cultures, knowledgeable as well in the exchange value of plants.[88] This was one of many gateways through which floriated wares made their way to Native American polities. Patterned cottons, like chintz and calico, thereafter became a favourite, a fact frequently observed by colonial travellers and administrators. Calicoes spread widely along the eastern seaboard of North America, approved as part of settler supplies and soon a trading post staple. The 'Indian Goods' stocked at Fort Pitt in 1761, for example, included both calico and flowered ribbon.[89] The noted trader and

[86] I thank Katie Pollock for constructing a data set of imported clothing into Hudson's Bay Company trading forts, 1689–1770. HBC York Factory, Post Account Book, 1689–1690.

[87] Thomas, *Entangled Objects,* pp. 4, 125.

[88] For botanic practice among Native American communities, see Nancy J. Turner and Dawn C. Loewen, 'The Original "Free Trade": Exchange of Botanical Products and Associated Plant Knowledge in Northwestern North America' *Anthropologica* 40:1 (1998): 49–70; Nancy J. Turner, *Ancient Pathways, Ancestral Knowledge: Ethnobotany and Ecological Wisdom of Indigenous Peoples of Northwest North America,* vols. 1 and 2 (Montreal and Kingston, ON: McGill-Queen's University Press, 2014).

[89] DuPlessis, *Material Atlantic,* pp. 116–117; Timothy J. Shannon, 'Dressing for Success on the Mohawk Frontier: Hendrick, William Johnson, and the Indian Fashion' *William and Mary Quarterly* 53:1 (1996), pp. 21, 38;

diplomat William Johnson included an even wider range of patterned wares among his trade goods and gifts for Native American allies in what is now upper New York State about the same period. Similarly, Native American elites adopted the use of tea and pottery accoutrements, which explains the blue and white ceramics found in Great Lakes archaeological sites.[90]

The circulation of tea through Indigenous communities suggests growing contact with ceramics, many of which were decorative.[91] Certainly, the Kanienkahagen (Mohawk) and other members of the Six Nations Confederacy had ready access to imports, positioned as they were along the chain of rivers and lakes linked to major ports. A visitor to the Mohawk Valley in the mid-1700s reported that 'several of the Indians who lived close to the European settlements had learned to drink tea'. And William Johnson included tea paraphernalia among his gifts to chiefly families.[92] Archaeological remains from the British Fort Hunter, a site west of Albany in upstate New York, are suggestive. Artefacts excavated from the chapel for Indigenous worshippers include teapots, teacups and saucers, with blue and white Delftware in greatest quantities and a singular absence of plain cream ware. Similar findings were made at another site on the Mohawk River.[93] Like the calico shirt, these goods were thereafter 'reconstituted socially'.[94] It is of little surprise that shifts in Native American stylistic motifs were initially traced to the main fur trade routes, along which the mass of imports flowed.[95]

An Irish writer described the standard apparel, everyday wear and more celebratory attire of Great Lakes and St Lawrence River-based Indigenous peoples in the 1790s. He notes that 'when they dress themselves to visit their friends, they put on a short shirt, loose at the neck and

---

[90] Timothy Shannon, 'Dressing for Success on the Mohawk Frontier'.

[91] Alexander Henry, *Travels and Adventures in Canada and the Indian Territories between the Years 1760 and 1776* ... (New York: I. Riley, 1809), p. 326;

[92] Quoted in Shannon, 'Dressing for Success', p. 20.

[93] Kevin Moody and Charles L. Fisher, 'Archaeological Evidence of the Colonial Occupation at Schoharies Crossing State Historic site, Montgomery County, New York' *The Bulletin: Journal of the New York State Archaeological Association* 99 (1989), pp. 7–8.

[94] Thomas, *Entangled Objects*, p. 125.

[95] Alfred G. Bailey, *The Conflict of European and Eastern Algonkian Cultures, 1504–1700* (Toronto: University of Toronto, 1937, repr. 1979), p. 151. This issue is discussed at length in Sherry Farrell Racette, 'Sewing Ourselves Together: Clothing, Decorative Arts and the Expression of Metis and Half Breed Identity', unpublished PhD, 2004, University of Manitoba.

wrists, generally made of coarse figured cotton or calico of some gaudy pattern, not unlike what would be used for window or bed curtains at a common inn in England'. He might disparage their choices, yet the cultural preferences of these communities were clear: women as well as men wore shirts made of decorative floral print fabric.[96] A comment by the British settler Catherine Parr Traill confirms this aesthetic partiality. Residing near Peterborough, between Lake Ontario and Lake Huron, in the 1830s she recorded the persistence of local Anishinaabeg women who were captivated by 'a gay chintz dressing-gown belonging to my husband'. They came 'by turns ... to look at 'gown' ... and when I said 'no gown to sell', they uttered a melancholy exclamation of regret, and went away'.[97] Parr acknowledged as well their skill with the needle and capacity to make to order whatever was required.

The process of close-looking, of visually assessing the material world, is shaped by cultural priorities and training, as are the means of acting on these sightings.[98] Patterned textiles and pottery permeated North America, and Indigenous people saw, assessed and used these wares, looked closely and responded with creative energies, integrating elements of this imagery into their botanic knowledge systems. Like other world communities, they evaluated and translated globalized floral iconography as streams of embellished materials infused their communities. This accounts, in large part, for the shift in iconography from geometric to more floral designs by Native American embroiderers. Calico or a decorated blue-and-white cup became something else when acquired by Indigenous Americans, who accumulated day-to-day experiences of translation. As Ruth Phillips observes, by the mid-1800s, 'the adoption of floral iconography in north-eastern Aboriginal art was one of the most rapid and dramatic changes in the history of Native North American art'.[99] Transition processes were lengthy and variable; thereafter, Native

---

[96] Isaac Weld, *Travels through the States of North America, and the Provinces of Upper and Lower Canada during the Years 1795, 1796, and 1797*, 4th ed. (London: John Stockdale, 1800), pp. 456–457.

[97] Parr Traill, p. 169; see also Sherry Farrell Racette, 'My Grandmothers Loved to Trade: The Indigenization of European Trade Goods in Historic and Contemporary Canada' *Journal of Museum Ethnography* 20:20–21 (2008): 69–81.

[98] Lianne McTavish, 'Learning to See: Vision, Visuality, and Material Culture, 1862–1929' in her *Defining the Modern Museum: A Case Study of the Challenges of Exchange* (2012).

[99] Phillips, *Trading Identities*, p. 155.

Americans' connection to and effect on globalizing material culture was incontrovertible. The spiritual and aesthetic sensibilities Indigenous women brought to botanic practice were enormously resonant.[100]

In this context, Phillips offers a sharp critique of previous generations of scholars who observed this evolving aesthetic and questioned the 'authenticity' of floriated Indigenous arts following contact and transcultural exchange. These critics denigrated the value of these goods, whose motifs reflected new styles and evolving priorities.[101] They decried stylistic influences deemed 'western', expecting stasis among Native American needleworkers, even as changes flowed worldwide. This view was perhaps a variant of the Braudelian claim that static material traditions persisted among all but European elites until the nineteenth century. Certainly, twentieth-century judgements by many Western-trained scholars scorned the aesthetic innovations of various world communities inspired by new globalizing influences, deeming this artistry less authentic to these cultures. The new analyses Phillips pioneered offer a fuller understanding of such creative works.

Indigenous North American artists responded to early global forms, as Asian-made goods connected heterogeneous cultures and sparked innovations. John Guy opines that the 'legacy of the Indian textile trade to the development of an international language of design was long lasting and profound'.[102] Guy's focus is Asia, but this impact extended over a far wider terrain. I argue that close attention to the global casts a sharper light on an artistic trajectory that includes Native American needleworkers.[103] It also problematizes the European role as mediators and acknowledges the wider contributions made thereafter by Indigenous artists. Ruth Phillips points to the 'multivalency' of botanic imagery, which 'rendered floral motifs mutually appropriable into Native and non-Native contexts of artistry and use'.[104] Just as Native Americans

---

[100]   Sherry Farrell Racette, *The Flower Beadwork People* (Regina: Gabriel Dumont Institute, 1991); Nathalie Kermoal, 'Métis Women's Environmental Knowledge and the Recognition of Métis Rights' in Nathalie Kermoal and Isabel Altamirano-Jiménez, eds., *Living on the Land: Indigenous Women's Understanding of Place* (Athabasca, AB: University of Athabasca Press, 2016), pp. 107, 127–137.

[101]   Phillips, *Trading Identities,* pp. 156–157; and for the Red River Metis experience, Racette, 'Sewing Ourselves Together', pp. 1–26.

[102]   Guy, 'One Thing Leads to Another', p. 27.

[103]   Racette, 'My Grandmothers Loved to Trade'.

[104]   Phillips, *Trading Identities,* p. 157.

embraced printed and painted calicoes for the value they ascribed to these goods, so too, they translated motifs of distant origins and complex genealogy for the meanings they inferred.[105] More generally, decorative and functional artefacts made by Indigenous people were collected or amassed by settlers, visitors and military based in the Americas, goods traded widely.[106] Production for the market became increasingly vital for Native Americans over the late eighteenth and nineteenth centuries, as access to land and opportunities for their farmers, hunters, trappers and traders were increasingly constrained.

This mid-nineteenth-century beaded firebag demands our closest attention. Indigenous embroiderers employed diverse techniques and materials with many creative adaptations, with Red River Métis women termed the 'Flower Beadwork People' as a consequence of their seminal works.[107] Plates 6.5A and 6.5B offer front and back views of a beaded firebag from the Red River settlement of the Hudson's Bay Company territory in what is now Manitoba. This exquisite bag was made in the mid-1800s and bought by the 9th Earl Southesk, a Scottish nobleman hunting and adventuring through the northern plains. Firebags, designed and made by Indigenous women for family and friends or for sale, were an essential part of men's attire in this broad landscape.[108] The iconic Asian vase and floral motif is reinterpreted here in stunning detail revealing innovation and mastery in equal measure. The three-dimensional beading marks the hand of a virtuoso needlewoman, most probably a Métis practitioner of the arts. She may have received formal schooling in Red River if she was the daughter of an HBC administrator. We cannot know what objects she saw, what texts she read or the combined inspirations that led her to produce this work. But the wider context of her patterning is clear, and her links to the iconography of globalized Asian wares are apparent.[109] News of Southesk's impending visit circulated well in advance of his

---

[105] Phillips, *Trading Identities*, p. 158.
[106] Phillips, *Trading Identities* and 'Reading and Writing between the Lines'.
[107] Farrell Recette, 'Sewing Ourselves Together', p. 4.
[108] Peers, 'S BLACK Bag'; Susan Berry, 'Recovered Identities: Four Métis Artists in Nineteenth-Century Rupert's Land' in Sarah Carter and Patricia McCormack, eds., *Recollecting: Lives of Aboriginal Women of the Canadian Northwest and Borderlands* (Edmonton: Athabasca University Press, 2011), pp. 46–47; and described in James Carnegie Earl of Southesk, *Saskatchewan and the Rocky Mountains: A Diary and Narrative of Travel, Sport and Adventure . . . in 1859 and 1860* (Edinburgh: Edmonston and Douglas, 1875), p. 203.
[109] Farrell Recette, 'Sewing Ourselves Together'.

arrival at Red River, and she prepared for this opportunity, ensuring she had the highest calibre goods to sell. Needlework of this type was a notable activity within Native American communities, for 'on the Great Plains, a woman's path to dignity, honour, and long life lay in the correct and skilled pursuit of the arts'.[110] Southesk himself offered a somewhat supercilious assessment of his exchanges, deeming Indigenous women 'most serviceable to us in dressing skins and heads, drying meat, and mending or making clothes'. However, their sharp appraisal of his trade goods put him slightly on the defensive:

I was glad to find among my stores a parcel of beads exactly to their taste. It amused me to see that fashion reigned here as imperiously as in more civilised lands; some fine, richly-coloured, oval beads, the size of pigeon's eggs, which I considered my best and which a year or two before would have been generally admired, were despised and out of date, while the little trashy white ones, no bigger than a pin's head, were highly appreciated. Perhaps the small beads were valued as useful for embroidery, in which the Indian and half-breed women excel.[111]

As Nicholas Thomas reminds us, 'exchange is always, in the first instance, a political process, one in which wider relationships are expressed and negotiated in a personal encounter'.[112]

The anonymous creator of this firebag employed twenty-five colours of miniscule beads to create its textured surface. Tassels and fringes are treated in a traditional style and strung with beads. Strawberries were placed on the tabs of the bag, a fruit of time-honoured significance. On occasion, borrowings from other Indigenous communities are evident on bags of this type, and the use of varied botanic imagery was common-place.[113] The totality of this firebag reflects multistep translation.[114] These arts must feature more prominently in global history, for they lay out important creative claims within a broad discursive paradigm.

In many parts of the Americas, Indigenous girls and women received training in missionary schools. This tuition has been emphasized in many histories, the assumption being that only formal colonial instruction

---

[110] Janet C. Berlo and Ruth B. Phillips, *Native North American Arts* (Oxford: Oxford University Press, 1998), p. 116, quoted in Berry, 'Recovering Identities', p. 33.

[111] Southesk, *Saskatchewan and the Rocky Mountains*, p. 124.

[112] Thomas, *Entangled Objects*, p. 7.   [113] Berry, 'Recovering Identities', p. 47.

[114] For an overview of Southesk's travels and collecting, see www.royalalberta museum.ca/exhibits/online/southesk/index.cfm, accessed 7 June 2016.

could account for the transformation in needlework design. Yet even as missionaries pursued their schooling of Indigenous children, reorienting the embroidery of Native American girls, the agency of objects continued.[115] And while this schooling was important in crafting souvenirs for settlers, visitors and collectors in Europe, the agency of things was also a dynamic force, and globalized trade played its instructive role.[116] Needlework reveals the ways in which Indigenous peoples interacted with global and colonial forces, preserving cultural production while claiming space within new economic, political and cultural contexts.

The Wendat of Wendake are a case in point. They settled near Quebec City after 1650, and built strong relationships with French and then British allies, supplying warriors and military materiel in the form of snowshoes, canoes and other goods. Over the eighteenth century they marketed a wider array of wares 'within a framework of political and social relations'.[117] Following the change of regime in 1763 with the defeat of the French, the Wendat were guaranteed their right to continue commercial relations with the British military posted near their community.[118] They leveraged this to build a broad mercantile network through the expanding sale of embroidery arts and souvenir craft. In the 1770s, leading Indigenous families in the St Lawrence River region sent sons to Dartmouth College in New Hampshire to acquire an English education. Subsequently, men and women of traditional chiefly families led efforts to conserve their culture and community while expanding opportunities for employment, focusing on making culturally defined goods for the market.[119]

---

[115] Chris Goden and Yvonne Marshall, 'The Cultural Biography of Objects' *World Archaeology* 31:3 (1999): 169–178. For discussion of Métis girls' re-education in design by Catholic nuns, see Jan Morier, 'Metis Decorative Arts and Its Inspiration' *Dawson and Hind* 8 (1979): 28–32.

[116] Phillips, 'Reading and Writing between the Lines' and *Trading Identities*. See also David W. Penny, 'Floral Decoration and Cultural Change: An Historical Interpretation of Motivation' *American Indian Culture and Research Journal* 15:1 (1991): 53–77.

[117] Anne de Stecher, 'Souvenir Art, Collectable Craft, Cultural Heritage: The Wendat (Huron) of Wendake, Quebec' in Janice Helland, Beverly Lemire and Alena Buis, eds., *Craft, Community and the Material Culture of Place and Politics, 19th–20th Century* (Aldershot, UK: Ashgate, 2014), p. 45. I am deeply indebted to Anne de Stecher for her many insights and conversation on this and related topics.

[118] Alain Beaulieu, 'Les Hurons et la Conquête', *Recherches Amérindiennes au Québec* 30:3 (2000): 56–60.

[119] De Stecher, 'Souvenir Art, Collectable Craft, Cultural Heritage', pp. 44–46.

Ruth Phillips, Anne de Stecher, Jonathan Lainey and others have illuminated the extraordinary capacity and artistic practice of this community.[120] The 1800s brought increasingly severe conditions as settlers encroached on Wendat territory. Building the market for their embroidered goods was a crucial option, with expanded sales of house-wares, craft and souvenirs. Traditional materials like moosehair and porcupine quills, vividly dyed, were embroidered on birch bark or textile objects for Euro-American and European buyers. Over genera-tions, Indigenous artists adapted and revised many kinds of goods through what Ruth Phillips terms 'historical processes of negotiation', encompassing 'dialogic ... change'.[121] These measures exemplify the ways in which Indigenous peoples engaged with the modernity of imperialism across generations, exhibiting 'a keen sense of how history was being made at their expense ... they worked mightily to prevent it from taking total hold of their polities and their lives'.[122] The Wendat depended on strategic opportunities, expressed in material form. Marguerite Vincent Lawinonkié (1783–1865) was a celebrated embroiderer from a family of chiefs, and her artistry was instrumental in diplomatic gifts and other ceremonial affairs. She and her husband, Paul Picard, developed the business well beyond local sales, pushing the distribution of souvenir arts throughout Quebec, Ontario and New York, particularly to major tourist sites like Niagara Falls. Figurative and floral motifs typified the 'splendid Indian work' reaching a wide range of commercial outlets.[123] As with other Native American com-munities, the imposition of colonial strictures required initiatives, some of which were commercially oriented.

[120]   Phillips, *Trading Identities;* Berlo and Phillips, *Native North American Arts;* De
        Stecher, 'Souvenir Art, Collectable Craft, Cultural Heritage' and 'Wendat Arts
        of Diplomacy: Negotiating Change in the Nineteenth Century' in Thomas
        Peace and Kathryn Magee Labelle, eds., *From Huronia to Wendakes:
        Adversity, Migrations, and Resilience, 1650–1900* (Norman, OK: University of
        Oklahoma Press, 2016), pp. 182–208. And personal communication.
[121]   Phillips, *Trading Identities*, p. 156. The extent of precontact floral decorative
        motifs among diverse Indigenous communities remains to be fully assessed.
        Certainly botanic materials of all sorts represented a major element of cultural
        and economic activity.
[122]   Antoinette Burton, 'Introduction: Traveling Criticism? On the Dynamic
        Histories of Indigenous Modernity' *Cultural and Social History* 9:4 (2012),
        p. 492.
[123]   De Stecher, 'Souvenir Art, Collectable Craft, Cultural Heritage', pp. 45–47.

My final examples of Wendat embroidery are outside the chronological remit of this volume, but vital to a full understanding of the
cosmopolitan markets now in place and their significance for communities of embroiderers such as the Wendat.[124] Aside from the tens
of thousands of embroidered moccasins made in Wendake, plus
snowshoes and souvenir crafts, embroiderers made fashion items
for local and international sales.[125] Their products sold through
merchants like the Quebec-based trader that ultimately became the
modern high-end retailer Holt Renfrew; in the nineteenth century
the founder's distribution links extended nationally and internationally. This company was launched in 1837 by an Irish-born merchant
who sold quality haberdashery and next branched into the sale of
high-value fur garments, in Lower Canada and then in Britain. In
time, a member of a prominent Wendat family rose to become
manager of the fur department in this company. These commercial
alliances proved fruitful, and Wendat exhibited their wares at industrial exhibitions in Quebec, Montreal and Paris, as well as being advertised to locals and tourists in newspapers, directories and almanacs.[126]
The size and range of their manufactures bespeaks their determined
intervention in a colonial capitalist economic system. Equally, it demonstrates the aesthetic space they claimed. Their distinctive floral products
aligned with broad design trends and, at the same time, distinguished

---

[124] I thank my collaborators in the project 'Object Lives & Global Histories in
Northern North America' for rich discussions on embroidered arts, in
particular Susan Berry, Cynthia Cooper, Judy Half, Jonathan Lainey, Laura
Peers and Anne Whitelaw. www.objectlives.com

[125] Brian Gettler, 'Economic Activity and Class Formation in Wendake, 1800–
1950' in Thomas Peace and Kathryn Labelle, eds., *From Huronia to Wendakes:
Adversity, Migrations, and Resilience, 1650–1900* (Norman, OK: University of
Oklahoma Press, 2016), pp. 144–181; for the late 1800s, see Gordon M. Sayre,
'Self-Portraiture and Commodification in the World of Huron/Wendat Artist
Zacharie Vincent', *American Indian Culture and Research Journal* 39:2
(2015), p. 19. An estimated 140,000 moccasins and 7,000 snowshoes were
made in Wendake at that date.

[126] Gettler, 'Economic Activity and Class Formation', pp. 153, 157; Jean Benoit,
'Renfrew, George Richard' in *Dictionary of Canadian Biography*, vol. 12,
University of Toronto/Université Laval, 2003. See www.biographi.ca/en/bio/re
nfrew_george_richard_12E.html, accessed 12 May, 2016. *Cherrier's Quebec
City Directory, 1874*, 14th ed. (Quebec: A. Coté & Co., 1874), p. 31. Cynthia
Cooper, McCord Museum, Montreal, has uncovered the significant extent of
Wendat commercial networks into the twentieth century.

Figure 6.5 Embroidered Glengarry-style cap, *c.* 1840. Huron. Made of wool, silk and moosehair. 2011.154.97. Ralph T. Coe Collection, Gift of Ralph T. Coe Foundation for the Arts, 2011. Metropolitan Museum of Art, New York.

their work from generic globalized goods. Object study reveals their important interventions.[127]

Wendat artistic production included pieces for fashion-conscious consumers. Fashions in this period privileged change and innovation, and referenced countless imperial and global connections.[128] Producers in many world regions hoped for niche markets such as the ones the Wendat secured. Wendat needlewomen deftly directed their energies to create distinctive items like the Glengarry bonnet or cap in Figure 6.5, a favourite male accessory after 1800. The Glengarry bonnet was an element of Highland dress, formalized in the 1790s as headwear for the Glengarry Fencibles and thereafter a feature of Highland and Scottish regiments in Great Britain and colonies, adopted as well by other squadrons. By the early 1800s it was 'worn by half the

---

[127] Such aesthetic interventions and creative development of souvenir arts are vividly explored in Phillips, *Trading Identities,* demonstrating the initiatives of many First Nations peoples in these creative arts. Penny, 'Floral Decoration', pp. 62–68.

[128] For transformations in men's dress and material culture in this context, see Beverly Lemire, '"A Question of Trousers" and "Men of the Word": British Mariners, Consumer Practice and Material Culture in an Era of Global Trade, c. 1660–1800' *Journal of British Studies* 54:2 (April, 2015): 288–319.

army as a most convenient undress, serving as a night-cap, and a neat military cap by day'.[129] Civilians were also drawn to this headgear, including men prizing military mnemonics in their self-fashioning. This Indigenous-embroidered creation alluded to both its military ancestry and its colonial context. Apparel was political. For generations, male colonial settlers in the Americas adopted elements of Indigenous dress for diplomatic, functional or sporting purposes, purposefully appropriating symbolic Indigenous dress to assert their new colonial intent.[130] Imperial and military allusions assumed increasing importance in Western male attire, both for adults and youth, fashions apparent in colonial precincts.[131] The proximity of British military regiments to Wendake and Wendat mastery of military iconography makes this bonnet a logical choice for these makers.[132]

Using trademark moosehair embroidery, with a lavish floral design, the juxtaposition of influences is striking. Leading exponents of Wendat embroidery demonstrated astute understanding of imperial fashion and its politics. This bonnet engaged rhetorically with a globalized imperial marketplace – in some respects a variant of the Turkish fez often sported in leisure hours by middle-class Victorian males. This accessory nods to imperial aspiration within the paradigm of uniformed manhood and

---

[129] *Sketches of the Character, Manners, and Present State of the Highlanders of Scotland: With Details of the Military Service of Highland Regiments . . .,* 3rd ed. (Edinburgh: Archibald Constable and Co., 1825), vol. 1, pp. 136, 431.

[130] Weld, *Travels through the States of North* America, p. 455; Shannon, 'Dressing for Success on the Mohawk Frontier'; Linda Baumgarten, *What Clothes Reveal: The Language of Clothing in Colonial and Federal America* (New Haven: Yale University Press, 2002), pp. 65–75; Catherine Cangany, 'Fashioning Moccasins: Detroit, the Manufacturing Frontier, and the Empire of Consumption, 1701–1835' *William and Mary Quarterly* 69:2 (2012): 265–304; Gillian Poulter, *Becoming Native in a Foreign Land: Sport, Visual Culture, and Identity in Montreal, 1840–1885* (Vancouver: University of British Columbia Press, 2009), pp. 33–36.

[131] As with many imperial fashions, this cap was also advertised for boys, as well as being a fashion for men. *The Lady's Newspaper* (London, England), Saturday, 15 January, 1848; 'Toddles's Highland Tour' *Every Boy's Magazine* (London, England), Thursday, 1 December, 1864; p. 43; 'Modes De Paris for April, 1870'. *The Ladies' Treasury* (London, England), Friday, 1 April, 1870; p. 60. For cultural cross-dressing, see Tara Mayer, 'Cultural Cross-Dressing: Posing and Performance in Orientalist Portraits' *Journal of the Royal Asiatic Society* 22:2 (2012): 281–298.

[132] Haudenosaunee embroiderers made similarly stunning bonnets with beaded embellishments. For example, 2011.154.191, Metropolitan Museum of Art, New York; ME978.58.3 and M12592, McCord Museum, Montreal.

global empire.[133] However, Victorian males required no arduous travels, as distribution networks carried confections from far-flung regions to imperial metropoles. Feeding these markets served Wendat interests.

Indigenous makers positioned their products within a cosmopolitan, imperial fashion complex, showcasing their aesthetic mastery with a variety of products, serving female as well as male fashions. The exquisite embroidery on the black broadcloth woman's jacket commands attention (Plate 6.6). It incorporates the material emblems of Wendat needlework – moosehair and porcupine quillwork – in a stylish garment from the 1860s or 1870s. Its gusseted shape would fit over the widest bustle and enfold the body of a modish woman. The Huron Wendat enjoyed contact with elites in colonial Canada, including Lady Elgin, the wife of the governor general of Canada (1847–1854).[134] Embroiderers highly placed in Wendake turned their connections to advantage, discerning fashion trends and the best ways to interpret these vogues. The use of black broadcloth offers a dramatic background with every border finely outlined – a garment devoid of irony, claiming its cachet through outstanding execution. Fashionability was realized through Native American hands. The red wool pumps from the later nineteenth century are further convincing examples of Wendat fashionable arts (Plate 6.7). Other instances survive in major museum collections.[135] These objects signal the astute eye of the designer/maker, deft material translation and the broad reach of Wendat artistry within globalized commercial networks.

Nineteenth-century imperial metropoles were awash with fashions shaped by long run global contacts and commercial linkages, including Asianized styles and adaptations. The Kashmir shawl is one such, shipped in volume to Europe from the Indian subcontinent over the eighteenth century and the focus of intensive imitation by European manufacturers after 1800.[136] Woven, printed and embroidered patterns

---

[133] Jennifer Craik, 'The Political Politics of the Uniform' *Fashion Theory* 7:2 (2003), pp. 129–132.

[134] De Stecher, 'Wendat Arts of Diplomacy', pp. 193–197.

[135] An incomplete pair of black wool slippers demonstrates the steps taken in the manufacture of these and similar fashion footwear. 51.2348a–b, moosehair embroidered slipper set in four pieces, on wool broadcloth. Huron Wendat, 1800–1850. Museum of Fine Arts, Boston. See also another Glengarry cap, 2013.646, mid-1800s.

[136] Fashion inspiration flowed in all directions, not just to Euro-American centres of power. For shawls from Kashmir, see Michelle Maskiell, 'Consuming Kashmir: Shawls and Empires, 1500–2000' *Journal of World History* 13:1

abounded within world markets, with distinctive variants from discrete cultures. Material mixing was routinized even as racial hierarchies hardened. Native American embroiderers were acknowledged experts, hailed in some British needlework journals, even as Indigeneity was derided.[137] Western fashions in the long eighteenth and nineteenth centuries incorporated layered products of empire, signs (sometimes ironic) of a seasoned worldliness and a shared participation in the globalized imperial world. The contexts and meanings of these uses are much debated: appropriation and acculturation, or translation, 'embodied and experiential'.[138] The moosehair and quill work embroidery crafted by Wendat makers represented distinctive interpretations of global floral genre, as souvenir, furnishing or fashion. These arts grew from complex inspirations and their history is vital to this narrative of events. Importantly, some of these works *were* accounted fashion and mark the expansive production of these artists. Wendat embroiderers made distinctive contributions to world fashion that must be celebrated and explained. This Native American community and its makers claimed artistic space in a fully globalized world.

Conclusion

Early modern globalization was expressed in tactile and visual forms, translated and adapted by those swept up in these forces or engrossed by the new commodity modes. And in this respect K. N. Chaudhuri's observation bears repeating, for global trade was indeed 'instrumental in the creation of a language of signs with an immense range of significance'.[139] This process of material adaptation was aesthetic and performative, ultimately generating a new visual *lingua franca* that facilitated a chorus of communication. Capitalist endeavours drove the great circulation of cargoes, at the same time carrying needleworkers to new locales where they plied their craft and intensified cross-cultural exchange. Corporate entities did not intend this communication in signs – it was not their priority. Rather, an unintended discourse proceeded as an

(2002): 27–65; see also, Onur Inal, 'Women's Fashions in Transition: Ottoman Borderlands and the Anglo-Ottoman Exchange of Costume' *Journal of World History* 22:2 (2011): 243–272.

[137] Phillips, *Trading Identities*.
[138] Phillips, 'Reading and Writing between the Lines', p. 111.
[139] Chaudhuri, 'Trade as a Cultural Phenomenon', p. 210

adjunct of global ventures. Small investments sustained the many workshops where new interpretive motifs were devised and sewn. Households
were additional sites of generative design, including settings with multi-
ethnic membership (slave and free). It is too reductive to see commercial
fashion alone as an explanation for this transformation in style, as long-
held cultural and spiritual beliefs fed into these new modes of expression.
The sites of burgeoning cosmopolitan material culture had no single point
of origin; rather this discourse was impelled by recurring translations and
paraphrases building a momentum that persisted across centuries.
Globalized stitchery projects emerged from many communities, including
those clearly at risk from colonizing forces such as the Wendat of
Wendake. They turned this creative phenomenon to their advantage.

The eye of the needle demands close attention and foregrounds a
different sort of historical evidence. Conclusions about the early global
era must take into account the sensory and aesthetic changes in play,
the new learning taking place, the agency of common people and the
translational processes driven by myriad groups, including those resisting the intended extinction of their cultures. Close attention to this
material culture offers deeper understanding of the processes underway. These artefacts demonstrate the inspiration, persistence and creative force released as, stitch by stitch, needles translated the global.

7 | Conclusion
Realizing Cosmopolitan Material Culture

Contemporary globalization is the subject of heated debate, with many voices raised to condemn the heightened connections that define the twenty-first century. Critiques vary. But a vocal contingent harken back to a lost golden age before these extensive links and pathways were established, reflecting nostalgically on what they assume were more settled and segregated polities with little disruption from commerce – a blithe history with little basis in fact. They little recognize the deep-seated ties that weave through our shared global past, ties that grew tighter in countless ways from the 1500s, evident in material culture, consumer habits and aesthetic practices. The profound ruptures that followed oceanic contacts in the 1490s produced different dimensions of material life, founded on commodity politics of new kinds. A closer look at this past soon makes clear the countless material adaptations that reshaped societies in past centuries, as global trade recast consumption and material life. That is my focus in this volume.

One of the striking themes in this book is the growth of cosmopolitan material culture, a by-product of early modern globalization as disparate world people and commodities connected in new ways. Worldwide linkages enabled a wider range of women and men to routinely access more diverse media. Their industrious labours enabled them to acquire things to augment comfort, enact fashions or discover new forms of respite from hard labour. However, engagement with the wider world and its orders was not always voluntary. The scale of involuntary contact demarcated this period from all previous eras, including European encounters with Native American peoples and the mass enslavement of Africans to power plantation production. Nonetheless, even those enmeshed in this imperial apparatus shaped their material culture from global commodity flows as they could, even though constrained. Constraints of various kinds and severity moulded the contexts of consumption for the majority of world populations even as material life evolved.

The globalized trade in fabric and furs, and the re-dressing of populations are additional landmarks. The textile trade was foundational to
these new commercial networks, including accelerated sales of silks
and cottons outside Asia. This commerce inaugurated new parameters
of taste and levels of comfort in many polities. Silver from the Americas
set a new pace of exchange, with American specie shipped across the
Pacific, linking Spain's Pacific colonies with New Spain and China. The
results were transformative. The extensive consumption of silk by
creoles in New Spain reflects just one facet of this trans-Pacific bond.
Throughout, textiles of different sorts were introduced to communities
formerly served by a narrower set of options. The flow of cargoes
through new channels disrupted and unsettled the material status
quo, with unexpected results. The accelerated fur trade in northern
climes is a case in point, demanding a rethinking of the categories of
'new' and 'old' luxury. This period witnessed a dramatic and many-
sided expansion of fur trade networks far beyond their previous span
with attendant revisions in material culture. The new Manchu dynasty
in China promoted the cultural force of fur throughout its empire and
beyond, demanding ever-larger quantities from ever-greater distances.
The power of this capacious market altered consumption practices of
many kinds. Attempts to evade Qing sumptuary edicts (including the
illicit wearing of furs) preoccupied the aspiring ranks of that society
and frustrated regulators. This fur trade heightened points of social
tension; and deep economic consequences echoed in China and in other
regions and regimes.

European contact with the Americas was initially driven by their
desire for Asian riches. These contacts sparked European colonial ambition, with profound political repercussions at each generation. Fertile
land and prolific silver drove colonization in America's southern latitudes. In the north, furs sustained an expansive commerce for generations. The North American fur trade set unprecedented commercial
systems in motion, expanding the production of fur products in
Europe, while aligning Indigenous hunters and traders with the commercial networks of Eurasia. Trade relations linked countless Indigenous
societies with systems of global provisioning, bringing the demands of
Indigenous Americans to a global stage. Wool blanketing was foundational to the North American fur trade, as was patterned cotton cloth
from India or the West. This fur trade represents a quintessential global
system, demanding new strategic responses from Native Americans now

'enmeshed in a spider web of seventeenth- and eighteenth-century exchange processes.'[1]

The volume of clothing multiplied in tandem with the greater quantities of cloth and peltry. And the nature of clothing changed as well. Traditional sumptuary codes founded on material hierarchies were challenged by the heightened capaciousness of trade and the wilfulness of citizenry. Officials legislated consumption in the hopes of an acquiescent populace, often finding the opposite. Sumptuary systems were shaken at every compass point by the growing tidal wave of goods. In colonial precincts new categories of race and rank were constructed through bruising material contests. Colonial legislators aimed to fix the servile status of African slaves, but this fixity was often evaded through creative dress. Printed Indian cotton handkerchiefs exemplify the commodities used in countless functional and generative ways. This includes the creation of a headscarf style demonstrating the resolute perseverance of women of colour in Caribbean and American plantation societies. Sumptuary legislation could shape but not crush aspirational intent. At the same time, the ever-larger secondhand markets enabled wider choice in every developing economy, from the very poor seeking decency to those who longed to look rich(er) for social or strategic advantage. Importantly, industrious opportunities expanded markedly at every stage of sale, recycling, repair and resale in innumerable regions. This facet of industriousness involved dynamic market-oriented exchange that engaged ever-larger numbers of women in the secondhand clothing sector in micro and main-street enterprises. Clothing ventures took many shapes.

The growth of readymade uniform apparel paralleled global and imperial ambitions, with the dressing of seafarers and military launching readymade to new heights. Uniforms offered virtual standardization, a discipline that contrasted sharply with the wider choices at hand. Readymade, standardized apparel served administrative purpose, helping to sustain grand plans and designs. Keeping the men in their service recognizably clothed required a new technology of production, one more fully recorded in Europe though apparent elsewhere, serving comparable aims. Discipline and systematization drove the

---

[1] Susan Sleeper-Smith, 'Cultures of Exchange in a North Atlantic World' in Susan Sleeper-Smith, ed., *Rethinking the Fur Trade Cultures of Exchange in an Atlantic World* (Lincoln: University of Nebraska Press, 2009), pp. xvii–xviii.

making and use of this apparel among populations critical to imperial ambitions: mariners, military and the enslaved. Vast new institutional systems marked these involuntary consumers and the readymade clothes they were assigned; their apparel was a disciplinary product of this age. The enforced dressing of subject populations would be a legacy bequeathed to future generations.

Commodities were accessed through a variety of strategies as the tempo of commerce accelerated. One of the defining features of the early modern world was the attempted policing by imperial office-holders, anxious to direct the 'explosion of commoditization.'[2] Bureaucracies on many continents introduced extensive regulations and robust taxation; and they remained incensed at the extralegal response of citizenry and foreigners who defied their commands. The scavenging of shipwrecks and beachcombing flourished on oceanic coastlines alongside capacious and sometimes-sophisticated smuggling networks. Cumulatively, these approaches allowed a wider access to commodity cargoes along worldwide waterways and brought cheaper goods to market in global communities, moving cargoes of impressive aggregate size and consistency. These unregulated flows of goods involved an unregulated set of actors, intersecting rank and regime in uncountable ways. Access to consumer goods was the driving aim. Heightened cosmopolitanism was the result. All earthly regions were touched, whether through customary or extralegal endeavours.

I focused on several of the most diagnostic features of the global history of consumption, including the diffusion of American tobacco. In this, as with other goods from the Americas, Europeans and then world communities learned the cultural forms of tobacco devised by Native Americans. This leaf was carried in the train of globalizing agents (merchants, missionaries and sailors) who embraced the knowledge of Indigenous Americans and became tobacco ambassadors in turn. Thereafter, each receiving region created richly varied routines redefining sociability and respite, routines that were centred on the ingestion of tobacco. Invention and adaptation spawned cosmopolitan tobacco cultures in countless locales, as with the blending of betel and tobacco quids in Southeast Asia, the spread of the hookah pipe from the

---

[2] Igor Kopytoff, 'The Cultural Biography of Things: Commoditization as Process' in Arjun Appadurai, ed., *The Social Life of Things: Commodities in Cultural Perspective* (Cambridge: Cambridge University Press, 1986), pp. 72.

Ottoman Empire to China, or the generalized use of cheap clay tobacco pipes across global terrains. Authorities soon learned of tobacco's value as a tool to discipline and tame labourers' spirits, and this stratagem was widely applied in scenarios of long-distance water transport by ocean, river or lake. The men toiling on these waters were essential to the global cargo system and tobacco became a quirt to drive this labour. This leaf was used as well to season African slaves and help reconcile them to servitude. This essential subject population was also pushed through promised access to this leaf. Coercion redefined consumption in profoundly inequitable conditions, inaugurating another disciplinary material regime distinct to this period.

At the same time, new racial categories were enacted in Western imperial realms with the help of tobacco advertising and material culture. The privileges of whiteness and the penalties imposed on colonized people of colour were laid out in widely circulating media, inculcating new racial norms in viewers and consumers. Daily habits of tobacco – purchase and use – included recurring visual instruction on the hierarchies enforced throughout imperial systems. Citizens learned the contexts of race through their habits. Tobacco exemplifies the complexities of form, usage and power that accompanied the spread of this commodity and the racialized consumption encouraged in this system.

The movement of people and goods engendered other important material forms as, region by region, needleworkers reoriented their designs, responding in visible ways to the material they saw. Floriated Asian designs resonated across broad cultural landscapes, inspiring translations and imitations fitted to local belief systems in which women figured prominently. The broad range of participants in this process denotes the profound effects of globalized aesthetics; tracing the path of needlework translation offers a means of gauging reactions among hybrid populations. Asian domestics and embroiderers relocated to colonial and European settings and intensified the impact of the 'language of signs' wrought through global trade.[3] Most importantly, Native American needleworkers wrote their own narrative responses to global material culture through expressive embroidery arts. Their works illuminate cosmopolitan material culture on a world scale.

[3] K. N. Chaudhuri, 'Trade as a Cultural Phenomenon' in Jens Christian V. Johansen, Erling Ladewig Petersen and Henrik Stevnborg, eds., *Clashes of Cultures: Essays in Honour of Niels Steensgaard* (Odense: Odense University Press, 1992), p. 210

Industrious habits increased markedly over this time period. Greater numbers of women and children were employed in the making of new wares, whether embroidering for Suzhou markets or spinning thread in northwest Europe. But wage earning did not constitute the sum of industriousness. Niche opportunities were cultivated in innumerable scenarios to take advantage of large and small-scale commodity flows, with or without legal sanction. These activities involved entrepreneurship as well as wage earning, including repair, recycling and resale in secondhand markets, a sector open and available to poor women, a fact I emphasized in previous chapters. These opportunities grew dramatically along with the heightened traffic in cloth, clothing and goods of all sorts. Poor people recognized the value in global commodities and took on laborious toil to secure their mite, confident in their ability to profit from their pains. Beachcombing, scavenging and sweeping ships' holds offered possibilities that became focused and routinized with the quickening tempo of trade. These demonstrations of industriousness were ineluctably linked to the more dynamic commercial systems set in place over this era. In this respect, it is now clear how Fernand Braudel's tripartite economic levels interacted. The exalted level of large-scale international commerce intersected not only with the 'so-called market economy' of local shops, fairs and markets, but also with the ubiquitous 'material civilization' that enveloped the earth.[4] Rural folk and fishers, fur trappers, artisans and merchants were touched by the energies unleashed through global processes. Material lives were transformed as a consequence.

A Japanese-made map from the early 1800s confirms the effects of global connections. Japan possessed a vibrant economy with a leadership that restrained foreign incursions, though licensed trade was allowed. The new world of goods evoked curiosity among those in this nominally hedged-in kingdom. This map of the world (Map 7.1) – a successor to an extant 1650 world plan[5] – confirms the persistent drive to secure cosmopolitan knowledge, a knowledge that accompanied the

---

[4] Fernand Braudel, *Civilization and Capitalism, 15th–18th Century, The Structures of Everyday Life*, vol. 1 translated by Siân Reynolds (New York: Harper & Row, 1985), pp. 23–24. French edition *Les structures de quotidian: le possible et l'impossible*, 1979.

[5] A map of the world, including a number of figures and ships, is held in the Beinecke Rare Book & Manuscript Library, Yale University. See brbl-dl.library.yale.edu/vufind/Record/4163423, accessed 6 May 2017.

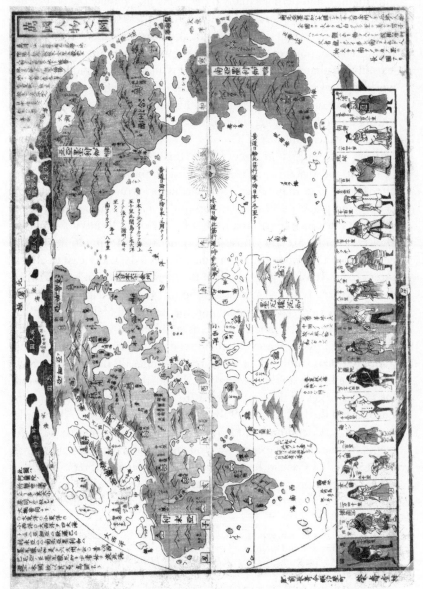

Map 7.1 *People of Many Nations* (*Bankoku jinbutsu no zu*), a map of the world with images of foreigners. 1800–1850. Nagasaki print. Fine Prints: Japanese, pre-1915. Library of Congress, Washington, DC.

circuit of cosmopolitan things. Despite prohibitions, a dedicated Japanese cartographer looked outward and assembled a mass of information about people, places and things that came with the now globalized world. His tutors likely included Dutch, Japanese and Chinese informants – and perhaps many others.[6] He likely knew the goods they traded at approved ports and perhaps knew local smugglers and heard their tales. He certainly knew the commodities foreigners desired from Japan. This mapmaker doubtless quizzed worldly seafarers and brokers, learning all that he could, anchoring his map with depictions of the world's peoples, with their particularities of dress and accoutrement on display. The mapmaker systematized his knowledge and sketched continents and oceans, along with those who populated these spaces and traversed wider routes.[7]

Every one of the subjects entered on this map is named by their place of origin and distance from Nagasaki, the authorized point of entry into Japan. The mapmaker's knowledge is strongest addressing the people and places of East Asia, noting the man from the Great Qing, 380 miles distance from Japan. Men from Korea, Ryukyu (Okinawa) and Hokkaido are the most proximate to this kingdom and are described with confidence. After which he styled a wider cast of adventurers from Russia, Tartary, India, the Netherlands, England, France, Iberia, Africa, North America and South America. Figures from the imaginary 'Country of Women' and the 'Country of Tiny People' are the only fictional members of this assembly. The mapmaker renders elements of dress, hair and armament that show a familiarity with those piloting global shipping, or anchored in Nagasaki harbour. He reckons, as well, with a wide geography, the northern sea ice in the arctic, the Great Lakes at the centre of North America, the sea surrounding Europe and the land termed 'Libya' (North Africa) thousands of miles from Japan. Coconuts and their source are another interest he documents. His spatial reckoning was touched by some of the same forces that resulted in Castelo Branco quilts and floriated pockets. This map was as much a product of the now globalized world as the tobacco he smoked, or the cotton robe he might wear, or the Chinese silk he

[6] For the expansion of mapping and the sale of maps in the Tokugawa period, tools and collaboration of Dutch and Japanese, see Kären Wigen, Sugimoto Fumiko and Cary Karacas, eds., *Cartographic Japan: A History in Maps* (Chicago: University of Chicago Press, 2016).

[7] I thank Anran Tu for her invaluable assistance with this map.

desired. Networks and circuits of exchange are confirmed on this map, combined with the distinctive peoples embedded in these systems.

Each region and each generation came to terms with the impact of global forces, embracing the new materials that enriched their lives, resisting coercive systems of consumption or toiling to secure a small slice of global cargoes. The power of fabric and fur, tobacco and pepper set the globalized system in motion.

Select Bibliography

Abbott, Elizabeth. *Sugar: A Bittersweet History* (Toronto: Penguin Group, 2008).

Adshead, S. A. M. *Material Culture in Europe and China, 1400–1800* (New York: St Martin's Press, 1997).

Affeldt, Stefanie. *Consuming Whiteness: Australian Racism and the 'White Sugar' Campaign* (Vienna: LIT Verlag GmbH & Co., 2014).

Ago, Renata. *A Gusto for Things: A History of Objects in Seventeenth-Century Rome*, translated by Bradford Bouley and Corey Tazzara, with Paula Findlen (Chicago: University of Chicago Press, 2013).

Alderman, John Robert. 'Bidar' in Navina Najat Haidar and Marika Sardar, eds., *Sultans of Deccan India 1500–1700, Opulence and Fantasy* (New York: Metropolitan Museum of Art, 2015), pp. 171–194.

Allerston, Patricia.'Reconstructing the Secondhand Clothes Trade in Sixteenth and Seventeenth-Century Venice' *Costume* 33 (1999): 46–56.

Ameisenowa, Zofia and W. F. Mainland. 'The Tree of Life in Jewish Iconography' *Journal of the Warburg Institute* 2:4 (1939): 326–345.

Andreas, Peter. *Smuggler Nation: How Illicit Trade Made America* (Oxford: Oxford University Press, 2013).

Andrews, Kenneth R. *Trade, Plunder and Settlement: Maritime Enterprise and the Genesis of the British Empire, 1480–1630* (Cambridge: Cambridge University Press, 1984).

Antony, Philomena Sequeira. 'Hindu Dominance in the Goa-Based Long-Distance Trade during the Eighteenth Century' in S. Jeyasella Stephen, ed., *The Indian Trade at the Asian Frontier* (New Delhi: Gyan Publishing House, 2008), pp. 213–230.

Antony, Robert J. ed., *Elusive Pirates, Pervasive Smugglers: Violence and Clandestine Trade in the Greater China Seas* (Hong Kong: Hong Kong University Press, 2010).

Appadurai, Arjun, ed. *The Social Life of Things: Commodities in Cultural Perspective* (Cambridge: Cambridge University Press, 1986).

Apperson, G. L. *The Social History of Smoking* (Middlesex, UK: Echo Library, 2006).

Ashworth, William J. *Customs and Excise: Trade, Production and Consumption in England, 1640–1845* (Oxford: Oxford University Press, 2003).

Ate, Richard. ed. *Behind Closed Doors: Art in the Spanish American Home* (New York: The Monacelli Press for the Brooklyn Museum, 2013).

Avery, Martha. *The Tea Road: China and Russia Meet across the Steppe* (Beijing: China Intercontinental Press, 2003).

Baghdiantz-McCabe, Ina. *A History of Global Consumption: 1500–1800* (Abingdon, UK: Routledge, 2015).

Baghdiantz-McCabe, Ina. *Orientalism in Early Modern France: Eurasian Trade, Exoticism and the Ancien Regime* (Oxford: Berg Publishers, 2008).

Bagneris, Mia L. 'Reimagining Race, Class, and Identity in the New World' in Amelia Peck, ed., *Behind Closed Doors: Art in the Spanish American Home, 1492–1898* (New York: Metropolitan Museum of Art, 2013), pp. 161–208.

Bailey, Alfred G. *The Conflict of European and Eastern Algonkian Cultures, 1504–1700* (Toronto: University of Toronto, 1937, repr. 1979).

Baker, T. C. 'Smuggling in the Eighteenth Century: The Evidence of the Scottish Tobacco Trade' *Virginia Magazine of History and Biography* 62 (1954): 387–399.

Bakewell, Peter and Jacqueline Holler. *A History of Latin America to 1825*, 3rd ed. (Oxford: Wiley Blackwell, 2010).

Ballantyne, Tony and Antoinette Burton, eds. *Bodies in Contact: Rethinking Colonial Encounters in World History* (Durham, NC: Duke University Press, 2005).

Ballantyne, Tony. 'The Changing Shape of the Modern British Empire and Its Historiography' *The Historical Journal* 53:2 (2010): 429–452.

Ballantyne, Tony. *Webs of Empire: Locating New Zealand's Colonial Past* (Vancouver: University of British Columbia Press, 2012).

Barahona, Victoria López and José Nieto Sánchez. 'Dressing the Poor: The Provision of Clothing among the Lower Classes in Eighteenth-Century Madrid' *Textile History* 43:1 (2012): 23–42.

Barbour, Richmond. 'The East India Company Journal of Anthony Marlowe, 1607–1608' *Huntington Library Quarterly* 71:2 (2008): 255–301.

Barnes, Ruth. *Indian Block-Printed Textiles in Egypt: The Newberry Collection in the Ashmolean Museum, Oxford* (Oxford: Clarendon Press, 1997), 2 vols.

Barrera, Antonia. 'Local Herbs, Global Medicine: Commerce, Knowledge, and Commodities in Spanish America' in Pamela H. Smith and Paula

Findlen, eds., *Merchants and Marvels: Commerce, Science, and Art in Early Modern Europe* (New York: Routledge, 2002), pp. 163–181.

Barrow, Thomas C. *Trade and Empire: The British Customs Service in Colonial America, 1660–1775* (Cambridge, MA: Harvard University Press, 1967).

Bauland, Micheline, Anton J. Schuurman and Paul Servais, eds. *Inventaires Après-Decès et Ventes de Meubles: Apports à une histoire de la vie économique et quotidienne (XIVe – XIXe siècle)* (Louvain-la Veuve: Acadèmia, 1988).

Baumgarten, Linda. *What Clothes Reveal: The Language of Clothing in Colonial and Federal America* (New Haven: Yale University Press, 2002).

Beckert, Sven. *The Empire of Cotton: A Global History* (New York: Alfred A. Knopf, 2014).

Beerbühl, Margrit Schulte. *The Forgotten Majority: German Merchants in London, Naturalization, and Global Trade, 1660–1815*, translated by Cynthia Klohr (London: Berghahn Books, 2007).

Bello, David A. *Across Forest, Steppe, and Mountain: Environment, Identity, and Empire in Qing China's Borderlands* (New York: Cambridge University Press, 2015).

Benedict, Carol. 'Between State Power and Popular Desire: Tobacco in Pre-Conquest Manchuria, 1600–1644' *Late Imperial China* 32:1 (2011): 13–48.

Benedict, Carol. *Golden Silk Smoke: A History of Tobacco in China, 1550–2010* (Berkeley: University of California Press, 2011).

Benton, Lauren. 'Legal Spaces of Empire: Piracy and the Origins of Ocean Regionalism' *Comparative Studies in Society and History* 47:4 (2005): 700–724.

Berdan, Frances F. *Aztec Archaeology and Ethnohistory* (Cambridge: Cambridge University Press, 2014).

Berg, Maxine. *Age of Manufactures 1700–1820: Industry, Innovation and Work in Britain*, 2nd ed. (London: Routledge, 1994).

Berg, Maxine. 'From Imitation to Invention: Creating Commodities in Eighteenth-Century Britain' *Economic History Review* 55:1 (2002): 1–30.

Berg, Maxine. 'In Pursuit of Luxury: Global History and British Consumer Goods in the Eighteenth Century' *Past & Present* 182:1 (2004): 85–142.

Berg, Maxine. *Luxury and Pleasure in Eighteenth-Century Britain* (Oxford: Oxford University Press, 2005).

Berg, Maxine and Helen Clifford, eds. *Consumers and Luxury: Consumer Culture in Europe 1650–1850* (Manchester: Manchester University Press, 1999).

Berlo, Janet C. and Ruth B. Phillips. *Native North American Arts* (Oxford: Oxford University Press, 1998).

Berry, Helen. 'Promoting Taste in the Provincial Press: National and Local Culture in Eighteenth-Century Newcastle-upon-Tyne' *British Journal for Eighteenth-Century Studies* 25 (2002): 1–17.

Berry, Mary Elizabeth. *Japan in Print: Information and Nation in the Early Modern Period* (Berkeley: University of California Press, 2006).

Berry, Susan. 'Recovered Identities: Four Métis Artists in Nineteenth-Century Rupert's Land' in Sarah Carter and Patricia McCormack, eds. *Recollecting: Lives of Aboriginal Women of the Canadian Northwest and Borderlands* (Edmonton: Athabasca University Press, 2011), pp. 29–59.

Bickham, Troy. '"A Conviction of the Reality of Things": Material Culture, North American Indians and Empire in Eighteenth-Century Britain' *Eighteenth-Century Studies* 39:1 (2005): 29–47.

Bickham, Troy. 'Eating the Empire: Intersections of Food, Cookery and Imperialism in Eighteenth-Century Britain' *Past & Present* (2008): 71–110.

Billings, E. R. *Tobacco: Its History, Varieties, Culture, Manufacture and Commerce* (Hartford, CT: American Publishing Company, 1875).

Bin Wong, R. *China Transformed: Historical Change and the Limits of European Experience* (Ithaca, NY: Cornell University Press, 1997).

Blondé, Bruno, ed. *Fashioning Old and New: Changing Consumer Preferences in Europe (Seventeenth-Nineteenth Centuries)* (Turnhout: Brepolis, 2009).

Blondé, Bruno. 'Tableware and Changing Consumer Patterns. Dynamics of Material Culture in Antwerp, 17th-18th Centuries' in Johan Veeckman, ed., *Majolica and Glass from Italy to Antwerp and Beyond. The Transfer of Technology in the 16th-Early 17th Century* (Antwerp: Stadt Antwerpen, 2002), pp. 295–311.

Blondé, Bruno, Natacha Coquery, Jon Stobart and Ilya Van Damme, eds. *Fashioning Old and New: Changing Consumer Patterns in Western Europe, 1650–1900* (Turnhout: Brepolis, 2009).

Blussé, Leonard. 'Chinese Century. The Eighteenth Century in the China Sea Region' *Archipel* 58 (1999): 107–129.

Blussé, Leonard. *Visible Cities: Canton, Nagasaki, and Batavia and the Coming of the Americans* (Cambridge, MA: Harvard University Press, 2008).

Blussé, Leonard and Diane Webb. *Bitter Bonds: A Colonial Divorce Drama of the Seventeenth Century* (Princeton, NJ: Markus Wiener, 2002).

Bockstoce, John. *Furs and Frontiers in the Far North* (New Haven: Yale University Press, 2009).

Boterbloem, Kees. *The Fiction and Reality of Jan Struys: A Seventeenth-Century Dutch Globetrotter* (Basingstoke, UK: Palgrave Macmillan, 2008).

Bourdieu, Pierre. *Distinction: A Social Critique of the Judgment of Taste*, translated by Richard Nice (French edition 1979, Cambridge MA, 1984).

Bowen, Huw. '"So Alarming an Evil": Smuggling, Pilfering and the English East India Company, 1740–1810' *International Journal of Maritime History* 14 (2002): 1–13.

Boyajian, James C. *Portuguese Trade in Asia under the Hapsburgs, 1580–1640* (Baltimore: Johns Hopkins University Press, 1993).

Braudel, Fernand. *Civilization and Capitalism, 15th to 18th Century, The Structures of Everyday Life*, vol. 1 translated by Siân Reynolds (New York: Harper & Row, 1985).

Breen, T. H. '"Baubles of Britain": The American and Consumer Revolutions of the Eighteenth Century' *Past & Present* 119 (1988): 73–104.

Breen, T. H. *The Marketplace of Revolution: How Consumer Politics Shaped American Independence* (New York: Oxford University Press, 2004).

Brewer, John. *Sinews of Power: War, Money and the English State, 1688–1783* (London: Unwin Hyman, 1989).

Bridenthal, Renate. ed. *The Hidden History of Crime, Corruption and the State* (New York: Berghahn Books, 2013).

Brook, Timothy. *The Confusions of Pleasure: Commerce and Culture in Ming China* (Berkeley: University of California Press, 1998).

Brook, Timothy. *Vermeer's Hat: The Seventeenth Century and the Dawn of the Global World* (London: Profile Books Ltd., 2008).

Brooks, Jerome E. *The Mighty Leaf: Tobacco through the Centuries* (New York: Little Brown, 1952).

Brouwer, C. W. 'Pepper Merchants in the Booming Port of al-Mukha: Dutch Evidence for an Oceanwide Trading Network' *Die Welt des Islams* 44:2 (2004): 214–280.

Brown, Jennifer S. 'A Partial Truth: A Closer Look at Fur Trade Marriage' in Theodore Binnema, Gerhard J. Ens and R. C. MacLeod, eds., *From Rupert's Land to Canada* (Edmonton: University of Alberta Press, 2001), pp. 59–80.

Brown, Kathleen M. *Foul Bodies: Cleanliness in Early America* (New Haven: Yale University Press, 2014).

Brown, Kathleen M. 'Native Americans and Early Modern Concepts of Race' in Martin Daunton and Rick Halpern, eds., *Empire and Others: British Encounters with Indigenous Peoples, 1600–1850* (Philadelphia: University of Pennsylvania Press, 1999), pp. 79–100.

Bruijn, Japp. R. *Commanders of Dutch East India Ships in the Eighteenth Century*, translated by R. L. Robson-McKillop and Prof. R. W. Unger (Woodbridge, UK: Boydell Press, 2011).

Buchner, Thomas and Philip R. Hoffmann-Rehnitz, eds. *Shadow Economies and Irregular Work in Urban Europe: 16th to Early 20th Centuries* (Vienna and Berlin: Lit Verlag, 2011).

Buckridge, Steeve O. *The Language of Dress: Resistance and Accommodation in Jamaica, 1760–1890* (Kingston: University of the West Indies Press, 2004).

Burke, Peter. 'Res et verba: Conspicuous Consumption in the Early Modern World' in John Brewer and Roy Porter, eds., *Consumption and the World of Goods* (London: Routledge, 1993), pp. 148–161.

Burke, Peter. 'Cultures of Translation in Early Modern Europe' in Peter Burke and R. Po-Chia Hsia, eds., *Cultural Translation in Early Modern Europe* (Cambridge: Cambridge University Press, 2007), pp. 7–38.

Burman, Barbara. 'Pocketing the Difference: Gender and Pockets in Nineteenth-Century Britain' *Gender & History* 14:3 (2002): 447–469.

Burton, Antoinette. 'Introduction: Traveling Criticism? On the Dynamic Histories of Indigenous Modernity' *Cultural and Social History* 9:4 (2012): 419–496.

Bushkovitch, Paul. *A Concise History of Russia* (Cambridge: Cambridge University Press, 2012).

Butel, Paul. *The Atlantic*, translated by Iain Hamilton Grant (London: Routledge, 1999).

Butler, Judith. 'Performative Acts and Gender Constitution: An Essay in Phenomenology and Feminist Theory' *Theatre Journal* 40:4 (1988): 519–531.

Cangany, Catherine. 'Fashioning Moccasins: Detroit, the Manufacturing Frontier, and the Empire of Consumption, 1701–1835' *William and Mary Quarterly* 69:2 (2012): 265–304.

Carlos, Ann and Frank D. Lewis, *Commerce by a Frozen Sea: Native Americans and the European Fur Trade* (Philadelphia: University of Pennsylvania Press, 2010).

Carney, Judith A. and Richard Nicholas Rosomoff, *In the Shadow of Slavery: Africa's Botanical Legacy in the Atlantic World* (Berkeley: University of California, 2009).

Caron, François and Joost Schouten. *A True Description of the Mighty Kingdoms of Japan and Siam.* Reprinted from the English edition of 1663, with Introduction, Notes and Appendixes by C. R. Boxer. (London: Argonaut Press, 1935).

Carson, Cary, Ronald Hoffman and Peter J. Albert, eds. *Of Consuming Interests: The Style of Life in the Eighteenth Century* (Charlottesville: University Press of Virginia, 1994).

Cassleman, Karen Diadick. *Lichen Dyes: The New Source Book*, 2nd ed. (Mineola, NY: Dover Publications, 2001).

Catsambis, Alexis, Ben Ford and Donny L. Hamilton, eds. *The Oxford Handbook of Maritime Archaeology* (Oxford: Oxford University Press, 2011).

Ch'ang, Chang Te. 'The Economic Role of the Imperial Household in the Ch'ing Dynasty' *Journal of Asian Studies* 31:2 (1972): 243–273.

Charpy, Manuel. 'The Scope and Structure of the Nineteenth-Century Secondhand Trade in the Parisian Clothes Market' in Laurence Fontaine, ed., *Alternate Exchanges: Secondhand Circulations from the Sixteenth Century to the Present* (Oxford: Berghahn Books, 2008), pp. 127–151.

Chassange, Serge. *Le coton et ses patrons en France, 1760–1840* (Paris: Editions de l'Ecole des hautes etudes en sciences sociales, 1991).

Chatterjee, Kumkum and Clement Hawes. *Europe Observed: Multiple Gazes in Early Modern Encounters* (Cranbury, NJ: Associated University Presses, 2008).

Chaudhuri, K. N. *The Trading World of Asia and the English East India Company, 1660–1760* (Cambridge: Cambridge University Press, 1978).

Chaudhuri, K. N. *Trade and Civilization in the Indian Ocean: An Economic History from the Rise of Islam to 1750* (Cambridge: Cambridge University Press, 1985).

Chaudhuri, K. N. 'Trade as a Cultural Phenomenon' in Jens Christian V. Johansen, Erling Ladewig Petersen and Henrik Stevnborg, eds., *Clashes of Cultures: Essays in Honour of Niels Steensgaard* (Odense: Odense University Press, 1992), pp. 208–219.

Cheng, Weichung. *War, Trade and Piracy in the China Seas (1622–1683)* (Leiden: Brill, 2013).

Chico, Beverly. *Hats and Headwear around the World: A Cultural Encyclopedia* (Santa Barbara, CA: ABC-CLIO, 2013).

Chin-keong, Ng. *Trade and Society, the Amoy Network on the China Coast, 1683–1735* (Singapore: Singapore University Press, 1983).

Christian, David. 'Silk Roads or Steppe Roads? The Silk Road in World History' *Journal of World History* 11:1 (2000): 1–26.

Ciriacono, Salvatore. 'Silk Manufacturing in France and Italy in the XVIIth Century: Two Models Compared' *Journal of European Economic History* 10:1 (1981): 167–172.

Clunas, Craig. 'Books and Things: Ming Literary Culture and Material Culture' in Frances Wood, ed., *Chinese Studies, British Library Occasional Papers* 10 (London: British Library, 1988), pp. 136–143.

Clunas, Craig. 'The Art of Social Climbing in the Ming Dynasty' *The Burlington Magazine* 133:1059 (1991): 368–377.

Clunas, Craig. *Superfluous Things: Material Culture and Social Status in Early Modern China* (Cambridge: Polity Press, 1991).

Clunas, Craig. 'Modernity Global and Local: Consumption and the Rise ofthe West' *American Historical Review* 104:5 (1999): 1497–1511.

Clunas, Craig. 'Things in Between: Splendour and Excess in Ming China' in Frank Trentmann, ed., *The Oxford Handbook of the History of Consumption* (Oxford: Oxford University Press, 2012), pp. 47–63.

Colburn, Forrest D. 'From Pre-Columbian Artifact to Pre-Columbian Art' *Record of the Art Museum, Princeton University* 64 (2005): 36–41.

Cole, W. A. 'Trends in Eighteenth-Century Smuggling' *Economic History Review* 10:3 (1958): 395–410.

Cole, W. A. 'The Arithmetic of Eighteenth-Century Smuggling: Rejoinder' *Economic History Review* 28:1 (1975): 44–49.

Colley, Linda. *The Ordeal of Elizabeth Marsh: A Woman in World History* (New York: Pantheon Books, 2007).

Collins, Brenda and Philip Ollerenshaw, eds. *The European Linen Industry in Historical Perspective* (Oxford: Oxford University Press, 2003).

Comaroff, John L. and Jean Comaroff. 'Fashioning the Colonial Subject: The Empire's Old Clothes' in John L. Comaroff and Jean Comaroff, eds., *Of Revelation and Revolution*, vol. 2, *The Dialectics of Modernity on a South African Frontier* (Chicago: University of Chicago Press, 1997), pp. 218–273.

Cope, R. Douglas. *The Limits of Racial Domination: Plebeian Society in Colonial Mexico City* (Madison WI: University of Wisconsin Press, 1994).

Coquery, Natacha. 'The Language of Success: Marketing and Distributing Semi-Luxury Goods in Eighteenth-Century Paris' *Journal of Design History* 17:1 (2004): 71–89.

Coquery, Natacha. 'The Semi-Luxury Market, Shopkeepers and Social Diffusion: Marketing Chinoiseries in Eighteenth-Century Paris' in Bruno Blondé, Natacha Coquery, Jon Stobart and Ilya Van Damme, eds., *Fashioning Old and New: Changing Consumer Patterns in Western Europe, 1650–1900* (Turnhout: Brepolis, 2009), pp. 121–132.

Corbin, Alain. *The Foul and the Fragrant: Odor and the French Social Imagination*, translated by Aubier Montaigne (Cambridge, MA: Harvard University Press, 1986).

Corner, David. 'The Tyranny of Fashion: The Case of the Felt-Hatting Trade in the Late Seventeenth and Eighteenth Centuries' *Textile History* 22:2 (1991): 153–178.

Courtwright, David T. *Forces of Habit: Drugs and the Making of the Modern World* (Cambridge, MA: Harvard University Press, 2001).

Craik, Jennifer. 'The Political Politics of the Uniform' *Fashion Theory* 7:2 (2003): 129–132.

Crooks, Peter and Timothy H. Parsons, eds. *Empires and Bureaucracy in World History: From Late Antiquity to the Twentieth Century* (Cambridge: Cambridge University Press, 2016).

Crouch, Christian Ayne. *Nobility Lost: French and Canadian Material Cultures, Indians, and the End of New France* (Ithaca: Cornell University Press, 2014).

Crowley, John E. *The Invention of Comfort: Sensibilities and Design in Early Modern Britain and Early America* (Baltimore: Johns Hopkins University Press, 2001).

Crowley, John. 'The Sensibility of Comfort' *American Historical Review* 104:3 (1999): 749–782.

Crowston, Clare. 'Engendering the Guilds: Seamstresses, Tailors, and the Clash of Corporate Identities in Old Regime France' *French Historical Studies* 23:2 (2000): 339–371.

Dahl, Camila Luise and Piia Lempiäinen, 'The World of Foreign Goods and Imported Luxuries: Merchant and Shop Inventories in Late 17th-Century Denmark-Norway' in Tov Engelhardt Mathiassen, Marie-Louise Nosch, Maj Ringgaard, Kirsten Toftegaard and Mikkel Venborg Pedersen, eds., *Fashionable Encounters: Perspectives and Trends in Textile and Dress in the Early Modern Nordic World* (Oxford and Philadelphia: Oxbow Books, 2014), pp. 1–14.

Dale, Stephen F. 'Silk Road, Cotton Road or . . . Indo-Chinese Trade in Pre-European Times' *Modern Asian Studies* 43:1 (2009): 79–88.

Dale, Stephen Frederic. *Indian Merchants and Eurasian Trade, 1600–1750* (Cambridge: Cambridge University Press, 1994).

Darnton, Robert. *The Great Cat Massacre: And Other Episodes in French Culture History* (New York: Basic Books, 1984).

Dauncey, Sarah. 'Illusions of Grandeur: Perceptions of Status and Wealth in Late-Ming Female Clothing and Ornamentation' *East Asian History* 25/ 26 (2003): 43–68.

Dauncey, Sarah. 'Sartorial Modesty and Genteel Ideals in the Late Ming' in Daria Berg and Chloe Starr, eds., *The Quest for Gentility in China: Negotiations beyond Gender and Class* (London: Routledge, 2007), pp. 134–154.

Davis, Natalie Zemon. 'Decentering History: Local Stories and Cultural Crossings in a Global World' *History and Theory* 50 (2011): 188–202.

Davis, Natalie Zemon. *Society and Culture in Early Modern France: Eight Essays* (Stanford: Stanford University Press, 1975).

Davis, Natalie Zemon. *The Gift in Sixteenth-Century France* (Oxford: Oxford University Press, 2000).

Dawdy, Shannon Lee. '"A Wild Taste": Food and Colonialism in Eighteenth-Century Louisiana' *Ethnohistory* 57:3 (2010): 389–414.

De Bruijn, Max and Remco Raben, eds. *The World of Jan Brandes, 1743–1808:*

De Groot, Joanna. 'Metropolitan Desires and Colonial Connections: Reflections on Consumption and Empire' in Catherine Hall and Sonya Rose, eds., *At Home with the Empire: Metropolitan Culture and the Imperial World* (Cambridge: Cambridge University Press, 2006), pp. 166–190.

De Jesus, Ed C. *The Tobacco Monopoly in the Philippines: Bureaucratic Enterprise and Social Change, 1766–1880* (Manila: Ateneo de Manila University Press, 1980).

De Mendonça, Maria Jose. 'Some Kinds of Indo-Portuguese Quilts in the Collection of the Museu de arte Antiga' in *Embroidered Quilts From the Museu Nacional de Arte Antiga, Lisboa* (London: Kensington Palace, 1978).

De Stecher, Anne. 'Huron-Wendat Visual Culture: Source of Economic Autonomy and Continuity of Traditional Culture' in Pierre Anctil, André Loiselle and Christopher Rolfe, eds., *Canada Exposed / Le Canada à découverte* (Brussels: Peter Lang, 2009), pp. 131–150.

De Stecher, Anne. 'Souvenir Art, Collectable Craft, Cultural Heritage: The Wendat (Huron) of Wendake, Quebec' in Janice Helland, Beverly Lemire and Alena Buis, eds., *Craft, Community and the Material Culture of Place and Politics, 19th-20th Century* (Aldershot, UK: Ashgate, 2014), pp. 37–58.

De Stecher, Annette. 'Wendat Arts of Diplomacy: Negotiating Change in the Nineteenth Century' in Thomas Peace and Kathryn Magee Labelle, eds., *From Huronia to Wendakes: Adversity, Migrations, and Resilience, 1650–1900* (Norman, OK: University of Oklahoma Press, 2016), pp. 182–208.

De Vries, Jan. 'The Industrial Revolution and the Industrious Revolution' *Journal of Economic History* 54 (1994): 249–270.

De Vries, Jan. *The Industrious Revolution: Consumer Behavior and the Household Economy 1650 to the Present* (Cambridge: Cambridge University Press, 2008).

De Vries, Jan and A. M. van der Woude, *The First Modern Economy: Success, Failure, and Perseverance of the Dutch 1500–1815* (Cambridge: Cambridge University Press, 1997).

Dean, Carolyn and Dana Leibsohn. 'Hybridity and Its Discontents: Considering Visual Culture in Colonial Spanish America' *Colonial Latin American Review* 12:1 (2003): 5–35.

Deceulaer, Harald. 'Secondhand Dealers in the Early Modern Low Countries: Institutions, Markets and Practices' in Laurence Fontaine, ed., *Alternate Exchanges: Secondhand Circulations from the Sixteenth Century to the Present* (Oxford: Berghahn Books, 2008), pp. 13–42.

Den Heijer, Henk. 'Africans in European and Asian Clothes: Dutch Textile Trade in West Africa, 1600–1800' in Veronika Hyden-Hanscho, Renate Pieper and Werner Stangle, eds., *Cultural Exchange and Consumption Patterns in the Age of Enlightenment: Europe and the Atlantic World* (Bochum: Verlag Dr. Dieter Winkler, 2013), pp. 117–130.

Dibbits, Hester. 'Between Society and Family Values. The Linen Cupboard in Early Modern Households' in Anton Schuurman and Pieter Spierenburg, eds., *Private Domain, Public Inquiry. Families and Life Styles in the Netherlands and Europe, 1550 to the Present* (Liversum: Verloren, 1996), pp. 125–145.

Dibbits, Hister. 'Pronken as Practice: Material Culture in The Netherlands, 1650–1800', in Rengenier C. Rittersma, ed., *Luxury in the Low Countries: Miscellaneous Reflections on Netherlandish Material Culture, 1500 to the Present* (Brussels: Pharo, 2010), pp. 135–158.

Disney, Anthony. 'Smugglers and Smuggling in the Western Half of the *Estado Da India* in the Late Sixteenth and Early Seventeenth Centuries' *Indica* 26:1 & 2 (1989): 57–75.

Douglas, Mary. *Thought Styles: Critical Essays on Good Taste* (London: Sage, 1996).

Douglas, Mary and Baron Isherwood, *The World of Goods: Towards an Anthropology of Consumption* (New York: Basic Books, 1979).

Drawings of a Dutch Traveller in Batavia, Ceylon and Southern Africa (Amsterdam: Waanders Publishers-Rijksmuseum, 2004).

Duffy, James. *Shipwreck and Empire: Being an Account of Portuguese Maritime Disasters in a Century of Decline* (Cambridge, MA: Harvard University Press, 1955).

Dugan, Holly. *The Ephemeral History of Perfume: Scent and Sense in Early Modern England* (Baltimore, MD: Johns Hopkins University Press, 2011).

Dusenbury, Mary M. *Flowers, Dragons and Pine Trees: Asian Textiles in the Spencer Museum of Art* (Manchester, VT: Hudson Hills Press, 2004).

Eacott, Jonathan. 'Making an Imperial Compromise: The Calico Acts, the Atlantic Colonies, and the Structure of the British Empire' *William and Mary Quarterly* 69:4 (October, 2012): 731–762.

Earle, Peter. *Sailors: English Merchant Seamen, 1650–1775* (London: Methuen, 1998).

Earle, Rebecca. 'Luxury, Clothing and Race in Colonial Spanish America' in Maxine Berg and Elizabeth Eger, eds., *Luxury in the Eighteenth Century: Debates, Desires and Delectable Goods* (Basingstoke: Palgrave Macmillan, 2003), pp. 219–227.

Earle, Rebecca. *The Body of the Conquistador: Food, Race and Colonial Experience in Spanish America, 1492–1700* (Cambridge: Cambridge University Press, 2012).

Earle, Rebecca. '"Two Pairs of Pink Satin Shoes!!": Race, Clothing and Identity in the Americas (17th–19th Centuries)' *History Workshop Journal* 52 (2001): 175–195.

Eastop, Dinah. 'Outside In: Making Sense of the Deliberate Concealment of Garments within Buildings' *Textile* 4:3 (2006): 238–255.

Ebben, M. A. 'Portuguese Financiers and the Spanish Crown in the North Sea Area in the First Half of the Seventeenth Century' in Juliette Roding and Lex Heema van Voss, eds., *The North Sea and Culture (1550–1800)* (Hilversum: Verloren, 1996), pp. 200–208.

Ehrenreich, Barbara and Deirdre English. *Witches, Midwives, and Nurses: A History of Women Healers*, 2nd ed. (New York: Feminist Press, 2010).

Elbl, Ivan. 'The Volume of the Early Atlantic Slave Trade, 1450–1521' *Journal of African History* 38:1 (1997): 31–75.

Elisonas, Jurgis. 'Notorious Places' in James L. McClain, John M. Merriman and Kaoru Ugawa, eds., *Edo and Paris: Urban Life and the State in the Early Modern Era* (Ithaca: Cornell University Press, 1994), pp. 253–291.

Ellinghaus, Katherine, Jane Carey and Leigh Boucher, eds. *Re-Orienting Whiteness* (New York: Palgrave Macmillan, 2009).

Erickson, Kirstin C. 'Las Colcheras: Spanish Colonial Embroidery and the Inscription of Heritage in Contemporary Northern New Mexico' *Journal of Folklore Research* 52:1 (2015): 1–37.

Escudero, Antonio Gutiérez. 'Hispaniola's Turn to Tobacco: Products from Santo Domingo in Atlantic Commerce' in Bethany Aram and Bartolomé Yun-Casalilla, eds., *Global Goods and the Spanish Empire, 1492–1824: Circulation, Resistance and Diversity* (London: Palgrave, 2014), pp. 216–229.

Fairchilds, Cissie. 'The Production and Marketing of Populuxe Goods in Eighteenth-Century Paris' in John Brewer and Roy Porter, eds., *Consumption and the World of Goods* (London: Routledge, 1993), pp. 228–248.

Faroqhi, Suraiya. 'Introduction, or Why and How One Might Want to Study Ottoman Clothes' in Suraiya Faroqhi and Christoph K. Neumann, eds., *Ottoman Costumes: From Textile to Identity* (Istanbul: EREN, 2004), pp. 15–48.

Faroqhi, Suraiya. *Subjects of the Sultan: Culture and Daily Life in the Ottoman Empire* (New York: I.B. Tauris & Co, 2000).

Faroqhi, Suraiya and Christoph K. Neumann, eds. *Ottoman Costumes: From Textile to Identity* (Istanbul: EREN, 2004).

Fatah-Black, Karwan. *White Lies and Black Markets: Evading Metropolitan Authority in Colonial Suriname, 1650–1800* (Leiden: Brill, 2015).

Fennetaux, Ariane. 'Women's Pockets and the Construction of Privacy in the Long Eighteenth Century' *Eighteenth-Century Fiction* 20:3 (2008): 307–334.

Ferreira, Maria João. 'Asian Textiles in the Carreira da Índia: Portuguese Trade, Consumption and Taste, 1500–1700' *Textile History* 46:2 (2015): 147–168.

Ferreira, Maria João Pacheco. 'Chinese Textiles for Portuguese Tastes' in Amelia Peck, ed., *Interwoven Globe: The Worldwide Textile Trade, 1500–1800* (New York: Metropolitan Museum of Art, 2013), pp. 46–55.

Finlay, Robert. 'The Pilgrim Art: The Culture of Porcelain in World History' *Journal of World History* 9:2 (1998): 141–187.

Finlay, Robert. *The Pilgrim Art: Cultures of Porcelain in World History* (Berkeley: University of California Press, 2010).

Finn, Margot. 'Slaves Out of Context: Domestic Slavery and the Anglo-Indian Family, c. 1780–1830' *Transactions of the Royal Historical Society* 19 (2009): 181–203.

Finnane, Antonia. *Changing Clothes in China: Fashion, History, Nation* (New York: Columbia University Press, 2008).

Finnane, Antonia. 'Chinese Domestic Interior and "Consumer Constraint" in Qing China: Evidence from Yangzhou' *Journal of the Economic and Social History of the Orient* 57 (2014): 112–144.

Fish, Shirley. *The Manila-Acapulco Galleons: The Treasure Ships of the Pacific* (Central Milton Keynes: AuthorHouse, 2011).

Fisher, John R. *The Economic Aspects of Spanish Imperialism in America, 1492–1810* (Liverpool: University of Liverpool Press, 1997).

Fisher, Michael H. *Counterflows to Colonialism: Indian Travellers and Settlers in Britain 1600–1857* (Delhi: Permanent Black, 2004).

Fisher, Michael H. 'Excluding and Including "Natives of India": Early Nineteenth-Century British-Indian Race Relations in Britain' *Comparative Studies of South Asia, Africa and the Middle East* 27:2 (2007): 303–314.

Fisher, Raymond Henry. *The Russian Fur Trade, 1550–1700* (Berkeley: University of California Press, 1943).

Floor, Willem. 'Arduous Travelling: The Qandahar-Isfahan Highway in the Seventeenth Century' in Willem Floor and Edmund Herzig, eds., *Iran and the World in the Safavid Age* (London: I.B. Tauris, 2012), pp. 207–236.

Flynn, Dennis O. and Arturo Giráldez. 'Born with a 'Silver Spoon': The Origins of World Trade in 1571' *Journal of World History* 6:2 (1995): 201–221.

Flynn, Dennis O. and Arturo Giráldez. 'Cycles of Silver: Global Economic Unity through the Mid-Eighteenth Century' *Journal of World History* 13:2 (2002): 391–427.

Fontaine, Laurence. ed. *Alternative Exchanges: Secondhand Circulations from the Sixteenth Century to the Present* (Oxford: Berghahn Books, 2008).

Fontaine, Laurence. *History of Pedlars in Europe*, translated by Vicki Whittaker (Cambridge: Polity Press, 1996).

Fontaine, Laurence. *The Moral Economy: Poverty, Credit and Trust in Early Modern Europe* (Cambridge: Cambridge University Press, 2014).

Fontana, G. L. and G. Gayot, eds. *Wool: Products and Markets 13th–20th Centuries* (Padova: Cleup, 2005).

Forster, Elborg and Robert Foster, eds. *Sugar and Slavery, Family and Race: The Letters and Diary of Pierre Dessalles, Planter in Martinique, 1808–1856* (Baltimore: Johns Hopkins University Press, 1996).

Fradera, Josep M. and Christopher Schmidt-Nowara. 'Introduction: Colonial Pioneer and Plantation Latecomer' in Josep M. Fradera and Christopher Schmidt-Nowara, eds., *Slavery and Antislavery in Spain's Atlantic Empire* (New York: Berghahn Books, 2013), pp. 3–6.

Francois, Marie. 'Cloth and Silver: Pawning and Material Life in Mexico City at the Turn of the Nineteenth Century' *The Americas* 60:3 (2004): 325–362.

Frick, Carole Collier. 'The Florentine *Rigattieri*: Second Hand Clothing Dealers and the Circulation of Goods in the Renaissance' in Alexandra Palmer and Hazel Clark, eds., *Old Clothes, New Looks: Second Hand Fashions* (Oxford: Berg Publishers, 2005), pp. 13–28.

Froide, Amy M. *Never Married: Single Women in Early Modern England* (Oxford: Oxford University Press, 2005).

Games, Alison. *The Web of Empire: English Cosmopolitanism in an Age of Expansion, 1560–1660* (Oxford: Oxford University Press, 2008).

Garrett, Valery. *Chinese Dress from the Qing Dynasty to the Present* (Tokyo; Rutland, VT; and Singapore: Tuttle Publishing, 2007).

Gazin-Schwartz, Amy. 'Archaeology and Folklore of Material Culture, Ritual, and Everyday Life' *International Journal of Historical Archaeology* 5:4 (2001): 263–280.

Geczy, Adam. *Fashion and Orientalism: Dress, Textiles and Culture from the 17th to the 21st Century* (London: Bloomsbury, 2013).

Gell, Alfred. *Art and Agency: An Anthropological Theory* (Oxford: Clarendon Press, 1998).

Gelman Taylor, Jean. 'Meditations on a Portrait from Seventeenth-Century Batavia' *Journal of Southeast Asian Studies* 37:1 (2006): 23–41.

Gelman Taylor, Jean. *The Social World of Batavia: Europeans and Eurasians in Colonial Indonesia*, 2nd ed. (Madison WI: University of Wisconsin Press, 2009).

Gerritsen, Anne and Giorgio Riello, eds. *The Global Lives of Things: The Material Culture of Connections in the Early Modern World* (Abingdon, UK: Routledge, 2016).

Gerritsen, Anne and Giorgio Riello, eds. *Writing Material Culture History* (London: Bloomsbury, 2015).

Gettler, Brian. 'Economic Activity and Class Formation in Wendake, 1800–1950' in Thomas Peace and Lathryn Labelle, eds., *From Huronia to Wendakes: Adversity, Migration, and Resilience, 1650–1900* (Norman, OK: University of Oklahoma Press, 2016), pp. 144–181.

Ghosh, Durba. 'Another Set of Imperial Turns?' *American Historical Review* 117:3 (2012): 772–793.

Giraldez, Arturo. *The Age of Trade: The Manila Galleons and the Dawn of the Global Economy* (Lanham, MD: Rowman and Littlefield, 2015).

Giusberti, Fabio. 'Dynamics of the Used Goods Market. Bolognese Drapers and Scrap Merchants in the Early Modern Era' in Alberta Guenzi, Paola Massa and Fausto Piola Caselli, eds., *Guilds, Markets and Work Regulations in Italy, 16th-19th Centuries* (Aldershot, UK: Ashgate, 1998), pp. 300–306.

Goden, Chris and Yvonne Marshall. 'The Cultural Biography of Objects' *World Archaeology* 31:3 (1999): 169–178.

Godinho, Vitorino Magalhães 'Portugal and the Making of the Atlantic World' *Review: A Journal of the Fernand Braudel Center* 28:4 (2005): 313–337.

Gokhale, B. G. 'Tobacco in Seventeenth-Century India' *Agricultural History* 48:4 (1974): 484–492.

Goldstone, Jack A. 'The Problem of the "Early Modern" World' *Journal of the Economic and Social History of the Orient* 41:3 (1998): 249–284.

Goldthwaite, Richard. *The Building of Renaissance Florence: An Economic and Social History* (Baltimore: Johns Hopkins University Press, 1980).

Goldthwaite, Richard. *Wealth and the Demand for Art in Italy, 1300–1600* (Baltimore: Johns Hopkins University Press, 1993).

Goodman, Jordan. *Tobacco in History: The Cultures of Dependence* (London: Routledge, 1993).

Goody, Jack. *The Culture of Flowers* (Cambridge: Cambridge University Press, 1993).

Goody, Jack. *The Theft of History* (Cambridge: Cambridge University Press, 2006).

Gordon, Andrew. *Fabricating Consumers: The Sewing Machine in Modern Japan* (Berkeley: University of California Press, 2012).

Gosden, Chris. 'What Do Objects Want?' *Journal of Archaeological Method and Theory* 12:3 (2005): 193–211.

Gottmann, Felicia. *Global Trade, Smuggling, and the Making of Economic Liberalism* (Basingstoke, UK: Palgrave, 2016).

Gould, Virginia Meacham. '"A Chaos of Iniquity and Discord": Slave and Free Women of Color in the Spanish Ports of New Orleans, Mobile, and Pensacola' in Catherine Clinton and Michele Gillespie, eds., *The Devil's Lane: Sex and Race in the Early South* (Cambridge, MA: Harvard University Press, 1997), pp. 232–246.

Grabowski, Jan and Nicole St-Onge. 'Montreal Iroquois *Engagés* in the Western Fur Trade' in Theodore Binnema, Gerhard Ens and R. C. MacLeod, eds., *From Rupert's Land to Canada* (Edmonton: University of Alberta Press, 2001), pp. 23–58.

Gradish, Stephen F. 'Wages and Manning: The Navy Act of 1758' *English Historical Review* 93:366 (1978): 46–67.

Grahn, Raymond. *The Political Economy of Smuggling: Regional Informal Economies in Bourbon New Granada* (Boulder: Westview Press, 1997).

Graubart, Karen B. 'The Creolization of the New World: Local Forms of Identification in Urban Colonial Peru, 1560–1640' *Hispanic American Historical Review* 89:3 (2009): 471–499.

Gray, Jane. *Spinning the Threads of Uneven Development: Gender and Industrialization in Ireland during the Long Eighteenth Century* (Oxford: Lexington Books, 2005).

Green Carr, Lois and Lorena S. Walsh. 'Inventories and the Analysis of Wealth and Consumption Patterns in St. Mary's County, Maryland, 1658–1777' *Historical Methods* 13 (1980): 81–104.

Greenfield, Kent Roberts. *Sumptuary Law in Nürmberg: A Study in Paternal Government* (Baltimore: Johns Hopkins University Press, 1918).

Grehan, James. *Everyday Life and Consumer Culture in 18th-Century Damascus* (Seattle: University of Washington Press, 2007).

Grehan, James. 'Smoking and "Early Modern" Sociability: The Great Tobacco Debate in the Ottoman Middle East (Seventeenth to Eighteenth Centuries)' *American Historical Review* 111:5 (2006): 1352–1377.

Greig, Hannah. 'Leading the Fashion: The Material Culture of London's *Beau Monde*' in John Styles and Amanda Vickery, eds., *Gender, Taste, and Material Culture in Britain and North America, 1700–1830* (New Haven, CT: Yale University Press, 2006), pp. 293–314.

Gungwu, Wang. 'Merchants without Empire: The Hokkien Sojourning Communities' in James D. Tracy, ed., *The Rise of Merchant Empires: Long Distance Trade in the Early Modern World* (Cambridge: Cambridge University Press, 1990), pp. 400–422.

Guy, John. *Woven Cargoes: Indian Textiles in the East* (London: Thames and Hudson, 1998).

Guy, John. '"One Thing Leads to Another": Indian Textiles and the Early Globalization of Style' in Amelia Peck, ed., *Interwoven Globe: The Worldwide Textile Trade, 1500–1800* (New York: Metropolitan Museum of Art, 2014), pp. 12–27.

Hall, Catherine. *Civilizing Subjects: Metropole and Colony in the English Imagination, 1830–1867* (Chicago: University of Chicago Press, 2002).

Hall, Catherine. 'Gendering Property, Racing Capital' *History Workshop Journal* 78 (2014): 22–38.

Hall, Catherine and Sonya O. Rose, eds. *At Home with the Empire: Metropolitan Culture and the Imperial World* (Cambridge: Cambridge University Press, 2006).

Hall, John Whitney. *The Cambridge History of Japan: Early Modern Japan*, vol. 4 (Cambridge: Cambridge University Press, 1991).

Hall, Stuart, Sut Jhally, Sanjay Talreja and Mary Patierno. *Representation and the Media* (Northampton, MA: Media Education Foundation, 1997).

Hamell, George R. 'Strawberries, Floating Islands, and Rabbit Captains: Mythical Realities and European Contact in the Northwest during the Sixteenth and Seventeenth Centuries' *Journal of Canadian Studies / Revue d'études canadiennes* 21:4 (1987): 72–94.

Hanley, Susan B. *Everyday Things in Premodern Japan: The Hidden Legacy of Material Culture* (Berkley: University of California Press, 1997).

Hansen, Karen Tranberg. *Salaula: The World of Secondhand Clothing and Zambia* (Chicago: University of Chicago Press, 2000).

Harley, C. Knick. 'Trade: Discovery, Mercantilism and Technology' in Roderick Flour and Paul Johnson, eds., *The Cambridge Economic History of Modern Britain* vol. 1 (Cambridge: Cambridge University Press, 2004), pp. 175–203.

Harms, Robert. *The Diligent: A Voyage through the Worlds of the Slave Trade* (New York: Basic Books, 2002).

Harrison, Anna and Kathryn Gill. 'An Eighteenth-Century Detachable Pocket and Baby's Cap, Found Concealed in a Wall Cavity: Conservation and Research' *Textile History* 33:2 (2002): 177–194.

Harte, N. B., ed. *The New Draperies in the Low Countries and England* (Oxford: Oxford University Press, 1997).

Harte, N. B. 'The Rise of Protection and the English Linen Industry, 1690–1790' in N. B. Harte and K. G. Ponting, eds., *Textile History and Economic History: Essays in Honour of Miss Julia de Lacy Mann* (Manchester: Manchester University Press, 1973), pp. 74–112.

Harvey, Karen. ed., *History and Material Culture: A Student's Guide to Approaching Alternative Sources* (London: Routledge, 2009).

Harvey, Karen. 'The History of Masculinity, circa 1650–1800' *Journal of British Studies* 44:2 (2005): 296–311.

Haskins, Victoria K. and Claire Lowrie. 'Introduction' in Victoria K. Haskins and Claire Lowrie, eds., *Colonization and Domestic Service: Historical and Contemporary Perspectives* (New York: Routledge, 2015), pp. 1–18.

Haynes, Douglas E., Abigail McGowan and Tirthankar Roy, eds. *Towards a History of Consumption in South Asia* (Oxford: Oxford University Press, 2010).

Helland, Janice, Beverly Lemire and Alena Buis, eds. *Craft, Community and the Material Culture of Place and Politics, 19th-20th Century* (Aldershot, UK: Ashgate, 2014).

Higman, B. W. 'An Historical Perspective: Colonial Continuities in the Global Geography of Domestic Service' in Victoria K. Haskins and Claire Lowrie, eds., *Colonization and Domestic Service: Historical and Contemporary Perspectives* (New York: Routledge, 2015), pp. 19–40.

Hoberman, Louise Schell. *Mexico's Merchant Elite, 1590–1660: Silver, State, and Society* (Raleigh: Duke University Press, 1991).

Hochmuth, Christian. 'What Is Tobacco? Illicit Trade with Overseas Commodities in Early Modern Dresden' in Thomas Buchner and Philip R. Hoffmann-Rehnitz, eds., *Shadow Economies and Irregular Work in Urban Europe: 16th to Early 20th Centuries* (Vienna and Berlin: LIT Verlag, 2011), pp. 107–126.

Hockley, Allen. *The Prints of Isoda Koryūsai: Floating World Culture and Its Consumers in Eighteenth-Century Japan* (Seattle: University of Washington Press, 2003).

Holcomb, Julie L. 'Blood-Stained Sugar: Gender, Commerce and the British Slave-Trade Debates' *Slavery and Abolition* 35:4 (2014): 611–628.

Hong-Schunka, S. M. 'Exchange of Commodities between Korea and Ryūkū' in Angela Schottenhammer, ed., *Trade and Transfer across the East Asian 'Mediterranean'* (Wiesbaden: Otto Harrassowitz KG, 2005), pp. 129–160.

Hood, Adrienne D. *The Weaver's Craft: Cloth, Commerce and Industry in Early Pennsylvania* (Philadelphia: University of Pennsylvania Press, 2003).

Howell, Martha. *Commerce before Capitalism in Europe, 1300–1600* (Cambridge: Cambridge University Press, 2010).

Hu, Minghi. ed. *Cosmopolitanism in China, 1600–1950* (Amherst, NY: Cambria Press, 2016).

Hudson, Pat. *The Genesis of Industrial Capital. A Study of the West Riding Wool Textile Industry, c. 1750–1850* (Cambridge: Cambridge University Press, 1986).

Hunt, Alan. *Governance of Consuming Passions: A History of Sumptuary Law* (Basingstoke: Macmillan, 1996).

Hunter, Janet and Penelope Francks, eds. *The Historical Consumer: Consumption and Everyday Life in Japan, 1850–2000* (Basingstoke, UK: Palgrave Macmillan, 2012).

Hyden-Hanscho, Veronika. 'Beaver Hats, Drugs and Sugar Consumption in Vienna around 1700: France as an Intermediary for Atlantic Products' in Veronika Hyden-Hanscho, Renate Piper and Werner Stadgl, eds., *Cultural Exchange and Consumption Patterns in the Age of Enlightenment: Europe and the Atlantic World* (Bochum: Verlag Dr. Dieter Winkler, 2013), pp. 153–168.

Ikegami, Eiko. *Bonds of Civility: Aesthetic Networks and the Political Origins of Japanese Culture* (Cambridge: Cambridge University Press, 2005).

Inal, Onur. 'Women's Fashions in Transition: Ottoman Borderlands and the Anglo-Ottoman Exchange of Costume' *Journal of World History* 22:2 (2011): 243–272.

Insoll, Tim. *The Archaeology of Islam in Sub-Saharan Africa* (Cambridge: Cambridge University Press, 2003).

Irwin, John and Margaret Hall. *Indian Embroideries* vol. II (Ahmedabad: Calico Museum of Textiles, 1973).

Ishii, Yoneo. ed., *The Junk Trade from Southeast Asia: Translations from the Tôsen fusetsu-gaki, 1674–1723* (Singapore: Institute of Southeast Asian Studies, 1998).

Israel, Jonathan I. *Dutch Primacy in World Trade, 1585–1740* (Oxford: Clarendon Press, 1989).

Jacob, Margaret C. *Strangers Nowhere in the World: The Rise of Cosmopolitanism in Early Modern Europe* (Philadelphia: University of Pennsylvania Press, 2006).

Jacobson, Matthew Frye. *Whiteness of a Different Color: European Immigrants and the Alchemy of Race* (Cambridge, MA: Harvard University Press, 1998).

James, E. O. 'The Tree of Life' *Folklore* 79:4 (1968): 241–249.

Jamieson, Ross W. 'The Essence of Commodification: Caffeine Dependencies in the Early Modern World' *Journal of Social History* 35:2 (2001): 269–294.

Javis, Michael J. *In the Eye of All Trade: Bermuda, Bermudians, and the Maritime Atlantic* (Chapel Hill, NC: University of North Carolina Press, 2010).

Johnson, Laura E. '"Goods to Clothe Themselves": Native Consumers and Native Images on the Pennsylvania Trade Frontier, 1712–1760' *Winterthur Portfolio* 40:4 (2005): 47–76.

Johnson, Laura E. 'Material Translations: Cloth in Early American Encounters, 1520–1750', unpublished PhD dissertation, 2010, University of Delaware.

Jones, Ann Rosalind and Peter Stallybrass, *Renaissance Clothing and the Materials of Memory* (Cambridge: Cambridge University Press, 2000).

Jones, Colin and Rebecca Sprang. 'San-culottes, *san café, sans tabac*: Shifting Realms of Necessity and Luxury in Eighteenth-Century France' in Maxine Berg and Helen Clifford, eds., *Consumers and Luxury: Consumer Culture in Europe, 1650–1850* (Manchester: Manchester University Press, 1999), pp. 37–62.

Jones, Evan T. 'Accounting for Smuggling in Mid-Sixteenth-Century Bristol' *Economic History Review* 54:1 (2001): 17–38.

Jung, Moon-Ho. *Coolies and Cane: Race, Labor, and Sugar in the Age of Emancipation* (Baltimore: Johns Hopkins University Press, 2006).

Karababa, Eminegül. 'Investigating Early Modern Ottoman Consumer Culture in the Light of Probate Inventories' *Economic History Review* 65:1 (2012): 194–219.

Karababa, Eminegul and Gulïz Ger. 'Early Modern Ottoman Coffeehouse Culture and the Formation of the Consumer Subject' *Journal of Consumer Research*, 37:5 (2011): 737–760.

Karl, Barbara. '"Marvellous Things Are Made with Needles": Bengal *colchas* in European Inventories, *c.* 1580–1630' *Journal of the History of Collections* 23:2 (2011): 301–313.

Karras, Alan L. '"Custom Has the Force of Law": Local Officials and Contraband in the Bahamas and the Floridas, 1748–1779' *Florida Historical Quarterly* 80:3 (2002): 281–311.

Karras, Alan L. *Smuggling: Contraband and Corruption in World History* (Lanham, MD: Rowman & Littlefield, 2010).

Kayoko, Fujita. 'Japan Indianized: The Material Culture of Imported Textiles in Japan, 1550–1850' in Giorgio Riello and Prasannan Parthasarathi, eds., *The Spinning World: A Global History of Cotton Textiles, 1200–1850* (Oxford: Oxford University Press, 2009), pp. 181–204.

Ken, Ivy. *Digesting Race, Class, and Gender: Sugar as Metaphor* (New York: Palgrave Macmillan, 2010).

Kent, H. S. K. *War and Trade in Northern Seas: Anglo-Scandinavian Economic Relations in the Mid-Eighteenth Century* (Cambridge: Cambridge University Press, 2008).

Keoke, Emory Dean and Kay Marie Porterfield. *Encyclopedia of American Indian Contributions to the World: 15,000 Years of Inventions and Innovations* (New York: Checkmark Books, 2003).

Kermoal, Nathalie. 'Métis Women's Environmental Knowledge and the Recognition of Métis Rights' in Nathalie Kermoal and Isabel Altamirano-Jiménez, eds., *Living on the Land: Indigenous Women's Understanding of Place* (Athabasca, AB: University of Athabasca Press, 2016), pp. 107–137.

Kisch, Herbert. *From Domestic Manufacture to Industrial Revolution: The Case of the Rhineland Textile Districts* (Oxford: Oxford University Press, 1989).

Kisluk-Grosheide, Daniëlle. 'Dirck van Rijswijck (1596–1679), A Master of Mother-of-Pearl' *Oud Holland* 111:2 (1997): 77, 84–85.

Klein, Cecelia F. 'Not Like Us and All the Same: Pre-Columbian Art History and the Construction of the Nonwest' *Anthropology and Aesthetics* 42 (2002): 131–138.

Klepp, Susan E. and Roderick A. McDonald, 'Inscribing Experience: An American Working Woman and an English Gentlewoman Encounter Jamaica's Slave Society, 1801–1805' *William and Mary Quarterly* 58:3 (2001): 637–660.

Klooster, Wim. *Illicit Riches: Dutch Trade in the Caribbean, 1648–1795* (Leiden: KILTV Press, 1998).

Klooster, Wim. 'Inter-imperial Smuggling in the Americas, 1600–1800' in Bernard Bailyn and Patricia L. Denault, eds., *Soundings in Atlantic History: Latent Structures and Intellectual Currents, 1500–1830.* (Cambridge, MA: Harvard University Press, 2009), pp. 141–180.

Klooster, Wim. 'Jews in Surinam and Curaçao' in Paolo Bernardini and Norman Fiering, eds., *The Jews and the Expansion of Europe to the West, 1450–1800* (New York: Berghahn Books, 2001), pp. 350–368.

Kolchin, Peter. 'Whiteness Studies: The New History of Race in America' *Journal of American History* 89:1 (2002): 154–173.

Konove, Andrew. 'On the Cheap: The Baratillo Marketplace and the Shadow Economy of Eighteenth-Century Mexico City' *The Americas* 72:2 (2015): 249–278.

Kopytoff, Igor. 'The Cultural Biography of Things: Commoditization as Process' in Arjun Appadurai, ed., *The Social Life of Things: Commodities in Cultural Perspective* (Cambridge: Cambridge University Press, 1986), pp. 64–92.

Kowaleski-Wallace, Elizabeth. *Consuming Subjects: Women, Shopping, and Business in the Eighteenth Century* (New York: Columbia University Press, 1997).

Kozub, Robert M. 'Evolution of Taxation in England, 1700–1815. A Period of War and Industrialization' *Journal of European Economic History* 32 (2003): 363–388.

Kriger, Colleen E. *Cloth in West African History* (Latham, MD: AltaMira Press, 2006).

Kriger, Colleen E. 'Silk and Sartorial Politics in the Sokoto Caliphate (Nigeria)' in Beverly Lemire, ed., *The Force of Fashion in Politics and Society: Global Perspectives from Early Modern to Contemporary Times* (Aldershot, UK: Ashgate, 2010), pp. 143–166.

Krishnamurthy, B. 'Indian Commercial Intermediaries and the French East India Company in Coromandel during the Seventeenth and Eighteenth Centuries' in S. Jeyaseela Stephen, ed., *The Indian Trade at the Asian Frontier* (New Delhi: Gyan Publishing House, 2008), pp. 173–192.

Kuwayama, George. *Chinese Ceramic in Colonial Mexico* (Los Angeles: Los Angeles County Museum of Art and University of Hawaii Press, 1997).

Kwass, Michael. *Contraband: Louis Mandrin and the Making of a Global Underground* (Cambridge, MA: Harvard University Press, 2014).

Lai, Walton Look and Chee Beng Tan, eds. *The Chinese in Latin America and the Caribbean* (Leiden: Brill, 2010).

Lana, Anna. 'Through the Needle's Eye: Embroidered Pictures on the Threshold of Modernity' *Eighteenth-Century Studies* 31:4 (1998): 503–510.

Lang, James. *Portuguese Brazil: The King's Planation* (New York: Academic Press, 1979).

Lázaro, Fabio López. *The Misfortunes of Alonso Ramíriz: The True Adventures of a Spanish American with 17th-Century Pirates* (Austin: University of Texas, 2011).

Lechler, George. 'The Tree of Life in Indo-European and Islamic Cultures' *Islamica* 4 (1937): 369–419.

Leibsohn, Dana. 'Made in China, Made in Mexico' in Donna Pierce and Ronald Otsuka, eds., *At the Crossroads: The Arts of Spanish America and Early Global Trade, 1492–1850* (Denver: Denver Art Museum, 2012), pp. 11–40.

Lemire, Beverly. 'The Theft of Clothes and Popular Consumerism in Eighteenth-Century England' *Journal of Social History* 24:2 (1990): 255–276.

Lemire, Beverly. *Fashion's Favourite: The Cotton Trade and the Consumer in Britain, 1660–1800* (Oxford: Oxford University Press, 1991).

Lemire, Beverly. *Dress, Culture and Commerce: The English Clothing Trade before the Factory* (Basingstoke, UK: Macmillan, 1997).

Lemire, Beverly. 'Consumerism in Preindustrial and Early Industrial England: The Trade in Secondhand Clothes' *Journal of British Studies* 27:1(1988): 1–24.

Lemire, Beverly. *The Business of Everyday Life: Gender, Practice and Social Politics in England, 1600–1900* (Manchester: Manchester University Press, 2005, reprinted 2012).

Lemire, Beverly, ed. *The British Cotton Trade* vols. 1–4 (London: Pickering & Chatto, 2010).

Lemire, Beverly. *Cotton* (Oxford: Bloomsbury, 2011).

Lemire, Beverly. 'The Secondhand Trade in Europe and Beyond: Stages of Development and Enterprise in a Changing Material World, c. 1600–1850' *Textile: Journal of Cloth and Culture* 10:2 (2012): 144–163.

Lemire, Beverly. 'An Education in Comfort: Indian Textiles and the Remaking of English Homes over the Long Eighteenth Century' in Bruno Blondé and Jon Stobart, eds., *Selling Textiles in the Long Eighteenth Century: Comparative Perspectives from Western Europe* (Basingstoke: Palgrave Macmillan, 2014), pp. 13–29.

Lemire, Beverly. 'Fashion Politics and Practice: Indian Cottons and Consumer Innovation in Tokugawa Japan and Early Modern England' in Shoshana-Rose Marzel and Guy D. Stiebel, eds., *Dress and Ideology: Fashioning Identity from Antiquity to the Present* (London: Bloomsbury Academic, 2014), pp. 189–210.

Lemire, Beverly. '"Men of the World": British Mariners, Consumer Practice, and Material Culture in an Era of Global Trade, c. 1660–1800' *Journal of British Studies* 54:2 (2015): 288–319.

Lemire, Beverly. 'A Question of Trousers: Seafarers, Masculinity and Empire in the Shaping of British Male Dress, *c.* 1600–1800' *Cultural and Social History* (2016): 1–22. http://dx.doi.org/10.1080/14780038.2016.1133493.

Leong-Salobir, Cecilia. *Food Culture in Colonial Asia: A Taste of Empire* (Abingdon, UK: Routledge, 2011).

Lewis, James B. *Frontier Contact between Choson Korea and Tokugawa Japan* (New York: Routledge, 2003).

Li, Lillian M. *China's Silk Trade: Traditional Industry in the Modern World, 1842–1937* (Cambridge, MA: Harvard University Press, 1981).

Licuanan, Virginia Benitez and José Llavador Mira, eds. *The Philippines Under Spain: Reproduction of the Original Spanish Documents with English Translation*, vols. 1–5 (1590–1593) (Manila: National Trust for Historical and Cultural Preservation of the Philippines, 1994).

Lightfoot, Kent G. 'Russian Colonization: The Implications of Mercantile Colonial Practices in the North Pacific' *Historical Archaeology* 37:4 (2003): 14–28.

Linebaugh, Peter. *The London Hanged: Crime and Civil Society in the Eighteenth Century* (London: Allen Lane, 1991).

Liu, Xinru. *The Silk Road in World History* (Oxford: Oxford University Press, 2010).

Liu, Yong. *The Dutch East India Company's Tea Trade with China, 1757–1781* (Leiden: Brill, 2007).

Llorca-Jaña, Manuel. *The British Textile Trade in South America in the Nineteenth Century* (Cambridge: Cambridge University Press, 2012).

Lockard, Craig. '"The Sea Common to All": Maritime Frontiers, Port Cities, and Chinese Traders in the Southeast Asian Age of Commerce, c. 1400–1750' *Journal of World History* 21:2 (2010): 219–247.

Loren, Diana D. *Archaeology of Clothing and Bodily Adornment in Colonial America* (Gainesville: University of Florida Press, 2010).

Lorimer, Joyce, ed. *Sir Walter Ralegh's Discoverie of Guiana* (Aldershot, UK: Ashgate, 2006).

Lorimer, Joyce. 'The English Contraband Tobacco Trade in Trinidad and Guiana, 1590–1617' in K. Andrews, N. P. Canny and P. E. H. Hair, eds., *The Westward Enterprise: English Activities in Ireland, the Atlantic, and America, 1480–1650* (Liverpool: Liverpool University Press, 1978), pp. 124–150.

Lubbock, Basil. *Barlow's Journal of his Life at Sea in King's Ships, East and West Indiamen and Other Merchantmen from 1659 to 1703*, vols. 1–2, (London: Hurst & Blackett Ltd., 1934).

Ludington, Charles. *The Politics of Wine in Britain: A New Cultural History* (New York: Palgrave Macmillan, 2013).

Lull, James. *Media, Communication, Culture: A Global Approach*, 2nd ed., (New York: Columbia University Press, 2000).

Lurvink, Karin. Beyond Racism and Poverty: The Truck System on Louisiana Plantations and Dutch Peateries, 1865–1920, PhD dissertation, Vrije Universiteit Amsterdam, 2016.

MacAulay, Suzanne P. *Stitching Rites: Colcha Embroidery along the Northern Rio Grande* (Tucson: University of Arizona Press, 2000).

MacLeitch, Gail D. *Imperial Entanglement: Iroquois Change and Persistence on the Frontiers of Empire* (Philadelphia: University of Pennsylvania Press, 2011).

MacLeod, Murdo J. *Spanish Central America: A Socioeconomic History, 1520–1720* (Berkeley: University of California Press, 1973, reprinted 2010).

Mancall, Peter C. 'Tales Tobacco Told in Sixteenth-Century Europe' *Environmental History* 9:4 (2004): 648–678.

Mancall, Peter C. 'The Raw and the Cold: Five English Sailors in Sixteenth-Century Nunavut' *William and Mary Quarterly* 70:1 (2013): 3–40.

Mancke, Elizabeth. *A Company of Businessmen: The Hudson's Bay Company and Long-Distance Trade, 1670–1730* (Winnipeg: Rupert's Land Research Centre, 1988).

Martin, Janet. 'The Land of Darkness and the Golden Horde: The Fur Trade under the Mongols 13th – 14th Centuries' *Cahiers du Monde russe et soviétique* 19:4 (1978): 401–421.

Martin, Janet. *Treasures of the Land of Darkness: The Fur Trade and Its Significance for Medieval Russia* (Cambridge: Cambridge University Press, 1986).

Maskiell, Michelle. 'Consuming Kashmir: Shawls and Empire, 1500–2000' *Journal of World History* 13:1 (2002): 27–65.

Matchette, Ann. 'Women, Objects, and Exchange in Early Modern Florence' *Early Modern Women* 3 (2008): 245–251.

Mathew, K. S. 'Indian Merchants and the Portuguese Trade on the Malabar Coast during the Sixteenth Century' in Teotonio R. De Souza, ed., *Indo-Portuguese History: Old Issues, New Questions* (New Delhi: Xavier Centre of Historical Research, 1984), pp. 1–12.

Mathiassen, Tov Engelhardt, Marie-Louise Nosch, Maj Ringgaard, Kirsten Toftegaard and Mikkel Venborg Pedersen, eds. *Fashionable Encounters: Perspectives and Trends in Textile and Dress in the Early Modern Nordic World* (Oxford and Philadelphia: Oxbow Books, 2014).

Matthee, Rudolph P. *The Pursuit of Pleasure: Drugs and Stimulants in Iranian History, 1500–1900* (Princeton: Princeton University Press, 2005).

Mauss, Marcel. *The Gift: Forms and Functions of Exchange in Archaic Societies*, translated by Ian Cunnison (London: Cohen and West Ltd., 1954).

Mayer, Tara. 'Cultural Cross-Dressing: Posing and Performance in Orientalist Portraits' *Journal of the Royal Asiatic Society* 22:2 (2012): 281–298.

Maynard, Margaret. *Fashioned from Penury: Dress as Cultural Practice in Colonial Australia* (Cambridge: Cambridge University Press, 1994).

Mazzaoui, Maureen. *The Italian Cotton Trade in the Later Middle Ages* (Cambridge: Cambridge University Press, 1981).

McCarthy, Conal. '"To Foster and Encourage the Study and Practice of Māori Arts and Crafts": Indigenous Material Culture, Colonial Arts and Crafts and New Zealand Museums' in Janice Helland, Beverly Lemire and Alena Buis, eds., *Craft, Community and the Material Culture of Place and Politics, 19th-20th Century* (Aldershot, UK: Ashgate, 2014), pp. 59–81.

McCarthy, William J. 'A Spectacle of Misfortune: Wreck, Salvage and Loss in the Spanish Pacific' *The Great Circle* 17:2 (1995): 95–108.

McCarthy, William J. 'Between Policy and Prerogative: Malfeasance in the Inspection of the Manila Galleons at Acapulco, 1637' *Colonial Latin American Historical Review* 2/2 (1993): 163–183.

McClellan, William Smith. *Smuggling in the American Colonial at the Outbreak of the Revolution: With Special Reference to the West Indies Trade* (1912, reprinted Westminster, MD: Heritage Books, 2007).

McCracken, Grant. *Culture and Consumption: New Approaches to the Symbolic Character of Consumer Goods and Activities* (Bloomington, IN: Indiana University Press, 1987).

McKendrick, Neil, John Brewer and J. H. Plumb. *The Birth of a Consumer Society: The Commercialization of Eighteenth-Century England* (London: Hutchinson, 1983).

McNeill, William H. *The Rise of the West: A History of the Human Community* (Chicago: University of Chicago Press, 1991).

McTavish, Lianne *Defining the Modern Museum: A Case Study of theChallenges of Exchange* (Toronto: University of Toronto Press, 2012).

Mendonça, Isabel. ed. *As Artes Decorativas e a Expansão Portuguesa: Imaginário e Viagem, Actas do II Colóquio de Artes Decorativas,* (Lisbon: FRESS/CCCM,i.p., 2010).

Mennell, Stephen. *All Manner of Food: Easting and Taste in England and France from the Middle Ages to the Present* (Chicago: University of Chicago Press, 1985).

Meuwese, Mark. 'The Dutch Connection: New Netherlands, the Pequots, and the Puritans in Southern New England' *Early American Studies* 9:2 (2011): 295–323.

Midgley, Clare. 'Slave Sugar Boycotts, Female Activism and the Domestic Base of British Anti-Slavery Culture' *Slavery and Abolition* 17:3 (1996): 137–162.

Midgley, Clare. *Women against Slavery: The British Campaign, 1790–1870* (London: Routledge, 1992).

Milgram, Lynne B. 'Refashioning Commodities: Women and the Sourcing and Circulation of Secondhand Clothing in the Philippines' *Anthropologica* 46:2 (2004): 123–136.

Miller, Christopher L. and George R. Hamell. 'A New Perspective on Indian-White Contact: Cultural Symbols and Colonial Trade' *Journal of American History* 73:2 (1986): 311–328.

Miller, Daniel. *Material Culture and Mass Consumption* (Oxford: Blackwell, 1987).

Miller, Marla R. 'Gender, Artisanry, and Craft Tradition in Early New England: The View through the Eye of a Needle' *William and Mary Quarterly* 60:4 (2003): 743–776.

Mintz, Sidney. *Sweetness and Power: The Place of Sugar in Modern History* (New York: Viking, 1985).

Mitchell, B. R. *British Historical Statistics* (Cambridge: Cambridge University Press, 1988).

Mol, Serge. *Classical Weaponry of Japan: Special Weapons and Tactics of the Martial Arts* (Tokyo: Kodansha International, 2003).

Mola, Luca. *The Silk Industry of Renaissance Venice* (Baltimore: Johns Hopkins University Press, 2000).

Molineux, Catherine. 'Pleasures of the Smoke: "Black Virginians" in Georgian London's Tobacco Shops' *William and Mary Quarterly* 64:2 (2007): 327–376.

Montaño, Mary. *Tradiciones Neuvomexicanas: Hispano Arts and Culture of New Mexico* (Albuquerque: University of New Mexico Press, 2001).

Moody, Kevin and Charles L. Fisher. 'Archaeological Evidence of the Colonial Occupation at Schoharies Crossing State Historic site, Montgomery County, New York' *The Bulletin: Journal of the New York State Archaeological Association* 99 (1989): 1–13.

Morantz, Toby. 'Economic and Social Accommodation of the James Bay Inlanders to the Fur Trade' in Shepard Krech, ed., *The Subarctic Fur Trade: Native Social and Economic Adaptations* (Vancouver: University of British Columbia Press, 1984), pp. 55–80.

Moreno Claverias, Belén. 'Luxury, Fashion and Peasantry: The Introduction of New Commodities in Rural Catalan, 1670–1790 in Beverly Lemire, ed., *The Force of Fashion in Politics and Society* (Aldershot UK: Ashgate, 2010), pp. 67–93.

Mu, Chi'en. *Traditional Government in Imperial China: A Critical Analysis*, translated by Chü-tu Hsüej and George O. Totten (Hong Kong: The Chinese University of Hong Kong, 1982).

Mui, Hoh-Cheung and Lorna Mui. 'Smuggling and the British Tea Trade before 1784' *American Historical Review* 74:1 (1968): 44–73.

Mui, Hoh-Cheung and Lorna Mui. '"Trends in Eighteenth-Century Smuggling" Reconsidered' *Economic History Review* 74:1 (1975): 44–73.

Muir, Edward. *Ritual in Early Modern Europe*, 2nd ed. (Cambridge: Cambridge University Press, 2005).

Mukherjee, Soma. *Royal Mughal Ladies and Their Contribution* (New Delhi: Gyan Publishing House, 2001).

Muldrew, Craig. *Food, Energy and the Industrious Revolution: Work and Material Culture in Agrarian England, 1550–1780* (Cambridge: Cambridge University Press, 2011).

Muldrew, Craig. '"Th'ancient Distaff" and "Whirling Spindle": Measuring the Contribution of Spinning to Household Earnings and the National Economy in England, 1550–1770' *Economic History Review*, 65 (2012): 498–526.

Murray, Tim. *The Archaeology of Contact in Settler Societies* (Cambridge: Cambridge University Press, 2004).

Nash, Elizabeth. *Seville, Cordoba, and Grenada: A Cultural History* (Oxford: Oxford University Press, 2005).

Nash, Robert C. 'The English and Scottish Tobacco Trades in the Seventeenth and Eighteenth Centuries: Legal and Illegal Trade' *Economic History Review* 35:3 (1982): 354–372.

Náter, Laura. 'The Spanish Empire and Cuban Tobacco during the Seventeenth and Eighteenth Centuries' in Peter A. Coclanis, ed., *The Atlantic Economy during the Seventeenth and Eighteenth Centuries: Organization, Operation, Practice, and Personnel* (Chapel Hill, NC: University of North Carolina Press, 2005), pp. 252–276.

Nellis, Eric. *Shaping the New World: African Slavery in the Americas, 1500–1888* (Toronto: University of Toronto Press, 2013).

Nenadic, Stana. 'Middle-Rank Consumers and Domestic Culture in Edinburgh and Glasgow, 1720–1840' *Past & Present* 145 (1994): 122–156.

Newell, Aimee E. *A Stitch in Time: The Needlework of Aging Women in Antebellum America* (Athens, OH: Ohio University Press, 2014).

Newson, Linda A. and Susie Minchin, *From Capture to Sale: The Portuguese Slave Trade to Spanish South America in the Early Seventeenth Century* (Leiden: Brill, 2007).

Nierstrasz, Chris. *Rivalry for Trade in Tea and Textiles: The English and Dutch East India Companies (1700–1800)* (Basingstoke, UK: Palgrave Macmillan, 2015).

Nishiyama, Matsunosuke. *Edo Culture: Daily Life and Diversions in Urban Japan, 1600–1868*, translated and edited by Gerald Groemer (Honolulu: University of Hawai'i Press, 1997).

Nogues-Marco, Pilar. 'Bullionism, Specie-Point Mechanism and Bullion Flows in Early 18th Century Europe', unpublished PhD dissertation, 2010, Institut d'Etudes Politiques de Paris.

North, Michael. 'Art and Material Culture in the Cape Colony and Batavia in the Seventeenth and Eighteenth Centuries' in Thomas Da Costa Kaufmann and Michael North, eds., *Mediating Netherlandish Art and Material Culture in Asia* (Amsterdam: Amsterdam University Press, 2014), pp. 111–128.

North, Michael. 'Production and Reception of Art through European Company Channels in Asia' in Michael North, ed., *Artistic and Cultural Exchange between Europe and Asia, 1400–1900* (Aldershot, UK: Ashgate, 2010), pp. 89–108.

Northrup, David. 'Globalization and the Great Convergence: Rethinking World History in the Long Term' *Journal of World History* 16:3 (2005): 249–267.

Norton, Marcy. 'Tasting Empire: Chocolate and the European Internalization of Mesoamerican Aesthetics' *American Historical Review* 111:3 (2006): 660–691.

Norton, Marcy. *Sacred Gifts, Profane Pleasures: A History of Tobacco and Chocolate in the Atlantic World* (Ithaca: Cornell University Press, 2008).

Norton, Marcy and Daviken Studnicki-Gizbert. 'The Multinational Commodification of Tobacco, 1492–1650' in Peter C. Mancall, ed., *The Atlantic World and Virginia, 1550–1624* (Chapel Hill, NC: University of North Carolina Press, 2007), pp. 251–273.

Notehelfer, Fred G. 'Notes on Kyōhō Smuggling' *Princeton Papers in East Asian Studies* I (1972): 1–32.

O'Brien, Patrick K. 'The Political Economy of British Taxation, 1660–1815' *Economic History Review* 41 (1988): 1–32.

O'Hanlon, Rosalind. 'Manliness and Imperial Service in Mughal North India' *Journal of the Economic and Social History of the Orient* 42:1 (1999): 47–93.

Ogilvie, Sheilagh. '"So that Every Subject Knows How to Behave": Social Disciplining in Early Modern Bohemia' *Comparative Studies in Society and History* 48:1 (2006): 38–78.

Ogilvie, Sheilagh. 'Consumption, Social Capital, and the "Industrious Revolution" in Early Modern Germany' *Journal of Economic History* 70:2 (2010): 287–325.

Ommer, Rosemary and Nancy J. Turner. 'Informal Rural Economies in History' *Labour/Le Travail* 53 (2004): 127–157.

Ormrod, David. *The Rise of Commercial Empires: England and the Netherlands in the Age of Mercantilism, 1650–1770* (Cambridge: Cambridge University Press, 2003).

Overton, Mark, Jane Whittle, Darron Dean and Andrew Hann. *Production and Consumption in English Households, 1600–1750* (London: Routledge, 2004).

Palmer, Alexandra and Hazel Clark, eds. *Old Clothes, New Looks: Secondhand Fashion* (Oxford: Berg Publishers, 2005).

Parent, Anthony S. Jr. *Foul Means: The Formation of a Slave Society in Virginia, 1660–1740* (Chapel Hill, NC: University of North Carolina Press, 2003).

Parke, Thomas. *Human-Built World: How to Think about Technology and Culture* (Chicago: University of Chicago Press).

Parker, Rozsika. *The Subversive Stitch: Embroidery and the Making of the Feminine* (London: The Women's Press Ltd., 1984).

Parthasarathi, Prasannan. 'Rethinking Wages and Competitiveness in the Eighteenth Century: Britain and South India' *Past & Present* 158:1 (1998): 79–109.

Parthasarathi, Prasannan. *The Transition to a Colonial Economy: Weavers, Merchants and Kings in South India, 1720–1800* (Cambridge: Cambridge University Press, 2001).

Pearce, Cathryn. *Cornish Wrecking, 1700–1860: Reality and Popular Myth* (Woodbridge, UK: Boydell Press, 2010).

Peck, Amelia. ed. *Interwoven Globe: The Worldwide Textile Trade, 1500–1800* (New York: Metropolitan Museum of Art, 2013).

Peers, Laura. '"Almost True": Peter Rindisbacher's Early Images of Rupert's Land, 1821–26' *Art History* 32: 3 (2009): 516–544.

Peers, Laura. '"Many Tender Ties": The Shifting Contexts and Meanings of the S BLACK Bag' *World Archaeology* 31:2 (1999): 288–302.

Peloso, Vincent C. *Race and Ethnicity in Latin American History* (New York: Routledge, 2014).

Pettigrew, William Andrew. *Freedom's Debt: The Royal African Company and the Politics of the Atlantic Slave Trade* (Chapel Hill, NC: University of North Carolina Press, 2013).

Phillips, Carla Rahn and William D. Phillips. *Spain's Golden Fleece: Wool Production and the Wool Trade from the Middle Ages to the Nineteenth Century* (Baltimore: Johns Hopkins University Press, 1997).

Phillips, Ruth. 'Reading and Writing between the Lines' *Winterthur Portfolio* 45:2/3 (2011): 107–124.

Phillips, Ruth. *Trading Identities: The Souvenir in Native North American Art from the Northeast, 1700–1900* (Seattle: University of Washington Press, 1998).

Picton, John and John Mack. *African Textiles* (London: British Museum Press, 1979).

Pierce, Donna and Ronald Otsuka, eds. *At the Crossroads: The Arts of Spanish America and Early Global Trade, 1492–1850* (Denver: Denver Art Museum, 2010).

Plankensteiner, Barbara. 'Salt-Cellar' in Helmut Trnek and Nuno Vassallo e Silva, eds., *Exotica: The Portuguese Discoveries and the Renaissance Kunstkammer* (Lisbon: Calouste Gulbenkian Museum, 2001), pp. 93–94.

Podruchny, Carolyn. *Making the Voyageur World: Travellers and Traders in the North American Fur Trade* (Lincoln, NE: University of Nebraska Press, 2006).

Podruchny, Carolyn. 'Unfair Masters and Rascally Servants? Labour Relations among Bourgeois, Clerks and Voyageurs in the Montreal Fur Trade, 1780–1821' *Labour/Le Travail* 43 (1999): 43–70.

Pomeranz, Kenneth. *The Great Divergence: China, Europe, and the Making of the Modern World Economy* (Princeton: Princeton University Press, 2000).

Poulter, Gillian. *Becoming Native in a Foreign Land: Sport, Visual Culture, and Identity in Montreal, 1840–1885* (Vancouver: University of British Columbia Press, 2009).

Pratt, Mary Louise. *Imperial Eyes: Travel Writing and Transculturation* (London: Routledge, 1992).

Preda, Alex. 'The Turn to Things: Arguments for a Sociological Theory of Things' *Sociological Quarterly* 40:2 (1999): 347–366.

Price, Jacob M. *Tobacco in Atlantic Trade: the Chesapeake, London and Glasgow* (Aldershot, UK: Valorium, 1995).

Price, Jacob M. *The Tobacco Adventure to Russia: Enterprise, Politics, and Diplomacy in the Quest for the Northern Market for English Colonial Tobacco, 1676–1722* (Philadelphia: American Philosophical Society, 1961).

Price, Jacob M. *France and the Chesapeake: A History of the French Tobacco Monopoly, 1674–1794, and its Relationship to the British and American Tobacco Trade*, 2 vols. (Ann Arbor: University of Michigan Press, 1973).

Price, Jacob M. 'Glasgow, the Tobacco Trade, and the Scottish Customs, 1707–1730' *Scottish Historical Review* 175 (1984): 1–36.

Pritchard, James. *In Search of Empire: France in the Americas, 1670–1730* (Cambridge: Cambridge University Press, 2004).

Quataert, Donald. 'Clothing Laws, State and Society in the Ottoman Empire, 1720–1829' *International Journal of Middle East Studies* 29: 3 (1997): 403–425.

Quataert, Donald. ed., *Consumption Studies and the History of the Ottoman Empire, 1550–1922* (Albany, NY: SUNY Press, 2000).

Racette, Sherry Farrell. *The Flower Beadwork People* (Regina: Gabriel Dumont Institute, 1991).

Racette, Sherry Farrell. 'Sewing Ourselves Together: Clothing, Decorative Arts and the Expression of Metis and Half Breed Identity', unpublished PhD, 2004, University of Manitoba.

Racette, Sherry Farrell. 'My Grandmothers Loved to Trade: The Indigenization of European Trade Goods in Historic and Contemporary Canada' *Journal of Museum Ethnography* 20: 20–21 (2008): 69–81.

Randle, Tracy. '"Consuming Identities": Patterns of Consumption at Three Eighteenth-Century Cape Auctions' in Laurence Fontaine, ed., *Alternate Exchanges: Secondhand Circulations from the Sixteenth Century to the Present* (Oxford: Berghahn Books, 2008), pp. 220–241.

Randles, Sarah. 'Material Magic: The Deliberate Concealment of Footwear and Other Clothing' *Parergon* 30:2 (2013): 109–128.

Raveux, Olivier. 'Space and Technologies in the Cotton Industry in the Seventeenth and Eighteenth Centuries: The Example of Printed Calicoes in Marseilles' *Textile History* 36:2 (2005): 131–145.

Raveux, Olivier. 'Fashion and Consumption of Painted and Printed Calicoes in the Mediterranean during the Later Seventeenth Century: The Case of Chintz Quilts and Banyans in Marseilles' *Textile History* 45:1 (2014): 49–67.

Ray, Arthur J. 'Indians as Consumers' in Carol M. Judd and Arthur J. Ray, eds., *Old Trails and New Directions: Papers of the Third North American Fur Trade Conference* (Toronto: University of Toronto Press, 1980), pp. 255–271.

Rediker, Marcus. *Between the Devil and the Deep Blue Sea: Merchant Seamen, Pirates and the Anglo-American Maritime World* (Cambridge: Cambridge University Press, 1987).

Rediker, Marcus. *The Slave Ship: A Human History* (New York: Viking, 2007).

Regaignon, Dara Rossman. 'Intimacy's Empire: Children, Servants, and Missionaries in Mary Martha Sherwood's "Little Henry and His Bearer"' *Children's Literature Association Quarterly* 26:2 (2001): 84–95.

Reid, Anthony. *A History of Southeast Asia: Critical Crossroads* (London: Wiley Blackwell, 2015).

Reid, Anthony. 'An "Age of Commerce" in Southeast Asian History' *Modern Asian Studies* 24:1 (1990): 1–30.

Reid, Anthony. 'From Betel Chewing to Tobacco-Smoking in Indonesia' *Journal of Asian Studies* 44:3 (1985): 529–547.

Reinarz, Jonathan. *Past Scents: Historical Perspectives on Smell* (Champaign, IL: University of Illinois Press, 2014).

Ribeiro, Fernando Rosa. *The Portuguese in the Creole Indian Ocean: Essays in Historical Cosmopolitanism* (Basingstoke, UK: Palgrave Macmillan, 2015).

Rich, E. E. 'Russia and the Colonial Fur Trade' *The Economic History Review* 7:3 (1955): 307–328.

Richards, John F. 'The Seventeenth-Century Crisis in South Asia' *Modern Asian Studies* 24:4 (1990): 625–638.

Richards, Rhys. 'A "Lost Galleon?" The Spanish Wreck at Taumako' *The Journal of Pacific History* 34:1 (1999): 123–128.

Richardson, Catherine, ed. *Clothing Culture, 1350–1650* (Aldershot, UK: Ashgate, 2004).

Richardson, Catherine. *Shakespeare and Material Culture* (Oxford: Oxford University Press, 2011).

Richmond, Vivienne. *Clothing the Poor in Nineteenth-Century England* (Cambridge: Cambridge University Press, 2013).

Riello, Giorgio. *One Foot in the Past: Consumers, Producers and Footwear in the Long Eighteenth Century* (Oxford: Oxford University Press, 2006).

Riello, Giorgio. *Cotton. The Fabric That Made the Modern World* (Cambridge: Cambridge University Press, 2013).

Riello, Giorgio and Prasannan Parthasarathi, ed., *The Spinning World: A Global History of Cotton Textiles* (Oxford: Oxford University Press, 2009).

Riello, Giorgio and Tirthankar Roy, eds. *How India Clothed the World: The World of South Asian Textiles, 1500–1850* (Leiden: Brill, 2009).

Riello, Giorgio and Ulinka Rublack, eds. *The Right to Dress: Sumptuary Regulations in Comparative and Global Perspective, c. 1200–1800*, forthcoming.

Ritcher, Daniel K. *The Ordeal of the Longhouse: The Peoples of the Iroquois League in the Era of European Colonization* (Chapel Hill, NC: University of North Carolina Press, 1992).

Rivas Pérez, Jorge F. 'Domestic Display in the Spanish Overseas Territories' in Richard Aste, ed., *Behind Closed Doors: Art in the Spanish American Home, 1492–1898* (New York: Brooklyn Museum and The Momacelli Press, 2013), pp. 49–103.

Rive, Alfred. 'A Short History of Tobacco Smuggling' *Economic History* 1 (1929): 554–569.

Roberts, Luke S. 'Shipwrecks and Flotsam: The Foreign World in Edo-Period Tosa' *Monumenta Nipponica* 70:1 (2015): 88–122.

Robicsek, Francis. 'Ritual Smoking in Central America' in Sander L. Gilman and Zhou Xun, eds., *Smoke: A Global of Smoking* (London: Reaktion Books, 2004), pp. 30–37.

Roche, Daniel. *The Culture of Clothing: Dress and Fashion in the Ancien Regime*, translated by Jean Birrell (Cambridge: Cambridge University Press, 1994).

Roche, Daniel. 'Between a "Moral Economy" and a "Consumer Economy": Clothes and Their Function in the 17th and 18th Centuries', in Robert Fox and Anthony Turner, eds., *Luxury Trade and Consumerism in Ancien Régime Paris* (Aldershot, UK: Ashgate, 1998), pp. 219–229.

Roche, Daniel. *A History of Everyday Things: The Birth of Consumption in France, 1600–1800*, translated by Brian Pearce (Cambridge: Cambridge University Press, 2000).

Roediger, David R. *The Wages of Whiteness: Race and the Making of the American Working Class* (New York: Verso, 1991).

Roger, R. A. 'From Cultural Exchange to Transculturation: A Review and Reconceptualization of Cultural Appropriation' *Communication Theory* 16 (2006): 474–503.

Romaniello, Matthew P. and Tricia Starks, eds., *Tobacco in Russian History and Culture: From the Seventeenth Century to the Present* (New York: Routledge, 2009).

Rothschild, Emma. *The Inner Life of Empire: An Eighteenth-Century History* (Princeton: Princeton University Press, 2011).

Rublack, Ulinka. *Dressing Up: Cultural Identity in Renaissance Europe* (Oxford: Oxford University Press, 2010).

Rule, John G. 'Wrecking and Coastal Plunder' in Douglas Hay, Peter Linebaugh, John G. Rule, E. P. Thompson and Cal Winslow, eds., *Albion's Fatal Tree* (London: Allen Lane, 1975), pp. 167–188.

Rule, John G. and Roger Wells. *Crime, Protest and Popular Politics in Southern England, 1740–1850* (London: Hambledon Press, 1997).

Rupert, Linda M. *Creolization and Contraband: Curaçao in the Early Modern Atlantic World* (Athens, GA: University of Georgia Press, 2012).

Russell-Wood, A. J. R. *The Portuguese Empire: A World on the Move, 1415–1808* (Baltimore: Johns Hopkins University Press, 1998).

Sandberg, Brian. '"The Magazine of All Their Pillaging"': Armies as Sites of Secondhand Exchanges during the French Wars of Religion' in Laurence Fontaine, ed., *Alternate Exchanges: Secondhand Circulations from the Sixteenth Century to the Present* (Oxford: Berghahn Books, 2008), pp. 76–96.

Sander L. Gilman and Zhou Xun, eds., *Smoke: A Global of Smoking* (London: Reaktion Books, 2004).

Sanderson, Elizabeth C. *Women and Work in Eighteenth-Century Edinburgh* (Basingstoke, UK: 1996).

Sardar, Marika. 'Silk Along the Seas: Ottoman Turkey and Safavid Iran in the Global Textile Trade' in Amelia Peck, ed., *Interwoven Globe: The Worldwide Textile Trade, 1500–1800* (New York: Metropolitan Museum of Art, 2013), pp. 66–81.

Sayre, Gordon M. 'Self-Portraiture and Commodification in the Work of Huron/Wendat Artist Zacharie Vincent, aka 'Le Dernier Huron' *American Indian Culture and Research Journal* 39:2 (2015): 1–27.

Scalberg, Daniel A. 'The French-Amerindian Religious Encounter in Seventeenth and Early Eighteenth-Century New France' *French Colonial History* 1 (2002): 101–112.

Scammel, Geoffrey V. *The First Imperial Age: European Overseas Expansion, c. 1400–1715* (London: Routledge, 2004).

Schaffer, Talia. 'Berlin Wool' *Victorian Review* 34:1 (2008): 38–43.

Schama, Simon. *The Embarrassment of Riches: An Interpretation of Dutch Culture in the Golden Age* (Berkeley: University of California Press, 1988).

Schimmel, Annemarie. *The Empire of the Great Mughals: History, Art and Culture*, translated by Corinne Attwood (London: Reaktion, 2004).

Schlesinger, Jonathan. *A World Trimmed with Fur: Wild Things, Pristine Places, and the Natural Fringes of Qing Rule* (Stanford: Stanford University Press, 2017).

Schlesinger, Roger and Arthur P. Stabler, eds. *André Thevet's North America: A Sixteenth-Century View* (Kingston and Montreal, ON: McGill-Queen's University Press, 1986).

Schoeman, Karel. *Early Slavery at the Cape of Good Hope, 1652–1717* (Pretoria: Protea Book House, 2007).

Screech, Timon. 'Tobacco in Edo Period Japan' in Sander L. Gilman and Zhou Xun, eds., *Smoke: A Global History Smoking* (London: Reaktion Books, 2004), pp. 92–99.

Shah, Deepika. *Masters of the Cloth: Indian Textiles Trades to Distant Shores* (New Delhi: Garden Silk Mills, 2005).

Shammas, Carole. 'Consumer Behavior in Colonial America' *Social Science History* 6 (1982): 67–86.

Shammas, Carole. *The Pre-Industrial Consumer in England and America* (New York: Oxford University Press, 1990).

Shannon, Timothy J. 'Dressing for Success on the Mohawk Frontier: Hendrick, William Johnson, and the Indian Fashion' *William and Mary Quarterly* 53:1 (1996): 13–42.

Sharpe, Pamela. 'Literally Spinsters: A New Interpretation of Local Economy and Demography in Colyton in the Seventeenth and Eighteenth Centuries' *Economic History Review* 44:1 (1991): 46–65.

Shepard, Alexandra. 'Crediting Women in the Early Modern English Economy' *History Workshop Journal* 79 (2015): 1–24.

Shively, Donald. 'Sumptuary Regulation and Status in Early Tokugawa Japan' *Harvard Journal of Asiatic Studies* 25 (1964/1965): 123–164.

Silberstein, Rachel. 'Eight Scenes of Suzhou: Landscape Embroidery, Urban Courtesans, and Nineteenth-Century Chinese Women's Fashions' *Late Imperial China* 36:1 (2015): 1–52.

Slack, Edward R. 'The *Chinos* in New Spain: A Corrective Lens for a Distorted Image' *Journal of World History* 20:1 (2009): 35–67.

Slade, Toby. *Japanese Fashion: A Cultural History* (Oxford and New York: Berg Publishers, 2009).

Sladoviskii, Mikhail Iosifovich. *History of Economic Relations between Russia and China*, translated from Russian (Jerusalem: Israel Program for Scientific Translation, 1966).

Sleeper-Smith, Susan. 'Cultures of Exchange in a North Atlantic World' in Susan Sleeper-Smith, ed., *Rethinking the Fur Trade Cultures of Exchange in an Atlantic World* (Lincoln: University of Nebraska Press, 2009), pp. xvii–lxii.

Smallwood, Stephanie E. *Saltwater Slavery: A Middle Passage from Africa to American Diaspora* (Cambridge, MA: Harvard University Press, 2007).

Smart, Alan and Filippo M. Zerilli, 'Extralegality' in Donald M. Nonini, ed., *A Companion to Urban Anthropology* (Chichester, West Sussex, UK: John Wiley & Sons, 2014), pp. 222–238.

Smart Martin, Ann. *Buying into the World of Goods: Early Consumers in Backcountry Virginia* (Baltimore: Johns Hopkins University Press, 2008).

Smart Martin, Ann. 'Lustrous Things: Luminosity and Reflection before the Light Bulb' in Anne Gerritsen and Giorgio Riello, eds., *Writing Material Culture History* (London: Bloomsbury Academic, 2015), pp. 157–164.

Smith, Kate. 'Empire and the Country House in Early Nineteenth-Century Britain: The Amherts of Montreal Park, Kent' *Journal of Colonialism and Colonial History* 16:3 (2015). Project MUSE, doi:10.1353/cch.2015.0042

Smith, R. E. F. and David Christian, *Bread and Salt: A Social and Economic History of Food and Drink in Russia* (Cambridge: Cambridge University Press, 1984).

Sola-Corbacho, Juan Carlos. 'Urban Economies in the Spanish World: The Cases of Madrid and Mexico City at the End of the Eighteenth Century' *Journal of Urban History* 27:5 (2001): 604–632.

Spufford, Margaret. *The Great Reclothing of Rural England: Petty Chapmen and Their Wares in the Seventeenth Century* (London: Hambledon Press, 1984).

Staples, Kathleen A. and Madelyn C. Shaw, *Clothing through American History: The British Colonial Era* (Santa Barbara: ABC-CLIO, 2013).

Stearns, Peter N. *Consumerism in World History: The Global Transformation of Desire* (New York: Routledge, 2001 and 2006).

Stern, Philip J. and Carl Wennerlind. 'Introduction' in Philip J. Stern and Carl Wennerlind, eds. *Mercantilism Reimagined: Political Economy in Early Modern Britain and Its Empire* (New York: Oxford University Press, 2013).

Stevens, Simon. 'A Social Tyranny: The Truck System in Colonial Western Australia, 1829–99' *Labour History* 80 (2001): 83–98.

Stewart, Charles. 'Creolization: History, Ethnography, Theory' in Charles Stewart, ed., *Creolization: History, Ethnography, Theory* (Walnut Creek, CA: Left Coast Books, 2007), pp. 1–24.

Stobart, Jon. 'Selling (through) Politeness: Advertising Provincial Shops in Eighteenth-Century England' *Cultural and Social History* 5 (2008): 309–328.

Stobart, Jon. *Sugar and Spice: Grocers and Groceries in Provincial England 1650–1830* (Oxford: Oxford University Press, 2013).

Stobart, Jon and Ilja Van Damme, eds. *Modernity and the Secondhand Trade: European Consumption Cultures and Practices, 1700–1900* (Basingstoke: Palgrave, 2012).

Struwe, K. *Vore gamle Tropekolonier*, ed. Johannes Brøndsted, vol. 6 (Copenhagen: SAXO, 1967).

Styles, John. 'Involuntary Consumers? The Eighteenth-Century Servant and Her Clothes' *Textile History* 33:1 (2002): 9–21.

Styles, John. *The Dress of the People: Everyday Fashion in Eighteenth-Century England* (New Haven: Yale University Press, 2007).

Subrahmanyam, Sanjay. 'Holding the World in Balance: The Connected Histories of the Iberian Overseas Empires, 1500–1640' *American Historical Review* 112:5 (2007): 1359–1385.

Sugihara, Kaoru. 'The State and The Industrious Revolution in Tokugawa Japan' Working Paper No. 02/04, London School of Economics (2004).

Sussman, Charlotte. *Consuming Anxieties: Consumer Protest, Gender and British Slavery, 1713–1833* (Stanford: Stanford University Press, 2000).

Suzuki, Barnabas Tatsuya. 'Tobacco Culture in Japan' in Sander L. Gilman, Xun Zhou, eds., *Smoke: A Global History of Smoking* (London: Reaktion Books, 2004), pp. 76–83.

Svalesen, Leif. *The Slave Ship Fredensborg*, translated by Pat Shaw and Selena Winsnes (Indianapolis: Indiana University Press, 2000).

Takekoshi, Yosaburō. *The Economic Aspects of the History of the Civilization of Japan*, vol. 2 (London: Routledge, 1930).

Tanimoto, Masayuki. 'Cotton and the Peasant Economy: A Foreign Fibre in Early Modern Japan' in Giorgio Riello and Prasannan Parthasarathi, eds., *The Spinning World: A Global History of Cotton Textiles, 1200–1850* (Oxford: Oxford University Press, 2009), pp. 367–386.

Teonge, Henry. *The Diary of Henry Teonge Chaplain on Board HM's Ships Assistance, Bristol and Royal Oak 1675–1679* (London and New York: Routledge Curzon, 2006).

Terkelsen, Signe Groot and Vivi Lena Andersen. 'Red Heels: The Symbol of a Power Shift in 17th-century Copenhagen' *Archaeological Textiles Review* 58 (2016): 3–9.

Thirsk, Joan. 'The Fantastical Folly of Fashion: the English Stocking Knitting Industry, 1500–1700' in N. B. Harte and K. G. Ponting, eds., *Textile History and Economic History: Essays in Honour of Miss Julia de Lacy Mann* (Manchester: Manchester University Press, 1973), pp. 50–73.

Thirsk, Joan. *Economic Policy and Projects: The Development of a Consumer Society in Early Modern England* (Oxford: Clarendon Press, 1978).

Thirsk, Joan. *Alternative Agriculture. A History from the Black Death to the Present Day* (Oxford: Oxford University Press, 1997).

Thirsk, Joan. *Food in Early Modern England: Phases, Fads, Fashions 1500–1760* (London: Hambledon, 2007).

Thomas, Nicholas. *Entangled Objects: Exchange, Material Culture, and Colonialism in the Pacific* (Cambridge, MA: Harvard University Press, 1991).

Thompson, E. P. *Customs in Common: Studies in Traditional Popular Culture* (The New Press: New York, 1993).

Thrush, Coll. *Indigenous London: Native Travelers at the Heart of Empire* (New Haven: Yale University Press, 2016).

Thwaites, Reuben Gold, ed. *The Jesuit Relations and Allied Documents: Travels and Explorations of the Jesuit Missionaries in New France, 1610–1791 ... with English Translation and Notes*, vol. 48 (Cleveland: Burrows, 1899).

Tobin, Beth Fowkes. *Picturing Imperial Power: Colonial Subjects in Eighteenth-Century British Painting* (Durham: Duke University Press, 1999).

Trigger, Bruce. *Natives and Newcomers: Canada's 'Heroic Age' Reconsidered* (Montreal and Kingston, ON: McGill-Queen's University Press, 1985).

Turgeon, Laurier. 'French Fishers, Fur Traders and Amerindians during the Sixteenth Century: History and Archaeology' *William and Mary Quarterly* 55:4 (1998): 558–610.

Turgeon, Laurier. 'Material Culture and Cross-Cultural Consumption: French Beads in North American, 1500–1700' *Studies in the Decorative Arts* 9:1 (2001–2002): 85–107.

Turner, Nancy J. *Ancient Pathways, Ancestral Knowledge: Ethnobotany and Ecological Wisdom of Indigenous Peoples of Northwest North America*, vols. 1 & 2 (Montreal and Kingston, ON: McGill-Queen's University Press, 2014).

Turner, Nancy J. and Dawn C. Loewen, 'The Original "Free Trade": Exchange of Botanical Products and Associated Plant Knowledge in Northwestern North America' *Anthropologica* 40:1 (1998): 49–70.

Turner, Terence S. 'The Social Skin', reprinted in *HAU: Journal of Ethnographic Theory* 2:2 (2012): 486–504.

Twinam, Ann. *Purchasing Whiteness: Pardos, Mulattos, and the Quest for Social Mobility in the Spanish Indies* (Stanford: Stanford University Press, 2015).

Ulrich, Laurel Thatcher. *A Midwife's Tale: The Life of Martha Ballard, Based on Her Diary, 1785–1812* (New York: Vintage Books, 1990).

Ulrich, Laurel Thatcher. 'Of Pens and Needles: Sources in Early American Women's History' *Journal of American History* 77:1 (1990): 200–207.

Ulrich, Laurel Thatcher. *The Age of Homespun: Objects and Stories in the Creation of an American Myth* (New York: Knopf, 2001).

Usner, Daniel H. Jr. *American Indians in the Lower Mississippi Valley: Social and Economic Histories* (Lincoln: University of Nebraska Press, 1998).

Vainker, Shelagh. *Chinese Silk: A Cultural History* (Rutgers: Rutgers University Press, 2004).

Valsecchi, Pierluigi. *Power and State Formation in West Africa: Appolonia from the Sixteenth to the Eighteenth Century* (New York: Palgrave Macmillan, 2011).

Van Damme, Ilja. 'Middlemen and the Creation of a "Fashion Revolution": The Experience of Antwerp in the Late Seventeenth and Eighteenth Centuries' in Beverly Lemire, ed. *The Force of Fashion in Politics and Society: Global Perspectives from Early Modern to Contemporary Times* (Aldershot, UK: Ashgate, 2010), pp. 21–40.

Van den Heuvel, Danielle. *Women and Entrepreneurship. Female Traders in the Northern Netherlands, c. 1580–1815* (Amsterdam: Aksant Academic Publishers, 2007).

Van den Heuvel, Danielle. 'The Multiple Identities of Early Modern Dutch Fishwives' *Signs: Journal of Women in Culture and Society* 37:3 (2012): 587–594.

Van Deusen, Nancy E. 'Seeing *Indios* in Sixteenth-Century Castile' *William and Mary Quarterly* 69:2 (2012): 211–240.

Van Dyke, Paul A. ed. *Americans and Macao: Trade, Smuggling and Diplomacy on the South China Coast* (Hong Kong: Hong Kong University Press, 2012).

Van Dyke, Paul A. *Merchants of Canton and Macao: Politics and Strategies in Eighteenth-Century Chinese Trade* (Hong Kong: Hong Kong University Press, 2012).

Van Gent, Jacqueline. *Magic, Body, and Self in Eighteenth-Century Sweden* (Leiden: Brill, 2009).

Van Kirk, Sylvia. *Many Tender Ties: Women in Fur-Trade Society, 1670–1870* (Norman: University of Oklahoma Press, 1980).

Vaporis, Constantine Nomiko. *Tour of Duty: Samurai, Military Service in Edo and the Culture of Early Modern Japan* (Honolulu: University of Hawai'i Press, 2008).

Vaporis, Constantine Nomikos. *Voices of Early Modern Japan: Contemporary Accounts of Daily Life during the Age of the Shoguns* (Santa Barbara, CA: Greenwood, 2012).

Vaughan, Meagan. *Creating the Creole Island: Slavery in Eighteenth-Century Mauritius* (Durham, NC: Duke University Press, 2005).

Vicente, Marta V. *Clothing the Spanish Empire: Families and the Calico Trade in the Early Modern Atlantic World* (New York: Palgrave Macmillan, 2006).

Vickery, Amanda. '"Neat and Not Too Showy": Words and Wallpaper in Regency England' in John Styles and Amanda Vickery, eds., *Gender, Taste, and Material Culture in Britain and North America, 1700–1830* (New Haven, CT: Yale University Press, 2006), pp. 201–224.

Vigneault, Louise and Isabelle Masse, 'Les autoreprésentations de l'artiste huron-wendat Zacharie Vincent (1815–1886): icons d'une gloire politique et sprituelle' *Canadian Journal of Art History* 32:2 (2011): 41–70.

Wada, Yoshiko Iwamoto, Mary Kellogg Rice and Jane Barton, *Shibori: The Inventive Art of Japanese Shaped Resist Dyeing* (Tokyo: Kodansha International Ltd., 1999).

Wadsworth, A. P. and Julia de Lacy Mann. *The Cotton Trade and Industrial Lancashire 1600–1760* (Manchester: Manchester University Press, 1931).

Walsh, Lorena S. 'Urban Amenities and Rural Sufficiency: Living Standards and Consumer Behavior in the Colonial Chesapeake, 1643–1777' *Journal of Economic History* 43:1 (1983): 109–117.

Walvin, James. *Slavery in Small Things: Slavery and Modern Cultural Habits* (Chichester, UK: John Wiley & Sons, 2017).

Ward, Cheryl and Uzi Baram. 'Global Markets, Local Practice: Ottoman-Period Clay Pipes and Smoking Paraphernalia from the Red Sea Shipwreck at Sadana Island, Egypt' *International Journal of Historical Archaeology* 10:2 (2006): 135–158.

Warren, Jim and Kathleen Carlisle. *On the Side of the People: A History of Labour in Saskatchewan* (Regina: Coteau Books, 2006).

Warsh, Molly. 'A Political Ecology in the Early Spanish Caribbean' *William and Mary Quarterly* 71: 4 (October 2014): 517–548.

Warsh, Molly. 'Enslaved Pearl Divers in the Sixteenth Century Caribbean' *Slavery & Abolition* 31:3 (2010): 345–362.

Watt, James C. Y. *When Silk Was Gold: Central Asian and Chinese Textiles* (New York: Metropolitan Museum of Art, 1997).

Weatherill, Lorna. *Consumer Behaviour and Material Culture in Britain 1660–1760* (London: Routledge, 1988).

Weaver, Jace. 'The Red Atlantic: Transoceanic Cultural Exchanges' *American Indian Quarterly* 35:3 (2011): 418–463.

Weaver, Karol K. 'Fashioning Freedom: Slave Seamstresses in the Atlantic World' *Journal of Women's History* 24:1 (2012): 44–59.

Welch, Evelyn. 'New, Old and Second-Hand Culture: The Case of the Renaissance Sleeve' in Gabriele Neher and Rupert Shepherd, eds., *Revaluing the Renaissance* (Aldershot, UK: Ashgate, 2000), pp. 101–120.

Welch, Evelyn. *Shopping in the Renaissance: Consumer Culture in Italy, 1400–1600* (New Haven: Yale University Press, 2005).

Welch, Patricia Bjaaland. *Chinese Art: A Guide to Motifs and Visual Imagery* (North Clarendon, VT: Tuttle Pub., 2008).

Wells, Julia C. 'Eva's Men: Gender and Power at the Cape of Good Hope' in Tony Ballantyne and Antoinette Burton, eds., *Bodies in Contact: Rethinking Colonial Encounters in World History* (Durham, NC: Duke University Press, 2005), pp. 84–105.

Westermann, Mariët *A Worldly Art: The Dutch Republic 1585–1718* (New Haven: Yale University Press, 1996).

White, Richard. *The Middle Ground: Indians, Empire and the Republics in the Great Lakes Regions, 1650–1815*, 20th anniversary ed. (Cambridge: Cambridge University Press, 2011).

White, Shane and Graham White, 'Slave Clothing and African-American Culture in the Eighteenth and Nineteenth Centuries' *Past & Present* 148 (1995): 149–185.

White, Sophie. 'Geographies of Slave Consumption' *Winterthur Portfolio* 45: 2/3 (2011): 229–248.

White, Sophie. '"Wearing three or four handkerchiefs around his collar, and elsewhere about him": Constructions of Masculinity and Ethnicity in French Colonial New Orleans' *Gender & History* 15:3 (2003): 528–549.

White, Sophie. *Wild Frenchmen and Frenchified Indians: Material Culture and Race in Colonial Louisiana* (Philadelphia: University of Pennsylvania Press, 2013).

Whyman, Susan E. *Sociability and Power in Late-Stuart England: The Cultural Worlds of the Verneys 1660–1720* (Oxford: Oxford University Press, 1999).

Wickman, Thomas. '"Winters Embittered with Hardships": Severe Cold, Wabanaki Power, and English Adjustments, 1690–1710' *William and Mary Quarterly* 72:1 (2015): 57–98.

Wigen, Kären, Sugimoto Fumiko and Cary Karacas, eds. *Cartographic Japan: A History in Maps* (Chicago: University of Chicago Press, 2016).

Williams, Eric. *Capitalism and Slavery* (Chapel Hill, NC: University of North Carolina Press, 1944, repr. 1994).

Willmott, Cory. 'From Stroud to Strouds: The Hidden History of a British Fur Trade Textile' *Textile History* 36:2 (2005): 196–234.

Wills, John E. *1688: A Global History* (New York: W. W. Norton & Co., 2001).

Wills, John E. Jr. 'European Consumption and Asian Production in the Seventeenth and Eighteenth Centuries' in John Brewer and Roy Porter, eds., *Consumption and the World of Goods* (London: Routledge, 1993), pp. 133–147.

Winslow, Cal. 'Sussex Smugglers' in Douglas Hay, Peter Linebaugh, John G. Rule, E.P. Thompson and Cal Winslow, eds., *Albion's Fatal Tree* (London: Allen Lane, 1975), pp. 119–166.

Winter, Joseph C. 'Traditional Uses of Tobacco by Native Americans' in Joseph C. Winter, ed., *Tobacco Use by Native North Americans: Sacred Smoke and Silent Killer* (Norman: University of Oklahoma Press, 2000), pp. 9–58.

Wintle, Claire. 'Negotiating the Colonial Encounter: Making Objects for Export in the Andaman Islands, 1858–1920' in Janice Helland, Beverly Lemire and Alena Buis, eds., *Craft, Community and the Material Culture of Place and Politics, 19th-20th Century* (Aldershot, UK: Ashgate, 2014), pp. 143–160.

Woodward, Donald. '"Swords into Ploughshares": Recycling in Pre-Industrial England' *Economic History Review* 38:2 (1985): 175–191.

Yang, Bin. 'The Rise and Fall of Cowrie Shells: The Asian Story' *Journal of World History* 22:1 (2011): 1–25.

Yi, T'ae-jin. *The Dynamics of Confucianism and Modernization in Korean History* (Ithaca: Cornell University Press, 2007).

Yule, Henry and A. C. Burnell, eds. *Hobson-Jobson. A Glossary of Colloquial Anglo-Indian Words and Phrases, and of Kindred Terms.* (London: John Murray, 1903).

Yun-Casalilla, Bartolomé. 'The History of Consumption of Early Modern Europe in a Trans-Atlantic Perspective: Some New Challenges in European Social History' in Veronika Hyden-Hanscho, Renate Pieper and Werner Stangl, eds., *Cultural Exchange and Consumption Patterns in the Age of Enlightenment: Europe and the Atlantic World* (Bochum: Verlag Dr. Dieter Winkler, 2013), pp. 25–40.

Zahedieh, Nuala. 'The Merchants of Port Royal Jamaica and the Spanish Contraband Trade, 1655–1692' *William and Mary Quarterly* 43 (1986): 570–593.

Zahedieh, Nuala. 'Trade, Plunder and Economic Development in Early English Jamaica, 1655–1689' *Economic History Review* 39:2 (1986): 205–222.

Zahedieh, Nuala. 'London and the Colonial Consumer in the Late Seventeenth Century' *Economic History Review* 47:2 (1994): 248–250.

Zahedieh, Nuala. *The Capital and the Colonies: London and the Atlantic Economy, 1660–1700* (Cambridge: Cambridge University Press, 2010).

Zheng, Yangwen. *China on the Sea: How the Maritime World Shaped Modern China* (Leiden: Brill, 2012).

Zilfi, Madeline C. 'Whose Laws? Gendering the Ottoman Sumptuary Regime' in Suraiya Faroqhi and Christoph K. Neumann, eds., *Ottoman Costumes: From Textile to Identity* (Istanbul: EREN, 2004), pp. 125–141.

Index